STALIN'S SPY

STALIN'S SPY

RICHARD SORGE
AND THE
TOKYO ESPIONAGE RING

ROBERT WHYMANT

ST. MARTIN'S PRESS 🐾 NEW YORK

THOMAS DUNNE BOOKS.
An imprint of St. Martin's Press

Library of Congress Cataloging-in-Publication Data
Whymant, Robert.
  Stalin's spy: Richard Sorge and the Tokyo espionage ring / Robert
Whymant.
    p.   cm.
  Includes bibliographical references and index.
  ISBN 0-312-19339-4
  1. Sorge, Richard, 1895-1944. 2. Espionage, Soviet—Japan—
History—20th century. 3. Spies—Soviet Union—Biography.
I. Title.
  UB271.R92S579   1998
327.1247053'092—dc21
[B]   98-31574
                                                               CIP

First published in the United Kingdom by I.B. Tauris & Co Ltd

First U.S. Edition: December 1998

10 9 8 7 6 5 4 3 2 1

Contents

Foreword and Acknowledgements

The story of Richard Sorge, one of the most successful spies of modern times, is encrusted with myths, distortions and fabrications. The attempt to disentangle truth from fiction for this book has taken twenty years of detective work in Japan, Russia, Germany, China and the United States. In the quest for Dr Sorge, friends, acquaintances and enemies of the Red Army Intelligence officer were tracked down, as were surviving members of his ring and their families. Some of those interviewed died, alas, before the completion of this book. But I am happy to say that Ishii Hanako, who shared her recollections of her beloved Sorge with me, and Yamazaki Yoshiko, who provided information about her late husband, Branko Vukelic, are both in reasonably good health, living quietly in Tokyo and Yokohama respectively.

This account is based on interviews with many people with direct knowledge of the affair, hitherto unpublished material from Russian Defence Ministry and KGB files, German diplomatic archives and Japanese and German memoirs and official records. However, a good deal of our knowledge of the Sorge affair rests on the testimony he and his subordinates gave to Japanese interrogators. This evidence, obtained in prison, in a climate of fear, must be treated with caution. One of the most difficult tasks in piecing together Dr Sorge's story is to assess how much credence to give to testimony obtained in the shadow of the gallows.

To those who consented to be interviewed in person, or who responded to requests for information by letter or telephone, I extend heartfelt thanks. Their names are cited in the Notes. I owe a special debt of gratitude to Eta Harich-Schneider, who talked to me about Sorge three years before her death in 1986. Mrs Harich-Schneider's perspective was invaluable: no one was closer to Sorge in his final weeks of freedom.

I am indebted to Ryu Otomo for his unstinting help in unearthing and elucidating many Japanese sources. Professor Christopher Andrew of Corpus Christi College, Cambridge, was kind enough to explain how Soviet intelligence services used 'sigint' – intelligence derived from intercepting and analysing signals – to back up Sorge's reports.

'So many lies have been written, so many distortions,' said Mrs Harich-Schneider. She worried that I might perpetuate the fictions, and begged me to record what really happened. This book is an attempt to fulfil that wish. However, even today large areas of the life and work of a remarkable espionage agent are cloaked in mystery. Much remains to be illuminated. The file on Dr Sorge is not yet closed.

Direct speech has been used sparingly to bring to life some key episodes in this book. In such cases, dialogue is based on recollections of participants or reconstructed from the judicial records without embellishment. Direct speech is recreated in concordance with the known facts and evidence, and sources are cited in the Notes following the text.

In Japanese names this book follows the Japanese style of giving the surname first, with the personal name second.

STALIN'S SPY

The Accident

AT AROUND three o'clock on the morning of 13 May 1938, a roll of thunder broke the silence of Toranomon, close to the government offices in the heart of Tokyo. A powerful motorcycle swung round the corner by the South Manchurian Railway building, and snarled up the road that leads to the American embassy. The embassy compound, then as now, straddles a hill at the top of this road, forming a T-junction. Here, the rider of the motorcyle veered left, and roared up the steep dark lane that skirts the embassy's south wall.

A moment or two later, the policeman at the embassy gate heard a resounding bang and a metallic clatter. Running up the slope to investigate, he found the wreckage of a motorcycle, buckled in a head-on collision with the stone wall. His torchlight picked out human teeth scattered among the metal debris. The man who lay bleeding in the road was a foreigner, later identified as a German journalist, Richard Sorge. Dr Stedefeld, an American doctor who lived near the embassy, was summoned to give first aid. Soon afterwards Prince Urach, a friend of Sorge staying at the Imperial Hotel, hurried to the scene.

The two of them had begun drinking early in the evening, finally staggering out of the Rheingold bar in the small hours. Urach had urged Sorge to take a taxi, or walk home, on no account to ride the motorcycle home. Sorge had laughed, in his usual cavalier way. He was not one to heed the voice of timidity. If he was too drunk to drive, he was also too drunk to care about the consequences.

Urach was appalled by what he found. Scarcely able speak through his bleeding mouth, Sorge made a painful effort to convey an urgent wish to Urach. 'Tell Clausen to come at once,' he mumbled.

§ At his home in Roppongi, Max Clausen was torn from sleep by the urgent ringing of the telephone. When he heard that Sorge was badly injured and on his way to St Luke's hospital by ambulance, he was filled with apprehension. Dressing hurriedly, he drove as fast as he could to the modern medical centre in the Tsukiji district.

Sorge was in very bad shape, on the verge of losing consciousness, and unable to talk clearly. Clausen later recalled what happened when he arrived at the hospital in the early hours of the morning:

> Displaying the will-power which I always found so remarkable, he pulled out of his coat pocket the intelligence reports in English, and the American currency which it was essential no one see, and passed them to me – and then slipped into unconsciousness, as if finally freed of a huge burden.[1]

Clausen hurriedly concealed these items. His next stop was Sorge's little house in Nagasaka-cho. There he removed all documents, including a diary, that were likely to arouse suspicion.

He completed his nerve-racking task in the nick of time. Around dawn, Rudolf Weise, who as chief of the official German news agency was the most senior among the German journalists, arrived to seal Sorge's house and property. It was a close shave that sent a chill down Clausen's spine: 'I shuddered at the thought that our secret work might have been exposed if Weise had arrived before me. What worried me too was that it would have seemed strange that an apparent outsider like myself was at the house at such a time.'[2]

It was true that Sorge and Clausen were sometimes seen in each other's company over a beer at the German Club, but no one quite understood why the gifted journalist and intellectual consorted with a humdrum, unrefined businessman like Clausen. That was why Prince Urach was puzzled by Sorge's insistence that the fellow be summoned at once to St Luke's. No one ever imagined that the bond between them was allegiance to the Soviet Union, or that they were comrades in a spy ring serving the Red Army.

Clausen was shaken. The espionage network had been built up with painstaking care, and it could all come crashing down because of this one reckless act. The Japanese were obsessed by the belief that spies lurked everywhere, and for that reason foreigners were accorded the closest scrutiny. If discovered by the police, the documents Sorge carried on his person were bound to provoke awkward questions.

It would have been forgiveable if Clausen had inwardly cursed his chief. Accumulated grievances would over time corrode his loyalty to Sorge, and the events of this night may have been among the first. Yet however intense his annoyance, when he watched Sorge writhing in agony at the hospital, he was struck by amazement and admiration at his display of fortitude.

An ordinary man in such a condition – most of his front teeth smashed, huge gashes on the jaw and forehead – would have fainted, but Sorge had somehow hung on until Clausen arrived. It was, he was forced to admit, the sign of an exceptional sort of person:

> When I rushed to the hospital after the telephone call, he was unable to speak, but even then he had his wits about him. Only after he had handed me the important confidential papers, and the other things – only when these were safely in my hands – did he lose consciousness ... Once again, I could not help but be impressed by his strong nature.[3]

The date of this harrowing episode stuck in Clausen's mind and, almost exactly four years later, he explained why to Japanese interrogators: 'It happened to be Friday the Thirteenth, which is the day Europeans and Americans hate most.'[4]

On Saturday 14 May readers of the *Japan Advertiser* could read the following item in the popular 'Social and General' column, immediately below the notices about the imperial court.

'Dr. R. Sorge, correspondent here of the *Hamburger Fremdenblatt*, was in St. Luke's International Center yesterday after a motorcycle accident early in the morning. His injuries were reported serious.'

Miyake Hanako, his girlfriend, found out about the accident from a telegram sent by his maid: 'Sorge injured come immediately.' She hurried to his house in the Nagasaka-cho district of the capital, and after hearing the maid's confused version of events, took a taxi to St Luke's. Sorge was in a pitiful state. His head was swathed in bandages, his jaw wired together, his left arm tied in a sling.

'I burst into tears when I saw him,' Hanako remembers. 'I couldn't stop crying. Only with much effort did I manage to pull myself together. I asked if he recognized me. To my relief, he gave a little nod. I held his hand, and after a while, said I'd come again the next day. There wasn't much I could do. I wanted to sleep there, beside his bed. But the hospital wouldn't allow it.'[5]

§ In the 1930s St Luke's was the most up-to-date centre of Western medicine in Japan. Foreigners who distrusted Japanese hospitals brought their ailments to Dr Elliot and his American-trained medical staff. In this rare oasis of hygiene, most expatriates' babies came into the world, and were greeted by a strong whiff of linoleum polish and disinfectant.

The bedside bibles with the imprint of the Episcopal Church of America reminded patients whom they had to thank for the fine building and first-rate care. It was a hospital run by American missionaries that succoured an agnostic Soviet agent in his hour of need and restored him to health and active duty.

Installed in a private room on the second floor, Sorge was soon receiving a steady stream of visitors – though his lips were so badly gashed that even when the bandages were removed, it was painful for him to utter more than a few words at a time.

Diplomats and secretaries from the German Embassy, press colleagues and fellow members of the Nazi Party's Tokyo branch came to commiserate with the correspondent of the *Frankfurter Zeitung*, Germany's leading newspaper.(The *Japan Advertiser* had got his affiliation wrong.) Sorge was a man who commanded respect and attention, as was apparent the moment a black limousine, with a swastika flag fluttering on the bonnet, swept onto the hospital forecourt and discharged the German ambassador's wife, Helma Ott.

Helma was a striking lady, tall even by European standards – the Japanese thought she resembled a *matsu no ki*, a pine tree – and very slender. Her hair was thoroughly grey, although she was a mere forty-four years of age, and her complexion shone with the freshness of a much younger woman. On one of her first visits she brought a get-well telegram from her husband, Eugen Ott, who had only recently been appointed ambassador of the Third Reich to Japan.

At this very moment, Ott was on his way to Berlin to discuss his new duties with Hitler's foreign minister, Joachim von Ribbentrop, and anticipated an audience with *Reichskanzler* Adolf Hitler himself. There is no doubt that, but for this pressing journey, the ambassador would have made an immediate bee-line for St Luke's. To Germany's top diplomat in Tokyo, Sorge was not only a journalist like no other. He was a personal friend, much liked and admired, who occupied a very special place in the Otts' domestic arrangements.

Over the coming weeks, Helma put in regular appearances at the hospital, to the detriment of her functions as the German colony's First Lady. 'I have to go now, my patient is waiting,' she would tell surprised hosts at social events, before rushing off. It was perhaps inevitable that this excessive solicitude provided the colony's matrons with a stimulating topic whenever they met for coffee and gossip.[6]

Even before this, the nature of Frau Ott's relationship with Dr Sorge had given rise to censorious whispers. The rumours about an affair were not without foundation, either. But – and this the busybodies could not know – the romance had already run its course. The passion was all spent, as far as Sorge was concerned. Helma, though, continued to look for fire in the dead ashes.

§ Among those who arrived to lift the patient's morale was Prince

Albrecht von Urach, his saviour on the night of the accident. At first sight, he and Sorge seemed ill-assorted. In temperament, they were virtual opposites. The prince, a scion of the Royal House of Württemberg, was easygoing, restrained in his manner and effete in appearance (though Hanako thought him elegant and good-looking).

Sorge, on the other hand, was dogmatic, boisterous and immoderate in most respects, especially in his appetite for women and drink. Urach, the correspondent for the Nazi Party newspaper *Volkischer Beobachter*, thought Sorge amusing and eccentric, as well as a skilled and knowledgeable writer. His noble rank gave him automatic entry to the smartest circles in Germany and Japan, and he was close to everyone that mattered in the German Foreign Ministry. This made him a useful companion.

No doubt Sorge felt rather more at home in the company of Major Erwin Scholl, the assistant military attaché, who drove over frequently to St Luke's. Scholl, a native of East Prussia, regarded Sorge as a good comrade and close friend. On arriving in January 1936, he was delighted to discover that Sorge had served in the same student battalion in Flanders in late 1914. The communion of the trenches was the strongest of bonds, creating instant and total trust. As a matter of course, Scholl spoke all too frankly about his work, not knowing that Sorge passed on the most important information to Moscow. Their comradeship was cemented by a shared passion for women and alcohol and a boyish delight in the telling of coarse anecdotes. In the past two years, the military attaché and the journalist had drunk their way across Tokyo in the uproarious fashion of two soldiers just back from the front.

We do not have a complete record of Sorge's visitors during his stay at St Luke's, but it would be surprising if these did not include Captain (later Rear-Admiral) Paul Wenneker, the naval attaché at the German embassy. Blond, blue-eyed, ramrod-straight, Wenneker was an epicurean after Sorge's heart (rumour had it that he had sampled every one of the Ginza's 2,000 bars). Sorge bowed to Captain Wenneker as one of very few men who could, literally, drink him under the table. The naval attaché was one of his very best sources in the embassy, innocently revealing precious secrets that swiftly found their way to Russia.

Hans-Otto Meissner, a young third secretary, fell into a different category. A sense of duty rather than friendship took him to the hospital. Posted to Tokyo in 1936, Meissner at first saw Sorge as 'the enigma of the German colony' and its 'mystery man'. But as he learnt more about the journalist, he had formed his own opinion. Sorge, he decided, was a 'gay, dissolute adventurer with a brilliant mind and an unassailable conceit'. One visit to St Luke's confirmed his impression that Sorge exerted an enviable magnetic power over women. It was the day an earthquake jolted the building: as the ground shook, three young nurses tore into the room and hurled themselves on Sorge's bed to protect him from falling plaster.[7]

We know too that a slim, balding man with round spectacles came to the hospital at least twice. Branko de Vukelic, a 34-year-old Yugoslav, was the espionage network's photographic expert. To cover his illegal activities, he worked as a journalist with Havas, the French news agency. On one visit to the patient he brought with him the Havas bureau chief, Robert Guillain. Guillain was new in Tokyo and keen to become acquainted with the *Frankfurter Zeitung* correspondent, whose praises Vukelic had sung.

'No one is better connected than Sorge. He's the closest friend of the German ambassador,' said Vuki, as the Yugoslav was known to all his friends. 'It was a terrible accident. But he's on the mend. The doctors have done a marvellous job of repairing his broken jaw. Why don't we go and see him? It's a good chance for you to meet and have a chat.'[8]

Max Clausen also came to visit the patient, on one occasion bringing his wife. Anna Clausen was an overweight, motherly woman, nearing forty – the same age as Max, a plain, stocky man with a sly grin and an ingratiating manner. They looked comfortable together, a plump, homely couple who would not have drawn a second glance on a street in Europe. There was a stern, puritanical streak in Anna, who regarded Sorge as a rotten influence on her husband. This latest drunken escapade lowered her opinion of him another notch.

§ Sorge was not idle during these weeks in hospital. He suffered from giddy spells at first, but as soon as they wore off he resumed work, heavily bandaged though he was. Visitors plied him with rumours and shop-talk, from which he distilled information to relay to his controllers. It was, most likely, the first time that St Luke's had served as a clearing-house for Soviet Intelligence.

Scholl's visits proved especially valuable. At the bedside, he passed on the latest information gathered from his Japanese contacts at General Staff Headquarters. And as usual, he asked for Sorge's help. One of his duties as military attaché was to compile reports on Japanese military affairs for his superiors in Berlin. It had become his habit to discuss these reports with Sorge, deferring to the journalist's superior understanding of Japan. Sometimes he lazily let Sorge draft the reports for him, so complete was his faith in the journalist's reliability. As Sorge observed, 'He brought me a lot of information and asked me what I thought. He wouldn't report anything important back to the home country without discussing it with me first, and asking my opinion, especially if the information was not confirmed.'[9]

For protection, the reports for Moscow had to be encoded before transmission. Sorge's network had its own code, which substituted figures for the letters of the alphabet. Random figures were added to make the system more secure, using tables in the *German Statistical Yearbook* for 1935. Before being sent overseas, Sorge had been taught cipher techniques by Fourth Department specialists and had committed the code to memory. No other member of the Tokyo network knew how it worked.

Up to May 1938, Clausen was unaware of the contents of the messages he tapped out in Morse code, and Sorge had no reason to discuss them with him. This was standard practice. For obvious reasons, a wireless operator is better off not knowing the meaning of the secret communications he is handling. As Sorge explained to a police interrogator: 'Only the person in charge of the intelligence group knows the method of encoding and decoding. But after the accident occurred I was at a loss how to handle it alone.'

Now that he lay injured in hospital, it struck him that it would be a great convenience if Clausen took over the chore. To cover himself, Sorge sent a message to Moscow explaining that he was ill – without the details – and seeking permission to initiate Clausen in the coding technique. His controllers in the Fourth Department gave their approval, and Sorge told Clausen how to proceed. 'You must memorize what I'm telling you. Take no notes. After transmission, destroy your work-sheets. Under no circumstances leave code materials where they could be found.'

From this point, Clausen took over the coding work in addition to his wireless duties. He was now able to read the outgoing and incoming traffic. The consequences of this would be devastating, and Sorge would later reproach himself for a grave error of judgement.

The accident had yet another legacy. After cosmetic surgery, Sorge's sensual features took on a fiercer, almost demoniac appearance. Still more alarming, some friends would later notice symptoms of an emotional imbalance and severe psychological disturbances. They decided these could only be attributable to the shock to the nervous system caused by that dreadful motorcycle crash.[10]

Part One

CHAPTER ONE

Child and Soldier

THE EARLIEST existing photo of Richard Sorge shows an infant at eight months, astride a high round table, as if on a throne, eyeing the camera sternly. At his side, a woman with a faint smile grips one tiny foot, in case the boy is minded to spring from this perch onto the four children seated below. An imposing father with a luxuriant beard towers above the brood, one arm akimbo, gazing into the distance with the air of a man well satisfied with his position in the world.

This family portrait is dated June 1896. The Sorges then lived in a sprawling wooden house shaded by acacias in Sabunchi, near the dusty city of Baku, Azerbaijan. The father was a specialist in oil-drilling machinery, employed by the Swedish Nobel conglomerate, one of many highly paid foreign technicians who flocked to the oilfields on the edge of the Caspian Sea.

Even the mind-baking heat of summer was tolerable in their airy mansion. Expatriates lived as grandly as colonials, segregated from the Muslim inhabitants crowded into bare shanties. Skilled engineers like Richard Sorge senior could build up, within a few years, a comfortable nest-egg to take home. To the natives they were all intruders and infidels, whether Germans, Swedes, Americans or Russians.

A glimmering memory of this ambience stayed with Richard Sorge all his life. The family moved to Berlin two years after his birth, but that fleeting experience of an alien land imprinted itself on his boyhood days in Germany. In his own words: 'The one thing that made my life a little different from the average was a strong awareness of the fact that I had been born in the southern Caucasus and that we had moved to Berlin when I was very small.'[1]

The family settled in a comfortable middle-class neighbourhood, and Richard Sorge senior prospered in a senior position with a bank involved in the import of Russian naphtha. Germany was at peace. Sorge, when he composed a statement in prison, would remember this as a tranquil, comfortable phase of his life: 'Until the outbreak of the war, my childhood was passed amid the comparative calm common to the well-off bourgeoisie in Germany. Economic worries had no place in our home.' However, Richard, a sensitive child, became aware that his home was 'very different from the average bourgeois home in Berlin'.

Writing in prison, Sorge did not spell out the differences. But these may be readily imagined. The Sorges would have been less parochial than most of their neighbours, more aware of a world beyond the frontiers of Kaiser Wilhelm's Germany. His father had spent much of his adult life working overseas, his mother, Nina, was Russian, and he had been born in a remote corner of Tsarist Russia. 'The Sorge household was slightly unusual, and so my childhood had something peculiar about it which set me, and my brothers and sisters, apart from ordinary children.'

The transition to school life made him more conscious of the differences between himself and other boys. From Easter 1905, when he was nine, until the war began in 1914, Sorge attended junior and middle school in Lichterfelde. Here, pupils were force-fed a stern diet of discipline, petty rules and loyalty to Kaiser and country; he chafed against the inflexibility of Prussian schooling. The early stirrings of a staunchly independent spirit can be detected in his account of those school years: 'I was a bad pupil, defied the school's regulations, was obstinate and wilful and rarely opened my mouth.' But if a school subject appealed to him, he threw himself into it with enthusiasm: 'In history, literature, philosophy, political science, and – it goes without saying – in athletics, I was far above the rest of the class, but in other subjects I was below average.'

There is a certain poignancy in this recollection. The 46-year-old man typing a statement in a Japanese prison is emphatic about his physical prowess as a youth. During one interrogation, he informs police that in 1912 and 1913 he trained hard in the fast walk, long jump and high jump with an eye to taking part in the Olympics. It is the voice of a man who can no longer run or jump, but wants his interrogators to know that he was a formidable athlete until he was lamed on the battlefield in the First World War.

At fifteen he discovered the joys of German literature, absorbing the works of Goethe and Schiller and 'struggling in vain to understand the history of philosophy and Kant'. The plays of Schiller were nothing less than a revelation. *Louise Millerin*, *Don Carlos* and *The Robbers* were the sort of reading that had aroused the social conscience of many a young man before him. No wonder the French Revolution – which translated into fact the inflammatory message of Schiller's *Sturm und Drang* theatrics

– seized the imagination of the young Sorge. He was enthralled by *The Robbers*, in which the hero, Karl Moor, becomes a criminal, and the leader of murderers, when he sees no other way of rectifying the injustices of his society.

There can be no doubt that this theme appealed greatly to the adolescent Sorge and produced a lasting influence. Villainy was justified if used to fight villainy. Victory over injustice demanded moral and physical sacrifice. (But what did Sorge make of Schiller's ending, where Karl Moor abandons his Robin Hood existence and surrenders to a clergyman, and by so doing acknowledges that there is a moral power stronger than his own individual will?)

The young Sorge also showed a keen interest in the society in which he lived, devouring newspapers to learn about political developments: 'I knew Germany's current problems better than the average grown-up … At school I was known as "Prime Minister".'

An early influence was Friedrich Adolf Sorge, a pioneering revolutionary and close comrade of Karl Marx. 'I knew how my grandfather had served the labour movement,' Sorge wrote in prison. In fact Friedrich Adolf was not his grandfather but a great-uncle, and it is not clear why he claimed a closer kinship with this distinguished forebear, a tireless organizer of the American working class who had died in 1906. No doubt he immersed himself in Friedrich Adolf's many tracts and magazine articles on the labour movement, though his conservative father would hardly have encouraged such reading: 'Father was, unmistakeably, a nationalist and imperialist … he was always strongly conscious of the property he had amassed while abroad and of his social position.'

As a young man, Sorge took part in the *Jugendbewegung*, the Youth Movement, whose innocent pleasures included long hikes through mountain forests, and the singing of songs that celebrated the honest purity of the great German *volk*. Sorge shared the Pan-German ideals of his generation, and was deeply patriotic. But his political views were not yet formed when the war brought his schooldays, and an untroubled existence, to an abrupt end.

§ Richard Sorge was eighteen when Kaiser Wilhelm II declared war on the Tsar's Russia in August 1914. During the school holiday he and a group of friends had been hiking in Sweden. They caught the last boat home, and found the railway stations milling with men in uniform recalled to their units.

A patriotic high-tide swept Germany. Young men like Richard threw away their books and seized their rifles with enthusiasm. The war was a 'purgative', and the beginning of 'a new zest for life', in the words of a young German novelist of the time. That is exactly what Richard must have felt. He swallowed whole the truism of the age that a man's education was not complete without experience of the army. School headmasters vied to provide the most recruits from their classrooms. The impetuous Richard Sorge needed no prodding.

Only after signing the enlistment papers did he tell his mother. Nina Sorge was a warm, loving mother, immensely proud of her youngest child. Richard was an adoring son. Her consternation when he told her he had obeyed the call to the colours can be readily imagined. Richard senior, a staunch nationalist, would have approved, but he did not live to see his son in uniform. He died in 1911, at the age of fifty-nine, leaving a comfortable legacy to his family. Unfortunately, Richard Sorge reveals nothing of his relationship with his father. One suspects the boy was swayed by the father's enthusiastic recounting of the military triumphs and empire-building of the great Bismarck.[2]

From Sorge's account of his march into battle, we catch a glimpse of a nature that determines his later destiny. We see a full-blooded, high-spirited youth, rushing into the fray, heedless of personal danger and impatient to escape the stifling tedium of bourgeois life. 'What drove me to make this decision was an urge to seek new experiences, to free myself from school studies, and from a life that seemed utterly meaningless to an eighteen-year-old, and the general excitement created by the war.'

Richard volunteered on 11 August, underwent basic training that he described as 'completely inadequate' and was posted to a student battalion of the Third Guards Field Artillery Regiment. In late September he was sent into action. He spent his nineteenth birthday on the battlefield by the banks of the Yser, in Flanders. On 11 November he experienced his baptism of fire. The German student battalions, ordered to storm French and Belgian positions, advanced in closed formation and were mown down by machine-gun fire. Thousands died, with patriotic songs on their lips. 'This period may be described as "from the classroom to the battlefield" or "from the school-bench to the slaughter-block",' Richard noted sardonically, recalling the innocence of the student volunteers used as cannon-fodder by the Prussian war minister, General Erich von Falkenhayn.

A photograph of Sorge the soldier shows a striking youth, with deep-set eyes and a large, well-sculpted face. The full-lipped mouth and strong jaw make a forceful impression. The handsome image is complemented by the military uniform. The worst nightmares of war still lay ahead.

§ In the muddy trenches of Flanders, Richard started to brood on the futility of war. On this same soil, for centuries, battle after battle had been fought for important reasons that no one could remember. Who had benefited?

> None of my simple soldier friends ever desired annexation or occupation. None of them ever understood the meaning of our efforts. Nobody knew the real purpose of the war, not to mention its deep-seated significance.
>
> Most of the soldiers were middle-aged men, labourers and craftsmen. Almost all of them belonged to labour unions, and the majority were Social Democrats. There was one real leftist among them, an old stone-mason from Hamburg, who refused to talk to anybody about his political beliefs.
>
> We became close friends, and he told me about his life in Hamburg, and the persecution and unemployment he had experienced. He was the first pacifist I had come across. He died in action in the early days of 1915.

In the early summer of 1915, Sorge was wounded by shrapnel from Belgian artillery and evacuated to a military hospital in Berlin. The period of convalescence was used for study. He also found time to sample some lectures at the Medical Department of Berlin University.

The homecoming proved a disheartening experience. Wartime shortages had stimulated profiteering and the black market, and the poor could barely feed their families. Men had gone to war carrying in their hearts a noble ideal of a better Europe in which Germany would occupy its rightful place. But the country that Richard saw now was a cesspit of greed, materialism and corruption.

He also began to doubt Germany's motives in waging war, suspecting that territorial expansion and hegemony over Europe were the true aims. But he overcame his qualms and volunteered for frontline duty before his allotted convalescence period was up, restless to be in the thick of the action once more. This time he was sent to the Eastern Front. Again he was wounded, and had to be evacuated to Berlin for medical treatment.

In hospital Richard attacked his books once again, and took his final school exam. The school-leaving certificate, issued by the Royal Examination Commission in Berlin, is dated 19 January 1916. His ability in German, French, English and religious instruction is assessed as 'satisfactory', in history, geography, mathematics, physics and chemistry as 'good'. Against physical training, a subject Richard adored, there is a blank space: he was too seriously injured to take the test. The certificate shows that Richard has risen in rank since first enlisting in the army: he is described as a bombardier in the 43rd Field Artillery Regiment Reserve.

He returned to a homeland that looked grimmer with every day that passed. National consensus on the certainty of victory had faded. The economy was in decay, there were cases of starving war widows, and he could observe with his own eyes the impoverishment of the middle classes in Berlin. The bourgeoisie were slipping to the economic level of the proletariat, and consoling themselves with the myth of German spiritual superiority. The spectacle of 'these ignorant and arrogant representatives of the "German spirit"' filled Sorge with revulsion.

The German leaders' rhetoric about fighting for a prosperous and harmonious Europe sounded increasingly hollow. Germany, along with Britain and France, was bereft of ideas on how to make the world a better place. The dawning of this realization had a profound effect on Sorge. 'Ever since that time, and regardless of the race of the people, I did not have any time for claims of spirituality and idealism trumpeted by a nation at war.'

What he saw and heard in his periods of convalescence in Berlin forced him to re-examine the values of the middle class from which he sprang, and the patriotic ideals he had believed to be worth dying for. Yet once again his restless nature drove him to back to the Eastern Front in the spring of 1916. As he explained: 'I felt that I would be better off fighting in a foreign land than sinking deeper into the mud at home.'

Rejoining his unit, he found that the morale of his fellow-soldiers was sinking. Many of them were coming to realize the futility of the war, and the need for sweeping social and political change. 'The notion was gradually forming that a violent political change was the only way of extricating ourselves from this quagmire.'

In lulls in the fighting in the Minsk sector, Richard listened to leftists offering radical prescriptions for not just ending this war, but eliminating the causes of the endless repetition of wars in Europe.

> As was my habit, I merely listened to these discussions and asked questions; I still had no convictions, knowledge or resolution. The time was ripe, however, for me to pass from my long period of fence-sitting to the final decision.
>
> It was then that I was wounded for the third time. This time seriously. I was hit by a great deal of shrapnel, two pieces of which smashed bones.

In a field hospital at Königsberg, in what was then East Prussia, Richard came across a young nurse who opened his eyes to a new world of ideas. She and her father, a doctor, were both radical socialists, and they happily took the young soldier under their wing. 'They gave me my first detailed account of the state of the revolutionary movement in Germany ... for the first time I heard of Lenin.'

While changing bandages and bathing his terrible wounds, the young woman – whose identity is unknown – drip-fed him socialist theory. She painted pictures of a better, more just world, and explained how this could be achieved. Books by Marx and Engels, Kant and Schopenhauer piled up beside his bed. She stimulated his intellectual curiosity, prescribing her favourite works on economics, history and the fine arts. This education lasted many months, interrupted by a series of operations on his shattered legs. It was a period of the most agonizing pain and the greatest bliss: 'Despite the seriousness of my treatment and the excruciating pain ... I was happy for the first time in many years.' He would always remember the debt he owed to the 'very cultured and intelligent nurse' he had met in Königsberg. As he wrote in his prison statement, 'My strong will to study – by which I sometimes feel driven even now – stems from that period.'

When he left hospital, the surgeons had saved his legs, but the left was two centimetres shorter than the right. Henceforth, he would never walk properly. Spasms of pain recurred to torment him in later life. But – as is true of many people with a physical disability – he was driven by an urge to prove himself fitter and abler than other men.

As a spy, he would find a way to turn a handicap into an asset. The war wounds were a badge of courage (he sometimes rolled up his trouser legs to display the scars to drinking companions), a surer testimonial than the Iron Cross, Second Class, he had been awarded 'for gallantry'. The limp was a bond with other veterans of the trenches. Faced with the visible proof of Sorge's sacrifice for the fatherland, German officials were more easily induced to part with confidential information.

Richard was now unfit for military service, and returned to his books. In any case, he had lost his boyish appetite for the adventure of war:

> At this time, that is, during the summer and winter of 1917, I came to feel most intensely that the Great War was meaningless, and would reduce everything to ruins. Already several millions had perished on each side, and who could predict how many more millions would go the same way?

His political awareness had been sharpened by the nurse at Königsberg, and his ideological formation had begun. He resumed his studies at Berlin University, switching from medicine to politics and economics, seeking answers to the ills of society in the tenets of socialism. In Germany, the situation cried out for radical change. The mighty economic machine had crumbled, capitalism was disintegrating, there was desperate poverty. 'I myself, in common with countless members of the proletariat, could feel the collapse through hunger and constant food shortages.'

Like many bourgeois families, the Sorges were struggling to make ends meet. Raging inflation had whittled away his father's inheritance. Eventually Nina Sorge was obliged to give up the comfortable home in middle-class Lichterfelde and move to a rented apartment in a less salubrious district of Berlin.

Richard's experiences had implanted the hatred for war that remained a constant factor in his life. His convictions were moulded by the nightmare he had lived through, and the shattering spectacle of Germany's decay.

> The World War from 1914 to 1918 exercised a profound influence upon my whole life. Had I been swayed by no other considerations, this war alone would have made me a Communist.

Like many other young Germans, Richard Sorge had become a radical in the trenches. And what they saw on the return to the homeland, after years of blood and dirt on the battlefield, reinforced their yearning for draconian remedies. By the autumn of 1918 Germany was rotting from despair and hate, and on the brink of chaos. Food and fuel were scarce. Malnutrition hastened the spread of a terrible influenza epidemic. Hungry and jobless, the haggard survivors from the military fronts were open to the ideas of extremists.

In early November 1918, the major naval port of Kiel was taken over by sailors singing revolutionary songs, a mutiny that quickly spread to other North Sea ports. A left-wing uprising in Munich deposed Germany's oldest monarchy. Revolt erupted in Berlin, where Karl Liebknecht and Rosa Luxemburg, leaders of the radical left, dreamed of imitating the Russian revolution and turning Germany into a republic of workers' and soldiers' councils.

On 9 November 1918 the discredited Kaiser Wilhelm II was forced to abdicate, and two days later the humiliating surrender terms of the Allies were accepted by a new social democratic government. Although the generals and the civilian elite were responsible for the defeat, it was the new centrist leadership who would bear the stigma of signing a soul-destroying armistice.

Millions of Germans were profoundly shaken by these events, none more intensely than a 29-year-old army corporal recovering in hospital from a poison gas attack. Adolf Hitler took the nation's defeat as a personal affront, and reacted by blaming the Marxists and Jews for breaking the moral backbone of the people. 'So it had all been in vain,' Hitler wrote later in his autobiography *Mein Kampf.* 'In vain the death of two million.'

Despite his deep disgust at the betrayal by scoundrels 'in the pay of enemy propaganda', Hitler was not minded to join battle against the enemy marching in the streets. Many like-minded veterans volunteered for special units commanded by reactionary officers who stormed out to crack heads and suppress revolutionary activity. But Hitler decided to take a different path when he learnt of Germany's defeat and the end of the monarchy: 'There followed terrible days and even worse nights. In these nights hatred grew in me, hatred for those responsible for this deed. In the days that followed, my own fate became known to me ... I, for my part, decided to go into politics.'

The war was over, but the Allied navies kept up a blockade, depriving Germany of food and fuel. The flu epidemic raged unabated in the winter of 1918–19. Count Harry Kessler, diplomat and man-about-town, noted in his diary that within six months of the armistice 700,000 children, old people and women had succumbed. 'The German people, starved and dying by the hundred thousand, were reeling deliriously between blank despair, frenzied revelry and revolution.'

Any young man who had endured the hell of the front line could not help but clench his fists in indignation at the bitter fruits of peace. Some raged at the left-wingers and Jews who had stabbed Germany's fighting men in the back, and girded themselves for revenge. Others, like Sorge, cheered the collapse of the old imperial order and its warmongers, and believed that militarism would be defeated once and for all only by drastic surgery. To Sorge, it looked like a promising moment to recreate in Germany the revolution achieved by Bolshevik leaders in Russia. He was soon to discover that this vision was not shared by the broad masses, who – for the time being – remained loyal to a more democratic brand of socialism.

CHAPTER TWO

Student and Revolutionary

RICHARD WAS twenty-two years of age when the Bolshevik Revolution shook the world in November 1917. Its effect on a young man in search of something to believe in was stunning. As he wrote later, this was the first time in the long history of the international labour struggle that the exploited masses had broken their chains and overthrown their oppressors. Was not this the cure for the evils of society, the absolute solution for all the problems of poverty, inequality and injustice that the world had been waiting for? Richard was 'plunged into a confusion of the soul'.

The Russian Revolution was a turning point in Richard's life. It showed him the way the workers' struggle must take, in every country, and inspired him to commit himself heart and soul to the cause of achieving a revolution in Germany: 'I resolved not only to support the movement theoretically and ideologically, but to actually become part of it myself.'[1]

He started to translate his convictions into actions as soon as he was discharged from the army in 1918. In the early part of that year he transferred his studies from Berlin to Kiel University, where he had his first taste of conspiratorial work among revolutionaries. The high point was the mutiny of the German navy fleet in October 1918. Richard prowled the docks of Kiel harbour, where he stealthily handed out leaflets to sailors, urging them to join the workers' struggle against capitalist tyranny: 'I conducted secret lectures on socialism to groups of sailors and dock workers.'

It was in Kiel that Richard came to the attention of an economics professor, Dr Kurt Gerlach, and his wife Christiane, who held regular political salons for young people at their home. Christiane describes how she and Sorge became acquainted in this vignette:

My husband had lived many years in England and was in sympathy with the idea of a German revolution. Late autumn 1918, winter 1919! Painters

20

were talking about new art, poets were breaking with all the traditions and a young student of my husband sat silently among the guests: Richard Sorge, son of a well-off German father and a Russian mother, born in Baku.

He had gone through the war, and he limped from a shot-away knee. In the lecture-room, in seminars, he was less reserved than in our salons, and it was soon clear that my husband favoured him over all the others. A friendship developed between the two of them; we called Sorge by his nick-name Ika, and when my husband moved to the Technical College in Aachen, he took him along as his assistant.[2]

Something about Richard – 'Ika' – sparked more than a casual interest in Christiane. She was drawn by the 'unusual face' and blue eyes: 'In his clear, sharp eyes there lay infinite distance, and loneliness, everybody could feel that.'

The following few years were eventful. Richard spent part of 1919 at Hamburg University working on his thesis on consumer co-operatives, and in August he was awarded a doctorate in political science '*mit Auszeichnung*' (with distinction). Once again, he became involved in shadowy activities, organizing a socialist group for students. At some point he moved to Aachen at Gerlach's invitation, and became assistant lecturer at the Technical College. And it was in Aachen, on 15 October 1919, that Richard joined the German Communist Party.

§ Eager to make his mark in the party, Richard accepted an exacting assignment. To recruit miners into the party, he took a job at a coal-mine near Aachen and organized cells at various pits in the industrial Rheinland. Life in the mines was tough and dangerous, he recalled later, especially hard because his war wounds still brought on spasms of pain. 'But I never regretted the decision. The experience as a miner was no less valuable than the experience of the battlefield, and my new vocation was equally significant to the party.'[3]

In March 1920, German military officers launched a *putsch* in an attempt to seize political power. The communists responded by rallying for a general strike, and Richard Sorge joined the Aachen strike committee. There is evidence that Richard also belonged to the party's military committee in the Ruhr, which organized fit young followers to do battle in the streets with the 'counter-revolutionaries'. In the words of a friend, he was 'quite incapable of staying out of a fight others had joined'.[4]

We know from his contemporaries that Richard was a militant who proudly bore the bruises of brawls with an assortment of reactionaries.

In his prison statement, however, he is silent about the violent episodes in this incandescent period of his life. His account of these adrenalin-filled years is fragmentary and selective, and seems deliberately designed to confuse his captors.

It was said of Sorge by those who knew him in the 1920s that the footloose young man was 'not marriage material'. The sad outcome of his union with Christiane Gerlach suggests that this may well have been true.

Early in 1919, Richard suddenly turned up on the doorstep of the Gerlachs' house in Aachen. The doorbell rang one evening and Christiane went to see who was there.

> Outside stood Ika. It was as if a stroke of lightning ran through me. In this one second something awoke in me that had slumbered until now, something dangerous, dark, inescapable.
> Ika never pushed. He did not need to court people, they rushed to him, men and women. Did he perhaps have more subtle means for bending them to his will?[5]

Christiane's husband, Kurt, resigned himself to the situation. Sorge was younger, spellbinding and disarming. As we know from many sources, women found him hard to resist, and men, it seems, found him hard to hate. The Gerlachs agreed on an amicable divorce, and Richard and Christiane were married in May 1921.

This was not quite what Richard had envisaged: apparently he had hoped to live with Christiane without going through the formalities of marriage. There was no deception involved – he had told her he saw marriage as a bourgeois curse. As modern socialists, he said, they should have no truck with marriage vows.

That was true, but it was not the only reason for Richard's reluctance to commit himself to Christiane. He relished his freedom as a 'wanderer, who can keep nothing in his hands' and expanded on this theme in a letter to a close friend, Erich Correns, dated 29 October 1919: 'In no way, not even internally, do I need another person to be able to live; I mean to really live, not simply vegetate. I have no attachments any more. I am so completely rootless that the road is where I really feel at home.'

In February 1920 Richard and Christiane set up home together in Solingen, where he had found a job with a newspaper, the *Voice of the Miners* (published by the Communist Party). It soon became evident that the police were keeping a close watch on him, and looking for an excuse to chase him out of town. By living 'in sin' with Christiane, he was giving the police the excuse they needed. Richard explained his predicament in a letter to Correns on 19 April 1921:

> Because they [the police] naturally want to throw me out of Solingen, but have no grounds to do so, they will try to use the pretext that this is creating a public scandal. To the bourgeois, living together constitutes creating a public scandal. It annoys both of us, but we will have to bite the sour apple.[6]

The sour apple was marriage. In 1922, we find the legally married couple in Frankfurt. Gerlach, who bore no grudge, arranged a job for Richard at a foundation for social and economic research he had helped to set up. We have the following description of Sorge in this period: 'Ika, tall, well-built, with a full head of hair, gave an impression of strength. His features, although sallow, were attractive, with a strong, prominent forehead, which made his eyes seem very deep-set.'[7]

For two years, including a spell when the Communist Party was outlawed, Sorge held responsible positions that indicate the esteem in which he was held by party leaders. His remit included liaison between Frankfurt and the central committee in Berlin, handling party funds and organizing propaganda materials.

In April 1924, Sorge was chosen to act as bodyguard for Soviet VIPs attending the party's Ninth Congress held in Frankfurt. The Comintern had sent several powerful figures, including Dimitri Manuilsky and Solomon Rozovsky, as delegates. Richard, conscientious and meticulous, not only organized security and accommodation for the Russians, but also shepherded them around Frankurt in their free time.

One day he brought them to the house that Christiane had tastefully furnished with antiques and a fine collection of modern and rare old paintings.[8] Christiane was not impressed by their peasant manners: 'My mind wanders back and I see them sitting on my violet sofa, eating peanuts which they had brought with them. They simply threw the shells on the carpet.'[9]

The Russians were well contented, however. By the end of their visit, they had decided that their efficient and charming escort was the sort of young man the Soviet Union could use to good advantage. 'At the close of the session, they asked me to come to Comintern Headquarters in Moscow that year to work for them.'[10]

Richard – undoubtedly flattered that these eminent revolutionaries had recognized his ability – was happy to accept, with the proviso that he must first complete his scheduled tasks for the German party. The abortive uprising on 23 October 1923 had shown that the German

Revolution was no longer round the corner, as he had believed and hoped. He was bitterly disappointed by the fiasco, and decided he could do more useful work elsewhere.

Very early one morning in October 1924, Richard and his wife crossed the Soviet border. Christiane was not buoyed by what she saw: 'The first impression of Russia: infinitely melancholy!' she wrote.[11]

CHAPTER THREE

Moscow, 1924-29

MOSCOW WAS bleak, stricken with poverty and permeated by fear. 'Everybody calls everybody a spy, secretly, in Russia, and everybody is under surveillance. You never feel safe,' observed a friend of the Revolution in 1921.[1]

Richard Sorge was blind to the imperfections of the Soviet Union, or justified them – like many starry-eyed visitors from capitalist countries – on the grounds that the Revolution was still in its infancy. He 'saw everything in black and white', noted a friend, and would brook no criticism of the workers' paradise. In high spirits he went to work at the headquarters of the Comintern, the organization founded by Lenin in 1919 to spread revolution throughout the world. He was assigned to the international liaison department, OMS, which he described in his prison statement as the 'Comintern Intelligence Division'.

His job was to collate information – some from published sources, some from Comintern agents – and compile reports on the labour movements and on economic and political conditions in Germany and other countries. The confidential analyses he prepared were channelled to high-ranking officials including Otto Kuusinen, the Comintern's secretary-general, Iosif Pyatnitsky, the head of OMS, and Dimitri Manuilsky of the Communist Party Central Committee. Other reports by Sorge were published in the Comintern's organs or the Communist Party theoretical journal. These appeared under his pseudonyms, 'R. Sonter' and 'I.K. Sorge'.

Richard and Christiane lived in the Hotel Lux, a regular haunt of officials of the Comintern and visiting foreign communists and trade union delegates. Hotel residents were kept under close watch by the secret police: the Soviet government did not trust visiting comrades and wanted to know what they were doing and saying.[2]

Social life was very restricted. The couple visited the German Club each week, where there were a few German books but little else in the way of entertainment. Christiane found it a depressing place. The club appears to have livened up when Richard was elected its president; he was an able organizer, and one of his accomplishments in 1926 was the setting up of a Pioneers Group for the children of the city's German residents.

Richard was not an easy person to live with, Christiane had discovered. He was self-contained, with deep inner resources, and although he was fond of her, she felt he could as easily have lived without her. 'No one, ever, could violate the inner solitude, it was this which gave him his complete independence – and perhaps explained the hold he had over people.'[3]

There was a happy interlude when they went their own ways one summer holiday. Richard travelled to Baku, which had become the capital of the Azerbaijan Socialist Republic, to visit his birthplace. The house had been turned into a convalescent home; a glorious acacia tree still shaded the veranda, as it had – so neighbours told him – at the time of his birth thirty years ago. From Baku, Richard went on to the Black Sea resort of Sotchi, where his wife was holidaying with a girlfriend.

But the marriage quickly came under strain. On some evenings, she was left alone in the Hotel Lux, and Richard would give her no clue where he was going, who he was meeting. 'A tormenting anxiety came over me. I could sense ever more clearly that our paths were moving apart through the same providence that once had made us collide with one another.'[4]

The isolation and tedium of her life in Moscow became unbearable, and she suggested that it might be better if she went home. Make up your own mind, Richard said. He could not tie her to him, and he himself refused to be tied.

The parting, in the autumn of 1926, on a cold Moscow railway platform late at night, was forever etched in her memory. 'We acted as if we would meet again soon. But as the train moved off, I could not stop the flood of tears. I knew it was the end of our life together, and he must have known it too.'[5]

Sorge, restless and ambitious, was not happy sitting at a desk and pined for adventure. His chance came in 1927, when he was sent to Scandinavia, the first of many journeys to Europe. These were exciting missions – helping to organize national communist parties under the wing of the Comintern, reporting on communist penetration of labour unions, analysing the economic and political situation in the countries he visited.

By his own account, he was sent to England in the spring of 1929, staying there about ten weeks, to report on the miners' strike, the state of the trade unions and the strength of the British Communist Party. He visited mining districts and 'saw for myself how deep the crisis was'. Years later, Japanese interrogators extracted only part of the story from their prisoner. It appears that his true mission in England involved collecting sensitive military information from a Soviet spy inside the British Intelligence organization MI6.

During his stay in London he was accompanied by Christiane. It is clear from her recollections that the mission was very risky. After an interval of many years, she recalled that the purpose was to meet a very important agent. The couple went together to the rendezvous on a street corner. At Sorge's bidding, Christiane kept her distance while the two men talked, and stood watch for signs of danger. It is possible that the agent was Charles 'Dickie' Ellis, a senior MI6 officer, who in the course of a convoluted career appears to have passed secrets to both the Germans and the Soviets. If he had been entrusted with an assignment of this nature Sorge would certainly not have sought contact with members of the British Communist Party, who would be well known to the police.[6]

On such clandestine journeys Richard travelled on a false passport with an assumed identity, playing cat-and-mouse with police forces that kept tabs on local communist organizations. He was in his element. 'He took to conspiracy like a fish in water. He would flash an amused smile at you, his eyebrows raised in disdain for being unable to tell you where it was he had spent his last year,' recalled Hede Massing, a friend from Richard's Frankfurt days.

When they met in Berlin in 1929, she found him largely unchanged by some four years in Moscow. He was utterly discreet about his work, but was amusing and eloquent all the same. As for his first assignment, he told her that it was in 'some Nordic country (he never said which) where he lived "high among the mountains" and where his company were "sheep, mostly". He would ramble on about the human qualities of sheep once one got to know them.'[7]

Richard developed an aptitude for intelligence work, but sorting out the internal problems of communist parties in Europe was not to his taste at all. From his experience in the field, he concluded that it was a mistake to combine intelligence gathering and party organization work. An intelligence agent who mixed with known communists was bound to attract the attention of the police sooner or later. So on his return to Moscow in 1929, he set out his proposals for separating the espionage activities from the functions of a Comintern operative in a 'frank analysis' for his superiors.

However, there is little doubt that Sorge was sparing with the truth when he explained to the Japanese authorities the motives for his switch from the Comintern to Red Army Intelligence towards the end of 1929. His transfer coincided with a crisis in the Comintern which cast a shadow over all those in its service. During 1929 Nikolai Bukharin, chairman of its Executive Committee since 1926, was swept aside in a witch-hunt against 'class enemies', losing his Comintern position and then his place in the Politburo. With the persecution of Bukharin, the talented foreign communists he had nurtured – Sorge among them – were deprived of a protector, and they too were harried and expelled from the Comintern. But Sorge hid this from the Japanese – he did not want them to think he was anything other than master of his fate.

The fact was that Sorge was feeling increasingly insecure in the Comintern. At one point he learnt by chance that the reports he sent to Moscow were being filed away unread, a discovery that both hurt his pride and dented his idealism. It brought home how exposed his position had become. Yet the only hint he gave the Japanese of this unsatisfactory state of affairs is a throwaway line in his prison statement: 'The Comintern had no interest in the political intelligence I gave them.'[8]

Happily for Sorge, his talent for clandestine activities had come to the notice of General Jan Karlovich Berzin, founder and director of the Fourth Department, the section of Soviet Military Intelligence operating networks of agents in foreign countries. (It is possible that Berzin's department had a hand in the sensitive intelligence assignments that took Sorge to Scandinavia, Britain and Germany during his Comintern years.) The general was seriously short of capable men, and glad to be able to extricate Sorge from an uncomfortable situation.

When Richard transferred to the Fourth Department in 1929, the Far East was a major focus of Soviet interest. After revolution failed to take hold in Western Europe, Soviet leaders had set their sights on the colonies of Western capitalist powers in Asia. Seen from Moscow, the most likely starting point for a revolution that would spread throughout Asia was China. But Soviet intelligence efforts in China had suffered serious reverses.

In a savage change of policy, Chiang Kai-shek, the Kuomintang leader, had decided to destroy the communists with whom he had formed a temporary alliance. Most of their leaders had been executed or had fled underground. Diplomatic relations between Moscow and Chiang Kai-shek's government in Nanking were severed after charges that the Soviet Union was using its consulates for espionage.

China was in the midst of civil war, but no systematic intelligence was reaching the Fourth Department on such vital matters as the comparative military strengths of the Nanking government of Chiang Kai-shek and its foe, the Chinese Red Army. The Russians, as yet undecided which horse to back, badly wanted to know which of the two armies was most likely to emerge triumphant. Berzin's priority was to rebuild his shattered China network and he planned to send Alex Borovitch, a colonel in his Far Eastern section, to Shanghai with an experienced wireless operator to restore effective operations. Sorge was told he would be the third man in this team.

In a briefing, Berzin explained to Sorge that he needed regular reports on the military capabilities of the Nanking government and the Chinese communists. No time should be lost in reopening wireless communications. Sorge put forward a proposal to report on the political and social as well as the military situation, and Berzin assented. Sorge was enthusiastic about his new mission: 'I decided to engage in this work partly because it was congenial to one of my temperament and partly because I was attracted by the new and extremely complicated state of affairs in the Orient.'[9]

In the autumn of 1929, Richard was initiated into the duties of a Red Army Intelligence officer. The Fourth Department's Far East section instructed him in military aspects, and other specialists briefed him on the political goals of the Soviet government and party with regard to China. Basic training in the use of codes and ciphers followed. He was given the code-name 'Ramsay', which would remain unchanged until the summer of 1941.

In November Sorge travelled to Berlin, where he made arrangements to contribute articles to two specialist journals devoted to agriculture and sociology. This was to be his legal cover. Carrying a valid German passport in his own name, he set out from Marseilles in December aboard a Japanese ship. Together with his two comrades, he reached Shanghai some time in January 1930.

CHAPTER FOUR

Shanghai Days

RICHARD SORGE and his two companions blended easily into Shanghai's rich racial stew. They found not the China of bamboos and willows, but a pulsating city with the tallest skyscrapers in Asia, wide boulevards and many pink faces of Westerners among the local inhabitants.

Over half of Shanghai was governed by foreign powers; in the International Settlement, which had its own municipal council, police force, customs authorities and volunteer force, the British ruled the roost. Ninety years earlier, British merchant adventurers had set up a trading port on swamp and mud on the Huangpu, ten miles inland from the Yangtze, Asia's greatest river. In 1930 the visitor found a great, thriving commercial centre, throbbing with enterprise, raw greed, and every pleasure its inhabitants could devise. Foreign residents were often at a loss to describe the magic of the city and tended to fall back on the convenient cliché: unique.

Shanghai was unique in the degree of Western penetration of China, and unique in another sense. The foreign concessions harboured countless Chinese intellectuals, dissenters and revolutionaries fleeing persecution by the Kuomintang authorities. The underground headquarters of the Chinese Communist Party was here; as well as the thriving gangster underworld and the Kuomintang tycoons. Shanghai was a magnet for adventurers, profiteers and spies of every nationality.

China was in anguish at the time Sorge arrived in 1930. Chiang Kai-shek had established himself as the supreme warlord, but much of the vast country was prey to rival warlords and bandits. Thousands of Chinese were dying every day – if not from starvation or banditry, then from the predations of communist and government forces locked in a vicious civil war. But for the foreign residents and the Chinese elite of Shanghai, the war may as well have been on another planet.

In February 1930 Agnes Smedley, the celebrated correspondent of the *Frankfurter Zeitung*, described the mood in the hedonistic city in an article entitled 'Civil War in China – what comes next?'

In the big cities, and especially Shanghai, life follows its normal carefree pattern. There are opulent official receptions and balls, new banks opening, the establishment of great financial groupings and alliances, gambling on the stock exchange, opium-smuggling, and mutual insults by foreigners and Chinese under the aegis of extra-territoriality. And there are night clubs, brothels, gambling clubs, and tennis courts and so on. And there are actually people who call this the beginning of a new era, the birth of a new nation. That may be true for a certain class of Chinese: for the merchants, bankers, racketeers. But for the Chinese peasantry, that is for 85 percent of the Chinese people, all this is like a life-destroying plague.

One of Agnes Smedley's admiring readers was Richard Sorge, and he sought her out soon after his arrival. Starting out in a strange city, it was essential to build up connections. A letter from the Foreign Ministry in Berlin, addressed to the German consul-general, recommended him as a journalist planning to write about Chinese agrarian conditions. But he appears to have had little else in the way of introductions. Smedley, whom he had never met, proved a generous supplier of contacts, as he recalled in his prison statement: 'The only person I knew I could depend on in China was Agnes Smedley, of whom I had first heard in Europe. I enlisted her help in establishing my group in Shanghai and particularly in selecting Chinese co-workers.'[1]

She was an exceptional woman, who had battled her way to fame from an impoverished childhood spent in the coal-mining camps in Colorado. A tireless champion of the oppressed, she had passionately espoused the causes of Indian independence from Britain, and the liberation of women. Her international reputation was established with the publication of an autobiographical novel, *Daughter of Earth*, which appeared in a German edition in 1929, and which Sorge had almost certainly read. Arriving in Shanghai in the spring of 1929 on an assignment for the *Frankfurter Zeitung*, she found exciting new challenges. The Chinese woman was a virtual slave, sexually, economically and socially; a symbol of the backwardness of society. The Chinese peasant was cruelly exploited by the governing classes.

To these victims of oppression, the struggle of the Chinese revolutionary movement offered hope, and Smedley threw herself into this new cause with heart and soul. By the time Sorge called on her, she had developed many contacts in the underground Chinese Communist Party. She was in her element in Shanghai, a haven for Chinese intellectuals and political dissenters fleeing persecution.

What did Richard make of this unusual woman? No doubt he was impressed by her physical courage, her feisty contempt for authority

and the firmness of her convictions, and he respected her skills as a
crusading journalist. They were both communists, both convinced they
were called to help free the world's oppressed from servitude and misery.

Smedley was not beautiful in any conventional way. The short-
cropped hair and prominent chin gave her a mannish air, which she
deliberately cultivated. By her own account, she tried to compensate for
her physical unattractiveness by developing her brains. According to
one female contemporary, Smedley in 1930 was: 'an intelligent working
woman in appearance. Simply dressed, thin brown hair, full of life, big,
grey-green eyes, in no sense pretty, but a well-proportioned face. When
she strokes her hair back, one sees the great dome of the forehead.'[2]

She was three and a half years older than Sorge – they must have
met for the first time around her thirty-eighth birthday (23 February
1930.) They apparently became lovers before they became friends.
Mature women seem to have held an appeal for Sorge, as we shall see.

According to a friend of Smedley, she and Sorge spent the late spring
and summer together in Canton (Guangzhou).[3] The newcomer from
Germany enthralled her, and she was in a state of bliss for the brief
duration of an intensely satisfying romance. A letter written on 28 May
1930 to a close female friend is revealing about them both:

> I'm married, child, so to speak – just sort of married, you know; but he's
> a he-man also, and it's 50-50 all along the line, with he helping me and
> I him and we working together or bust, and so on; a big, broad, all-sided
> friendship and comradeship. I do not know how long it will last; that
> does not depend on us. I fear not long. But these days will be the best
> in my life. Never have I known such good days, never have I known
> such a healthy life, mentally, physically.[4]

Smedley, whose crusade for equal rights for women included the right
to sexual gratification, was plainly fulfilled by her manly lover. For
Sorge, the attachment was also rewarding in a practical sense. Smedley's
connections were wide-ranging, and she generously opened doors for
him and provided valuable information. In his prison statement, he
counted her as part of the Shanghai network: 'I used her as a direct
member of my group, and her work was completely satisfactory.'[5]

Smedley, however, did not regard herself as a 'member' of any group.
She was aware Sorge was working for Moscow, but was unsure whether
he served the Comintern or a department of Soviet Military Intelligence.
Chafing against authority of any kind, Smedley was not a woman to let
herself be slotted into an organization. She later wrote that her
sympathies always lay with the communists and that she had actively

assisted the communist movement in China, but had never joined the party.

The couple arrived in Canton in the early part of May and for a few idyllic weeks they travelled together in southern China, an area ruled by warlords. The treaty port of Canton was, after Shanghai, the most important commercial centre under foreign control. Here, three years earlier, Chiang Kai-shek's troops had crushed a communist uprising and massacred thousands of people – including most of the Soviet consulate's staff. Communist and labour union leaders – those who survived – were trying to reorganize. Beneath the surface, the city seethed with unrest.

Richard made the international concession in Canton his base for field trips to investigate conditions in the province, which adjoined the British colony of Hong Kong. By the time he left the city, he had established a network of willing helpers to report on the Nanking government's moves to exert authority over the southern warlords. These, and informants in other parts of China, provided a steady stream of intelligence on Chiang Kai-shek's quest for administrative unity and internal order. Over the following months, he relayed to Moscow his assessments of the relative strengths of the Chiang Kai-shek regime and its principal enemies.

One of the first priorities for the trio of agents – Alex Borovitch, Richard Sorge and Seppel Weingarten – was the improvement of radio communications between Moscow and Shanghai. This work was already under way when the new team arrived. Max Clausen, Weingarten's colleague from the Fourth Bureau's technical department, had been sent to China in the autumn of 1928. By the time he met Sorge in January 1930, Clausen had established radio contact between Shanghai and Vladivostok, and installed transmitting equipment for a Red Army spy group based in Harbin.

Clausen, who was thirty-one years of age in 1930, was a dedicated communist. He was the son of a poor shopkeeper in northern Germany, and his convictions had been moulded by his personal experience of poverty. His parents could afford only the barest education for the boy, and he was happy to find a job in the merchant navy. As an activist in the German Seamen's Union, Clausen attracted the attention of Soviet Intelligence and was invited to Moscow, where he was given a month's training at the Red Army wireless school before being assigned to an existing *apparat* in Shanghai.

After a spell in Harbin, Clausen returned to Shanghai, where he encountered a widow, Anna Wallenius, a refugee from the Russian

Revolution. She and her late husband had settled, like thousands of other White Russians, in Shanghai, a kaleidoscope of over thirty nationalities. Anna detested communism; when she fell in love with Max, she had no inkling that he was an ardent communist and Soviet agent. She became his common-law wife, and it would be several years before the Fourth Department gave him permission to legalize the union.

A few months after arriving in Shanghai, Sorge's superior, Alex Borovitch, had to leave in a hurry – the Shanghai police were on his tail. From then on Richard had charge of their network, and would remain his own boss for the rest of his career as an intelligence officer. No one in Shanghai, except for the tiny band of Fourth Bureau agents, knew who Sorge really was. He had two other identities, one completely phoney, one corresponding to his legal cover. Chinese collaborators knew him as Mr Johnson, an American journalist, and assumed he was working for the Comintern. Then there was Dr Sorge, the writer of articles like 'The soy-bean harvest in Manchuria', 'Good Sesame Harvest in China' and 'China's Growing Peanut Exports', published in the *Deutsche Getreïde-Zeitung* (German Grain Newspaper) in Berlin.

This was the persona the German community knew and came to respect. Richard found his most valuable sources of information on the Nanking government's military strength among the fifty German officers advising Chiang Kai-shek's armies. As a war veteran, he could approach such men with confidence. The limp from a war wound was an obvious testimonial.

Germany was seeking to increase its prestige in China by assisting the reorganization of the Chinese army and supplying armaments. The growth of German influence was a source of great concern to the Soviet Union, but it was Japanese expansion that posed a more immediate threat to Soviet interests in China. This was brought home by an explosive event in 1931. On the night of 18 September the South Manchurian Railway near Mukden was dynamited by unknown perpetrators. The Kwantung Army, the Japanese garrison in Manchuria, put the blame on the Chinese, and occupied Mukden after a heavy bombardment of Chinese troops. In little more than a month, almost all of Manchuria was under Japanese control. On 1 March 1932, 'Manchukuo' was proclaimed a republic, and Pu-yi, a puppet of Japan, installed as regent.

This act of aggression, euphemistically labelled the Manchurian Incident by Japan, was the spark that led to the conflagration in the Pacific ten years later. The direct effect was to upset the delicate balance of interests between Japan and the Soviet Union. In Sorge's words:

After seizing control of Manchuria, Japan had an incentive to play an extremely active role in East Asia. Furthermore, it was easy to see that the conquest had bolstered her determination to make that role a dominant and exclusive one. The direct effect of the Manchurian Incident on the Soviet Union was to bring her face to face with Japan in a vast border region hitherto more or less neglected from the standpoint of national defense.[6]

The Manchurian Incident prompted international condemnation, but the major powers were careful not to provoke Japan and conceded that the Japanese had special rights and interests in Manchuria. The Chinese were enraged by the weak-kneed response of the world community. Anti-Japanese demonstrations flared up in cities across China. The tension boiled over in Shanghai, when Japanese residents demanded that the army 'punish' the Chinese for their insolence. Armed clashes occurred at the end of January 1932. A landing force of Japanese marines attacked Chapei, the Chinese quarter of Shanghai, and after weeks of bitter fighting, Chinese troops were driven out of the city. Foreign residents in the International Settlement observed the battle from the windows of the Cathay Hotel and other vantage points. Acrid smoke wafted across from the burned-out Chinese quarter.

The fighting presented Sorge with an irresistible challenge. By his own account, he was close to the battle lines. It appears that he was so enthused by the heroism of the Chinese soldiers and their student supporters that he may have lent a hand at the barricades. What is certain is that he seized the chance to assess at first hand the fighting capabilities of the Chinese forces and their morale.

Chiang Kai-shek's German military advisers, several of whom Richard had befriended, held that one Japanese soldier was worth between five and ten Chinese. It was not valour in combat but superior discipline, organization and military equipment that gave the Japanese forces the overwhelming advantage. Sorge had seen the Chinese put up an impressive defence. The Nineteenth Route Army deployed in the battle at Shanghai was one of the best Chinese fighting units. Moreover it was strongly entrenched, and the Japanese attackers chose to hammer away with frontal attacks, instead of bringing their superiority in field manoeuvring into play. But Sorge was forced to conclude that Chinese government troops – mostly ill-armed and ill-disciplined – were not ready for war against the formidable Japanese military machine.

Such a war, however, now appeared inevitable. The 'Shanghai Incident' reinforced Sorge's view that Japan was bent on further conquest, and posed a more serious threat to China's survival than the imperialism of the Western powers. From this point on, Sorge wrote later, 'I found

myself compelled to deal with the problem of Japan as a whole, and I
decided to do so in a general way while still in China. As a start, I
embarked on a course of study by which I sought to become thoroughly
familiar with Japanese history and diplomatic policies.'[7]

§ 'Can you introduce to me a Japanese to help improve my knowledge
of Japan's policy towards China?' Richard asked Agnes Smedley when
he returned from Canton in November 1930.[8]

She had put Sorge in touch with many young Chinese committed to
the struggle against imperialism, and he had pressed a number of them
into service as informants and couriers. Now he was eager to meet her
Japanese friends, who opposed their country's encroachment in China
and for whom there might be a role in his network. Smedley agreed to
help, and arranged a meeting that would have enduring consequences.
The man she introduced, at a restaurant on the Nanking Road, was
Ozaki Hotsumi, a newspaper correspondent with a thorough understanding of Chinese affairs, and completely in tune with her progressive
views. 'Johnson is a fine man,' she had assured Ozaki.

Smedley's friend, six years younger than Sorge, was unremarkable in
appearance. Ozaki had chubby cheeks, a prominent nose for a Japanese,
gentle eyes and a ready smile. He introduced himself, not without pride,
as the correspondent of the *Osaka Asahi*, Japan's leading newspaper.
Smedley had told Sorge that he was one of his country's leading
specialists on China.

The two men quickly established a rapport. Ozaki was affable, interesting and ready to help. They recognized each other's intellectual
ability, and before long discovered shared interests. Ozaki was married
– he delighted in pulling out photos of his baby daughter from his
wallet – but he was, as a friend put it, a 'hormone tank' with a
compulsion for chasing women.

Ozaki's entanglements with women began when he was a student in
Tokyo. A certain Yaeko, a married woman well known to his family,
followed him to Japan from Taipei and became his mistress, abandoning
him when the hardships of life with an impecunious student became
unbearable. Marriage vows were never a hindrance to his womanizing.
In 1927 he married Eiko, the former wife of his eldest brother Honami
– a novel arrangement in Japan in those days. This did not deter the
tireless pleasure-seeker from pursuing other women who took his fancy.
He took delight in entertaining friends with tales of his extramarital
conquests, giving the impression he was an incorrigible *enpuka*, ladies'
man. Eiko could hardly have been unaware of these infidelities, which

she seems to have borne with the tight-lipped fortitude of the traditional Japanese wife.[9]

Henceforth, Ozaki began to enlighten Sorge – who continued to pose as 'Johnson' the American journalist – about Japanese intentions in China, and the politics of the Nanking government. As a reputed correspondent, he had excellent contacts in the Japanese official and business community in Shanghai. On a subterranean level, he was also assisting the Chinese Communist Party's organization in that city. Ozaki had declined to join the Communist Party, in either Japan or China, and could be more effective because his name was not on a police black-list.

Through Ozaki, Sorge was introduced to two other Japanese in Shanghai who agreed to gather political and military information. Mizuno Shigeru was a bright-eyed young idealist whose work for the ring was cut short when he was deported as a student agitator. Kawai Teikichi was a footloose journalist, a *Shina Ronin*, an adventurer who had migrated to China to try his luck.

Ozaki's life was transformed by his encounters with two Westerners in Shanghai. After his arrest, he observed: 'If I reflect deeply, I can say that I was indeed destined to meet Agnes Smedley and Richard Sorge. It was my encounter with these people that finally determined my narrow path from then on.'[10]

§ Richard had acquired a powerful motorcycle, which he rode at break-neck speed through Shanghai's teeming streets. One day, in September 1931, the inevitable happened. He skidded, crashed, and broke a leg. In hospital, leg encased in plaster, he laughed off the injury: his body was already so battered by the wounds of war, what difference did another scar make? He had not outgrown his reckless streak and constantly put his courage to the test, even though he was now, as commander of a Red Army unit, a person with responsibility for the lives of others.

One of his hospital visitors was Ruth Kuczynski, alias Werner, a young German communist who responded eagerly to Richard's invitation to work for the espionage ring. She was a willing assistant and offered the use of her house for clandestine meetings, while she stood sentry. Ruth, a strong-willed and energetic woman, formed a deep attachment to her recruiter, whom she found irresistible. She trusted him with her life and, to prove it, rode pillion on those wild motorcycle jaunts, clinging to Richard as they rocketed, engine straining, down the Nanking Road and out into the leafy suburbs, the oriental Surrey where the foreign *taipans* (heads of merchant houses) lived.

Ruth, though married with a baby (her husband, Rolf Hamburger, was an architect employed by the Shanghai Municipal Council) was enamoured. When the time came for Richard to leave, at the end of 1932, the sense of loss was overwhelming. She threw herself with immense vigour into her work for Soviet Intelligence and served with zeal and courage, proving herself as one of Moscow's most effective secret agents.

Another of Sorge's collaborators, Max Clausen, also experienced the frisson of riding on the back seat of the motorcycle. But while Ruth delighted in the exhilaration of danger, such escapades left Clausen quaking with fear. Like Sorge, Ruth had nerves of steel. Clausen did not.[11]

§ During these years Sorge moved mainly in German circles, cultivating as sources of information the military advisers, diplomats and business-men who had access to the highest echelons of the Nationalist govern-ment. No doubt he had at least a nodding acquaintance with some of the Anglo-Saxon journalists known to Smedley. He may, also through Smedley, have come into contact with an English expatriate, Roger Hollis, the future chief of British counter-intelligence.

Roger Hollis lived and worked in Shanghai's International Settlement for at least part of the time when Sorge was based in the city. The young man, who had dropped out of Oxford University without taking a degree, arrived in China in 1927 to try his luck as a freelance journalist. The following year he found a more secure job with the British Amer-ican Tobacco Company (BAT). His career in China ended in 1936, cut short by illness, and he returned to England. After two difficult years Hollis landed a position with Britain's security service, MI5. He is remembered by some colleagues as a colourless and self-effacing man, but promotion came quickly, and in 1956 he climbed the final rung to the post of director-general.

In the 1980s, Hollis (who had died in 1973) was publicly denounced as a 'mole' and traitor serving the Soviet Union. The allegations, in two sensational books on the subversion of British intelligence agencies, were based in part on Hollis' Shanghai days, where the seeds of his 'treachery' were supposedly sown. Hollis was alleged to have converted to communism while in China, and to have formed an association with three communist agents in Shanghai: Agnes Smedley, Arthur Ewert and Ruth Kuczynski. According to one account, he may also have met Richard Sorge during this period.[12]

It is tantalizing to surmise that Hollis and Sorge met, and that they caroused together in Shanghai's louche bars (both were 'good bottle men' and fond of women), but the connection is unproven. Nor is there any evidence that the future spy chief was enlisted – in China or anywhere else – into the ranks of 'Stalin's Englishmen'.

What is beyond doubt, however, is that Ruth Kuczynski, the dedicated spy who ran a highly effective network in Britain during the 1940s, was first recruited and given her initial training by Sorge in Shanghai. It was Sorge, with his unerring eye for talent, who took her under his wing and provided Soviet Military Intelligence with the agent code-named Sonia – a woman described as 'the most successful female spy of all time'.[13]

§ The romance between Sorge and Smedley soured after a few months, as she had predicted. Why this happened is not known. Quite possibly, she tired of his promiscuity. Smedley was a passionate advocate of sexual freedom for men and women, in theory at least, but noble sentiments expressed to large audiences did not mean she was immune to jealousy in her private life.

By the time Sorge left Shanghai late in 1932, he owed a huge debt of gratitude to this remarkable woman – most of the Chinese in his network had been recruited with Smedley's help. But the extent of that debt became clear only later, when Ozaki Hotsumi, introduced by Smedley in Shanghai, became Sorge's most important collaborator in Japan. In the light of what we now know about their intense relationship, Sorge's description of Smedley sounds strikingly ungracious and insensitive: 'Smedley had a good educational background and a brilliant mind, and made a good journalist, but she was not someone to marry. In short, she was a mannish woman.'[14]

Women played a more active part in Sorge's network in Shanghai than in Japan. Besides Agnes Smedley and Ruth Kuczynski, he recruited at least two Chinese women. One of these, the agent code-named 'Mrs Chui', he described as 'a native Cantonese, who fitted into our network extremely well'.

It is all the more surprising then, to hear his scathing views on women's lack of aptitude for espionage: 'Women are utterly unsuited to espionage work. They have no understanding of political and other affairs and I have never received satisfactory information from them. Since they were useless to me, I did not employ them in my group.'[15] Possibly, Sorge made this statement to protect the women on the fringe of his network in Japan. It certainly does not fit in with what we know about his operation in Shanghai.

CHAPTER FIVE

'Tokyo Wouldn't Be Bad'

ON HIS return to Moscow in January 1933, Sorge was given a 'warm welcome' by General Berzin and congratulated on his three productive years in China.

This first mission had established Sorge's reputation in the Fourth Department as an able organizer, bold in gathering military information, and skilful at analysing political and economic affairs. A new assignment was not discussed at this stage, and Sorge settled down to writing a book on Chinese agriculture. A scholarly work, he believed, would enhance his standing as an expert on the Orient.

This interlude in Moscow brought contentment. Before leaving for Shanghai he had formed a close attachment with Yekaterina Maximova, or Katya, as she was known to her friends, a drama student who had been assigned, possibly by the internal security service, to teach him Russian. Surviving photos of Katya show a pretty, dark-eyed girl with a wistful smile. She believed in Soviet communism ardently and idealistically. While Richard was away, she had given up her drama studies to take a job in a factory, eager to play a part in the expansion of industrial output. Their mutual affection had survived the long separation; and now he moved into her cramped basement flat and enjoyed a few months of domestic bliss. He studied more Russian, wrote his book, and went with Katya to the theatre.

In prison, Sorge explained how he came to be assigned to Tokyo by the Fourth Department.

> It was around the end of April that same year. Berzin summoned me. He said, I know I promised you could complete your book. Sorry, but I can't keep my promise. I have to ask you to go abroad again. Where did I want to go?
>
> So I said, there were three places in Asia I'd like to go. North China, Manchuria, and – half as a joke – I said Tokyo wouldn't be bad. That was at the first meeting. Two weeks later Berzin summoned me again. He told me: we are interested in what you said about giving Tokyo a try.[1]

Berzin told Sorge that it was in Japan that his skill and experience were most badly needed.

Japanese expansion after the Manchurian Incident had swept away the buffer of Chinese sovereignty, and ousted Russia from its zone of influence in North Manchuria. Pressed up against the Soviet frontier was a large and aggressive Japanese army that saw Russia as its traditional enemy, and communism as an insidious form of poison gas. The dislike was mutual. Every middle-aged Russian could recall the humiliations at the hands of the upstart Asian state – the thrashing of their army at Port Arthur, the sinking of the imperial fleet in the Tsushima Strait in the early years of this century.

And now the bayonets of the Kwantung Army in this thick wedge of Manchuria were pointed against the Soviet Union in three directions – the Soviet Maritime Province in the East, the boundless steppes of Siberia in the north, and the Soviet-protected state of Outer Mongolia in the west.

Soviet defences in the Far East were weak, and undermined by low morale stemming from the severe privations of the past winter – including actual famine – which resulted from Stalin's emphasis on high-speed industrialization. Fears about Japanese designs on the Soviet Far East were amply confirmed by intelligence gathered by intercepting Japanese communications. Breakthroughs in signals intelligence – sigint – had provided the Fourth Department with alarming clues to what the Japanese were really thinking.

'First and foremost, we need to know what Japan's real intentions are towards our country,' said General Berzin, outlining the nature of Sorge's mission in Tokyo. He continued:

> Obviously, the central question is whether or not Japan is scheming to attack us. The military seem to be trying to rule the roost in Tokyo. From what we know of the army's attitude since the takeover of Manchuria, there is every reason to believe that easy victory has whetted their appetite for conquest. They are hungry for more territory.
>
> You will concentrate on investigating what direction this expansion will take. Naturally, we need accurate data on Japanese military capabilities, especially any reorganization and buildup of army and air units in preparation for an attack.[2]

Berzin feared that extreme anti-Soviet elements were now in a position to determine Japanese policy. The take-over of Manchuria had shown that a Japanese garrison overseas could dictate policy to the home government – a case of the tail wagging the dog.

The Fourth Department apparently had no network in Japan at this

critical juncture. The main source of intelligence, apart from sigint, was
the 'legal organization' – the Soviet Embassy, trade office and Tass news
agency in Tokyo. Earlier attempts by the department to insert agents
into Japan had ended in embarrassing failure.

§ In the little time that remained before setting out for Japan, Sorge
pored over books and newspapers in Moscow's libraries to broaden his
knowledge of the little-known country that was to become his new
home. From his preliminary research, he gathered that most Japanese
accepted that expansion to the Asian continent was unavoidable. They
believed that Japan could not feed its population of nearly 70,000,000
in the home islands with their existing acreage of cultivable land.
Japanese across the social spectrum were obsessed with the notion that
population density – ten times greater than the world average – was the
root cause of their social and economic difficulties.

Japan was a 'have-not' nation, denied its rightful place in Asia by the
Western powers growing fat on the natural resources of their colonies.
There were other iniquities. Not only hot-headed nationalists but also
moderate academics pointed to the unfairness of worldwide restrictions
on Japanese immigrants and Japan's predominantly textile exports. In
short, expansion of territory by thrusting out towards the Asian mainland was justified on the simple grounds that it was essential for Japan's
very survival.

China, overcrowded though it was, exerted a magnetic power over
Japanese seeking more living space, for cultural and geographic reasons.
China's weakness, which the Western powers had thoroughly exploited
by occupying 'treaty ports', made it an easy prey. Japan had been a late
starter in the imperialism stakes, acquiring Taiwan in a war with China
in 1894–95, annexing Korea, a Chinese protectorate, a few years later,
and striking out in Manchuria in 1931.

But would Japan be content with these possessions? Or would the
smell of social and national decay tempt it to take a deeper bite at the
carcass of China? As one of his duties in Tokyo, Sorge was instructed
to pay close attention to Japanese ambitions to expand its frontiers on
the Asian mainland. Japan's moves in China had a direct bearing on its
strategy towards other nations.

'We want you to keep us fully informed on Japan's policy towards
China,' Berzin told Richard. 'This will give us a good idea of Japanese
intentions towards the motherland. The course of Japan's relations with
other countries can readily be deduced from her China policy.'[3]

§ Richard's tranquil life with Katya in the gloomy basement apartment soon came to an end. The thought of another long separation saddened them both, but he accepted the new assignment joyfully. Once again, his craving for adventure conquered the humdrum instinct for domestic happiness shared with one woman.

However, before leaving, he made a significant concession to the detested rules of bourgeois society, and the rigid bureaucracy of the Soviet Union. He suggested that they should formalize their relationship, purely for practical purposes: in this way, Katya's existence would be recognized by the Fourth Department. As the wife of a Red Army officer serving overseas she could draw on his salary, and mail would be passed on. Katya was a free spirit, and shared Richard's disdain for the straitjacket of marriage. But she allowed herself to be persuaded – a decision she would later have cause to regret.

They went through the formalities, and became man and wife without ceremony and celebration. The bureaucrats took their time processing the papers. The document certifying that Yekaterina Maximova was Sorge's wife is dated 8 August 1933. By then, he had reached New York on his way to Japan.[4]

In prison Sorge misled his interrogators about his relationship with Katya, whom he described as his 'lover'. Poignantly, he added: 'If I were in Moscow, I think we would be living together and married.'[5]

§ On his westward journey to Tokyo, Sorge first made his way to Berlin to refurbish his protective cover as a journalist. In Japan, un-assailable credentials and influential introductions would be vital. These could only be obtained in Germany, a country transformed since his last visit in 1929.

Adolf Hitler had seized power and launched the revolution of the Third Reich. By the time Richard reached Berlin, towards the end of May, German democracy had been destroyed. Those communist leaders who had not been murdered or imprisoned had fled the country; the party's rank-and-file had humbly submitted to the new order.

Entering Germany in this turbulent period was fraught with danger for Sorge. He would have been acutely aware that the police files, which the Nazis had taken over, might well record his activities in the communist movement. It was a calculated risk. He could take comfort from the fact that the Gestapo apparatus was still in its infancy, and bureaucratic chaos reigned. Besides, many ex-communists had switched allegiance to the Nazis, so his past did not necessarily mark him out as an enemy of Hitler's regime.

His first step was to obtain a new passport; for that he re-established residency, reporting to a police station in Berlin on 1 June. In filling out the inevitable official forms, Richard made it seem that he had come to Germany direct from China; his past five months in Moscow were 'lost'. After giving the matter some thought, he decided to wait until he reached Japan before applying for Nazi Party membership, rather than risk scrutiny of his background while he was still in Germany. In 1933 a party card was not yet an essential requirement for a working journalist.

During his few weeks in Germany, Sorge worked on strengthening his professional status. The cover of a foreign correspondent had served him well during three years of espionage work in Shanghai. While he considered the role of businessman the ideal cover, it did not suit his temperament. Didactic by nature, he enjoyed writing dense, serious articles which would be read by experts rather than laymen. He had already had made a name for himself with learned articles on Chinese agriculture, but now he sought new outlets for his work. One of these was the influential *Zeitschrift für Geopolitik* (Journal of Geopolitics), which agreed to take articles on subjects like Japan's army and the agriculture and development of Manchuria.

The journal was the creation of Dr Karl Haushofer, a university professor well known for his theories on the influence of geography on politics, an expert on Japan and a great admirer of the Japanese, and a friend of powerful Nazis, among them Hitler's crony, Rudolf Hess.

A visit to Munich to pay personal homage to the esteemed Dr Haushofer proved rewarding. In preparation, Richard had steeped himself in Nazi ideology and terminology, and had ploughed through Hitler's *Mein Kampf*. Dr Haushofer was impressed, and provided Richard with letters of introduction to the German ambassadors to Japan and to the United States.

During this visit Haushofer may have mentioned the name of a certain Lieutenant-Colonel Eugen Ott, who had been in his office only a few weeks earlier for a briefing prior to travelling to Japan for a new posting. Ott's name also came up in a conversation with Dr Zeller, the respected chief editorial writer of the *Tägliche Rundschau* in Berlin. Sorge enquired whether the newspaper would be interested in contributions from Japan. It would indeed, said Zeller, who had read some of Sorge's articles on China.[6]

Both men had served in the Great War, which created an immediate *esprit de corps*, and they reminisced about their experiences in the trenches. In the course of the conversation, Zeller was reminded of an officer with whom he had served, a close personal friend. 'There's a man you must meet when you are over there. A good friend of mine. He left only recently for Japan,' Dr Zeller said. 'He's an exchange officer with a Japanese artillery regiment in Nagoya. The name is Ott. Lieutenant-Colonel Eugen Ott.' Dr Zeller wrote out an introduction to this officer, and Richard must have felt a warm glow when he read this sentence: 'You can rely on Sorge in every respect – politically and personally.'[7]

§ By early July Richard decided it was too risky to linger any longer in the Nazi lions' den. 'In the present commotion here, interest in my person could become excessive,' he advised Moscow. Before leaving Berlin on his journey to Japan via New York and Vancouver, he reported to the Fourth Department on what he had accomplished during two months in Germany:

> I cannot say that I have achieved my goal one hundred percent. There were a lot of things I simply couldn't manage. But to stay longer to get other newspaper accreditations would be pointless. One has to make the most of things as they are. It's unbearable playing the role of idler. I have to get on with work. At present all I can say is that the prerequisites for my future work are more or less on hand.[8]

Part Two

CHAPTER SIX

'A Man of Consequence'

AT ONE p.m. on 6 September 1933, the Canadian Pacific liner *Empress of Russia* docked at Yokohama. The last haul through Tokyo Bay was slowed by choppy seas whipped up by the last gasp of a powerful typhoon. Now the sky was clear but for a few tiny clouds. Passengers making their way down to the wharf felt the clamping heat of late summer. They were welcomed by a powerful aroma of rotting fish mingled with human waste rising from the harbour.

As usual the ship's manifest was carried by the *Japan Advertiser* the following day. The small foreign community, marooned so far from home, liked to keep track of the comings and goings. Among the arriving passengers listed they would have found a 'Mr R. Sorge', a name that meant nothing to most, if not all, of the newspaper's readers.

Richard Sorge was travelling under his own name, and with a genuine passport of the German Reich. But in the jargon of his secret trade, he came as an 'illegal'. There were also intelligence officers working, under various guises, in the Soviet Union's legal organizations in Tokyo. Sorge, however, was unprotected by diplomatic immunity. The success of his mission in Japan – and his own survival – would depend on a secure cover, and operational skills that had been honed by his apprenticeship in Europe as an agent of the Comintern's Intelligence Department, and his service in Soviet Military Intelligence in China.

The country in which Sorge would spend the next ten years was made to sound alluring by the Japanese Government Railways Official Guide for 1933:

> Japan, land of high romance, whose emergence from feudalism and rise to the status of a great power is still the wonder of the modern world, stretches, the Ultima Thule of Asia, for 2,900 miles along the eastern coast of that continent from the Kurile Islands in the north ... to Formosa (Taiwan) in the south.

Japan had not quite emerged into the modern world, however, and that of course was part of its charm for the visitor from the West. There were trams in the city streets and one-yen taxis, but there were also man-powered rickshaws (though these were fast disappearing); on the Ginza, women in kimonos mingled with so-called *moga* (modern girls) in skirts with hemlines that had risen above the knee for the first time in history; since the 1920s, traditional samisen music had had to co-exist with novelties from the West like jazz and the tango. Westernization had brought the aeroplane, waterworks, and Heinz tomato ketchup. There was also a new-fangled democratic system, but the idea of govern-ment based on the will of the masses was still not firmly rooted by the early 1930s.

It had become almost a cliché for foreign writers to observe that Japan was living with one foot in the past and the other in the present. A travelogue by the German journalist Friedrich Sieburg opined that the Japanese 'are at one and the same time a modern and a feudal people. They live – this has to be repeated whatever aspect we consider – in two ages, at the same time. As an official slogan puts it with commendable frankness: Japan still hobbles on two uneven feet.'[1]

Friedrich Sieburg, who arrived in Japan in 1938 and spent some time travelling around the country with Sorge, was impressed by the contrasts between the new and the old. When he went to the plaza facing the Imperial Palace, he was struck by the loyalty and devotion shown by the Japanese to the emperor, their divine overlord:

> the people look towards the palace, arms pressed against their sides, and bow deeply to the ground. All do this – strollers, schoolchildren, house-wives out shopping, families seeing the sights of Tokyo, farmers who have just arrived at the station, soldiers on leave, or who are leaving for the front the next day.

The belief that government should be based on the august will of the Emperor was deeply ingrained. Democracy was only acceptable to the ruling elite if it did not challenge the existing social order, sanctified by the emperor's position at its apex. Conservatives were as alarmed by demands for liberal democracy and popular sovereignty, on the English model, as they were by the introduction of socialism and Marxism, stimulated by the Russian Revolution.

In 1925 a strict law was enacted to control subversives – that is, anyone attempting to undermine the *kokutai*, the Japanese form of government as embodied in the emperor system. The Peace Preservation Law targeted not only communists and anarchists, however; bureaucrats, police and politicians used it to stifle dissent by liberals, socialists,

Christians and pacifists. For the next twenty years, this law served as an all-purpose instrument to deal with 'thought criminals' (*shisohan*), which in practice meant those opposed to Japan's military expansionism.

By the time Sorge arrived, the brief flowering of democracy was over. The assassinations of the prime minister, finance minister and leading industrialists in 1932 marked the effective end of government by parliamentary means. The rule of law was breaking down. Military chieftains were usurping decision-making – as the 1931 take-over of Manchuria had demonstrated.[2]

A fatal flaw in the government system was the custom of restricting the posts of war and navy ministers to officers on the active list, which meant that the military could dictate the fate of cabinets. The most influential figure in Japan was therefore not the prime minister, or even the emperor – the supreme commander of the armed forces – but the war minister, General Araki Sadao, a rabid ideologue and a leading exponent of totalitarian Shinto. Worse was to come. As the 1930s progressed, 'Japan was ruled, and her policies determined, not by any true system of government but by an anarchy of terror.'[3]

The ascendancy of the military filled Stalin with dread. It seemed inevitable that the hot-heads in the Japanese military would prevail and would precipitate a conflict against the Soviet Union, which was totally unprepared to wage a large-scale war.

On 7 September 1933, the day after Sorge arrived, the US ambassador to Japan, Joseph Grew, recorded in his diary that talk of war with Russia was in the air. The rumours had hardened by 8 February 1934, when Grew wrote: 'The army has complete confidence in its ability to take Vladivostok and the maritime provinces and probably all the territory up to Lake Baikal.'[4]

§ Organizing an espionage network in this charged atmosphere was particularly hazardous for an Occidental. All *gaijin* (outside persons), suffered the rigorous scrutiny of the police. Foreigners were automatically deemed to be trouble-makers and a source of cultural infection. A fair-haired, blue-eyed Caucasian was especially conspicuous. In Shanghai's International Settlement no one spared a Westerner a second glance. In the whole of Japan, there were a mere 8,000 Europeans and Americans, alien beings who attracted inquisitive stares and unwelcome attention wherever they went.

The Japanese concern with espionage was studied with fascination by Albrecht Haushofer – son of the famous scholar Sorge had visited in Munich – who had produced a detailed report on the subject (Rudolf

Hess, who was now deputy Führer of Germany, had lent a hand with this project). It is probable that Sorge was acquainted with this document, which made no bones about the pecularities of the island race: 'Every Japanese when he goes abroad considers himself to be a spy; and when at home he takes upon himself the role of spy-catcher. I suggest that this preoccupation with espionage is ingrained in the Japanese.'[5]

In a land obsessed with spies and instinctively hostile to foreigners, Sorge's success would hinge on creating an impeccable image of status and authority. Form – as he would have realized from his observation of the Japanese in China – mattered far more than substance. The new arrival carried a letter of introduction to the Foreign Ministry's press section from the Japanese ambassador to the United States, Debuchi Katsuji, and this he presented when he paid a courtesy call and applied for his foreign correspondent's identity card in the first few days.

However, Sorge assumed that, in measuring him up, Japanese officials would take a cue from the German embassy: 'I thought that if I got close enough to win the confidence of the embassy, I would appear more reliable in the eyes of the Japanese. And that the embassy would serve as a bulwark against any doubt about me that might arise.'[6] Furthermore, his experience in Shanghai had taught him that security was relatively loose in German missions far from home, and that diplomats and military personnel in isolated postings usually welcomed the company of a well-informed, congenial compatriot:

> When I came to Japan I remembered how successfully I used the German Consulate-General in Shanghai and the German military advisers to the Nanking government for my intelligence activities in China. So I set out to conduct intelligence activities in Japan using, first and foremost, the German Embassy in Tokyo.[7]

General Berzin had stressed the importance of penetrating the German Embassy. The Russians were convinced that Germany and Japan were developing closer ties, and feared that this would lead to an encircling alliance. One of Sorge's duties was to monitor these disturbing moves. This could only be done by gaining the complete trust of embassy staff, and inducing them to part with confidential information they would not ordinarily give to a journalist.

Three days after his arrival, Sorge set out from his hotel, the Sanno in Akasaka, to register as a German national new to Japan, a normal formality. The embassy, pleasantly situated on a hill overlooking the Imperial Palace, was a modest establishment in 1933, staffed by an acting ambassador and five other diplomats, two service attachés and two typists. The new ambassador, Herbert von Dirksen, was not due to arrive until December.

Sorge presented letters of recommendation supplied by the editor of *Zeitschrift für Geopolitik* to two of the staff. Karl Knoll, the counsellor, and Hasso von Etzdorff, a secretary at the embassy, had, it turned out, both served as privates in the German army. Sorge's own wartime experience helped greatly in establishing a personal rapport. It was an auspicious start to the crucial endeavour of forging connections.

§ Some time that autumn, Richard took a train to Nagoya, four and a half hours away from Tokyo. Lieutenant-Colonel Eugen Ott was assigned as a liaison officer with the Third Artillery Regiment, and engaged in a study of the Japanese army's intelligence organization.[8] Ott, then forty-four years old, was a military man from head to toe. The upright bearing, the stiff manner, the large angular face that looked as if it was hewn from granite, all suggested a typical Prussian officer, although in fact Ott came from the more relaxed environment of Swabia.

Nagoya, where he had spent a miserable summer, was a dreary industrial sprawl of porcelain and textile factories and foul-smelling smokestacks. There were few foreigners, and any German visitor would have relieved the tedium. It would have afforded him special pleasure to discover that Dr Sorge, who was six years his junior, was charming and witty, and enjoyed a game of chess. In addition he displayed, for a newcomer, a good grasp of the Japanese political situation.

Once again, Sorge's impressive army record created an immediate atmosphere of mutual trust and understanding. After his arrest, Sorge stressed the significance of this bond. 'I think one of the reasons we became so close was because of my background, serving as an ordinary German soldier in the First World War, and being wounded. Ott too had served in the war as a young officer.'[9] If Ott was at first wary of the newcomer, any doubts would have melted away when he opened the letter of recommendation from his close friend, Dr Zeller, assuring him that: 'You can rely on Sorge in all respects.'

As far as we know, it was by mere chance that Sorge encountered Helma Ott and the children soon afterwards. Out hiking amid the rice-fields, under a deep blue sky that the Japanese describe, proprietorially, as *nihonbare* (the clarity of Japan's sky), he saw a car approaching. Inside was Ott, with a European woman and two small children. The German officer and the woman got out to greet him. 'This is my wife, Helma. And that' – he pointed to the little girl, who had also clambered out of the car – 'is Ulli. And my son, Podwick.'

Helma Ott's great height and prematurely grey hair gave her a regal air. She walked with a stoop, a habit formed, perhaps, from constantly bending to reduce the gap between herself and her shorter husband. Sorge kissed her hand, then crouched to address the sweet-looking girl, who wore her blonde hair in little plaits. 'Ulli, my little one, how old are you?' Ulli rolled her eyes timidly. But the stranger seemed kind, and she was quickly won over by his pleasant manner and warm smile. 'I'm seven,' she declared. 'This is my brother. He's old. He's already eleven.'

With characteristic energy, Sorge applied himself to an intensive study of Japan, concentrating particularly on history, literature and the rice culture, which he regarded as the key to understanding *yamato-damashii*, the Japanese national spirit. As he explained later, he set himself the goal of becoming a recognized *Japan-Kenner*, an authority on Japan.

In his prison memoir, he stated categorically that he owed his commanding position in the embassy to the knowledge acquired through study: 'Without this knowledge, that is, without my detailed research, certainly none of the embassy staff would have cared to discuss things with me or to consult me on confidential matters.'[10]

§ By the end of 1933, he was confident enough to contribute a first political essay to the *Tägliche Rundschau*. In Sorge's words, this was 'very well received in Germany' and raised his standing among the diplomats.

In these early months, his knowledge of Japan was shallow, yet by sheer force of personality he impressed them with his superior wisdom. Sorge had a didactic streak, and the panache and self-assurance to 'explain' an arcane country in which he had so recently arrived. Incisive analysis was his forte. In a surprisingly short time, he acquired a reputation as an authoritative journalist who probed beneath the deceptive surface of Japanese politics.

Even Herbert von Dirksen, who arrived as head of mission in December, soon got into the habit of picking Sorge's brain. This was all the more remarkable given that Dirksen was haughty, tight-lipped and suspicious of journalists as a breed. By his own account, Sorge had accomplished his goal of gaining a firm foothold in the German Embassy by the autumn of 1934. Thus, within a year of arriving in Japan, 'I was regarded as being a man of consequence.'[11]

The Fourth Department now had eyes and ears inside the Nazi citadel in Tokyo, and access to inside information of great value to Soviet strategic planning. In methodical fashion, Sorge laid the groundwork for his mission in the early period before attempting to feed intelligence to his superiors. This meticulous, unhurried approach paid off. Later he summed up the first phase of his work in Japan:

> The point I would like to make from the start is that by successfully approaching the German embassy in Japan and winning the complete trust of the embassy people, I had the foundation for my subsequent intelligence activity, and that I could only conduct such activity once I had this foundation beneath me.[12]

One of his first moves was to make himself a card-carrying National Socialist. He applied through the Nazi organization in Japan, and his party card shows that he was admitted, with membership number 2751466, on 1 October 1934. Routine checks into his background were conducted by NSAPD officials in Berlin, but these clearly yielded nothing that aroused suspicion.

Joining the party was a sensible precaution. The German community was not uniformly pro-Nazi – it included a number of Jews and independent-minded people hostile to Hitler – but the party was tightening its grip on Germans living overseas. The embassy had its quota of heel-clicking zealots who donned brown shirts on Nazi festivals and roared their approval of the Führer. 'The German embassy is absurdly Nazi, and officials don't even say thank you to kindly former Jewish friends who sent flowers to greet them on their return from leave,' observed the wife of a British diplomat in January 1934.[13]

With the party badge in the lapel of his jacket, Sorge's acceptance was complete. It has been held as truth by some writers that he played the Nazi to the hilt, but the evidence suggests that in the company of the Germans he wanted to impress he made no pretence of blind loyalty to the party. Indeed, he was often scathing about the NSAPD and its leaders. 'Sorge made no secret of his aversion to National Socialism,' noted a senior German diplomat.[14]

After his arrest, Sorge expressed the view that Eugen Ott could not have mistaken him for a loyal Hitler-man: 'Ambassador Ott certainly would not have believed I was a straight-down-the-line Nazi in my outlook on life and ideological position.'[15] Generally, Sorge's harsh criticism of the party was not taken amiss. It was seen as additional proof of his individualism, eccentricity and disarming candour. Such frankness was exceptional in the embassy, where everyone guarded his tongue out of fear that informants of the German secret service might be listening. But 'playing the Nazi' was simply not in Sorge's nature. His camouflage could not be bettered – it was his own skin. However, prominent members of the German community believed Sorge to be sound enough to lead the Nazi organization in Japan. During interrogation, Sorge recalled the invitation with evident relish:

> In 1934 the leader of the Nazi organization in Japan went home, and that
> left the section here without a chief for a time. Some Germans members
> asked me to take over the position. Privately I thought it was absurd, but
> I went at once to Ott, who was then military attaché, to talk it over. Ott
> took the matter to Ambassador Dirksen and they both said I should go
> ahead and become the organization's chief, and then the Nazis would
> gain a rational leader.[16]

Sorge cited this as an instance of the esteem he enjoyed in the embassy, where his unconventional manner was much appreciated.

> That's just an anecdote, but it shows how well liked I was by Ott and
> Dirksen, as a somewhat unusual character. In short, I was regarded by
> Ambassador Ott and the other people in the embassy as a leading journal-
> ist of the *Frankfurter Zeitung*, but a proper eccentric. And as I mentioned
> already it was thanks to my peculiarities, learning and lack of ambition
> that I gained such extraordinary trust.[17]

These remarks to the prosecutor reveal as much about how Sorge saw himself as about the opinion of him held by others.

Wisely perhaps, Sorge turned down the post of local Nazi branch *Leiter*. The organization made use of his services in other ways. Political guidance meetings were held for Germans living in Japan, and Sorge was invited as an instructor. On one occasion, the subject he chose to speak on was the Comintern. Sadly, no record survives of what the Soviet agent told his audience. We may suspect that Sorge enjoyed the irony of lecturing to the Nazi faithful on Comintern techniques for spreading revolution – techniques he knew from first-hand experience and had personally put into practice.[18]

CHAPTER SEVEN

The Ring Takes Shape

THE FOURTH Department assigned a wireless operator, code-named 'Bernhardt', to the Tokyo network in October. Sorge greeted the new arrival and his wife in the lobby of the Imperial Hotel. He explained that wireless communication with Moscow must be established quickly, but that 'Bernhardt' first had to set up his protective cover as a business-man, and also had to build the radio equipment himself.

Another comrade was already in Tokyo, waiting anxiously for some-one to contact him with the pre-arranged signal. Branko Vukelic had arrived at Yokohama with his Danish wife, Edith, on 11 February 1933, after a six-week sea journey from Marseilles. They had left a year-old son, Paul, with Edith's mother in Denmark, and expected to be back in France within two years.

Vukelic, twenty-nine, slim, with receding hair, was a Yugoslav from Croatia who had chosen exile in Paris. He wore wire-rimmed spectacles, was passionately fond of political debate, and resembled countless other intellectuals who battled to build a better world over coffee and cigarettes in Left Bank cafés. But the year before, he had been offered a chance to translate his ideals into reality. A certain Comrade Olga, an 'energetic, sporty type', had invited him to carry out intelligence work for the Comintern.

Vukelic at first objected that he was not a heart-felt communist, and so hardly suitable for such a mission. 'I hardly think I'd make a spy. My only military experience is four months service spent in army barracks,' Vukelic said. His father had made a career in the army, but he himself was too much of an individualist to accept military discipline. But Comrade Olga, whom he believed to be a former captain in the Red Army, brushed this aside. 'Our task is nothing like that of the spies in Oppenheim's detective stories,' Olga reassured him.

The object of his mission would be to defend the Soviet Union from war so that it could build an impregnable socialist state, strong enough to deter intervention by capitalist countries. Vukelic allowed himself to be persuaded. In his prison statement he explained why: 'Even if revolution could not be realized in our time, at least one country that had endured the precious struggle to establish socialism would continue to exist, to preserve the idea of the socialist revolution for future generations.'[1]

He was puzzled by the decision of the Moscow Centre to assign him to Japan. 'They say the scenery in Japan is beautiful. I only wish it was me that was going,' said Comrade Olga, when she eventually revealed his destination. She made it perfectly clear that as a Comintern agent he was on his own, and must have nothing to do with the Soviet Embassy in Japan:

> We depend on young communists like you, and sympathizers in foreign countries to gather intelligence. Soviet embassies are strictly watched by police. If something goes wrong, the Soviet Union would be jeopardized if it was linked to Comintern activities. What's more, the Comintern and Soviet diplomatic agencies don't necessarily see eye-to-eye.

Branko and Edith embarked on this journey to the other side of the globe with trepidation. Japan was a land of mystery, the mission was ill-defined, and he had been given no training. Soon after their arrival, they found that they had not been given adequate funds to maintain a Western living standard for more than a brief period. The lack of preparation became painfully obvious. It struck him that the Comintern was not the power-house of intelligence he had once imagined.

As protective cover for his secret mission, Branko had made arrangements to contribute articles on Japan to a French magazine and a Yugoslav newspaper. This he considered to be a 'threadbare camouflage'. Moreover, the payments he received barely covered the rent. Edith, a qualified gymnastics teacher, found part-time jobs at two colleges in Tokyo, the Tamagawa Gakuen and Bunka Gakuin. For ten months the couple scraped a living, until they were finally rescued by Sorge. He sent 'Bernhardt' to their apartment to make the initial contact, and went round himself the following day.

Sorge said later that Vukelic was in pitiable shape – ill, homesick and broke – by this point. Though he was the leader of the network, he had had no say in the selection of this operative, and apparently he was not overly impressed. Perhaps Vukelic, garrulous and light-hearted, did not meet his exacting standards for an intelligence agent. Until the very end, Vukelic could never shake off a feeling that he was an 'outsider' and that Sorge did not consider him to be 'a serious type'.

§ Before leaving Moscow, Sorge had told General Berzin that a Japanese associate would be indispensable for the Tokyo unit. A suitable man had been recruited from the large Japanese community on the West Coast of the United States, and had landed in Yokohama on 24 October. Every day since his arrival, Miyagi Yotoku, a 30-year-old artist, scanned the classified ads column of the *Japan Advertiser* for a pre-arranged signal. It finally appeared on 6 December 1933, under the rubric 'Wanted to Buy': 'Ukiyoe prints by old masters. Also English books on same subjects. Urgently needed.' This advertisement was placed – at 5 sen a word – by Vukelic, at the direction of 'the boss', as he called Richard Sorge.

Like Vukelic, Miyagi had been approached to undertake an ill-defined mission in Japan by the Comintern. Later he described his recruiters as 'a Japanese–American agent of the Comintern, Yano Toru' and 'a white man from the Comintern of unknown nationality.'

Miyagi was sixteen when he left his native Okinawa for the United States to join his father, who had emigrated in search of work. His great love was art, which he studied at a college in San Diego. In 1931 he joined the Communist Party in the belief that communism would eliminate injustices and create an equitable society. His convictions were shaped by his own bitter experiences. Okinawans were treated like a low-caste people by the Japanese; and as an Oriental, he was no stranger to discrimination in the United States.

However, Miyagi did not jump at the chance to serve the communist cause by working in Japan. He was suffering from tuberculosis, and his condition had improved in the dry climate of southern California. Moreover, the recruiters did not specify the nature of his work in Tokyo, though there was no doubt it would be illegal. All they said was: 'Go to Tokyo and you will be given instructions on your duties by a contact man in Tokyo. You'll be back in just a month.'

That was in July. Miyagi had accepted, against his better judgement, travelled to Japan, and in December finally discovered what duties he was expected to carry out. After answering the advertisement, his first contact was with Branko Vukelic. Neither gave their real names. Each man carried half of a dollar bill to establish their bona fides. This led to Miyagi's first encounter with Richard Sorge, outside the Ueno Art Gallery. For purposes of recognition, Sorge wore a black tie, Miyagi a blue tie that day.

At their first meeting, Sorge looked over the Okinawan to assess how he could be fitted in, and only later explained the role Miyagi would play.

Sorge didn't say clearly I should do intelligence work, but he asked me
about Japanese political and military matters. He said he was working for
the Comintern, but was not trying to set up any organization. But I
realized some time in December that my mission was intelligence work
for the Comintern. In January 1934 I was asked by Sorge to work for
him in Japan, and I agreed.[2]

Although he had no love for the Japanese, Miyagi was not enthusiastic
about accepting the role of traitor. He took some time to make up his
mind. 'It would have been a different matter conducting this work in
America. But what was the position of a Japanese who did this in
Japan?'[3]

What finally swayed him was Sorge's argument that the main purpose
of the unit's espionage activity was to avert war between Japan and the
Soviet Union. Miyagi was offered the chance to work for peace – the
customary pitch used by recruiters for Soviet Intelligence. Miyagi the
idealist could not turn his back on that. Yet he appears to have assented
reluctantly, for he urged Sorge to look around for someone better
qualified for this kind of work to take over as soon as possible. 'So I
participated in the ring, fully aware that this activity was against the laws
of Japan, and that I would be executed in wartime for my espionage.'[4]

Sorge said that he would try to find a replacement, but nothing came
of this promise. Perhaps he never looked. It would not have been
simple to find anyone as capable, diligent and conscientious as Miyagi.
He was stuck in Japan, in a job he did not want, and was never to see
the United States again.

§ In December 1933, after nearly four months of living in hotels, Sorge
rented a house in Nagasaka-cho, a quiet residential quarter in Tokyo's
Azabu borough. The district he chose was lower middle class: neighbours included an engineer working for Mitsui Mining and a clerk at
a credit union.[5] The house was unpretentious, a wooden two-storey
structure squeezed alongside two similar houses in a tiny compound.

For someone engaged in perilous clandestine work, Sorge seemed
untroubled by the lack of privacy. The houses were so close, they
shared each other's aromas. Visitors could be easily observed from the
nearby Toriisaka police station. By one account, police officers had a
clear view into the first-floor rooms. Possibly he selected this house
precisely because it was an unlikely setting for the nerve-centre of an
espionage ring.

Compared to foreign diplomats and businessmen in Tokyo, Sorge
lived in modest surroundings (whatever the drawbacks, he stayed at the

same address for almost eight years, right up until his arrest). Some of Sorge's German visitors found the dwelling tiny, spartan and impossibly untidy. As in any Japanese home, shoes were removed in a tiny concrete vestibule. The ground floor consisted of a living room of eight tatami mats,[6] a four-and-a-half-mat dining room, kitchen, bathroom and toilet – the Japanese 'squatting' variety. A narrow stairway led up to the first floor, where Sorge had his study, crowded with bookcases, filing cabinets, a sofa and a large wooden desk. A carpet covered the eight tatami mats. Adjoining was a six-mat bedroom, where mattresses – *shikibuton* – were piled to give the effect of a Western-style bed.

On a fine day sunlight bathed the upstairs corridor, where the telephone was placed. By pushing back the sliding windows here, Sorge could walk out onto a shaky wooden verandah where he kept a few potted plants. When Helma Ott visited Nagasaka-cho, she decided that Sorge's domestic arrangements were too exposed to public view, and took it upon herself to measure the windows and fit flower-patterned curtains.

Sorge followed a strict routine, rising around five each morning, making do with very little sleep, and then soaking in the cramped wooden bath downstairs. An elderly maid arrived to make breakfast, which followed a spell of brisk exercise with a chest expander. He read every line of the (American-owned) *Japan Advertiser*, and spent most of the morning at the typewriter. Before leaving Europe Sorge had made arrangements to write articles for the Dutch financial newspaper *Algemeen Handelsblatt*, and this became an important outlet after the Nazis closed down the liberal newspaper *Tägliche Rundschau* in December 1933.

After lunch, without fail, he took an hour's nap. Thus invigorated, he left the house and headed, invariably, for the Domei News Agency, where the German News Agency was located. He visited the embassy on a regular basis and often called at the German Club, where there was a reading-room with recent newspapers from home. After five p.m. he was usually to be found at the Imperial Hotel bar; and later in the evening he might attend one of the parties with which the German businessmen and diplomats sought to relieve the tedium of their lives.

Sorge – a sparkling conversationalist, and refreshingly indiscreet – was a welcome guest at these social occasions. Among German ex-patriates, he acquired a reputation as an eccentric, hard-drinking, fast-living bachelor who succumbed willingly to the many temptations of the flesh on offer in Tokyo. He became an habitué of a number of Ginza establishments, such as the Florida Dance Hall, where he paid to tango with girls in elegant evening-gowns, and of the Silver Slipper,

Rheingold and Fledermaus bars. Heavy drinking is part of the journalist's culture, but Sorge indulged to excess.

It is in Japan that we find the first signs of unbridled, chronic alcoholism. Sorge, observed his friend Prince Urach, would pass through all the stages of the drunkard – 'exultation, tearful misery, aggressiveness, paranoia and megalomania, delirium, stupor, and the grey solitude of the hangover that can only be relieved by more alcohol'.[7]

An American journalist who sometimes spent the small hours drinking with Sorge, as a fellow correspondent, suggests that haunting the bars and chasing women were 'a calculated part of his masquerade. He created the impression of being a playboy, almost a wastrel, the very antithesis of a keen and dangerous spy.'[8]

§ Japanese society was like a sea anemone that closed up at the approach of a marauder. Sorge realized that as an outsider, and an alien, he could not hope to penetrate its inner layers. Only a well-placed Japanese would have access to sensitive political and economic information that the newspapers could not print. As he constructed his *apparat* in those early months, the problem of how to recruit such an informant was in the forefront of his mind.

Miyagi, who had spent half his life in America, and lacked the right social background, would have difficulty developing connnections in the higher reaches of this clannish society. But Sorge knew of one man who was well qualified to fill the gap in his network. Ozaki Hotsumi, the journalist who had assisted him in Shanghai, had attended the same elite schools as many prominent public figures and was accepted in the circles that mattered. He was building a reputation as a China expert, was well versed in politics and ideologically sympathetic. And, not least, Ozaki was not compromised by association with the outlawed Japan Communist Party. Sorge decided to seek his help once again.

After four exhilarating years in Shanghai, Ozaki had returned to the Osaka headquarters of the *Asahi* in February 1932, taken up a job on the foreign desk, and settled into a tranquil suburban existence with his wife and young daughter. One day in late May, when Ozaki had just turned thirty-three, a stranger called on him at the *Asahi* building. The man, introducing himself as Minami Ryuichi, an artist, said he had come on behalf of a foreigner whom Ozaki had known in Shanghai. This foreigner was now in Japan, and was eager to arrange a meeting. Ozaki was on his guard, suspecting that this stranger might be in the pay of the police: 'I thought at first he might be a spy sent by police who had found out about our Shanghai activities.'[9]

After talking a little longer, it dawned on Ozaki that the foreigner in question must be the man he had known as 'Johnson'. His hunch was confirmed that same evening, when Ozaki took 'Minami' to dinner at a Chinese restaurant for a longer chat. The artist was affable company, and Ozaki felt sufficiently at ease to invite him to visit his home. This was when he assented to meet the foreigner. 'Afterwards I learnt that this Minami Ryuichi was Miyagi Yotoku, and that he was a member of the American Communist Party,' Ozaki later recalled.[10]

In early June 1934, Richard Sorge and Ozaki Hotsumi met in Nara. The rendezvous had been arranged to take place by the steps that lead down from the Kofukuji temple to the Sarusawa-ike (the Monkey Swamp Pond). They had not met for two years, and we may suppose that they greeted one another warmly.

In Shanghai they had held one another in high esteem. Sorge had been impressed by Ozaki's political flair and deep understanding of China. The Japanese journalist had warmed to Sorge's refreshing lack of pomp and artificiality. There was no trace in his manner of the condescension that many Westerners in Shanghai could not hide in their dealings with Japanese and other Asians.[11] They talked beside the large, oval pond, which caught the reflection of the nearby Five-Layered Pagoda. There would have been many sightseers, for the first days of June in the Kansai area were pleasantly warm, with just a hint of cloud.

Few of those Japanese tourists gazing dutifully at the temples would have been as familiar with the history of this attractive city as Sorge was. For him, the Nara era twelve hundred years ago summed up all that was best – and irrevocably lost – in the Japanese character: the aesthetic values of sculptors, painters, master builders, the poets whose wistful odes, in the *Manyoshu* (Collection of Myriad Leaves) Sorge could appreciate even in translation.

A path winds along the bank of the pond, behind a line of gnarled willows, and perhaps the two men strolled here while they talked. They may have paused for refreshment at the little tea-house on the edge of the pond. Somewhere in this attractive setting, Ozaki agreed to a proposition that would change the course of his life.

'I have something to ask of you,' said Sorge. 'I want your help to find out more about the situation in Japan. Not about China, but about Japan. I would like to have information from you on the political, economic and military situation and get your opinion on these matters.' Ozaki replied: 'I will do whatever I can to help you.'[12] From Ozaki's testimony, we gather that the matter was quickly decided. He did not ask for time to think things over before giving Sorge his answer. Writing in prison, he summed up the brief exchange in these terms: 'I was asked by Sorge to co-operate in his intelligence activities in Japan, and I readily accepted his proposition, deciding to work together with Sorge on intelligence activities.'[13]

That Ozaki agreed 'readily' to co-operate with Sorge has perplexed some Japanese scholars. They find it hard to accept that a man of Ozaki's intellectual and social standing accepted on the spot, and did not have to wrestle with his conscience. Some authorities on the case prefer to assume that Ozaki was pressured by his inquisitors into confessing that he was a willing recruit to Soviet Intelligence.

This is impossible to prove. As the evidence stands, Ozaki apparently needed no persuading to join Sorge's network, although this act made him a traitor working against the interests of his motherland. His fateful decision required a level of courage and a breadth of vision that surpass the bounds of ordinary understanding.

Why did Ozaki, a family man, assured of a good career, embark on what he knew to be the 'difficult and unprofitable enterprise' of espionage for the Soviet Union? His earlier life provides some clues. He was born of humble parents in Tokyo on 1 May 1901. Immediately after his birth the Ozaki family moved to Taiwan, a Japanese possession, and he grew up as part of the privileged colonial class.

In 1919 he entered the elite *Ichiko* (First Higher School) in Tokyo, and went on to Tokyo Imperial University in 1922. His political awareness was sharpened by the arrests the following year of leaders of the newly formed Japan Communist Party. The killing of many communists and labour leaders made a deep and lasting impact. At the Imperial University, as a member of a social science study group, he discovered the appeal of Marxism. Undoubtedly he was a convinced communist by the time of the mass round-up of Communist Party members and sympathizers in 1928. But this crack-down demonstrated the wisdom of his decision to avoid formal party ties.

In Shanghai, as a young reporter for the *Asahi*, he gravitated towards Chinese Communist Party circles. The Japanese seizure of Manchuria and the attack on Shanghai had a profound effect on Ozaki's thinking. Japan's sabre-rattling along Manchuria's border with the Soviet Union made it clear where his duty lay. As a believer in world revolution, Ozaki realized the importance of protecting the revolution in Russia from that country's most bellicose adversary, Japan.

After his arrest, he explained what drew him to work with Sorge:

> I came to think that of all our fields of activity, the role of defending the USSR was one of the most important. And for that defence, our most

important mission was to provide accurate information to the Comintern or the Soviet government on the internal situation in Japan – the strongest of the world powers opposed to the Soviet Union – so they could take counter measures. Because at that time, the Japan Communist Party was so ineffectual as to be non-existent. Sometimes I thought secretly that to be a communist in Japan engaging in this difficult and unprofitable enterprise was something to be proud of.[14]

In Shanghai, Ozaki formed the same impression as Agnes Smedley – that Sorge was working for the Comintern. Sorge appears to have encouraged Ozaki in the illusion, leading him to believe that he had been registered as a 'member' of the Comintern.

During his years as a spy, Ozaki remained unaware that he was working for Red Army Intelligence. He did not know that a dossier in the Fourth Department listed him as a principal in the Tokyo unit from the summer of 1935, when Sorge reported to his superiors in Moscow. No doubt Sorge, and his masters, thought that foreign communists would more readily serve the Communist International than Soviet Intelligence, and this was why Ozaki, Miyagi and Vukelic were all deliberately misled.

At the reunion in Nara, Ozaki did not learn Sorge's real name. He still believed him to be an American, called 'Johnson' or simply 'John'. It was a long time before he discovered his true identity. 'Around 1935, I heard from John's mouth that one parent was German and the other Russian, and so I thought that he had both German and Russian nationality.'[15] Then in September 1936 he found out Sorge's real name, quite by accident. They both attended a reception at the Imperial Hotel, where someone 'introduced' Ozaki to the man he had already known for almost five years: 'I would like you to meet Dr Sorge, a German journalist.'

§ Eugen Ott was appointed senior military attaché at the German Embassy in Tokyo in April 1934, and promoted to the rank of colonel. With immense relief the family left Nagoya and moved to Tokyo, which offered many more diversions. Their new home was a modest wooden structure in the Nagai Compound, a calm refuge with lawns and trees only a minute or two from Shibuya, one of Tokyo's busiest railway terminals. Here Ulli played happily with the children of diplomats and businessmen from America and Europe. Among her friends was a little Jewish boy – until the Gestapo tightened its grip on the German colony in Tokyo in 1936, and such liaisons became inadvisable.

Richard became a regular visitor, leaving the Imperial Hotel around seven to career along Aoyama Avenue on his newly acquired motorbike. Frequently he stayed for dinner, after which he and Colonel Ott played chess until late at night, drinking cognac and discussing the Hitlerian revolution taking place in Germany. On these relaxed occasions, they would pool information about the growing ascendancy of the military in Japan and the impotence of the nation's civilian leaders. Ott was well versed in the internal dynamics of the Japanese army and was personally acquainted with a number of influential middle-ranking officers, such as Colonel Oshima Hiroshi, a Germanophile and admirer of Hitler, and the spy chief and political intriguer Colonel Doihara Kenji.

Ott relied on Sorge's discretion; it was understood that this information was not intended for publication. Sorge reciprocated by offering perceptive analysis of political and diplomatic developments, based on voracious reading, intelligent deduction, and (from early 1935) Ozaki's insights. In the military attaché's eyes Sorge was no run-of-the-mill journalist, but an astute observer with scholarly interests and an excellent grasp of Japan's political realities. The colonel somehow gained an impression that Sorge's command of Japanese had helped him to penetrate the bamboo curtain. The truth was that Richard, finding insufficient time for study, never advanced beyond a rudimentary knowledge of the language.

In the early autumn of 1934, when the military attaché undertook a tour of Manchuria, he asked Sorge to accompany him (having sought the approval of Ambassador Dirksen). This invitation attests to the special position that the Soviet agent had built up within a year of arriving in Tokyo. The journey yielded a wealth of information on the military and economic aspects of Japan's reconstruction of Manchukuo, the new name for Manchuria, and no doubt some useful contacts in the Kwantung Army occupying the vast territory. On his return, Sorge sat down and compiled a lengthy overview of the situation in Manchuria, which he showed to Ott. Impressed, the colonel forwarded the report to his superiors in the High Command in Berlin, where it was well received. This brought Sorge further commissions for in-depth studies that greatly enhanced his standing both in the embassy in Tokyo and at army headquarters in Berlin.

Before long, the Otts came to treat Sorge – 'Uncle Richard' to little Ulli – as part of the family. They were all so close that it was perhaps inevitable that a love affair blossomed between him and Helma, and inescapable that the colonel would find out about it. It appears that Helma had ceased to derive satisfaction from her marriage, and that she and her husband had slept in separate beds since the early 1930s.[16]

A friendship that promised to become a gold-mine of intelligence might have been wrecked by Richard's sexual delinquency. Once again, we see him ruled by impulse, rather than reason, and relishing the *frisson* of pursuing a married woman as he did the excitement of riding his motorcycle in an alcoholic haze. But Ott reacted with admirable composure to the discovery of Helma's infidelity. By one account – which has an apocryphal ring – he raised a glass and shouted 'Your health, Sorge! Let's drink to what's to be!'[17] One of his favourite epithets for Sorge was '*der Unwiderstehliche*', the irresistible one, and perhaps he had fallen under Sorge's spell. He did not allow the affair to come between them. Besides, he was sure that the romance would soon blow over, and events proved him right.

§ In the first week of January 1935 Sorge was notified of the arrival in Tokyo of the Soviet agent 'Ingrid', and went to the Imperial Hotel to meet her. She had been sent by the Fourth Department, and he would have been curious to discover why his superiors had deemed it necessary to assign someone else to Japan – 'his' territory.

The new arrival was Aino Kuusinen, the estranged wife of Otto Kuusinen, the Finnish secretary of the Executive Committee of the Comintern. Sorge had met her for the first time some ten years earlier in Moscow, when he went to work in the German secretariat of the Comintern. Like Richard, she had moved on, and now belonged to Red Army Intelligence.[18]

'Elisabeth Hansson' was the name in her Swedish passport. Her working name in the Fourth Department was 'Ingrid'. She had come with orders to penetrate the highest strata of society and government, posing as a writer, and issued with enough funds to live in style. By her own account, it was an unstrenuous assignment that afforded ample time for the study of Japanese culture and language. Many years later she would call this 'one of the happiest periods of my life'. Japan enchanted her. It was not the polite façade, but the self-control, and the concealment of personal tragedy behind a smile, that impressed her as the most worthy qualities of the Japanese.[19]

Her instructions were to operate independently from Sorge, but to communicate with Moscow, and receive funds via his organization. What no one in the Fourth Department realized was that Aino had undergone a change of heart by the time she arrived in Japan: she was utterly disenchanted with communism. Her previous mission to the United States for the Comintern had been the catalyst. The 'free air' she had breathed in America had changed her ideas about Stalin's Russia, and when she returned to find some of her best friends had been purged the sense of disillusionment was complete. She was overjoyed when General Berzin offered to send her to Tokyo on an espionage mission. Japan was becoming a police state, but compared with what she had seen in Russia, it seemed blissfully free.

She and Sorge got off to a shaky start. For their next rendezvous, one week later, he took her to one of his watering-holes – from her description it appears to have been the Fledermaus or the Rheingold. This 'German ale-house of the lowest kind' was not a place to invite a lady, she said firmly. Sorge shrugged off her complaint, evidently indifferent to her opinion of him.

For the next few months Aino busied herself establishing contacts in the Japanese press and the higher echelons of officialdom. She was not expected to begin intelligence activities until she was completely accepted in Japanese high society – assuming that was feasible.

§ Tension between the Soviet Union and Japan in the early months of 1934 underlined the importance of Sorge's primary mission – namely, investigating whether the Japanese army was planning an attack on Soviet territory in the Far East. On Sorge's instructions, Miyagi prepared a report on the army's attitude towards the Soviet Union, which concluded that an onslaught was imminent. However, he had no sources in the High Command, and relied on newspaper and magazine articles and street gossip for his information.

Sorge did not allow the war scare to distract him from the task of organization. He went about the construction of the ring with meticulous care. In his view, intelligence work could only begin in earnest when all the pieces were in place:

> In the period from the autumn of 1933 until the spring of 1935, the execution of our duties was completely out of the question. The time was spent in getting to grips with the especially difficult Japanese situation. We had to organize the group and lay a foundation before beginning active operations.[20]

By the time the first phase was completed, Sorge had gained acceptance in the German Embassy – to a degree he believed to be 'absolutely unprecedented' – and general recognition as an active and capable journalist. In particular he had cultivated Colonel Ott, the senior military attaché, and Captain Paul Wenneker, the naval attaché who arrived in 1934, and he was held in high esteem by the ambassador.

Moreover, he had proved the feasibility of operating in a hostile environment where police were obsessed with spies – to the point of raiding an art shop and confiscating eighteenth-century prints that showed Nagasaki harbour. Foreigners were continuously followed by police or their armies of informants. Sorge worked on the assumption that he was being watched – by the ordinary police at the Toriisaka station, the *Tokko* (Special Higher Police) or the *Kempei* (military police), or by all three.[21]

As he was fully aware, his maid was frequently questioned by police, and the house searched when he was absent on a trip to China. Even at the Imperial Hotel he sensed that policemen were watching him. Nonchalantly, he adjusted to the perpetual surveillance: 'This was standard procedure for all foreigners. I was not the only foreigner under suspicion.'[22] To divert suspicion, he collected the match-boxes of restaurants, bars and pleasure houses (in the red-light district of Honmoku) that he patronized, and left them for the maid to find. In this way she could report to the police on nocturnal activities that he had no reason to hide.

Soon after first arriving in Tokyo, he sent a wireless message to Moscow boasting that he had sized up the police and their methods: 'I get the impression of leading them by the tip of their noses.'[23] In prison, he aired the view that Japanese police worried too much about minutiae, and couldn't see the wood for the trees: 'I believe they waste time gathering trivial, valueless things.'[24]

However, the first arrest of a foreigner under the savage Peace Preservation Law showed how unwise it was to underestimate the police. In March 1934 William Bickerton, a young New Zealander teaching at the *Ichiko* high school, was picked up and charged with 'dangerous thoughts' and 'communistic activities'. During questioning by the Tokko interrogators, he was repeatedly beaten, but refused to confess and was freed after the intervention of the British Embassy. Sixty years after the event, documents released by Moscow prove conclusively that there was substance to the charges, and that Bickerton had indeed played a liaison role between the Comintern and Japanese Communists.[25]

§ Towards the end of 1934, Sorge received word that Ozaki was being transferred to Tokyo to join the staff of the *Asahi's* research organization, the Society for the Study of East Asian Problems (*Toa Mondai Chosakai*). This was excellent news: Sorge badly needed Ozaki's help in Tokyo, and they were now able to meet regularly.

Ozaki indulged his epicurean tastes by fixing many of these rendez-vous at high-class restaurants (*ryotei*) or houses of assignation where geisha might be summoned (*machiai*). On some occasions they met at

Lohmeyer's, a German restaurant, or the Rheingold, a German bar. To explain away his frequent meetings with the foreigner, Ozaki told acquaintances that he had been requested by his superiors at the *Asahi* to guide the foreign journalist. 'It's a burden (*onimotsu*)! But I could hardly refuse!'[26]

Sorge was satisfied that he had the components of a workable *apparat*, but there was one major weakness – the absence of assured channels of communication with Moscow. Radio contact could not be relied on, mainly because the wireless operator, 'Bernhardt,' was obsessed by fear of being caught. In Sorge's words, 'he was extremely timid and did not send half the messages I gave him'.

As a result, he was having to rely on smuggling material out of Japan by courier. Vukelic, who was put in charge of the ring's photographic work, copied Sorge's reports on rolls of microfilm, which could be secured beneath the carrier's clothing. But this method was unsatisfactory. A special journey had to be undertaken to Shanghai, and months might pass before material left Japan for Moscow.

The ring urgently needed a wireless operator with strong nerves, Sorge explained in a message to Moscow in the spring of 1935. Now that the exploratory part of his mission was complete, he asked to be recalled for consultations, to report on progress and discuss the next phase. In May he received instructions to return without delay.

CHAPTER EIGHT

Moscow, Summer 1935

'I'M GOING to spend the summer in the United States,' Sorge told Helma and Eugen Ott. 'I want to do some sight-seeing and look up some old friends there. Need to have a break from Japan once in a while.' This account was true in two respects: Sorge did travel to the United States on his way to Moscow, and on his return by the same route we know he arranged to meet at least one old friend.

In Moscow, Sorge discovered that some of his associates in the Fourth Department had disappeared. The most important change was the replacement of General Berzin, the 'old man' for whom he felt deep respect and affection, by a new director, General Semyon Petrovitch Uritsky.

Sorge's prison statement gives no hint that he was disturbed by the changes he found. When he reported to the new chief, he gained the impression that Uritsky was keenly interested in the work he was doing. Sorge related his experiences in establishing the ring and spoke of the 'bright prospects' for future operations. The new director encouraged Sorge to press ahead with his foremost duty of investigating Japanese intentions. He was particularly keen to stress that Sorge should pay close attention to the development of relations between Japan and Germany, which appeared to be moving in the direction of a *rapprochement* aimed against Russia.

Sorge asked for *carte blanche* to develop his relations in the German Embassy by feeding officials there with a certain amount of information. This, he believed, would induce them to volunteer information of major importance. Uritsky gave his approval, and left it to Sorge's discretion to decide what to give to the Germans. In his own words: 'I was given permission to supply a certain amount of information to the embassy, in order to strengthen my connections there.'[1] This give-and-take was to prove a highly effective means of consolidating his position in the embassy.

Another important item of business during his stay in Moscow was the selection of a new wireless operator. At Sorge's request, the Centre had pulled the nervous 'Bernhardt' out of Tokyo, and possible replacements were discussed. Sorge suggested that Max Clausen, with whom he had worked in China, might be suitable.

After his recall to Russia in August 1933, Clausen's fortunes were at a low ebb. He was banished from Moscow for more than a year – a penalty for unsatisfactory work, he would tell Japanese interrogators. His fall from grace possibly had more to do with an act of insubordination – flatly refusing to leave Shanghai without Anna, his White Russian common-law wife.

When Sorge was in Moscow, he found that Clausen had been posted to the Red Army's wireless school, and entrusted with developing a portable transmitting and receiving set. With Uritsky's approval, Sorge proposed to Clausen that he join him in Japan. Clausen was happy with the new assignment. As he wrote in prison: 'I was very proud when Moscow put me in charge of the wireless operations of the Tokyo intelligence network. I came to Japan as an enemy of the Japanese Government and, as I thought, as a friend of the Japanese people.'[2]

The Seventh Congress of the Comintern was being held in Moscow that summer, and Sorge had hoped to attend. But the risk that he might be recognized, and that word of his presence in Moscow could get back to Germany or Japan, was too great. He was therefore given strict orders to stay away from the congress and the foreign delegates.

In prison, Sorge gave little away about this interlude in Moscow. He admitted to renewing contact with the Comintern leader, Otto Kuusinen, and Grigori Smoliansky, a friend who had left his job as first secretary of the Central Committee. According to his prison statement he saw Clausen frequently to discuss their joint work in Japan, and spent some time with specialists of the 'Code and Eastern sections' reviewing the network's codes and ciphers. Otherwise, he claimed in his statement, he had few engagements: 'My social life was very restricted.'[3]

The available evidence suggests, however, that while in Moscow he held a number of reunions with personal friends whose names he chose not to reveal. Ignace Poretsky (alias Ludwig Reiss), an NKVD agent employed previously by the Fourth Department, and his wife, Elizabeth, saw a lot of Sorge that summer. They were among a select group of trusted friends who could talk to him frankly about the horrors that Russians were living through. Stalin's purge of the followers of his great rival, Trotsky, which began with the Fifteenth Party Congress in 1927, had claimed countless victims. Sorge learnt that many people he knew personally had been arrested – one was the illustrious Grigori Zinovyev, his mentor when he was a novice at the Comintern. The fear of arbitrary arrest affected people everywhere, in big cities like Moscow, and in tiny country villages. No one was immune to Stalin's attacks of paranoia. Sorge listened sullenly, refusing to believe that Stalin's rule was evil.[4]

However, one friend gained a different impression of Sorge in August 1935. Niilo Virtanen, who worked in the Comintern's secretariat, invited him to dinner in the restaurant of the Hotel Bolshaya Moskovskaya and was surprised to find how much he had changed. The old self-assurance and idealism had faded. Drinking heavily, Sorge gave vent to his anguish.

He admitted quite openly that he was tired of working as a spy for the Russians, but saw no possibility of breaking free to start a new life. He sensed that he was in danger in the Soviet Union, but he could not return to Germany, because the Gestapo would pick him up. The only choice left to him was to go back and resume his espionage activities in Japan. But he feared that, even in Japan, he wouldn't survive all that long.[5]

Coming from the mouth of a dedicated communist and proud Red Army officer, this was a shocking confession. We do not know what induced Sorge to reveal his innermost feelings that evening in August – was it the vodka, or was it a reaction to his faithful friend Virtanen's admission that he was completely disillusioned with Stalin's regime?

The vignette recorded by Aino Kuusinen is arresting, for it jars with the conventional image – the brashly self-confident spy motivated by ruthless devotion to his masters. Here we catch the first glimpse of a crack in Sorge's loyalty. What emerges from this and later clues is a lonely prisoner of his espionage mission, struggling with doubts, and torn between hope and fear of returning to Russia. By Aino's account, Sorge went back to Japan to resume clandestine operations because he had no other options. He was supremely skilful and courageous, but all the same, it seems, he was something of a reluctant spy.

§ Katya had waited two long years for this moment. They shared a few weeks of domestic contentment, the first time they had spent together as man and wife. Richard was approaching forty, and ready to give up his wanderings in exotic countries in favour of the ordinary ideal of married bliss. But he was subject to military discipline, and the Fourth Department expected him to resume espionage operations in Tokyo at the end of the summer. Sorge won a promise from the director that he would be replaced within a year or two, and this may have eased the pain when he told Katya he was being sent overseas again. He left in late August, begging her to write regularly and assuring her it would not be too long before he came home to settle down.

'I left Moscow by plane,' Sorge wrote in prison. There are many conspicuous omissions and discrepancies in his account of the return journey, and the sojourn in Russia – not least his statement that he left Moscow at the end of July, after a brief trip 'lasting only about fourteen days'. He told interrogators that he passed through Holland, where he destroyed the false passport with an Austrian name on which he had travelled to Russia, and became Richard Sorge again. He visited a tailor in New York to pick up a suit, forgetting that he had used a different name for the fitting three months earlier, and he did some sight-seeing.

One of the few certain facts is that on the way back to Japan Sorge looked up an old friend, Hede Massing, who was spying in America for the Soviet secret police apparatus. For their first encounter in six years, they went to the Café Brevoort in New York for dinner. What struck her was that Sorge had been transformed by his years of working as an intelligence agent for the Soviet Union.

Her impressions are worth quoting in full. She noted that Richard

> had been transformed into a boisterous, hard-drinking man. Little of the charm of the romantic, idealistic scholar was left, though he was still startlingly good-looking. His cold blue eyes, slightly slanted and heavy-browed, had retained their quality of looking amused for no reason at all; his hair was still thick and brown, but his cheeeks and the heavy, sensuous mouth were sagging, his nose was thinner.
>
> It was a very different man, this Ika with whom I had dinner in the Café Brevoort in 1935, from the one who took me to dinner in Berlin at the end of the year 1929.[6]

Sorge was back in Tokyo at the end of September after an absence of four months. When German diplomats and press colleagues enquired where he had been all this time, he put on a bravura performance: 'Oh, I took a peek at California, looked up some old friends. And then I was in Pittsburgh, the steel centre. Good grief, the Japanese don't have a chance of matching American steel production, even if they conquer the whole of China!'[7]

He went into raptures describing the statuesque American women he had encountered: 'The girls over there are fully grown! They've got legs, none of these stumps of muscle like the Japanese women.' But he was forced to concede that American girls were more trouble to deal with than their Japanese sisters – they were not self-effacing and malleable, like the little women in Japan.[8]

CHAPTER NINE

'It's Hard Here, Really Hard'

ON THE warm, drizzly evening of 4 October 1935, the Rheingold bar and restaurant in Nishi-Ginza hummed with activity. Helmut Ketel's little establishment was a magnet for homesick German businessmen, technicians and sailors, but the clientele invariably included a sprinkling of Japanese academics, artists or middle-ranking army officers with fond memories of student or cadet days spent in Germany. Papa Ketel, as he was universally known, had recreated a little corner of the *Vaterland* in Tokyo, complete with Berlin pancakes washed down with Holsten beer, and maudlin hits from Berlin played on the new-fangled electric gramophone.

The essence of the Rheingold was *Gemütlichkeit,* created from German aromas, food, music, and the jovial bark of the shrewd proprietor greeting customers. On top of all that the Rheingold boasted something never to be found in a *Bierstube* in Hamburg or Bremen: pretty Japanese waitresses, fetching in their dirndl frocks and pinafores, who served table but also brought a smile to lonely customers with their giggly ways and mispronounced German phrases. Each of these girls was personally selected by Papa Ketel for her looks and a semblance of good breeding, and given a new name. There was a Bertha, a Dora, an Irma – and an Agnes, who spoke her first hesitant words to Richard Sorge that evening, and so diverted her life into a new, unimaginably turbulent channel.

'Who is the foreigner talking to Papa?' Agnes – the bar-name of Miyake Hanako – asked her friend Bertha, who had worked there longer and knew all the regulars.[1] Sitting in a booth against the wall, Hanako saw a middle-aged foreigner, with prominent forehead and high cheek-bones, wavy chestnut hair and blue eyes – a very *gaijin* (foreign) face. There was nothing flashy about him, nothing remarkable that drew her attention, but Hanako was wide-eyed and curious about all the strange Western people who came to the Rheingold.

'He hasn't been in recently, but he used to come here a lot,' Bertha told her. 'He's a nice man. Doesn't speak Japanese. But he's very generous.' This was useful information. Papa didn't pay salaries, and the girls relied on tips – and there were plenty of stingy clients who tried to wriggle out of paying.

Since it was Hanako's turn to serve, she went over to take the blue-eyed foreigner's order. He turned his bright smile on the waitress, and examined her with evident interest. The girl Sorge saw was not a beauty in the conventional sense. Plumpish, with a dimpled moon face and soft babyish features, she gave a bashful impression that was only partly contrived. Hanako had worked in bars before she came to the Rhein-gold, but she had preserved an innocent manner that made a customer think this was her first day in this trade. There was something both flirtatious and demure in the way she fluttered her eyelashes at a man; a fey grace that could well have both teased and intrigued Sorge.

Papa Ketel made the introductions. 'This is Dr Sorge. And today happens to be his birthday.' '*Soo desu, soo desu,*' the man said, in a deep, gravelly voice. 'I am Sorge.' He offered her his hand – a very large hand – and she took it, smiling shyly, not sure how to respond. Papa tactfully got up and left them together, and Sorge beckoned to Hanako to sit beside him. 'Agnes, how old are you?' he said in English.

'*Ich bin dreiundzwanzig Jahre*' (I'm twenty-three), the girl replied. She was in fact twenty-five, but she looked a good deal younger, and foreigners were hopeless at guessing the age of a Japanese. 'I am forty today. So let's drink champagne together to celebrate.'

Hanako had worked at the Rheingold for a year, but still felt un-comfortable when foreigners stared at her, as Sorge did now. Every time she looked up from beneath her long eyelashes she found him gazing steadily. She blushed, and prayed that Bertha or one of the other girls would come and rescue her. He was trying to say something, in a mixture of German and English, neither of which she knew at all well. The gramophone was blaring a tearful melody, and all around foreigners were declaiming in loud, guttural voices. But she somehow managed to catch his drift.

'I am happy today ... tell me, Agnes, what would you like? I want to give you a present.' Hanako, plucking up courage, replied, 'If you want to give me a present, I like a record. I like music.' Sorge nodded. 'So we will go together and buy one tomorrow.' Taking out a notebook he jotted down the time and place, and made quite sure Hanako had understood. He did not stay long, and left a large tip when the bill came. When he had gone, Hanako asked Bertha whether this foreigner had a particular favourite among the waitresses. 'Not really. Dora sometimes sits with him. But he doesn't ask for anyone in particular.'

The following day, Hanako went to the appointment in a music shop in the Ginza. True to his promise, Sorge bought her the records she wanted – operatic arias – and some Mozart sonatas that he was personally fond of. Afterwards he took her to Lohmeyer's, a German restaurant nearby, where the staff greeted him by name. Over lunch, mixing English and Japanese, he told her a little more about himself and his work as a journalist. When they parted Sorge said he wanted to see her again, and, after some hesitation, she agreed.

§ Two months after Sorge's return to Tokyo, Max Clausen arrived in Yokohama aboard the *Tatsuta Maru* from San Francisco. Hidden in his clothing were two small vacuum tubes for the wireless set he planned to build from scratch. Before they parted in Moscow, he and Sorge had agreed to go to a certain bar near the Ginza every Tuesday until they made contact. But on the day after Clausen's arrival, Friday 29 November, there was a fancy-dress party at the German Club in Tokyo, and here they bumped into each other by chance – Sorge was decked out that evening like a Berlin sausage-vendor. They arranged to meet the following day at the Blue Ribbon bar, where Sorge encouraged Clausen to construct, as soon as possible, a new transmitter to replace the bulky equipment left behind by his timid predecessor 'Bernhardt'.

This task tested Clausen's skill and ingenuity to the fullest. Patiently, he combed little shops in the Ginza and Shimbashi area for wireless parts and for copper wire to build the tuning coils. Since private individuals were forbidden to own transmitters, considerable care was needed to avoid attracting attention to these purchases. Piecing the equipment together and testing it took several weeks, and it was not until February 1936 that radio communication with Moscow was up and running.

With Clausen's arrival, the core of the ring was in place. Branko de Vukelic, the only other foreigner in Sorge's network, handled photography. His work involved photographing documents to be sent out to Moscow on microfilm, and developing incoming microfilm which brought instructions from Moscow (and occasional letters to Sorge from Katya).

In addition, Vukelic collected whatever information he could from the British and French diplomats and the Western journalists he cultivated. He had talked his way into a reporter's job at the French news agency, Havas, which gave him access to the Domei News Agency, where he could pick up news that could not be published because of censorship rules. But, as Sorge would tell interrogators, the Yugoslav was not in a position to learn anything about truly sensitive Japanese political and military matters. For high-grade intelligence Sorge relied on Ozaki, and to a lesser extent Miyagi, his loyal Japanese co-workers. In his own words, 'I must admit that I owe my immense success to Ozaki and Miyagi.'[2]

Ozaki Hotsumi had a superb grasp of complex issues. His talent lay in cutting to the heart of the information he amassed, without neglecting to explain the context of arcane events. This was so valuable that Sorge made it a rule to wait for Ozaki's analysis before sending reports on major developments to Moscow. Ozaki had a simple, modest explanation for his success in gaining information: an affable personality. 'By nature I am a sociable person. I like people. I can make friends with most people. Moreover I like to be kind to people. Not only is my circle of friends wide, I am on intimate terms with most of them. My sources of information have been these friends.'[3]

§ Sorge was a resourceful intelligence agent with an aptitude for drawing out the best in his small team. He ran the network in a relaxed fashion, with minimal discipline. By his own description it was not a strict organization, though the approach to work, he said, was 'certainly not loose'.

They were neither bound by contract nor motivated by gain: 'We had no fixed contracts, or regulations, but worked for Moscow as a group cemented by ideology as communists, and definitely not by thought of money or profit.'[4]

Sorge was not always even-tempered, and friction was bound to arise at times between men of very different personalities. In his prison memoir, Vukelic recalled being sharply rebuked by Sorge for carelessness. And we know from another witness that on one occasion when Sorge was on the telephone to Vukelic, he shouted and stamped his feet with uncontrollable anger. Such outbursts were rare, and Vukelic respected Sorge as an able leader. When he or Clausen were required to carry out a certain task, Sorge never gave orders – he explained what the job was, suggested how to carry it out, and asked for their views on the best approach.

> In fact, Clausen and I were fairly awkward customers and often had our own way. Nevertheless, over the whole nine years, apart from once or twice when he lost his temper, he never threw his weight around. And even when he was angry he simply appealed to our political conscience or friendship toward him, never to other motives.[5]

Ozaki, too, remained steadfast in his admiration for Sorge. The entry into his life of two foreigners – Sorge and Smedley – had devastating consequences, yet after his arrest he was full of praise for them: 'Both were true to their principles, able, and committed to their beliefs, and enthusiastic in their work.'[6]

An embittered Clausen saw a different side of his chief, sharing with his interrogators this savage indictment of Sorge: 'He would destroy his best friend if it were necessary for communism ... He was a firm communist, yet he was a man who could not bear up under certain conditions ... Sorge's character as a man was not of the best.'[7]

To friends, Sorge's most serious flaws were dogmatism, intolerance of other people's viewpoints, and a complete lack of a sense of humour: 'With Sorge there was only irony and sharp sarcasm: there were no nuances. He lived in a world of black and white: but the world is coloured.'[8]

But beneath the cynic's armour beat a deeply compassionate heart. The genuine sympathy he felt for the weak and exploited is not in doubt. For instance, the writer Friedrich Sieburg, who came to know Sorge well, was touched by his disinterested concern for the women driven by poverty to work in the mean brothels of Tokyo's Tamenoi district: 'Sorge was obsessed by the fate of all these girls who had been ruthlessly sent to big cities, and had developed a charming habit of chatting with them in his broken Japanese, teasing them and showing them little kindnesses. He was unbelievably popular in this milieu.'[9]

§ Aino Kuusinen, the Fourth Department's 'mole' in Japanese high society, was startled when she was ordered to return to Moscow. It was November 1935, and she had been in Tokyo for less than a year. The summons filled her with alarm.

On her return, she found the Fourth Department in confusion. No one would explain why General Berzin had been replaced as head of the organization he had created. Her recall from Japan appeared to be a symptom of the chaos that prevailed. General Uritsky, whom she met for the first time, told her there had been a 'mistake'. She was to return to Japan, continue her language studies and extend her range of contacts. Uritsky had no specific tasks to give her, but he suggested she write a favourable book about Japan that would raise her stock in that country and smooth her infiltration of influential circles.

To her surprise, Aino was advised to keep away from Sorge, and left in no doubt that the director was dissatisfied with the Ramsay ring. Clausen had asked her to pass on a request for $20,000 capital to start up a business as his protective cover, and the general's reaction was an explosion of fury: 'Those rascals – all they do is drink and spend money. They won't get one kopeck!'[10]

Sorge had clearly fallen from favour since the departure of his mentor General Berzin. Aino discovered this in December 1935, a very few months after Sorge's visit to Moscow. Could Sorge have failed to sense the tension in the Fourth Department when he reported to Uritsky in the summer? Was he blind to the 'state of utter confusion' described by Aino?[11]

He was too perceptive to miss the chill in the air, the hostility to those, like himself, associated with Berzin. Some feeling of foreboding prompted the bleak confession in the Hotel Bolshaya Moskovskaya in August in which we find the first glimmering of disenchantment with Stalin's Russia. When this is coupled with the director's disparaging remarks, a picture forms of a doubt-ridden spy labouring for capricious and ungrateful masters. In this light, the shield of cynicism that struck his acquaintances so forcefully is more easily understood. So too is the pursuit of oblivion through alcohol and women, a quest that grew more frantic as successive attempts to escape from Japan proved futile.

§ In the early hours of 26 February 1936, in driving snow, 1,500 troops of the elite First Division marched out of barracks to stage a revolt against the government. Acting under the orders of disaffected young officers, the rebels seized strategic points in Tokyo. Murder squads proceeded to wipe out 'liberal influence around the throne' – the intention being to eliminate eminent public figures who did not support the army's expansionist schemes in Asia.

Takahashi Korekiyo, the veteran finance minister, was the insurgents' first victim. About the same time, another squad of assassins burst into the official residence of the prime minister, Admiral Okada Keisuke. Here they shot and killed his brother-in-law, Colonel Denzo Matsuo, mistaking him for Okada, who fled to a toilet, where he remained hidden for two days. Other victims were the lord keeper of the Privy Seal, Viscount Saito, and the inspector-general for military education, General Watanabe. The grand chamberlain, Admiral Suzuki, was seriously wounded.

Second Lieutenant Yukawa Yasuhiro, twenty-two, described how he led a rebel detachment in the attack on police headquarters.

We walked from Azabu to the Metropolitan Police Department at Sakura-damon, climbing up the staircase, firing machine guns to break open staircase doors while a different company started negotiations with top police officers.

There was no bloodshed, because police backed away when they heard our machine guns. We stationed two machine guns on the roof and then waited for a flashlight signal from the Imperial Palace grounds that would mean friendly troops had occupied the palace.[12]

The rebels entrenched themselves around the Imperial Palace and government buildings, including the War Ministry. The German Embassy in Nagata-cho was in the line of fire. Dirksen, the ambassador, who happened to be in Nagasaki that day, hurried back to Tokyo.

The embassy was in a virtual state of siege. Along with the entire diplomatic corps, Dirksen and his senior military attaché, Colonel Ott, were at a loss to explain the causes of the unprecedented mutiny, and baffled by the failure of the authorities to crush it swiftly. Dirksen and Ott turned to their oracle, Sorge, whose judgement in political and economic matters had been sound on previous occasions. They were not disappointed. Sorge saw an excellent chance to strengthen his position in the embassy, and plunged into the work of illuminating the enigma both for his masters in Moscow and for the German mission in Tokyo.

After his arrest, Sorge listed five occasions when the entire network operated at full stretch to gather and interpret intelligence for the Fourth Department. The first of these was the *putsch* of 26 February 1936. Armed with a camera and his press card, Sorge reconnoitred rebel lines in the heart of Tokyo. His attention was caught by a stand-off between soldiers and marines on the road between the Foreign Ministry and Navy Ministry. The navy was not prepared to stand idly by, he concluded, and this was indeed the case – it turned out that battleships in Tokyo Bay had their guns trained on rebel positions.

Miyagi translated the young officers' manifesto and pamphlets and newspaper articles, and surveyed the opinion of ordinary people, who tended to be either indifferent or firmly on the side of the rebels. At an early stage, the artist-spy ventured a prediction that the mutinous young officers were doomed. Miyagi thought the crushing of the rebellion would represent victory for the army faction that wanted to expand into China, and defeat for young, radical officers pressing for a strike against Russia. For the immediate future, he concluded, Russia was safe. The darker side of the coin was that the army would proceed to tighten its grip on the affairs of the nation.

Ozaki Hotsumi, stationed in the *Asahi*'s stronghold in Yurakucho, close to the Ginza, was able to give Sorge up-to-the-minute reports as events unfolded. An in-depth study of the drama proved especially valuable. Ozaki identified the miserable conditions of the farmers as a root cause of the unrest. Most of the rebel soldiers came from country districts, and were influenced by the grinding poverty they had seen or personally experienced. (Farmers made up half the population, but, including landlords, had only 18 per cent of the national income. So dire was the poverty in some areas that farmers were forced to sell their daughters – the sisters of men like these rebels – into prostitution. In some villages, government notices urged local people: 'Consult with officials before you trade your daughters!')

However, Ozaki made the point to Sorge that the young officers' ideology, though anti-capitalist, was not left-wing. He foresaw two likely consequences of the revolt – first the growth of right-wing influence in Japan, and second a sharper anti-Soviet tilt in Japanese foreign policy.

Using the findings of Ozaki and Miyagi, Sorge was able to produce his own detailed report on the mutiny, which he submitted to Dirksen, Ott and Wenneker at the embassy. This authoritative analysis was seen in Berlin by, among others, General Georg Thomas, chief of the German army's economic department. Thomas was so impressed that he commissioned Sorge to compile a special study of the mutiny for his department.

At the same time Sorge was reporting to Moscow on the disturbances in Tokyo. Clausen was still experimenting with his new radio, so most of the material was sent out by courier. The package of microfilm smuggled out of Japan included confidential documents Ott had obtained from the Japanese army. The military attaché allowed Sorge to read through these documents, and he found a chance to photograph them surreptitiously. This was the first time that he used a pocket camera to copy material on the embassy premises. Soon it would become a routine practice.

The perplexing 26 February incident was the first real test of the network's capabilities, and showed how information could be recycled to meet the needs of different masters. Intelligence gathered by the ring ended up not only in Moscow but in Berlin. Sorge's stock soared in the embassy, and more official secrets came his way. An office was placed at his disposal by a grateful ambassador. In May, his prestige was further enhanced by the publication of his study of the revolt in the influential *Zeitschrift für Geopolitik*.

§ The 26 February episode turned out to be a watershed, establishing beyond doubt that in Japanese politics the bullet was mightier than the ballot. The revolt was put down, eighteen officers court-martialled and shot, and the army temporarily discredited. But, as Miyagi had predicted, the ascendancy of the army in national life was unstoppable. The result was the triumph of the policy of unfettered expansion on the Asian continent.

A few weeks after the mutiny Sorge could see for himself which way the wind was blowing. The ministers for war and the navy justified the coming massive increases in army and naval expenditure by claiming that Japan's hands had been 'forced by the naval programme of the United States and the warlike preparations made by Soviet Russia in the Far East.'

As Ozaki impressed on Sorge, the threat to the Soviet Union posed by Japan would henceforth grow, and vigilance was essential. The Japanese army was possessed by a yearning to conquer the Asian continent. This presupposed the destruction of Soviet power: 'Thus ever since the Manchurian Incident there has been a constant risk that Japan will attack the Soviet Union.'[13]

§ In the winter of 1935–36 Sorge built up the Soviet spy ring, consolidated his position in the German Embassy and pursued his cover profession as a journalist. He also found time to woo Hanako. On his frequent visits to the Rheingold, it was understood among the waitresses that only Hanako would sit beside him. On her days off work, he invited her to lunch, took her shopping, and they communicated in the simple Japanese of small children. This went on for several months.

'In spring 1936, just after the *Niniroku* affair [26 February army revolt], he said he was going on a journey to Mongolia and what present should he bring back?' Hanako reminisced, many years later.

> So I said, a camera! He didn't show up in the Rheingold for a while, and then one summer evening he came in with this camera – made in Germany, a really good one. That made me happy. I'd never owned a camera before.
>
> Not long after that, on my day off, he took me out to dinner and asked me to go home with him. He said he wanted me to see something interesting. I suppose it was asking for trouble, but I said yes. I didn't feel nervous or anything. We bought some chocolate at the German Bakery in Yurakucho and took a taxi.
>
> His house was in Azabu, at Nagasaka-cho, down a long slope as far as Toriisaka police station, then you turned left. We got out and walked into a narrow lane, and his house was at the end. Foreigners wouldn't have thought it anything special, but it was an up-to-date middle-class house as far as Japanese were concerned.

We went up to the second floor, and into a ten-mat room which was cluttered up with two desks, books and papers everywhere, and every wall covered in maps, maps all over! There were books and a gramophone even in the *tokonoma* [an alcove in which a scroll or painting is hung]. Oh, and a low sofa as well on one side.

Well, I ate some of the chocolate. He made coffee and he had a bottle of something and a soda syphon. Sorge showed me a tile he brought back from Mongolia, and explained its history, which went over my head. I was more interested in an antique gold buckle, inlaid with a red jewel. He saw me looking at this and said I could have it.

Then he started to fool around a bit. He pulled out a sword from the *tokonoma* and danced around the room swinging it – not that there was much space to dance in. And he burst out laughing, and I laughed, and then he played some records. I can't remember what he put on. He knew I liked Italian opera. He was fond of Mozart and Bach.

He must have got tired, changing records, and winding up the gramophone, and he came and sat beside me on the sofa. Then without warning he was pressing me down with that powerful body of his. I was so surprised I couldn't speak. Then he had one arm round me, and his other hand was caressing my breasts and my stomach. His hand reached my skirt and I found my voice.

'Don't! Don't!' I put up strong resistance, writhing and trying to escape. Sorge simply said: 'Why?' I shouted something like: 'Terrible! Terrible!' And he let go. He sat there and looked at my face – I must have looked on the point of crying. He helped me up, and I straightened my skirt. I told him I was leaving. So he took me up to the top of the hill and found a taxi and gave me some money. So that was that. I got in, and looked at him standing there, looking miserable. And I too felt sad when I left him that night.

I was relieved when he came to the Rheingold a few days later. We made another date, went to buy some records, and had dinner. Again he invited me to his house, and I went. I suppose I knew what was going to happen. He was forty-two by Japanese reckoning, and a bachelor. I was twenty-six, so I knew what I was doing, coming to the place of a man I liked. When he embraced me I resisted, just a little, but I didn't cry out, I closed my eyes. All feeling of fear was gone.

One night not long after that he came to the Rheingold late at night, and waited until I finished work, and took me home on his motorbike. I can tell you I was trembling. He was drunk, and drove flat out. I clung to him for dear life. That was the first night for me to sleep in his bedroom.

I had a little apartment where I lived by myself. But soon after that night together I packed my things, and went to Sorge's house. I spent half the week with Sorge at Nagasaka-cho, and because he was so busy, I spent a few days each week at my place.[14]

§ A few months after Sorge left Moscow, he received news that Katya was pregnant. The baby was expected in May. In a reply dated 9 April 1936, he rejoices at the prospect of being a father:

> there will soon be someone else who belongs to us both. Do you remember our agreement about names? I'd like to alter the agreement so that, if it's a girl, she has your name ... I have sent you a parcel with things. I hope it gives you pleasure and you can use it when the difficult time for you is over and you can be elegant again. Today I'll arrange a second parcel with things for the baby.

But some mishap apparently occurred, for in the summer of 1936 he is writing:

'I have got a short message from home and now know that everything turned out quite differently than I hoped.' There is no further reference to a child in the letters, and it has been assumed that Katya terminated the pregnancy. Mystery surrounds this episode.[15]

The letter, written less than a year since Sorge left Moscow to resume his clandestine work, is permeated by sadness. He itches to return to Russia, but knows it is an impossible dream. He cannot discuss his mission, or even reveal in what country he is living; all he can say is that 'it is hard here, really hard.'

> I'm tormented by the thought that I am getting old. I'm seized by the mood to be back home quickly, back home in your new apartment. But for the time being that's all dreams ... speaking strictly objectively, it is hard here, really hard. Yet it's better than could have been expected ... I ask you to make sure that I get news from you at every opportunity, because I'm terribly lonely here.

Sorge was plagued by loneliness. It was a nagging illness that numerous love affairs, and the devotion of Hanako, relieved without curing. The pain of a solitary life, burdened with secrets he can never share, resonates in the surviving letters to Katya, and in some of his correspondence with the Fourth Department. We sense the acute frustration caused by his enforced sojourn in Japan, cut off from the spiritual nourishment of Russia, dreading old age and fearful of the future. This was the inner person concealed behind the brash, cocksure facade.

§ To her great satisfaction, Aino Kuusinen, alias 'Ingrid', returned to Japan in mid-September 1936, with instructions to resume her infiltration of high social circles. She had added a new string to her bow, having completed a book entitled *Smiling Japan*. This dwelt on the virtues of Japan and the Japanese, and so delighted officials in the Foreign Ministry that they arranged an English translation of the Swedish original. As she had calculated, this positive portrayal of Japan ensured that she was warmly received by prominent officials and aristocrats.

The Swedish author Elizabeth Hansson – as her passport identified her – was invited to Emperor Hirohito's garden party and to a reception at the Imperial Palace. This was not quite the coup for Soviet Intelligence that it seems. From her account, we can gauge that she felt more warmth for Hirohito than for Stalin. In her heart, she had already defected from the Soviet Union, where her brother and many friends were now in prison.[16]

Aino struck up a cordial relationship with Prince Chichibu, the emperor's brother, to whom she ascribes 'democratic views' – unlike those of Hirohito. But her memoirs provide tantalizingly few details about her contacts at the Japanese court. Indeed, her mission as an agent of the Fourth Department in Tokyo remains something of a mystery. The prison testimonies of Sorge and Clausen add little to our knowledge of 'Ingrid'. For some fourteen months she studied Japanese and immersed herself in oriental philosophy – a restful assignment for a Soviet spy. We do not know whether she earned her keep by feeding information to the Fourth Department. General Uritsky, who had complained about the extravagant expenses of the Sorge ring, approved ample money for Aino to live in elegance. In her memoirs she has little good to say about her superiors in Moscow, but she does pay tribute to their unusual generosity in funding her agreeable sojourn in Japan.[17]

§ The development of close relations between Japan and Germany, culminating in the anti-Comintern pact on 25 November 1936, confirmed the Soviet leadership's worst suspicions. In Moscow, as Sorge told his inquisitors, 'no doubt was felt that the chief target that bound the two countries together at that time was the USSR, or more precisely speaking, their hostility towards the USSR'.[18] Thanks to Sorge, the Russians were fully informed about the anti-Comintern pact, and the months of negotiations that went into it. This intelligence coup was the first major dividend of his intimacy with Senior Military Attaché Eugen Ott.

The German Embassy found out only by chance that secret talks on a German–Japanese alliance were being conducted in Berlin. The prime movers were Joachim von Ribbentrop, a senior Nazi functionary (later Hitler's foreign minister), Oshima Hiroshi, the Germanophile military attaché at the Japanese Embassy in Berlin, and Admiral Canaris, head of German Military Intelligence. This little clique went to great lengths to conceal the negotiations from meddlesome politicians and Foreign Ministry officials in both countries.

Hitler, impressed by the Japanese army's seizure of Manchuria in 1931 in defiance of world opinion, saw Japan as a useful ally in an anti-Bolshevik front. His belief – expressed in *Mein Kampf* – that the Japanese were a primitive race who borrowed all their culture from others had not changed, but now he hid his contempt for expediency's sake.

Japan, worried by Russia's hardening attitude, thought it made good sense to have a European ally capable of holding Russia in check. The idea of a pact with Germany held a strong appeal for the Japanese army. Its hawkish elements believed Germany would be a strong partner in a joint attack on the Soviet Union, and all army factions were agreed that a pact would bring an end to Germany's support for Chiang Kai-shek and weaken Chinese resistance to Japanese encroachment.

It was in early spring – shortly after the army revolt had been quelled – that Colonel Ott happened to hear about the negotiations from contacts at Japanese General Staff Headquarters. Unable to restrain his excitement, he told Sorge what he had heard:

> It's so hush-hush that neither Ambassador Dirksen nor myself were told anything about this. The talks must be extremely important. The ambassador has asked me to contact the General Staff in Berlin to find out what's going on behind our backs.
>
> I'm going to telegraph to Staff Headquarters using the army code, and I would like your help. You must swear not to tell anybody about the matter.

Sorge described what happened next:

> I agreed to Ott's request and went to his private house to help him encode the telegram. The matter was so secret that he couldn't ask anyone at the embassy for help with this.
>
> The query to the Army Staff headquarters brought no reply. Ott got very annoyed and let Dirksen know. He suggested Ott send another query using the army code. Do it together with Sorge, the ambassador said, and don't let anyone else see it. So Ott came to me again for help and we sent another coded telegram to Berlin asking for information.
>
> The outcome was that eventually an answer arrived from the German General Staff saying they couldn't give any details in a telegram, and telling Ott to ask the Japanese General Staff to brief him.[19]

Through this channel, Sorge was better informed than anyone in the German embassy, apart from the ambassador and senior military attaché, about the progress of the negotiation and the content of the anti-Comintern pact announced on 25 November. The official, published version of this pact against international communism was harmless enough: Japan and Germany agreed to exchange information and jointly combat the worldwide activities of the Communist International.

However, as Sorge reported to Moscow, the sting lay in a secret protocol, in which the Soviet Union was explicitly named as the target of the pact. The two countries pledged that if either became the subject of an unprovoked attack or threat of attack by the Soviet Union, they would consult on 'measures to safeguard their common interests' and take no measures that would 'ease the situation of the USSR'. It did not amount to a military alliance, but to the Soviet leadership it smacked of a sinister conspiracy by two hostile nations on its western and eastern borders.[20]

Sorge's account of this episode is of special interest for what it reveals about his familiarity with the most secret materials in the embassy: the codes used to protect communications with Berlin, including the code used exclusively by the German army. It is inconceivable that Sorge missed the opportunity to photograph the code materials and send them to Moscow, to help Russian specialists toiling to decrypt Germany's secret communications.

Another Soviet Intelligence officer claimed credit for warning Moscow about the secret preparations for a German–Japanese pact. Walter Krivitsky, the NKVD (secret police) Resident in The Hague, described how one of his agents got hold of the Japanese Embassy's code-book, and its files on the negotiations, in the summer of 1936: 'From then on all correspondence between General Oshima and Tokyo flowed regularly through our hands', wrote Krivitsky in memoirs published after his break with the Soviets.[21]

If this is true, Krivitsky pulled off a tremendous coup. Signals traffic between the Japanese Embassy in Berlin and Tokyo carried vital information on the development of relations between the Nazis and the Japanese. If the Soviets were in possession of Oshima's code-book, they could read the military attaché's secret reports to the Japanese government on his interviews with Hitler and other top German officials.[22] This material would have corroborated what Sorge was reporting on the German–Japanese negotiations. There is evidence that even before this – from the early 1930s – the Russians had access to raw intelligence about Japan which supplemented Sorge's dispatches from Tokyo.

Indeed, one leading expert on Soviet Intelligence claims that the most influential information obtained by the Soviet Union in the early 1930s derived from sigint – intelligence acquired by intercepting and decrypting secret communications between Japan and its embassies in foreign countries and between army units.[23] According to this authority, the Russians placed immense weight on sigint – not least because of Stalin's paranoia about his agents overseas. Human spies were prone to the weaknesses of the flesh and might turn into traitors. Sigint did not lie, nor could the most alert and nimble agent match it for speed.

But agents in the field could play a vital part in the complex task of penetrating a code system, and Soviet spy-masters instructed agents to steal material that would assist the code-breakers. Without doubt Sorge was expected to obtain the German Embassy's up-to-date tables used in navy and army codes and cipher instructions, and ship them to Moscow. Apparently, little effort was required. We know of two occasions when Eugen Ott, first as military attaché, and then as ambassador, handed the army codes to Sorge so that he could fulfil secret duties on behalf of Germany.

§ A week or two after the anti-Comintern pact was signed, Sorge took a short break from work. Together with Hanako, he travelled to the hot-spring resort of Atami, fifty miles south-west of Tokyo, some time in December 1936. Hanako, in her eighties, would reminisce about their first trip as a couple with wry amusement.

> 'Let's get away from Tokyo for a day or two', he said, and bought me a new suitcase. It was supposed to be a holiday, but he took his typewriter along too, and he was working all the time. He'd booked a room in the Sanno Hotel. It was a Western-style hotel, with proper beds, you see. The curious thing is, they served Japanese food. Sorge liked raw fish. He was the sort of person who could adapt to anything, anywhere. The hotel was about at mid-level of the big hill overlooking the bay. There was a hot-spring bath, and I remember Sorge took a very long soak. We had dinner in the room, and hot sake, and went to bed. He was very passionate, but gentle – not like a wild male animal baring his teeth. That wasn't Sorge's way. It was raining the next day and we stayed in the room. Sorge got on with his typing, and I looked out at the rain tap-tapping on the window pane.[24]

Hanako was a town-girl, and she quickly grew bored with Atami, grey and deserted at this time of year. Only one day away from Tokyo, and she already missed the bright lights and gaiety of the capital. At a loss, she lay down on the bed and occupied herself by writing a poem.[25]

After a while, Sorge stopped typing and came and lay down beside her. What is it, Miyako?' he asked, addressing her by the pet name he had chosen. 'What are you doing?'

'It's a poem. I'm trying to write a poem.'

'I think it is not interesting for you when I type, is it? But look at the rain, Miyako. If we go out, we ... we ...'

Sorge struggled to find the right word. Hanako helped him out.

'*Nureru – nu-re-ru* – we get wet. Don't worry. You type. I write my poem.'

She thought his Japanese had improved since she first met him just over a year ago. Now that they were together half the week, he was acquiring new vocabulary from her, jotting the words down in a notebook. He tried hard, but Japanese was a language that would take years to master, and Sorge clung to the hope that his stay in Japan would be short, as the director had promised.

'Miyako, do you want to study? Sorge will help you study. What do you want to study?' 'Singing. I want to study opera. Ever since I was a schoolgirl I have a dream of becoming a professional singer.'

'Sorge knows a German music teacher. When we go back to Tokyo I will take you to him immediately. Does that make you happy?'

Hanako cheered up at once. Sorge spent much of the day typing, and immersing himself in the hot-spring bath. The next day the rain cleared. They took a car from the hotel to Odawara, by the mountain road that passes through Hakone, and there they caught the train back to Tokyo.

'What a fine character he had!' says Hanako:

> When Sorge made a promise, he always kept it. True to his word, he arranged for me to have singing lessons with Dr August Junker, who taught at Musashino Music College, and supported me as much as he could. He bought me a piano, but it didn't fit into my apartment so he rented a house, and I started piano lessons. That was just like Sorge! He didn't buy luxuries for himself like gold watches or expensive clothes but when it came to helping me study, he gave me all the money I needed to fulfil my dream.[26]

§ Max Clausen made his first transmissions from the home of Gunther Stein, a journalist who arrived in Japan in 1936 as correspondent for the *Financial News* and *News Chronicle* of London. Stein, a German Jew who became a naturalized British subject, may have been involved in Soviet espionage before he came to Japan. In prison, Sorge described him as a 'supporter' of the ring. This almost certainly understated his role in the network.[27]

Stein placed his house at Clausen's disposal, and from an upstairs room the radio operator made his first contact with 'Wiesbaden' (Vladivostok) in the middle of February 1936. Clausen also operated the radio set from the Vukelic home, and from his own quarters. It was dangerous work. If police discovered the equipment, he would automatically be treated as a spy.

He assumed that Japanese monitoring agencies could detect the radio traffic, and this was indeed the case. Japanese authorities first intercepted unauthorized radio signals in 1937. Attempts were made to locate the source, but the Japanese lacked mobile direction-finders, and never got closer than a two-kilometre range. The Japanese deduced that a spy was operating from Tokyo – the traffic was in a code that government cryptanalysts failed to crack. They believed that the receiving station was in Shanghai at first, and from 1940 in the Soviet Far East.

Hauling the equipment to the transmission site was a nerve-racking business. The ingenious Clausen had compressed the radio set so that it fitted into a large briefcase, which looked innocent enough. But there were several close shaves that frayed Clausen's nerves. On one occasion he was stopped by police while driving home after operating from Vukelic's house. A policeman stepped into the road and asked where he was going.

> Vukelic was in the car clutching the black bag with the radio set, and my heart leapt at the thought we had been discovered. For some reason or other, the policeman merely remarked, 'Your headlights are off. Be more careful,' and walked away without examining our baggage or searching us.[28]

As a basic security precaution, the members of the group were referred to only by their code-names: Sorge was 'Ramsay' or 'Vix', Miyagi 'Joe', Ozaki 'Otto,' Vukelic 'Gigolo', Clausen 'Fritz', Gunther Stein 'Gustaf'. Code-names were also used for key locations and in-dividuals mentioned in communications with the Centre. Moscow was 'München', and the receiving station in Vladivostok 'Wiesbaden'. Ott was 'Anna', Wenneker 'Paul'.

Sorge believed that the most important protection for a secret agent was a watertight legal cover. In his view, the best camouflage was that of a merchant, which Clausen chose. With a supercilious air, Sorge commented:

> A man clever enough to take up espionage work as a career in the first place would not forsake his career for business, and even if he did, the chances are he would not succeed. Generally speaking, the mercantile class is made up of men of average or less than average intelligence, and the agent who assumes such a cover would be quite safe from detection by police.[29]

Sorge displayed a similarly condescending attitude towards Clausen, and no doubt believed that the merchant's cover suited the radio operator well.

Clausen himself said he had three principles for diverting suspicion: 'Act cheerfully in public, look stupid, and, especially, make it known I was interested in amateur radio.'[30]

§ Many of Sorge's reports were too long to transmit by wireless. These, along with the texts of Japanese and German documents, maps and diagrams, were recorded on microfilm and smuggled out of Japan by members of the ring. Until 1939, the handover of this material and the receipt of funds and instructions usually took place at a pre-arranged rendezvous with Moscow's liaison men in Shanghai or Hongkong.

Sorge himself took out the film cartridges, hidden under his clothes, on three occasions; Clausen and his wife, Anna, each undertook two courier journeys to Shanghai. Anna, who had married Max in Shanghai in August 1936 after finally being allowed out of the Soviet Union, was a reluctant collaborator. She was cajoled into serving as courier by a combination of veiled threats and promises that she could spend part of the ring's funds for personal shopping.

After the outbreak of the European war, in September 1939, these journeys were discontinued, chiefly because Hong Kong and Shanghai police intensified their scrutiny of German nationals. At Sorge's request, Moscow arranged that liaison would henceforth be conducted through Soviet emissaries in Japan. 'Illegals' operating in foreign countries were, in theory, forbidden to maintain contact with local Soviet missions. This was clearly a sensible rule for Japan: foreign diplomats were kept under close watch by police. It is therefore surprising to discover that – despite the likelihood that they were being followed – Soviet diplomats regularly held meetings with Clausen at his home and office.

On 27 January 1940, Max and Anna Clausen took their seats in the Teikoku Gekijo – the Imperial Theatre – facing the Outer Garden of the Palace. Their tickets had arrived in Clausen's post office box at the Tokyo Central Post Office earlier in the month, following radioed instructions from Moscow to prepare for a rendezvous. Clausen was carrying a small packet containing thirty-eight rolls of microfilm, which included material from the German Embassy that Sorge had photographed surreptitiously. After a few minutes a European slipped into the seat next to Clausen's. The exchange took place, unobserved, in the darkened theatre. The man passed Clausen an envelope with $5,000 dollars of funds for the ring.

Further rendezvous with the same 'man from Moscow' took place in the following months. Then, in November 1940, a new man, known to Clausen as 'Serge' took over the liaison role, and their meetings were held either at Clausen's office in Shimbashi or at his house in Hiroo-cho. From photographs that police showed Clausen after his arrest, the two were positively identified as Helge Leonidovich Vutokevich, head of the consular division of the Soviet Embassy, and Viktor Sergevich Zaitsev, second secretary at the Soviet Embassy.

§ The Sorge ring's most precious asset was Ozaki Hotsumi, whose growing fame as a China expert brought him ever greater access to his country's power-holders. One event in particular firmly established his professional standing: the conference of the Institute of Pacific Relations held at Yosemite, in California, in the summer of 1936. The IPR was a forum dedicated to fostering relations between Pacific Rim nations through the exchange of ideas and information. Through the good offices of a schoolfriend, Ushiba Tomohiko, Ozaki was invited to join the Japanese delegation as a recognized specialist on the 'China Problem' or *Shinamondai*, the term Japanese used for the chaos they felt only they could resolve.[31] In a speech to the conference, Ozaki was careful not to rock the establishment boat. Concealing his personal opposition to Japanese aggression, he skilfully rationalized Japan's expansionist policy in China.

Yosemite had two far-reaching consequences for Ozaki's advancement. First, he made important contacts in the Japanese delegation. His lifelong friendship with Saionji Kinkazu, grandson of the statesman Prince Saionji, began on board the ship to California, and his relationship with Ushiba was cemented. Both these young men moved in the most influential circles, and would prove to be invaluable connections. Second, his contribution at Yosemite enhanced his prestige and brought him to the notice of men of power. Then, in December 1936, his stock was boosted further by an article on a dramatic incident that occurred in China.

Chang Hsueh-liang, war-lord of Manchuria, kidnapped Chiang Kai-shek, leader of the nationalists (Kuomintang) in Sian, capital of Shensi province. Ozaki wrote an article for his newspaper predicting that the kidnapping would force the nationalists to smoke the pipe of peace with their sworn enemies, the communists, and make common cause to confront Japanese aggression. It took courage to venture such a prediction in the jingoistic climate of the time. But Ozaki was quickly proved right: the nationalists reluctantly agreed to form a common front with the communists as the price for Chiang's release.

In April 1937, the renowned journalist was invited to join the newly formed Showa Research Association, whose aim was to encourage distinguished political thinkers to apply their minds to finding alternatives to the policies of the right-wing extremists who espoused a totalitarian state and *hakko ichiu* (Japanese domination of East Asia). By joining this group, Ozaki won new and influential friends. One of these took him under his wing: Kazami Akira, the head of the association's section dealing with the 'China problem'. When Prince Konoye formed his cabinet in June 1937, Akira was appointed chief cabinet secretary, and the Showa Research Association served as the new prime minister's 'think-tank.'[32]

Following the outbreak of overt hostilities between Japan and China, Ozaki's China expertise was in increasing demand. Within days of a brief skirmish between Japanese and Chinese troops by the Marco Polo Bridge near Peking on 7 July, Ozaki forecast in a magazine article that the incident would 'develop on such a scale as to prove of the utmost significance in world history'.[33]

Ozaki's insights on the course of the 'China Incident' were of exceptional interest to Sorge; convinced of its importance, he directed all the members of the network to devote themselves exclusively to the issue. Ozaki predicted that the 'Incident' would not be settled at the level of local commanders, and would inevitably lead to a protracted war between Japan and China. Since the German Embassy looked to Sorge for an interpretation of the events in China, he conveyed Ozaki's views to the ambassador and military attaché as if they were his own: 'I told Dirksen and Ott, who laughed at first, but later understood. Probably only I and Ozaki held the opinion that the Marco Polo Bridge incident would trigger a long war between Japan and China. I reported this to Moscow, adding my own opinion.'[34]

Ozaki believed that because of the China Incident the danger of a Japanese attack on Russia had diminished, at least temporarily. If the Japanese army had its hands full in China, its ambition to destroy Bolshevism would have to be shelved for the time being. This assessment too was conveyed by Sorge both to the German Embassy and to his masters in Moscow.

Open warfare was soon raging across northern China, and in late July the Japanese captured Peking and Tientsin. They took Shanghai in November, and then the Chinese capital, Nanking, in December 1937. The Japanese had expected easy victories; the Emperor had been assured the fighting would be over in three months. But it was not to be. The invaders met dogged resistance from Chinese armies, both nationalist and communist, and were sucked ever deeper into the vast continent.

At first Japan had set out to 'chastise' the Chinese nationalist government, but the scope of its war objectives had swollen by January 1938 to the 'establishment of a new order'. Japanese soldiers went to war on a wave of public support, and the entire population and national resources were marshalled in what came to be known as the *seisen*, holy war, conducted under the leadership of the emperor himself. The *seisen*, portrayed in newsreels and newspapers as a series of glorious but hard-won victories, became a means to 'mobilize and control the population and repress any opposition, not just to the prosecution of the war, but also to the government'.[35]

For Sorge, the outbreak of war in China was a useful new opportunity to prove his indispensability to the embassy. By repeating Ozaki's views as if they were his own, Sorge built on his prestige, and was frequently called into the ambassador's office to give advice.

As a matter of course, Sorge was invited to join an embassy study group set up by Ott to investigate the Japanese army's mobilization and equipment and its performance in the China theatre. These study sessions, spread over several months, yielded a good quantity of useful reports on Japanese logistics, aircraft, training and troop dispositions, which Sorge photographed secretly and sent to Moscow.

On Kazami Akira's recommendation, Konoye brought Ozaki into his entourage as a cabinet consultant – *naikaku shokutaku* – in July 1938. Ozaki gave up his job at the *Asahi*, and moved into an office in the prime minister's official residence. On the inside track, with access to classified documents, he worked on reports proposing ways to cope with the 'China Incident'. However, he later stressed that he could not exploit his position to realize his political aims, because government policies had already been clearly laid down. 'Rather I used this position to gain a proper grasp of the actual direction of Japanese politics and to obtain accurate information ... so of course I passed on to Sorge the information I obtained in the cabinet.'[36]

In November 1937, Prime Minister Konoye acquired a new, informal advisory group, the *Asameshikai* (Breakfast Society). The initiative came from his two private secretaries, Ushiba Tomohiko and Kishi Michizo, who enlisted Saionji Kinkazu and Ozaki, and, over time, a number of other 'wise men' as members. The Breakfast Society offered scope for thrashing out policy ideas for Prince Konoye, though he did not attend the meetings himself.

Over *miso* soup, the members of the Breakfast Society freely pooled confidential information. Here too was a channel to the decision-makers in government. In this select clique Ozaki, as a leading political analyst, was listened to with due attention and respect. For nearly four years he lost no chance to colour the views of those in power. This attempt to exert political influence, he firmly believed, was every bit as important as the collection of official secrets.

Without needing to dissemble, Ozaki mixed with absolute assurance in Japan's elite circles. At the same time Sorge blended easily with the heel-clicking Nazi diplomats he despised, genial, ever ready to be of service, yet keeping a detachment and an edge of cynicism that enhanced his popularity. A group photo taken in the embassy garden on 22 September 1937 after a diplomatic wedding indicates how thoroughly Sorge had infiltrated the milieu. Posing stiffly with Count Mirbach, head of the press section, Colonel Ott, Helma Ott, Dirksen the ambassador, and Mrs Dirksen, Sorge looks every inch the embassy insider. The bridegroom is Hans-Otto Meissner, a third secretary who had arrived in Tokyo the previous year.

Though the two men were not on close terms, it was unthinkable for Meissner not to invite Sorge, a somewhat raffish figure, but a reputed correspondent and favourite of the ambassador. After all, 'Sorge was accepted by everyone, everywhere.'[37] The fellow had a 'brilliant mind', even if Meissner recoiled at his 'unassailable conceit'.[38]

Another young diplomat attending the wedding reception would recall this day, after an interval of more than half a century. 'Of course there was nothing about Sorge's behaviour that suggested he was anything other than what we all took him for. He was a respected journalist, an adviser to Dirksen and Ott, and he was completely at home in the embassy.'[39]

§ The German community in Japan was tiny – only 1,118 souls in 1933, according to the *Japan-Manchukuo Yearbook*, though the number was almost to double by 1940. The largest contingent was in Tokyo, but German missionaries were scattered far and wide across the islands.[40]

Germany seemed infinitely remote. A fast North Lloyd steamer took six weeks to reach Hamburg. The Trans-Siberian Railway could reach Berlin – via Shimonoseki, Pusan, Harbin, Manchuli and Moscow – in sixteen days if the traveller was in a hurry, until Hitler's onslaught on Russia severed that route in June 1941.

The few reminders of home were savoured hungrily. Perhaps the German Club offered the best refuge to the homesick. It shared premises with a cultural institute, the German–East Asia Society, in a modest single-storey building five minutes' walk from the embassy. A curving Japanese tiled roof crowned the gate, and the building was laid out round a garden with a pond and bamboos, which the visitor could survey through walls of glass.

The library and reading-room here were an oasis of calm, and Sorge called in frequently. German newspapers were available, a month out of date, and there was a decent collection of books, mostly on oriental culture. These included a curious volume by a German anthropologist who had measured the sizes of heads and other body parts of scores of young Japanese women; the book was illustrated lavishly with semi-nude photos.

Frieda Weiss, a pretty young woman working as a secretary in the German–East Asia Society's office, caught Sorge's eye. They chatted, and eventually he asked if she could help him with some typing. 'I typed out a long press report on the February 26 incident (the army revolt of 1936). In fact he asked me to become his assistant, but my eyes were bad, and I had to turn the offer down.'[41]

The German Club, on the other side of the garden, consisted of a hall for concerts and get-togethers, and a bar and restaurant. By the mid-1930s, the Tokyo branch of the Nazi Party gathered here regularly, and the hall resounded with the *Horst Wessel Lied* and fiery speeches. There were also study meetings, using primers like *The ABC of National Socialism*, and Sorge was among local notables enlisted to give lectures.

The flavour of home was recreated at establishments like Lohmeyer's, which had pig's trotters on the menu and sold first-class *Wurst* over the counter. The *Apfelstrudel* and Black Forest Cake at the German Bakery in Yurakucho were universally deemed to be excellent. In the Ginza there was the Rheingold restaurant and bar, and its less salubrious competitor, the Fledermaus, a tiny, dingy German-style bar where Sorge was sometimes to be found. His friend, the writer Friedrich Sieburg, was distinctly unimpressed when Sorge took him there one night: 'There was nothing Japanese about the place, except for one or two low-class serving girls who would come and sit with customers, put their arms round their necks and giggle affectedly.'[42]

When German businessmen and diplomats drew up guest-lists for their soirées, they invariably included Dr Sorge. Sometimes they had cause to regret inviting him. He would offend bourgeois sensibilities with risqué jokes, and flirted outrageously, making no distinction between married and unattached women. Frieda Weiss, a single woman in her thirties, describes him as a roaring *Salonlöwe* (salon lion). 'Women were fascinated by him, and if the men envied him, they tried hard not to show it.' She remembers a party at the German Club when he swung her round the dance floor in a fiery tango, a dynamo of human energy.

When he danced, the limp from his war wounds seemed to melt away. 'At any social occasion Sorge attended, he attracted a crowd of admirers, men and women. He was the life and soul of any party.'[43]

§ Aino Kuusinen – the Soviet agent 'Ingrid' – visited Sorge on urgent business one night in late November 1937. To her dismay, he was seriously drunk, sprawled on the sofa with an almost empty bottle of whisky at his side – a lamentable state for a man with such important responsibilities.[44] Intoxicated though he was, Sorge succinctly explained that Moscow had told him to relay a message to 'Ingrid'.

> We've all been ordered to go back to Moscow, and that includes me. You are to go back via Vladivostok, and await further instructions there. I don't know what's behind this order.
>
> Even if you find the atmosphere unhealthy in Moscow, you have no reason to be afraid. As for me, I'll comply with the order if it's absolutely essential. But when you see our chiefs I'd like you to pass on a message on my behalf. Tell them that all the remarkable connections I've made here will be wasted if I have to leave Tokyo. And tell them that in any case, I can't leave before next April.

As she was about to leave, Sorge made a curious remark that lodged firmly in her memory: 'You're a very intelligent woman. I have to confess I've never met a woman with such clear judgement. But my judgement is superior to yours!'[45]

On her return to Moscow in December, she found that the situation had further deteriorated since her last visit. General Uritsky, the director of the Fourth Department, had been arrested, and it was likely he had been executed. Many other Soviet Intelligence officers had been recalled from overseas, and had then vanished. Aino herself was arrested and imprisoned on trumped-up charges as an 'enemy of the people'. Only now, when it was too late, did she grasp what Sorge had meant by his words when they parted. Apparently, he was smart enough to sense the danger that threatened them both, and for his part had no intention of obeying the recall order.

Aino underwent a harsh interrogation, in the course of which she was clearly given to understand what the Soviet leadership thought of Sorge. Her inquisitors said that he had disappointed the expectations of people 'at the highest levels'. The intelligence he provided was not satisfactory, and he was spending too much money. There was no saving grace. The NKVD (secret police) interrogators even told her that Sorge had been ordered 'many times' to come back, and the order came from Stalin himself. And he had the nerve to disobey!

Aino was instructed to write a letter asking Sorge to return to Moscow. This made no sense to her – if he had ignored Stalin's order, she pointed out, why would he pay attention to her? The interrogators responded that Sorge would surely heed such a request if it came from such a close friend. That was a wrong assumption, Aino protested. She and Sorge were *not* close friends. Anything the NKVD had heard to the contrary was a groundless rumour.[46]

Aino's interrogation was conducted at the beginning of 1938. The mood in Moscow was savage. The elimination of Stalin's suspected enemies was well under way: both Berzin and his successor at the Fourth Department had been executed. Though Sorge had no direct knowledge of their fate, it is likely that he sensed the change.

Soviet agents everywhere were being ordered home – indeed, it was remarkable if someone was *not* recalled in 1937. It was a common practice to lure back top intelligence officers by appealing to their egos. The order might say that the agent's presence in Moscow was required in order to brief the leadership on the situation in the country where he or she was posted; possibly the order to Sorge was couched in similar terms.[47]

But Sorge was more circumspect. A surprising amount of news about the Terror reached Tokyo, and he had access to German, English and American newspapers which carried reports of the 'show trials' and the blood-letting. And in September 1937, the assassination in Switzerland of his old friend, Ignace Poretsky (alias Reiss), who had defected from the NKVD, made headlines round the world.

Aino had agonized over whether to obey the summons from Moscow. She thought she had a choice, as the Finnish proverb went, 'between a swamp and a muddy place'. Of course her name might be on Stalin's 'hit list'. But if she disobeyed, might not the Soviet government send agents to track her down? Although Sorge was unhappy in Japan and longed to return, as his letters to Katya reveal, he judged the current atmosphere to be too 'unhealthy' to make a move. Aino was convinced that he had made the right choice: 'If Sorge had obeyed the order to return at that time, he would have been liquidated, there is no doubt about it,' she wrote.[48]

§ Journalism for Sorge was not merely a façade for espionage, nor was the professional standing he acquired just a means to impress the embassy. He enjoyed writing for its own sake, and took pride in his careful coverage of Japan and China. Indeed, he applied himself to his cover job as assiduously as any of his press corps colleagues, and this despite the onerous demands of his clandestine work for Moscow.

From 1937 he contributed regularly to the *Frankfurter Zeitung*, a newspaper that, in his words, 'represented the highest standards of German journalism'.[49] Sorge was never offered a staff position and remained a 'stringer', without a formal contract, until the end. But he wrote prolifically. In 1940 and 1941 his articles, by-lined 'S', normally appeared four or five times each month.

In his prison memoir he noted with satisfaction that the *Frankfurter Zeitung* 'often praised me on the grounds that my articles elevated its international prestige'.[50] Morever, he added immodestly, he was recognized in Germany as 'the best reporter in Japan'. Not all the German diplomats would have agreed with this assessment. Count von Mirbach, the urbane head of the embassy's press section, considered Sorge to be a mediocre journalist with little culture. But Eugen Ott was in no doubt at all that Sorge was head-and-shoulders above the other correspondents. 'The man knows everything,' he liked to tell people.

Dutifully, Sorge attended the regular press conferences held by the Foreign Ministry, and by the Board of Information from 1940. But they yielded pitifully little in the way of news. An American press colleague recalled that the Foreign Ministry spokesman evaded questions, and almost never volunteered information. 'His manner plainly indicated that the conference was painful to him and that he was anxious to be finished with it'.[51]

The official obsession with secrecy prevented the Foreign Ministry from illuminating the dark recesses of government policy-making, but individual bureaucrats did make efforts to win the goodwill of foreign journalists. Kase Toshikazu, a junior member of the Foreign Ministry's information department, was instructed to cultivate the German correspondents, including Sorge. 'He came at least once a week to the press conference held at the Foreign Ministry. I often saw him sitting there with the other members of the foreign press,' Kase recalls.

Professionally, Sorge made little impression on the young diplomat, who had acquired good conversational German in his three-year stint at the Japanese Embassy in Berlin. 'He didn't show any special cleverness. I just took it for granted that he was rather commonplace – not an outstanding journalist. But a very nice man. That is usually the way with spies anywhere.'

Sorge, no doubt keen to broaden his range of official contacts, responded to Kase's overtures, and the two men established a friendly rapport. One day in 1936, he invited Kase to his house in Nagasaka-cho. 'He liked Bach, and put some records on while I was there. I remember we listened to the Brandenburg Concerto. He knew that I loved music. Everybody did who stayed in Germany at that time, towards the end of the Weimar Republic. Germany was considered as the world capital of music.' There was a young woman at the house, but Sorge did not introduce her, and he never learnt her name. This may have been Hanako, who took up residence in Sorge's house in the summer of 1936.[52]

§ In February 1938 Sorge was looking forward to returning to Russia sometime in the summer. He wrote to Katya:

> I could not keep my promise to return home last autumn. I don't know if you have lost patience already, while you wait for me ... I think, my love, that I can soon come home. I ask you if possible to wait to take your summer holiday until my arrival. Then we will both go together ... Until then goodbye my love (*Auf Wiedersehen meine Liebe*) Your Ika.[53]

Time and time again he had raised false hopes in Katya, only to disappoint her, but this letter has the ring of confident expectation. However, everything depended on the whim of his superiors. On 26 April 1938 we find him appealing to the director to be recalled: 'You are already familiar with the reasons for my persistent wish to return home. You know I am now into the fifth year of working here, and you also know how hard it is.' There is a peevish tone to this message that jars with the conventional image of the brave and dedicated spy. Though Sorge was both, his communications with the Centre reveal that he did not always grit his teeth and bear hardships with the fortitude expected of an elite Red Army officer.

The timing of this appeal is interesting. Sorge had refused orders to return to Moscow the previous year, and in November 1937 asked Aino to relay to the Director that 'I can't leave before next April.' We can only conjecture why Sorge preferred to remain in Japan until April. Did he have some reason to believe that the danger of liquidation would have passed by then?

Stalin's purges were still continuing, bloodily, in the spring of 1938, although the worst was over. (His friend from Comintern days, Niilo Virtanen – to whom he had confided his doubts in the summer of 1935 – was executed by a firing squad that year.) Sorge was suspect on two counts. First, he was a protégé of Jan Berzin, the purged director of the Fourth Department, and thus a Trotskyite by association. Second, he was a foreigner, and presumed to be a double agent, probably in the pay of the Germans. This he must have known, just as he must have known he would pay a heavy price for these two 'crimes' if he returned.

That he should have begged repeatedly to be recalled appears surprising. But was it not the same peculiar Russian craving for home that led so many of Stalin's agents to their doom?

§ In February, the position of German ambassador to Tokyo fell vacant with the departure of Dirksen, who was suffering from severe asthma attacks. A few weeks later the military attaché, Eugen Ott, who had been promoted to the rank of major-general the previous autumn, informed Sorge that Berlin had offered him the ambassadorship. 'Nobody knows about this yet, apart from Helma,' Ott said. 'I wanted to hear your opinion. Should I accept the position?'

We can only surmise what went through Sorge's mind. As ambassador, Ott would have a direct line to the power-holders of the Third Reich. There was a risk that Ott might be more aloof and circumspect as ambassador than he was as senior military attaché, and would restrict Sorge's access to confidential material. But possibly Sorge calculated that Ott's promotion would greatly enhance his own worth in the eyes of his superiors – and that they would dismiss out of hand his entreaties to return home in the near future.

'Don't take it,' Sorge advised. 'You'll lose your integrity if you do. As Hitler's ambassador, you'll be carrying out instructions completely at odds with your own deeply held convictions.' Sorge told a friend later that he had urged the military attaché not to take the position out of a sincere concern for Ott: a decent human being could not represent an immoral regime without himself becoming morally corrupted. How selfless the advice was is hard to gauge.[54]

However, Ott could not resist the power and the glory of the post of Hitler's plenipotentiary in Japan. On 28 April Ott was driven in a horse-drawn carriage to the Imperial Palace to present his credentials. The cherry blossoms around the moat blazed in bright sunshine as Ott, accompanied by his wife Helma, crossed the Hanzomon bridge into the palace grounds for the audience with Emperor Hirohito.

§ It was around this time that a rendezvous with a Soviet agent in Hong Kong had been arranged, to transfer a quantity of Sorge's microfilms, reports and letters and take receipt of funds for the Tokyo ring. Sorge told Ott that he planned to visit the British colony for his newspaper, and Ott asked him to act as courier for the German Embassy – compelling evidence of his total confidence in the journalist. A temporary diplomatic pass was issued which exempted him from customs and police examinations, and Sorge became, as he expressed it, a 'double courier to Manila and Hong Kong, carrying documents from both sides'.

Soon after his return, Sorge went on one of his drinking sprees. Returning home by motorbike in the early hours of 13 May his luck ran out. He was found battered and bleeding on the road beside the American Embassy, and rushed to St Luke's Hospital. This near-fatal accident had a number of significant repercussions.

When the bandages were peeled off and a series of cosmetic operations completed, Sorge's face was transformed. The furrows on the forehead ran deeper than before, the full lips were thinner, and the lines from his nose to the corners of his mouth much sharper. His mouth became infected and more teeth had to come out; false teeth were fitted, top and bottom, causing immense discomfort. For some time to come, whenever he tried to smile, he could only grimace. The contours of his face struck a woman who met him exactly three years after the accident as 'somewhat like a mask, demoniacal'.[55]

Hanako recalls the shock she experienced when she saw him in hospital the day after the crash: 'The impact had smashed his face against the handlebars of the motorbike. I thought his whole face was ruined for good. And worse, I was afraid it must have done something to his brain, and that he would be permanently brain-damaged.'[56]

Sorge suffered severe concussion, but X-rays showed no evidence of brain damage. The German ambassador, however, was convinced that the collision had affected Sorge's mental stability. Nearly four years on he reported to Berlin: 'He has been subject to nervous disorders, the after-effects of a skull fracture in a motor-cycle accident in 1938.'[57]

For some friends, the episode was a watershed in Sorge's life. They talked of the man they had known 'before the accident' and 'after the accident', as if the event had affected not only his appearance, but something more fundamental as well.[58]

Still prone to dizzy spells, Sorge left St Luke's Hospital and spent a short while recuperating at the ambassador's residence. Eugen Ott had left for Berlin for consultations with his superiors, and an audience with Hitler. Helma Ott was due to join him in Germany; she had a passage booked for 2 June.

For a few days, she lavished attention on the man she loved. Helma's affair with Sorge was now over, but she seized this chance to smother him with care and affection. Naturally, tittle-tattle in the German community was frenzied. If Helma hoped to regain Sorge's love by changing bandages and preparing soups while his gums healed she was to be disappointed. There is no hint of gratitude in his recollection of this episode to a friend: 'Yes, taking in someone helpless and forcing unwanted intimacy on them – she's good at that! Any hospital would have taken care of me as well. Just as soon as I could more or less move, I was off, out of the trap!'[59]

The accident was the final blow to Sorge's hopes of returning to Moscow. On 7 October 1938, he wrote a poignant letter to his beloved Katya.

> When I last wrote at the start of this year, I was so convinced we would spend the summer holiday together that I even made plans where the best place would be.
>   But I'm still here. I have misled you so often with my dates that I wouldn't be surprised if you've given up this eternal waiting ... I had an accident, which put me in hospital for several months. But now everything's alright again and I'm working as before.
>   I've certainly not become more beautiful. I've got some new scratches, and a lot less teeth. But I'll have false ones fitted. All that from a motorbike crash. So when I get back, you won't find me very beautiful. I look like a battered robber-knight now. In addition to the five wounds from the war I've got a lot of broken bones and scars.[60]

§ On 13 June 1938, General G. S. Lyushkov, an officer commanding NKVD forces in the Far East, fled across the border into Manchuria and sought the protection of the Japanese army. The defection alarmed the Russians and delighted the Japanese, who reaped an intelligence and propaganda windfall. Lyushkov was brought to General Staff Headquarters in Tokyo for interrogation and poured out information about Soviet military dispositions in the Far East, and about the seething discontent in the Red Army provoked by Stalin's draconian purge of senior officers. The general said he had decided to escape because he believed his own life was in danger.

Sorge was still recuperating from his accident and at first attached little weight to the defection, which Japanese newspapers trumpeted in triumphant headlines when the army released the news. But his superiors in Moscow took a grave view of the event. They learnt that Admiral Wilhelm Canaris, chief of Germany's Secret Military Intelligence Service (*Abwehr*) had dispatched a counter-intelligence colonel to debrief Lyushkov, and wanted to know what secrets he had betrayed.

On 5 September 1938, Clausen received and decoded the following radio message from the Centre.

> Ramsay. Make maximum effort to obtain copy of report which Canaris' courier received from Green Box [Japanese army] or result of his direct interview with Lyushkov. Cable all you know about it at once. Far East.[61]

Even for a skilful and resourceful operator like Sorge, this was a tough request, according to Clausen. 'It gave him a headache,' Max later told police.[62]

Major Erwin Scholl, the assistant military attaché, proved his unwitting saviour. Scholl was convinced of Sorge's reliability, and was quite ready to pass on what he knew about Lyushkov's debriefing by the German counter-intelligence officer. Sorge relayed this information to Moscow, adding his opinion that there was 'a danger of Japanese–German military action to exploit the weaknesses in the Red Army exposed in Lyushkov's report'.[63]

The report ordered by Canaris ran into several hundred pages. Scholl allowed Sorge to read the embassy's copy, and with great ingenuity he managed to photograph half of it. This was duly sent to Moscow on microfilm in January 1939. As a result, the Russians discovered how Japan and Germany viewed their military capabilities in the Far East and the condition of morale in the ranks. More important, the Red Army was able to make good deficiences in its defences, weed out dissenters and assess where the Japanese army was most likely to strike.

Sorge's 'coverage' of the Lyushkov defection was to prove invaluable when Soviet forces clashed with Japanese intruders at Nomonhan, a township on the border between Manchukuo and Mongolia, in May 1939. A localized, ferocious war (known as the 'Nomonhan Incident' in Japan) raged throughout the summer, and ended in a decisive victory for the Russians.

Thanks to Sorge's reports on the Lyushkov defection, Soviet commanders were privy to the Japanese army's estimate of Soviet military capabilities. This put the Russians at a great advantage in fighting the war at Nomonhan, according to a prosecutor who investigated the Sorge case. 'I believe this to be one of the most important tasks that Sorge accomplished for Moscow during his eight years in Japan,' Yoshikawa Mitsusada declared many years later.[64]

§ The agent 'Ramsay' persevered with his duties, but his masters in the Fourth Department must have shaken their heads at his lack of stoicism. We can easily imagine their reaction to his repeated requests to be recalled: he had disobeyed an order to return home in autumn 1937, and now he was forever grumbling about the hardships of his mission, as if he expected the life of a Red Army Intelligence officer to be a bed of roses!

A letter addressed to 'Dear Director', dated June 1939 and carried to Russia by courier, is shot through with discontent and pessimism. Sorge bemoans the fact that, owing to the weight of ambassadorial duties, Ott has become less accessible than before: 'Ott has at last become a figure of importance. As a result, he has much less time to go around with me and discuss things one to one. So the future looks dark to me.'[65] He laments that his best contacts in the embassy have left Japan – presumably a reference to the transfer of Major Scholl, the assistant military attaché, and Captain Wenneker, the naval attaché.[66]

And there is a further problem – it is becoming much harder to move about freely, now that the Japanese authorities have imposed tighter controls on foreigners. 'I have the impression that the best time for our activities here is completely finished, or at least will be soon.'

On a brighter note, he reports that the Tokyo ring is functioning properly. Clausen is doing a good job as wireless man, and liaison with Moscow is going smoothly. Then he comes to the point of the letter: he has had enough of Japan, and wishes to be replaced:

> However, I would like to repeat my earlier request. I'd like you to send new people. At the very least a co-worker who could replace me ...
>
> 'I've already lived here six years, nine years in the Far East. I was only able to be home very briefly. A year ago I endured a very bitter misfortune. Nine years really seems too much to endure.
>
> Please pass on my best wishes to Katya. Its unbearable for her to have to wait so long for my home-coming.
>
> Dear Director, please take personal responsibility for doing something about this matter.
>
> We continue to be your old, loyal and obedient workers. We send heartfelt greetings to all of you over there. Ramsay.

The director filed this away with Sorge's earlier messages on the same theme. No action was taken. The Fourth Department may have been dissatisfied with Sorge, but it was evidently short of agents qualified to fill his place.

§ There is no doubt that the recall of Scholl and Wenneker, two of Sorge's best sources, left a large gap. He had built up a close personal rapport with both, and they dispensed confidential information freely. However, it is hard to escape the impression that Sorge was exaggerating the effects of personnel changes in the German Embassy in order to justify his withdrawal from Japan.

The fact was that no replacement sent by Moscow could duplicate the position Sorge had attained in the embassy. He enjoyed the trust of Colonel Gerhard Matzky, the senior military attaché (who had taken over from Ott) and before long he was on excellent terms with the new naval attaché, Captain Joachim Lietzmann, who brought with him a letter of introduction from Wenneker.

Lieutenant-Colonel Nehmitz, the assistant air attaché, also welcomed Sorge's visits to his office, and this access was maintained when Lieutenant-Colonel Hans Wolfgang von Gronau arrived in early 1939 to assume the post of senior air attaché.

Moreover, the available evidence shows that Sorge's relationship with Ott was unaffected by his elevation to ambassador. General Ott continued his practice of showing him drafts of cables and reports and seeking his opinion before transmitting them to Berlin, and the other staff took their cue from the ambassador. To use Sorge's own words, 'They would come and say: "We have found out such and such a thing, have you heard about it, and what do you think?"'[67]

Sorge's request to be withdrawn from Japan was ill-timed. Border clashes that had all the makings of a major conflict had erupted in the desolate region between Mongolia and Manchuria in May. Japan's Kwantung Army was poised to seize control of Mongolia, threatening Russia's vital interests. The Soviet leadership desperately wanted to know if the clash at Nomonhan was the start of the long-anticipated Japanese attack on Siberia. Urgent instructions were radioed to the Tokyo ring to report whether troop reinforcements were on their way from Japan, foreshadowing a full-scale war.

Sorge mobilized his team of agents to investigate what the Japanese, with their usual understatement, termed the 'Nomonhan Incident': 'I ordered each [member] to devote himself to discovering Japanese plans for reinforcing its army along the border with Mongolia, and to collecting the materials which would allow me to judge how far this clash would escalate.'[68] According to Ozaki's assessment, the Japanese government would try to localize the conflict, and had no intention of risking an all-out war with Russia.

Vukelic visited the battle area with a party of other journalists invited by the Japanese army, and his observations proved useful. But it was Miyagi and a new recruit, Odai Yoshinobu, who provided critical information on the organization and equipment of army divisions, and the shipment of tanks, artillery and aircraft to the war zone.

Corporal Odai was Miyagi's 'find'. In three years of military service, he had been posted to Manchuria, and was in northern China after the start of the 'China Incident' in July 1937. His spell of active duty had given him first-hand experience of army conditions, morale and weaponry, and he had a good understanding of the composition of the army and troop dispositions.

Miyagi had come to know Odai when the younger man was a student at Tokyo's Meiji University. The connection was a mutual acquaintance, Kiyotake Yasumasu, an Okinawan like Miyagi, who happened to live next door to Odai. Kiyotake's left-wing ideas had made an impact on the student, and Miyagi knew where Odai's sympathies lay when he made the first approach in the early days of the 'Nomonhan Incident'.

In their discussion, Miyagi expressed the view that, as always, the farmers and workers in both countries would suffer most if war broke out between Russia and Japan. It was to avert such a tragedy that he, Miyagi, was sending various data to the Comintern. Was Odai willing to provide information about the Japanese army which would help the cause of peace? This tack proved effective. Odai replied that he had little access to secret matters and did not want money, but he agreed to co-operate without further persuasion. In the end he did accept a monthly retainer of fifty yen, a generous amount for an underpaid Japanese soldier.

Corporal Odai was the answer to Sorge's prayers. His Moscow controllers had pressed him repeatedly to improve the network's intelligence capabilities in the military field. In February 1939, the director ordered: 'It is essential that we bring in two or three Japanese army officers. Look into this as a matter of priority.' Two months later, on 13 April, the Fourth Department radioed impatiently that it was still waiting for an answer: was it possible or not to recruit Japanese army officers?

It was, Sorge believed, next to impossible. Penetration of the higher levels of the Imperial Japanese Army was out of the question, and even junior officers would be hard to ensnare. The army was a bastion of ultranationalists, conditioned to see Russia as their principal enemy, and itching to march into Siberia and the Maritime Provinces and teach the Bolsheviks a lesson they would not forget. 'This is not going to be easy,' Sorge told Clausen. He did not easily admit defeat, but he appeared to be at a loss on this occasion.[69]

No senior officers were recruited by the ring.[70] But Miyagi arranged for Sorge to size up his acquaintance Corporal Odai, and they met – once or twice, Sorge recalled – in a restaurant in Tokyo. In this way, Moscow Centre secured the services of an idealistic young man prepared to betray his country in pursuit of his utopian vision of social justice and world peace. Henceforth Odai was code-named 'Miki' in communications with Moscow. Despite his junior rank, he was to prove one of the network's most valuable assets.

Odai provided military secrets on a systematic basis, beginning in

June 1939.[71] Miyagi was also extremely active in gathering information on Japanese troop strength and equipment. Using these data, Sorge was able to relay intelligence estimates to the Red Army that doubtless served General Georgi Zhukov well when he launched a massive counter-attack on Japanese positions.

The Russians crushed their adversaries swiftly and decisively, and the war was over on 15 September. The Kwantung Army was humiliated, and every effort was made to keep the débâcle secret from the Japanese public. Remains of the thousands of Japanese killed in battle were brought home in small batches to hide the extent of the defeat.

The outcome of the war was a painful lesson for the Kwantung Army. The *bushido* (way of the warrior) spirit clearly could not overcome an enemy with superior firepower, mechanization and aviation. For decades Japan's military leaders had considered Russia to be Japan's only real hypothetical enemy. But the débâcle at Nomonhan shattered the confidence of the Japanese army, and sapped its will to risk a large-scale conflict with the Soviet Union.

While the hot-heads in the military licked their wounds, the Japanese threat to the Soviet Union retreated. Sorge summed up the favourable new situation in a long dispatch dated 24 January 1940.

> Difficulties with the economy, the fact that the war in China is dragging on, the defeat at Nomonhan, and finally German–Soviet co-operation – all these factors have shaken the position of the army within the leadership of Japan, and in the eyes of the Japanese people.
>
> The army has lost its prestige not only in domestic and foreign policy, but even in military affairs. Currently, the leadership is in the process of shifting to court circles and a group of big capitalists.
>
> The recent trend is for political parties and the navy to become more active, in the hope of gaining the upper hand.[72]

The curmudgeonly tone of certain messages from the Fourth Department to Sorge is striking. His superiors carped and cavilled, and rebuked him for failing to understand their needs. In prison, Sorge proudly told interrogators about the messages of congratulation he received for his work from Soviet leaders, and implied that his work was much admired. But the available evidence tells a different story: that his relationship with Moscow soured after his return to Tokyo in September 1935, and was beset by friction right up to the end.

A telegram dated 1 September 1939 – the day war broke out in Europe – gives an idea of what Sorge had to endure. The director is clearly in a foul temper.

I have to advise that your information on current military and political situation has deteriorated during the summer. Green [Japan] has begun important moves lately to prepare for war against Red [USSR] but we are not getting the valuable information which you must be fully aware of through Anna [Ott] ...

I stress you should do more to obtain this information and radio it as a matter of priority. You are greatly experienced and have a strong position with Anna, and what I ask and expect of you is information on crucial military and political matters. But you are evading this, and sending less important information.

The message goes on to tell Sorge to make better use of 'Joe' (Miyagi), 'Miki' (Odai) and 'Otto' (Ozaki) and suggests he pay them for each task they carry out for the ring.

Consider my advice and the importance of your work, and think of the deep trust that your mother country has for you. I expect to see an improvement in your work. Radio a reply when you receive this message.[73]

We can readily imagine Sorge's intense frustration at receiving this reproof – and it was not an isolated instance. His was a lonely, perilous existence in a hostile land, dedicated to protecting the Soviet Union from its enemies, and the reward was a succession of complaints from desk-men safely ensconced in Moscow. Did this treatment feed his disillusionment, traces of which we have already discerned? How could it have been otherwise?

It was Clausen who revealed to Japanese interrogators that his chief was not held in quite the high esteem that Sorge sought to depict after his arrest. Until 1938, when he learnt the code, he could not read the communications, but afterwards he discovered how frequently the Centre complained about unsatisfactory results. The radio operator was at pains to stress that at this stage he was faithfully transmitting Sorge's dispatches in full – so he bore no blame for any shortcomings in the performance of the Tokyo ring. The message of 1 September 1939 was one of many stern admonitions, Clausen said – not without a certain Schadenfreude, we may suspect. 'From then on he regularly got telegrams with scoldings and exhortations,' Clausen told his captors.[74]

§ The Fourth Department treated with incredulity Sorge's assessment that the defeat of the Kwantung Army at Nomonhan had eliminated the Japanese threat. Suspicions persisted that it was only a matter of time before Japanese militarists made another stab against the Soviet Far East, and Sorge was ordered not to relax his guard. Moreover, the Tokyo ring came under pressure to furnish more routine intelligence on

Japan's military capabilities and troop dispositions and data on Japan's war industry.

A radio message from the Centre on 19 February 1940 contained this directive:

> Exert utmost effort to obtain accurate diagrams of army and navy arsenals and civilian arms production capability in artillery, tanks, aircraft, automobiles, machine guns and so on.

A similar request was radioed from Moscow on 2 May:

> Send data on aircraft production facilities and heavy artillery factories. Precise figures on 1939 output. Report what steps being taken to increase production.

One lesson the Japanese had learnt at Nomonhan was the urgent need to expand and upgrade their war industry, and Sorge was well aware that harnessing industry to serve the requirements of the armed forces had become a national priority. But it was no simple matter finding out how many tanks and planes were being built – even bicycle production figures were a state secret. As usual, his masters failed to appreciate the immense obstacles that confronted an intelligence agent working in Japan.

Sorge considered how best to tackle the assignment. He first turned to Miyagi, and the ever-willing Okinawan devoted a good deal of time and effort to obtaining details of tank production at the factories of Hitachi and Nihon Diesel. A year or two ago, Sorge could have tapped the German businessmen and engineers he had cultivated; they had proved useful sources of information on Japan's steel, chemical and aviation sectors in the past. But the intensifying Japanese phobia about spies made them nervous, and he decided it was a waste of time approaching them. Besides, Sorge knew very well where most of the answers he wanted could be found. The embassy had extensive files on the war potential of Japanese industry: all he needed to gain access to this treasure trove was a plausible excuse.

While Sorge was pondering the problem, German officialdom provided the solution. On a summer's day in 1940, Colonel Gerhard Matzky, the military attaché, invited Sorge to his office, housed in a small building at the rear of the ambassador's residence. The two men got on well, although Matzky was a fervent Hitlerite. The colonel respected Sorge's abilities, and knew that he had found favour in high army circles in Berlin. The year before, Sorge had produced a 'Study of the Japanese Economy under Conditions of War in China' for

General Georg Thomas, chief of the German army's Economic Department. This had been so well received that General Thomas was now urging Sorge to provide a follow-up report on Japan's wartime manufacturing industries.

Sorge listened intently as Matzky conveyed the request from Berlin. It was a very delicate matter, he explained. The embassy did not wish word to leak out to the Japanese. The commission had been given to Sorge because he had an independent mind, and was totally reliable. 'General Thomas is anxious to know how the conversion of Japanese industry to meet wartime needs is proceeding,' Matzky said. 'He would like a full investigation of aircraft, automobile, tank, aluminium, synthetic petrol, iron and steel sectors – output production levels, production standards, that kind of thing.'

Since the start of hostilities with Britain in September 1939, Germany had hoped to coax Prime Minister Konoye's government into joining the war: 'have-nots' – Germany and Japan – against Britain, the arch-imperialist power. Germany's military strategists were therefore anxious to assess Japan's staying power in a conflict against a more formidable adversary than China. Its ability to fight a long-drawn-out war – and its usefulness as a war ally of Germany – depended on the potential of Japanese industry to supply the necessary war materials to its fighting forces. Sorge was delighted to be of assistance. Berlin's request dovetailed neatly with his clandestine assignment for Moscow; by providing his services to the Germans, he was able serve his Soviet masters all the more efficiently.

Matzky authorized Sorge to use whatever embassy documents he required, as he had done when Sorge was compiling his earlier economic report for Berlin. Conveniently, much of the leg-work was already done. Lieutenant-Colonel Nehmitz, the assistant air attaché, had paid discreet visits to the aircraft and precision instrument plants of Mitsubishi, Kawasaki, Nakajima and Aiichi Tokei Denki, and he gave Sorge the results of his research.

From the latter's own account, it is evident that he was not impressed with the material supplied by Nehmitz and Matzky. However, there was enough to piece together a picture of Japan's fast-expanding aircraft output. Then he turned his attention to Nissan and Toyota, which produced not only cars, but also trucks and personnel carriers – and gave low marks to their performance. As for the tank factory in Niigata, he stressed that its production was in a sorry state.

For material on Japan's aluminium and synthetic petroleum, Sorge had only to stroll across the garden to Dr Alois Tichy's economic section. In the files here, he found details of the German-supplied patents for the manufacture of synthetic gasoline from coal. Japan's navy and army were desperate to find alternative oil supplies and reduce their dependence on the oil-wells of the United States, and were conducting experiments using German technology. Dr Tichy also provided hard-to-obtain statistics on Japan's iron and steel manufacture. Sorge took notes, and actually recalled the figures during interrogation eighteen months later: iron production stood at an annual figure of 6 million tons, with eighteen months' to two years' inventory, while steel manufacture, boosted by modern German methods, reached 2 to 3 million tons annually.[75]

Colonel Matzky kept the designations and statistics of cars, aircraft and tanks in a notebook, and thought that Sorge would also need these for his study. 'Jot these down, will you?' he said. So Sorge took out his notebook – one with a grey cover – and put down the data Matzky was so keen to give him. 'Of course, all these statistics were secret,' Sorge observed to his interrogators.[76] Meticulously, and at a measured pace, he collected every scrap of information that might be of interest to Moscow. As he explained: 'All the material used for these two reports commissioned by Thomas, through Matzky, was of extreme importance, so I photographed all the documents I used in the embassy, unobserved, and sent them in stages to Moscow Centre.'[77]

Sorge gathered all the necessary files and took them to his office, in the press section on the second floor of the old Chancery building. Here it was possible to photograph the documents, with the Robot camera that fitted unobtrusively into the spacious pockets in his jacket. But the utmost caution was required. Count von Mirbach, the press section head, Richard Breuer, who dealt with information and propaganda, and Reinhold Schulze, the cultural attaché, were in adjoining rooms. Next door was the teletype machine, bringing in news from Berlin, and there was a constant to-and-fro along the corridor. There was a risk that someone might enter the office at any moment, and find him photographing the papers.

Photography became 'really dangerous work', in Sorge's words, as the embassy staff steadily increased in size in 1940. Privacy became ever more fragile. Fortunately, he was able to take some documents out of the embassy, and then he would use either the little Robot or the larger Leica camera at home.

Clausen remembered that on a visit to Sorge's house, he found his chief engrossed in copies of German Embassy files dealing with aircraft and tanks. This must have been early in 1941 – evidently Sorge took his time over this assignment. 'I believe he summed up the contents in English, and then gave me a draft message to radio. I transmitted it some time in the spring of 1941,' he told police.[78] But the quantity of material was so great that most of it had to be sent to Moscow by courier. Clausen said he handed over the microfilms to 'Serge' from the Soviet Embassy some time in early 1941.

Sorge's security precautions left much to be desired. His grey notebook containing Matzky's sensitive data, which ought not to have been in a journalist's possession, was simply left lying in his study; it was among the damning evidence police picked up when they searched the house after his arrest.[79]

§ From early 1939 Sorge's interest had focused on the course of negotiations between Japan and Germany directed towards concluding an alliance. Hitler, who was plotting war against Britain and France, hoped for a military alliance that would commit Japan to strike against British possessions in the Far East. But Japan, bogged down in the China war, would not be drawn, and the talks made little progress.

Annoyed by Tokyo's timidity, Germany negotiated a non-aggression pact with Russia in August 1939. The Japanese, engaged in a ferocious conflict with the Russians at Nomonhan, were appalled by Hitler's action. The pact smacked of an act of treachery, and made nonsense of the anti-Comintern pact they had concluded with Germany in 1936.

Germany and Japan drifted apart, and swastika flags disappeared from streets and shop-windows in Tokyo. However, by the summer of 1940, Nazi victories in Europe had fired the imagination of Japan's political and military leaders. They scented attractive opportunities for expansion on the cheap. Germany's conquest of France and Holland left Indochina and the Dutch East Indies as helpless 'orphans'. Japan, ogling their minerals and oil resources, was keenly interested in adopting them. Britain too was preoccupied by the threat of a German invasion, and appeared to be doomed: its colonies in the Far East, especially Hong Kong and Singapore, were both vulnerable and tempting.

An alliance with the victorious Germans now seemed to make good sense. Promoting ties with the Berlin–Rome Axis became the top priority of Prime Minister Konoye's second cabinet, formed in July 1940 with the inclusion of Foreign Minister Matsuoka Yosuke and War Minister Tojo Hideki, both strongly pro-German. The time for wavering between friendship with Germany and the Western democracies was over.[80]

In early September Foreign Minister Ribbentrop sent a special envoy, Heinrich Stahmer, to conduct discussions on a draft worked out in preliminary sessions in Berlin. The talks, held in Foreign Minister Matsuoka's private residence to preserve secrecy, lasted three weeks.

Sorge kept in close touch with Stahmer throughout the negotiations. From his vantage point in the embassy he had followed each stage of the *rapprochement* since Germany initiated the first tentative discussions at the end of 1938. During a visit to Tokyo in the spring of 1938, Stahmer had been impressed by Sorge's grasp of political issues, and he had mentioned to Ambassador Ott that his adviser was 'a splendid fellow with a first-rate mind'.

As the Stahmer–Matsuoka talks proceeded, Sorge was given access to the cables that the special envoy was sending on a daily basis to Ribbentrop in Berlin. As a result, Moscow learned the main thrust of the negotiations long before the public announcement of the Three Powers Pact. The most important point, which Sorge relayed at an early stage, was that: 'From the start, the Soviet Union was excluded from the scope of this alliance, which was mainly targeted at Britain and would only become operative against the US if the US joined in the war against Germany.'[81]

A hitch developed half-way through the discussions. The Japanese side – Prime Minister Konoye, in particular – fretted about Japan's obligations in the event that Germany and the United States went to war.

> While the German side favoured a narrower interpretation, the Japanese side preferred to keep the conditions ambiguous. Finally, both sides agreed that the treaty would become operative in case of an attack. And that it was up to each of the allies to decide to which attacking country it applied.[82]

Thanks to this loop-hole – which would prove of crucial importance – the talks could be wound up with lightning speed. On 27 September 1940, the world was taken by surprise by the announcement of the so-called Three Powers Pact. Tokyo had joined the Rome–Berlin Axis.

As described by Japanese leaders, the purpose of the new alliance was to restore justice to an unjust world, and to assure the three 'have-nots' of a fairer share of the cake monopolized by the 'haves' (America and Britain). Foreign Minister Matsuoka Yosuke summed up the shared goals at the Imperial Conference which sanctified the pact on 26 September: 'Germany wants to prevent American entry into the war, and Japan wants to avoid a war with the United States.'

The parties to the accord agreed to work together for a 'new order' in the world, a euphemism for replacing Anglo-Saxon supremacy with

Axis domination by all means including force of arms. Germany and Italy agreed that the Japanese sphere for creating the 'new order' was 'Greater East Asia'. Japan recognized its two partners as the leaders of the 'new order' in Europe.

The Three Powers Pact was a sinister document recognizing the three new master-races, with a curious preamble stipulating that 'all nations of the world be given each its proper place'. In Greater East Asia – which Matsuoka defined as stretching from Burma in the west to New Caledonia in the south – Japan considered its proper place to be that of elder brother and guardian to the more backward races.

But the principal significance of the alliance lay in emboldening the Japanese to pursue their goal of ruling East Asia. With new confidence they embarked on plans to break the Anglo-Saxon hold on Asia, secure in the belief that, if America attacked, Germany and Italy would make their moves against America.

The Three Powers Pact caught American officials off balance. They were more or less resigned to seeing Japan throw in its lot with the victorious Nazis sooner or later, but the swiftness with which the alliance was realized came as a surprise. The wall of secrecy guarding the negotiations had proved virtually leak-proof. Japanese newspaper editors were under strict instructions not even to mention Stahmer's presence in Japan, much less speculate on the purpose of his mission. 'We were all groping more or less in the dark,' wrote the American ambassador later.

For the past week or two foreign correspondents, too, had been chasing around in circles trying vainly to confirm rumours that Japan was about to form an alliance with Germany and Italy. 'Even some of the American press men thought up to five o'clock on the afternoon of the signature that the pact was to be signed in Tokyo, not Berlin, and some of my colleagues pooh-poohed the possibility of such an alliance up to the very day of its conclusion,' Grew recorded.[83]

It was late in the afternoon when foreign correspondents were informed that the Foreign Ministry was holding an emergency press conference at ten o'clock. They guessed that it concerned the rumoured alliance between Germany and Japan, but no one really had any idea.

Wilfred Fleisher, editor of the *Japan Advertiser*, found the Foreign Ministry compound in a state of turmoil: cars and motorcycles everywhere, Japanese newspapermen darting from one side to another, camera flashlights exploding constantly. Straightaway, ministry press officers put the Axis journalists in a separate room from the Anglo-Saxon press corps (or what was left of it by the autumn of 1940 – Fleisher counted a mere half-dozen colleagues that night. Many had packed their bags, and one popular figure had died in mysterious circumstances. Jimmy Cox, the Reuters correspondent, had 'thrown himself' from a window in *Kempei* headquarters on 29 July while being interrogated on charges of espionage.)

The larger German contingent, with Italian colleagues, were celebrating in the offices of Japanese officials to the loud clinking of beer bottles and hoarse shouts. A well-kept secret was out. 'The Japanese radio was already blaring out its announcement to the unsuspecting Japanese public, which had had no inkling of the momentous decision to which they were being committed.'[84]

At ten-thirty the two groups of journalists were summoned to the conference room. The cheeks of the German correspondents glowed from the beer. In this group was Richard Sorge. He was one of the tiny handful of people in Tokyo who knew what was going on, but of course he could not write about the negotiations for his newspaper. Moscow had been kept informed of every twist and turn, however. Tonight he had to behave as if he had been as much in the dark about the momentous events as his press colleagues.

It was, the American correspondent Relman Morin records, a 'hot night when the air was charged with electricity'. Ceiling fans whirred in the Foreign Ministry room where the announcement was made. 'With no preliminaries the spokesman said Japan had signed a treaty of mutual assistance with Germany and Italy.'[85]

Outside the *Asahi* premises in Sukiyabashi, the newfangled electric screen was flashing the news of 'the moving event (*kangeki*) of the century'. Passers-by paused to look up. A few streets away, in the Rheingold, boisterous German customers saluted Hitler and the Tenno with raised jugs of beer and threw sweaty hands around the shoulders of Japanese in a display of fraternity.

The newspapers reported next day that one enterprising beer-hall patron hoisted the three powers' flags, and a banner of congratulation, within minutes of the radio announcement. 'The great rejoicing over the successful conclusion of the Pact in all quarters was unmistakeable,' the German naval attaché recorded in his war diary.[86]

A glittering reception was held at the foreign minister's official residence to celebrate the signing, which had taken place in Berlin. Cabinet ministers, military leaders and German and Italian diplomats toasted the pact, Chancellor Hitler and Emperor Hirohito in succession. But one man was conspicuously absent. Prime Minister Konoye was anxious about how the United States would react to the alliance. That night he was indisposed, and had to miss the celebrations. As on a number of occasions, he took to his bed in a bad state of nerves.

The following day, Saturday, Ambassador Ott hosted a reception at the embassy, inviting Japanese and German journalists. It was a glorious sunny morning, and Stahmer, looking pleased with himself, strolled in the garden with some of the press people. With a satisfied chuckle he remarked that not a word had leaked out about 'his' treaty in advance.

Sorge, who attended the press function, also had cause to congratulate himself. A German diplomat who was present that day noted many years later: 'Dr Sorge certainly smiled inwardly, if he did not laugh out loud.'[87]

The *Asahi* that Saturday devoted most of its front page to the historic event. 'Japan, Germany, Italy, Three Powers' Alliance Achieved. Signing completed in Berlin' was splashed as the main headline. Lower down, a sub-heading declared: 'Very Significant for Relationship with the Soviet Union' over a few paragraphs reminding readers that Germany and Russia had concluded a non-aggression pact a year earlier. Without doubt, the Three Powers Pact would have a positive effect on Tokyo's relations with Moscow, the newspaper commented.

§ Japan held many attractions for Sorge. He was fascinated by its temples, Buddhist art and rice culture. The grace and delicacy of Japanese women were a constant source of delight. Sorties into the countryside were motivated by personal rather than professional curiosity. In his own words, 'My travels in Japan were made not for espionage purposes but to obtain a better knowledge of the country and its people.'[88]

In 1939 Sorge accompanied the writer Friedrich Sieburg on a long journey to Nara, Kyoto and the Ise Shrine at Yamada. With Ambassador Ott he visited the Kawana Hotel, near Ito, the tiny fishing port of Shizuura, on the west coast of the Izu Peninsula, Hakone and the Otts' summer residences in Akiya and Karuizawa. When he had time, he made brief trips to rural areas close to Tokyo. 'On Sundays I used to hike everywhere from Tokyo to the area west of Atami,' he wrote in prison.

He took great pleasure in the rituals of Japanese inns, savouring the coolness and aroma of *tatami*, the comfort of a *yukata* (light cotton kimono) after a long soak in an outdoor bath, the pampering by maids who giggled behind their hands at the strange guest's clumsy ways.

But the foreigner was always a lonely figure, and Sorge, like many other visitors to these islands, was afflicted by the depressing isolation.

Foreigners were like moths, drawn to a brightly lit room, eager to be accepted, but forced to flit outside the window, forever excluded. Sorge, who could not communicate with local people – except in the baby-talk he used with Hanako – would have felt cut off from life itself. The tiny German community did not provide the intellectual and cultural nourishment he craved, or satisfying companionship: he complained repeatedly that he had 'no friends'.[89]

During his seven years in Japan we sense that Sorge keenly felt himself to be the sad wanderer of the poem written in his student days – 'eternally a stranger who condemns himself never to know real peace'. By the autumn of 1940, his desire to leave Japan had turned into an obsession. In a letter to the director, he repeated his request to be relieved of his duties, complaining that the strains of espionage had grown intolerable. Max Clausen had suffered a heart attack, which he thought was not to be wondered at. 'Conditions in Japan would undermine the strongest constitution,' Sorge wrote, shortly after his forty-fifth birthday on 4 October.

> As for me, I have already told you that as long as the European War lasts, I will remain at my post. But the Germans here say the war will soon be over and I must now know what is to become of me. May I count on being able to return home at the end of the war?
>
> I have just turned 45 and have been on this assignment for eleven years. It is time for me to settle down, put an end to this nomad existence, and utilize the vast experience I have accumulated. I beg you not to forget that I have been living here without a break, and unlike other 'respectable foreigners' have not taken a holiday every three or four years. That may look suspicious.
>
> We remain, with health somewhat undermined it is true, always your true comrades and co-workers.

The letter resounds with anguish. Sorge worries that his masters have doomed him to grow old in a country where he has no roots and will never belong. His plea does not touch the stony hearts of the men with the power to decide his fate. We do not know how the director responded, but Sorge's wish was not granted, and he contemplated the bleak prospect of indefinite exile in Japan.

§ The more Clausen's business prospered, the less ardently he carried out the mission that had brought him to Japan. He had arrived in November 1935, with a 'strong communist spirit', to play his part in the Soviet espionage network, yearning for the overthrow of the Japanese capitalist system. As he wrote in prison: 'I had always thought the

Japanese were groaning under brutal government oppression, and so I believed after I arrived that I was working for the welfare of the people by opposing the political system ... I made the biggest mistake of my life.'[90]

By 1940 his company, which made blueprint presses, was making steady profits. His commitment to communism was wavering, and his zeal for radio work diminishing. Moreover, his relations with Sorge were less cordial than they appeared on the surface: 'He always treated me as a sort of servant since he had no one else to help him.'[91]

Clausen could not help but contrast Sorge's off-hand manner towards a man like himself, who had no high-school education, with his respectful treatment of an intellectual like Gunther Stein, a journalist who performed many useful services for the ring. From Clausen's testimony, we gain the impression that Sorge's condescending attitude rankled.[92] In prison, he had few kinds words to say about his chief. Sorge was 'terribly small-minded', left the hard work of collecting intelligence to the others, and tried to stay away from danger himself.

Possibly Clausen hoped to ingratiate himself with his captors by blackening Sorge's character. But one of his criticisms, at least, has an authentic ring – whenever his chief stayed home with some slight ailment, Clausen had to keep him company because Sorge could not bear to be alone. 'At the time I was seriously ill and under doctor's orders not to work, but Sorge asked me to work just the same as when I was fit. So it has to be said he didn't show consideration to other people.'[93]

In such grievances may lie the seeds of Clausen's perfidy. Had Sorge paid more attention to human relations, his radio operator might have remained loyal, despite his disenchantment with Soviet espionage. But by the end of 1940, a year in which he suffered a serious heart attack, Clausen was bitter and resentful. He was in a mood to inflict serious damage on the Tokyo ring, at the moment when it entered its most crucial phase.

An episode in the winter of 1940–41 ought to have alerted Sorge to the risk posed by Clausen's increasing absorption with making money. In autumn 1940, this message came in from Moscow: 'Because of the war, foreign exchange has become a problem and it has become awkward to remit money. So from now on remittances will be limited to 2,000 yen a month, and what is needed over and above this you should take out of Clausen's operating profits.'[94]

The Fourth Department believed that the time had come to get a return from its investment in Clausen's business. The company – 'M.

Clausen Shokai' – was certainly earning enough to cover a portion of the ring's running costs: in 1939 it reported a net profit of 14,000 yen.

The Sorge network's monthly outlays averaged 3,000 yen (about $700). Clausen drew a salary of 700 yen, and 175 yen for rent, and Sorge took out different amounts each month, sometimes as much as 2,000 yen, for his own expenses and those of Japanese members of the ring. Though Clausen handled accounts, he never found out how much salary Sorge received from Moscow.

The Centre kept a beady eye on expenditures, and would no doubt have been enraged to discover that Sorge was spending 150 yen a month for Hanako's living expenses, and even more on liquor and bar bills. By the standards of ordinary Japanese, both Clausen and Sorge lived high off the hog (a Japanese high-school teacher earned around 80 yen a month).

Faced with Moscow's demand, Clausen rebelled. He had worked hard to build up the firm, winning important firms like Mitsubishi, Mitsui, Hitachi and Nakajima, as well as the Ministry of the Navy, as clients. With full order books in Japan, Clausen had even set up a branch in Mukden in Manchuria to serve the Japanese military and commercial establishment in the colony. As he explained, 'At first I started this work as a camouflage, but as I came to dislike spy work and my communist beliefs began to falter I came to devote all my energy to running the business properly, invested all the money I had in it and worked as hard as I could.'

In a lengthy report, he set out the reasons why the company was unable to fund the espionage ring as the Fourth Department requested. The business was not going well; the small 4,300-yen profit for 1940 was needed for new equipment; the firm was carrying debts. 'It's impossible to take money out of this business ... Our business has a lot of expenses, while the profits are not as big as expected. The police here only allow a fifteen percent profit on deals. In addition the police regulate prices.'

Moreover, Clausen continued, it cost money to keep up his cover as a well-to-do foreign merchant:

Since I have a variety of jobs, I cannot live in a smaller house than the present one. When I came here five years ago, my monthly salary was enough to permit me to live reasonably well. However, the situation has changed completely, consumer prices have tripled, and I also have to be more careful about keeping up appearances. For that reason I have more expenses than I would wish for.

Also I am a member of the German Association so there are additional

expenses. For instance this winter again I have to pay 500 yen to the
stupid Winter Relief Charity, which goes very much against the grain.

Worried how Sorge would react to his refusal to bail out the Tokyo
ring, Clausen waited until January or February to show him the report.
Sorge accepted Clausen's explanations without further ado, and the
report was microfilmed and sent to Moscow.

After his arrest, Clausen admitted he had lied to the Russians, and
that his company had indeed made enough profits to support the spy
ring. He had defied the request, he told Japanese interrogators, because
he wanted to distance himself from the Russians.[95]

§ Hitler had always dreamed of overthrowing the Soviet regime and
controlling Europe from Britain to the Urals. The non-aggression pact
he signed with Stalin in 1939 was simply a short-term expedient to
secure Germany's rear for the conquest of Western Europe. The Führer's
emotional hatred of Bolshevism simmered as he waited for an opportune
moment to strike. In summer 1940, Soviet forces occupied the Baltic
States, and then advanced into Bukovina, close to the Romanian oil-
fields on which Germany depended. Hitler was enraged, and decided
he had to act before Soviet strength became too great. On 18 December
1940, Hitler authorized Case Barbarossa, the plan for the invasion of
the Soviet Union. The very existence of this directive was known only
to the most senior officers in Germany's High Command.

In late December, Sorge picked up alarming information from 'all the
military men' coming to Tokyo from Berlin – apparently a reference to
the German officers assigned to escort the couriers who carried the
diplomatic bag.

The gist was this: after sustained bombing of British cities and
military facilities, Hitler had given up hopes of an early invasion of
Britain. So he was turning his attention to the East. A powerful military
force, including units from France and the French coastal regions, was
being transferred to eastern border regions in both Germany and
Romania. Some eighty divisions were deployed here already and Germany had completed fortifications, which posed a grave strategic threat
to the Soviet Union.

Sorge tested the accuracy of this information on Colonel Alfred
Kretschmer, the senior military attaché who replaced Colonel Matzky.
Kretschmer had just arrived, and barely knew Sorge by this time (December 1940). However, Matzky, on the eve of his departure for Berlin,
introduced the *Frankfurter Zeitung* journalist to his successor, assuring

him that Sorge was highly regarded at German army headquarters and totally reliable. The two men discovered a strong bond. Like Sorge, Kretschmer had been severely wounded in the Great War. His nose had been blown away on the battlefield, and partly restored by cosmetic surgery.

The two appear to have got off to a good start, and before long Kretschmer was one of Sorge's firmest admirers in the embassy. Some time in late December, Sorge told him what he had heard, and Kretschmer confirmed the substance, but reckoned the figure of eighty German divisions poised on the border to be exaggerated. He also confided that his instructions on arriving were to advise the Japanese military authorities that the German build-up was a response to the massing of troops by the Soviet Union on its western border.

Kretschmer was aware what Hitler and his generals had in mind. He had left Berlin for Tokyo in November, and had heard from General von Paulus, then head of the operations section in the General Staff, about the early planning exercises for Case Barbarossa.[96]

Before the end of the year, Kretschmer was also given a broad hint of Hitler's intentions by Matzky, who had been appointed chief of the intelligence division of the German General Staff on his return, and promoted to the rank of general. Matzky sent his successor a carefully worded letter saying he hoped that the attack on 'the man with the red beard' (Barbarossa) which was being prepared 'at the particular request of one gentleman' (Hitler) would not be implemented.[97]

On 28 December Sorge drafted a radio message to Moscow: 'All the military men arriving in Japan from Germany are talking about Germany's deployment of some eighty divisions on her eastern borders including Romania, designed to influence Soviet policy.' Sorge went on to explain that if the Soviet Union responded to this provocation by taking any action prejudicial to German interests, Germany might use this as a pretext to occupy a large chunk of Soviet territory:

> Although Germany does not wish to, it will resort to this step if forced to by Soviet actions. Germany is aware the Soviet Union is not in a position to run the risk because Soviet leaders, especially after the Finland war, know very well that the Red Army needs at least another twenty years to bring its army up-to-date.[98]

This was an early warning – ten days after Hitler signed Directive Number 21, better known as Case Barbarossa – that the Soviet leadership would be unwise to place too much trust in the non-aggression pact of 1939. From this point on, Sorge kept his ears pricked for further evidence that the German High Command was planning to open a second front in the East.

Stalin, however, was unwilling to heed agents whose warnings implicitly questioned his judgement. He wanted to believe that the pact of friendship with Germany was his personal guarantee of peace on his western flank. While he distrusted and disregarded his most loyal servants, he was happy to trust in Hitler's good faith. Thus Stalin enjoyed the illusion that he had nothing to fear from Germany, that the threat from Japan was neutralized, and that Russia at the close of 1940 was in a stronger position than at any time since the Revolution.

While Hitler was busy with schemes to conquer the Soviet Union, his foreign minister, Joachim Ribbentrop, was proposing the adhesion of Russia to the Axis grouping to reinforce the alliance directed against Britain and America. As a prelude to this, Germany played the honest broker, trying to engineer an accommodation between Tokyo and Moscow.

Ambassador Ott was instructed to persuade Japan to patch up her old quarrels with the Soviet Union, and the result was encouraging. In a cable dated 11 November 1940, Ott reported to Berlin that Deputy Foreign Minister Ohashi Chuichi had told him that Japan welcomed Ribbentrop's efforts to improve its relations with Russia. Ribbentrop calculated that if Japan was released from anxiety about its rear – its frontiers with Russia – it might be induced to join Germany's war against Britain.

In the winter of 1940–41 Ambassador Ott was entrusted with selling the idea to Japanese leaders that an attack on Singapore – the British 'Pearl of the East' – would be of inestimable benefit to their nation. Summoning up all his powers of persuasion, Ott assured Foreign Minister Matsuoka and other senior officials that Japanese forces could easily pluck Singapore, because Britain was about to be brought to its knees by the *Wehrmacht* and could not divert resources to defend its colonies.

However, Hitler had suspended Operation Sea Lion – the invasion of Britain – on 12 October and Ott had to admit that, as far as he knew, no new date had been set. The Japanese listened politely to the German Embassy's proposal, but it was evident that they were waiting for the *Wehrmacht* to storm Britain's beaches before agreeing to help themselves to British settlements in the Far East.

Japan wanted the gain – the Asian and Pacific colonies of the Western democracies – without the pain of waging war. This preference for 'stripping the corpse' caused immense frustration among German diplomats and service attachés when they tried to embroil their new allies in Hitler's war. In the coming months, there would be recurring complaints in the embassy that Japanese foot-dragging was weakening the Three Powers Pact that had been launched with such fanfare and high hopes. With satisfaction Sorge picked up the signs of strain in the Axis, and reported them to Moscow.

Part Three

CHAPTER TEN

Winter and Spring 1941

THE YEAR of the Snake, 1941, was ushered in with solemn official warnings that things could only get worse for the Japanese people. 'In greeting the New Year, we are grimly determined to cope bravely with various difficulties and hardships, by bearing what is unbearable and unprecedented in the history of Japan,' said Prime Minister Konoye in a gloom-laden message to the nation.

Japan's war with China, still known by the euphemism 'China Incident', was hopelessly out of control, bleeding the nation of its youth and its material resources. Over a million Japanese soldiers were deployed across China, and well over a hundred thousand had died there in three-and-a-half years of conflict. There was no sign that China was prepared to yield and accept a negotiated settlement on Japanese terms. As the war dragged on it acquired a momentum of its own, and produced an ever greater hunger for raw materials that Japan could only satisfy by advancing into Southeast Asia. The empire-builders could hold on to their gains in China only by further military expansion to the south.

This was the grim strategic logic of the Greater East Asia Co-Prosperity Sphere, advanced as the Konoye cabinet's new objective for Japan's foreign policy. The Co-Prosperity Sphere concept was a thin veneer covering the true aim of Japanese control of oil, tin, rubber, rice and other essential resources abundant in Southeast Asia. These riches now lay within Japan's grasp. With the swastika flying over France and Holland, and Britain preoccupied with staving off a German invasion, the only obstacle to a Japanese march on the White Man's colonies was the United States.

The Konoye government naïvely believed that Washington would flinch before the combined might of the Axis Powers, and that by signing the Three Powers Pact Japan was empowered to take what she wanted in Southeast Asia with little risk of interference. The prevailing official view in Tokyo was that the appeasers had the upper hand in Washington.

But the mood was changing. On 1 January 1941, the US ambassador in Tokyo – who had tried so long and hard to conciliate the Japanese – noted in his diary that Japan was 'on the war path' and spoke of the 'utter hopelessness of a policy of appeasement'.

As a prelude to building a 'New Order in Greater East Asia including the South Seas', Prince Konoye had set about creating a 'New Structure' at home, a regimented state that would follow without question the dictates of the military. The 'New Structure' was inspired by the model of Italy and Germany, but instead of creating a single political party like the Fascists and Nazis, Konoye simply abolished parties altogether. In their place he created a totalitarian organization with the meaningless title Imperial Rule Assistance Association (*Taisei Yokusan Kai*). Labour unions were dissolved, the socialist movement was crushed, and vigilant *Tokko* and *Kempei* cracked down hard on 'dangerous thoughts'. All opposition to the foreign policy of expansionism was liquidated.

The quest for territory and raw materials was ennobled by intensive propaganda about bringing Japan's superior culture to lesser breeds of men in the 'eight corners of the world'. The Japanese were taught that this holy mission required selfless loyalty to the emperor and a readiness to endure hardships, the least of which were the perpetual food shortages. Martial airs and patriotic songs were played constantly on the radio. Frugality was demanded, gaiety discouraged. Bureaucrats busied themselves dreaming up new rules about food and dress, many so petty that people didn't know whether to laugh or cry.

On 28 September 1940 the Tokyo metropolitan government ordered that brides should avoid ostentatious and expensive wedding kimonos, and opt for short-sleeved versions. On 1 October a ban on driving to entertainment quarters was imposed – the National Police Agency said that this would save petrol and keep pleasure-seekers at home. In a perfectly serious statement, the authorities announced that concubines might no longer have telephones. The rich and powerful usually managed to find ways round the restrictions. For instance, golf, a costly and decadent Western sport, was frowned upon – but people were allowed to play if their purpose was to build up physical fitness.

While the nation's resources were being squandered by the Japanese army in China, rules on kimono sleeves seemed laughable to ordinary citizens. What concerned them was the absence of daily necessities. The writer Nagai Kafu told his diary that he spent New Year's Day huddled in his futon with a hot-water bottle to keep at bay the icy cold in his four-and-a-half mat room. There was no charcoal, not enough gas, and he could not stoke up his energy with rice, because that too was in short supply.[1]

Tokyo in February 1941 made a sombre impression on the newly arrived *New York Times* correspondent, Otto Tolischus. His previous posting was wartime Germany, and he recognized the symptoms of a nation at war. 'Tokyo already had a dimout, and the bright lights which, I was told, once rivaled those of Broadway were gone.'[2] Declining standards of living, shortages of daily necessities and imported goods, the poor quality of domestic whisky, the scarcity of taxis – these provoked the sort of grumbles from Japanese that he had got used to hearing from Germans.

The gloom was thickened by newspaper adverts for air-raid shelters. A five-person shelter was offered in the *Asahi* at a 'bargain' price of 150 yen, good value because it 'can be used as fire-proof and earthquake-proof storage room in normal times'. If that was too costly, Tokyoites could stock up with *bokuyohin* (air defence necessities) at the Itoya store on the Ginza: the pack contained a gas-mask, torch, megaphone, and black paper for pasting over windows. The adverts were grim reminders that the Japanese might not be spared the horror of air-raids in their next war, if they took on an adversary more formidable than China.

§ Branko Vukelic was blissfully happy in his second marriage. His young wife Yoshiko was the foreigner's dream-image of the Japanese woman: delicate, demure, devoted. And into the bargain she was intelligent, brave and resourceful. Was Sorge, who pined for a settled life with Katya, and dreaded solitude, pricked by envy at his assistant's good fortune in finding such a paragon to share his life?

On 26 January 1941, Branko and Yoshiko – now seven months pregnant – celebrated their first wedding anniversary. They recalled the accident that had brought them together, on Sunday 14 April 1935, at the Nogakudo, a theatre in Tokyo's Suidobashi district specializing in *No*, a form of classic Japanese opera. The only tickets left were for the morning performance, and fate allocated them adjoining seats.[3]

Branko, who was then thirty-one, fell in love on the spot with the pretty girl sitting in the next seat – or so he told her later. No doubt he was eager for romance, after the breakdown of his marriage to Edith. They were an ill-matched couple who quarrelled frequently, and Branko was intent on a divorce.

Branko cornered the young woman in the theatre lobby and found out that she was Yamazaki Yoshiko, a student of English at Tsuda

College in Tokyo. Yoshiko recalls her excitement when the foreigner approached her. 'I really wanted to try my English, but I was with my father and I didn't have the courage to talk to him anyway. It was very crowded, and I didn't feel well, so I went out for some air, and he followed me and asked me a question about the play.'

At the beginning, her interest in the foreigner was educational, rather than romantic. Branko, captivated by the woman, pursued her indefatigably, overwhelming her with his considerable wit and eloquence. 'I have 91 love letters starting from the next day, 15 April, until the date I agreed to marry,' Yoshiko recalls with a laugh. 'I didn't make it easy for him. I thought kissing meant marriage. When he tried to kiss me at the Fuji Five Lakes on a boat, I pulled down my hat and his kiss landed on that. He looked terribly disappointed.'

As she anticipated, her parents were fiercely opposed to her marrying a foreigner. At the best of times, well-to-do Japanese families shuddered at the thought of a foreign son-in-law. And by the early 1940s, many people, influenced by malignant propaganda, regarded such marriages as contamination of Japan's racial purity, and akin to treachery.

To compound Branko's problems, Sorge – 'the boss' – also objected when he broached the question of leaving Edith. 'If you divorce Edith, it must be because you want to marry another woman. In any case, it will make it harder to maintain the secrecy of the group,' Sorge said.[4]

Branko was insistent, and when Sorge realized his mind was made up, he arranged a settlement for Edith. It was essential that Edith be treated fairly. She knew too much about the workings of the Tokyo ring – the Vukelic household was one of Clausen's wireless bases – and there was a danger that a vengeful woman might betray it to the authorities.

After the couple separated in July 1938, Clausen was given the job of finding new accommodation for Edith. In September that year she settled in the Kami-Meguro district with 8-year-old Paul. Under the new arrangements, Edith allowed Clausen to use her home for transmissions, and helped out where she could, even carrying the bulky wireless equipment for Clausen after his heart attack. In return, Sorge arranged a special allowance for Edith and the boy. After an expensive legal procedure – complicated by the fact that Edith was Danish, Branko a Yugoslav citizen, that they had wed in Paris, and were now resident in Tokyo – the Vukelics' marriage was finally dissolved at the end of 1939.

A few weeks after the divorce came through, Yoshiko and Branko held a white wedding at the Nikolai Russian Orthodox church in the Kanda district. By then, her parents had resigned themselves to the inevitable and they attended the wedding, as did Yoshiko's four brothers and sisters. 'I was still the black sheep of the family, however,' she says.

Richard Sorge was not invited. Branko had to keep the wedding a secret from the 'boss'. He had sought Sorge's permission for the marriage, but the answer was an adamant 'No!' From Vukelic's testimony, we sense how much Branko's domestic problems irked Sorge, who was forced to point out the risks to the Tokyo unit. 'If you marry a Japanese woman, the ring will be more vulnerable to exposure. However devoted to you she is, if she discovers the nature of our work, there'll be a clash of loyalties and who knows whether she can be relied on to keep it secret?' Sorge said.[5]

But Branko could not hide his marriage indefinitely, and with some trepidation he confessed to what had happened. To his surprise Sorge showed no sign of anger. 'Now you're married it can't be helped,' Sorge told his subordinate. The fact remained that his orders had been disobeyed, and the matter would have to be reported to the Centre.

> Never tell your wife anything about the organization as long as you're in Japan. If possible, just go back to Yugoslavia to think things over, and obtain Moscow's approval to explain the situation to your wife and win her over to our cause. Otherwise, you'll have no alternative but to withdraw from the organization.[6]

So Branko was told to wait for instructions from the Centre. Sorge relayed to Moscow that Vukelic wished to return to his home country, and showed him the message he had sent. Moscow's response was that Vukelic should stay put in Japan for the time being. A week or two later, the war in Europe spilled over into Yugoslavia. Branko could not go home even if he wanted to, and the matter was shelved.

Before they married, Branko told Yoshiko about his communist convictions – heinously 'dangerous thoughts' of a kind that had catapulted hundreds of Japanese into prison. What he did not tell her was that he belonged to a spy group, and that this subterranean mission, not journalism, had brought him to Japan. Branko was anxious not to implicate Yoshiko in his dangerous work.

Edith, of course, had known the purpose of their journey to Japan, and played a minor but useful part in the operation. As for Max Clausen, he had told Anna about his clandestine activities for Russia only after they were married, and, as a devout anti-communist, she was not at all pleased.

It was not long after they moved into a little house in Sanai-cho that Yoshiko realized her husband was involved in some twilight business.

She was surprised to see a fat, rather coarse man – 'a typical German merchant' – come round about once a month with a heavy-looking document case, and then disappear into the spare bedroom upstairs for hours at a stretch.

Branko was forced to explain this mysterious visitor. The German, he told Yoshiko, was a comrade in an anti-war movement, headed by a man he referred to simply as 'the boss'. The aim of this movement was to prevent Japan from becoming embroiled in a war with the Soviet Union. Yoshiko thought this to be a worthy cause, and the fact that he was involved in the risky undertaking only deepened her respect for Branko.

Indeed, these stealthy activities appealed to this bright young woman's sense of adventure, and she asked to be allowed to help. Branko told her that when the mysterious visitor was busy transmitting, she could keep watch in case police or other unexpected callers came to the house. One day, the fat German carelessly left behind a receipt with his company's name, and that was how she discovered his name was Clausen.

As for 'the boss', he remained a shadowy figure. Branko spoke of him with respect. He was a splendid person, but he was also *darashinai* – he played fast and loose with women. At the same time he had a soft heart, and had wept over a letter from a woman he had left behind in Moscow – Branko had projected a microfilm, brought by courier, on to the wall of his room, and there was this letter in German that moved Sorge to tears.

Yoshiko never spoke more than a few words to Sorge, and these over the telephone. She came to recognize the husky voice when he called and asked her to summon Branko to the phone. Only many years later, when the newspapers carried photos of the Soviet spy, would she put a face to the voice. The closest she came to seeing him in the flesh was the day they all happened to be at Lohmeyer's restaurant. 'We were having lunch, when Branko said suddenly: the boss is sitting over there. Don't turn round. I did as I was told, and so I never laid eyes on Sorge.'

In those days of ferocious nationalism, a Japanese woman married to a foreigner had to develop a thick skin. She was forced to endure censorious remarks by 'patriotic' busybodies, and the intrusive attention of officials.

One day in 1940, Yoshiko and Branko were walking along the road beside Hibiya Park, a stone's throw from the Imperial Hotel, when a scowling police officer in uniform approached. 'He demanded to know what I was doing walking around with a foreigner at a time of grave crisis for Japan,' Yoshiko remembers.

> Here was I consorting with a foreigner, and the nation was surrounded by foreign enemies! He sounded really angry. Branko got quite upset. 'Leave her alone!' he told the policeman, in Japanese. 'She's my wife!' And he pulled out his passport to prove we were a legitimate couple. You just had to put up with that sort of meddling. People regarded you as a sort of traitor for marrying a foreigner.

§ From early 1941, while restrictions on civilian consumption were tightened, and simplicity and parsimony lauded as patriotic virtues, the press prepared the people for a great national emergency.

The mood of impending crisis darkened day by day. On 1 March – 'New Asia Day' – Tokyo's residents rose early, and observed the occasion by bowing, in their millions, in the direction of the Imperial Palace. The *Japan Times and Advertiser,* like the Japanese-language press, was reporting on 'measures to boost national defence'.

Youth associations were being mobilized to dig bomb-proof shelters, collect waste materials and cultivate waste land, and undertake 'other measures to boost national defence'. Cabarets and dance-halls, geisha houses of assignation and brothels were closing down for the day. 'Café hostesses, geisha and licensed prostitutes will engage in sewing handicrafts of various kinds, manufacture of envelopes, and other useful efforts. The proceeds will go to the national defence fund,' said the *Japan Times and Advertiser.*

Without the help of a translator the Japanese-language press was impenetrable, and Sorge, like other foreign journalists, read Tokyo's one surviving English-language newspaper each day with great care. It was known as a government mouthpiece, which had certain advantages for a foreign correspondent working under tight censorship. Sorge sprinkled many of his newspaper articles with *Japan Times and Advertiser* quotes, confident that they would safely pass the censor. Moreover, it conveyed a good impression of what was irking the government at any given moment, and, obliquely, of the tensions and fault lines in the nation's power structure – matters that Ozaki would later illuminate for Sorge.

But as a barometer of the mood of the people, Hanako served him well. She brought gossip from family and friends, relaying the grumbles at the rationing of daily necessities, the dearth of fresh vegetables and fish, the denial of simple pleasures. Her perspective belied the propaganda image of a united nation pulling together in a common endeavour that transcended class barriers.

How far from the truth that was. The sacrifices of ordinary people
to sustain the Holy War in China would have been bearable if they
were shared equally by all. But the rich continued to wallow in luxury,
and high officials showed little inclination to abstain from forbidden
pleasures. This is evident from the secret diary kept by Nagai Kafu, the
novelist. On 3 March 1941, he was once more moved to decry the
rottenness of the New Structure imposed by the nation's rulers. A woman
from Kanuma, in Tochigi Prefecture, who worked as a geisha, had told
him that there was still plenty of business, despite the government
restrictions on lavish entertaining. Her *machiai* (house of assignation)
was safe from police interference, she explained, because it supplied
geisha for important customers – including gentlemen from the *Tokko*,
the Special Higher Police, and high-ups in the *Taisei Yokusan Kai*, Konoye's
organization that had replaced political parties. 'The corruption of the
so-called New Structure runs rife on the dark side of the capital of the
Empire,' Nagai told his diary. 'I have to say it's really very curious.'[7]

§ In the first week of March, General Ott told Sorge about a top secret
telegram that had arrived from Berlin. Foreign Minister Ribbentrop had
again urged him to exert every effort to entice Japan to attack Singapore.

The ambassador was exasperated. For the past two months the
resources of the embassy had been devoted to the task of embroiling
Japan with Britain. The service attachés, the political and press departments, and Ott himself had worked overtime to nudge Japan into the
war. Wenneker, the naval attaché, had drawn up a full-scale Singapore
campaign plan for the guidance of the Japanese navy. There were some
powerful officers, like General Ishihara, who advocated an attack. But
mostly the Germans had met with scepticism in high military and
government circles. Evidently, Foreign Minister Ribbentrop did not
appreciate the difficulties of handling the Japanese.

'It's not surprising,' said Sorge, who was briefed about these exertions
by Ott himself. 'As you well know, Mr Ambassador, the Japanese are
past masters at pulling the wool over Westerners' eyes. I've told you
before, Japan will not be used as Hitler's cat's-paw. Was it not the great
Bismarck who said that every alliance is made up of a knight and his
horse? Well, Japan doesn't want to be the horse carrying the knight in
the Axis partnership!'[8]

This discussion took place a short while before General Ott left
Tokyo on a journey to Berlin, preceding Foreign Minister Matsuoka,
who was about to make a historic visit to Moscow, Berlin and Rome.
Before setting out, the ambassador listened carefully to Sorge's advice

on what approach to adopt in his all-important meetings in Berlin with Ribbentrop and Hitler.

He encouraged Ott to explain to his masters the limitations of the brotherhood of Germany and Japan. The two nations shared the same bed, and the same dreams of conquest, but co-operation was often grudging, and at the embassy the Germans grumbled constantly that they gave more than they took. Sorge would then join in and seek to exacerbate this resentment with his own interpretation of events. The wedge between Tokyo and Berlin was already there, it was just a question of driving it deeper. Every spark of friction he detected between the Axis partners warmed his heart; any sign of fissure in an evil alliance raised his spirits.

§ Prince Urach, an old friend, gave Sorge some useful insights into Germany's changing strategic priorities. Urach, a former journalist recruited to work for the press section of the German Foreign Ministry, explained that Ribbentrop still hoped for an aggressive Japanese policy towards Singapore – but not at the cost of provoking the United States to enter the war on Britain's side. Berlin was now leaning more to enlisting Japan's support in restraining the Soviet Union in the Far East. He heard from the German General Staff – to which he had close connections – that Germany was in favour of Japan strengthening its forces in Manchuria, so that it could apply pressure on Siberia.[9]

Sorge pricked up his ears. The implications of this information were disturbing. If the Germans wanted Japan to sit on the Russian bear's tail in the East, they were evidently planning an offensive in the West. And while Ribbentrop was still nagging Ott to engineer a Japanese attack on Singapore, it appeared that German strategic planning now envisaged a role for Japan in the conquest of Russia.

This emerged even more strongly from a discussion Sorge then had with General Kretschmer, the senior military attaché. He had received a letter from General Matzky, his predecessor – now the chief of the intelligence division of the German General Staff – who kept him in touch with the thinking of army leaders in Berlin. In the letter Matzky described the violently anti-Soviet tendencies of senior army officers, and other quarters, and left the attaché to draw his own conclusions. Colonel Kretschmer confided in Richard, and gave his own considered opinion: 'From what General Matzky says in his letter, it looks as if there's going to be a bitter struggle between us and Russia when the present war is over. That's the mood among our top brass and the people close to Himmler.'

But Kretschmer, who had once served as a Soviet specialist in the General Staff, did not share the fanatical anti-Soviet views of many of his fellow-officers: 'Now we come to the question of what contribution Japan should make as our ally. Well, Japan may feel it has a mission to combat communism in the Soviet Union. But I still think the priority is to get Japan to make a move against Singapore.' These discussions in the embassy persuaded Sorge that Germany planned to enlist Japan as a fellow belligerent in the invasion of Russia. His primary mission of discovering whether Japan intended to attack the Soviet Union was about to become more sharply focused, and more urgent.

§ Foreign Minister Matsuoka set out on his odyssey to Europe from Tokyo Station on 12 March after visiting the Meiji Shrine to report to the spirit of the Emperor Meiji. It was a momentous occasion. Matsuoka was the first Japanese foreign minister to venture outside his own borders since 1907, the newspapers pointed out. The journey to Berlin, Rome and Moscow and back would take nearly six weeks, much of the time rolling across Siberia in a special train laid on by the Russians.

The Sorge group had its own 'mole' in the Matsuoka entourage. Saionji Kinkazu, the aristocrat Ozaki had befriended when they attended the Yosemite conference in 1936, joined the delegation in his capacity of Foreign Ministry consultant. Before leaving, he told Ozaki that the journey was expected to yield few concrete results. Above all, it was intended to demonstrate Axis solidarity. Saionji, the adopted grandson of the nation's most eminent elder statesman, Prince Saionji Kinmochi, belonged to Konoye's circle, and was able to tell Ozaki on good authority that Matsuoka's brief was to study the European situation, and make no commitments in his talks with Hitler and Ribbentrop. The principal task assigned to Matsuoka was to improve relations with the Soviet Union by negotiating a non-aggression pact. On a stop-over in Moscow on 24 March, he proposed such a pact during a meeting with Soviet Foreign Minister Vyacheslav Molotov.

Matsuoka arrived in Berlin on 26 March, and was fêted like a visiting monarch. Red carpets were rolled out everywhere, cheering crowds waved Japanese flags, lamp-posts sprouted bunting, bands played the Japanese national anthem. Matsuoka, a dynamic, erratic man with a love of ostentation, was floating on air when he was hailed in the German and Italian media as the architect of the Axis, and the most capable member of the Konoye cabinet.

On 27 March, he was Ribbentrop's guest of honour at a luncheon. The Nazi Foreign Minister Ribbentrop tried to convince Matsuoka that

Japan's best interests lay in attacking Singapore, an action that would give it supremacy in Southeast Asia. Matsuoka, keeping to his instructions, carefully avoided making a commitment.

Hitler had ordered that Matsuoka be kept in the dark about Operation Barbarossa, Germany's plan to attack the Soviet Union. Although he had embraced Japan as a partner in the Axis, the Führer's distrust for the race he had scorned in *Mein Kampf* was undiminished. He suspected that if Japan knew about Barbarossa, she might betray the secret to Russia, Britain or America to gain an advantage.

By all accounts, the meeting between Hitler and Matsuoka was more like a bizarre monologue. Hitler became so heated in his conversation that he seemed to forget to whom he was talking. Raising his fist, pounding the table, he shouted excitedly, 'England must be beaten!' Matsuoka, a staunch admirer of the Führer, was impressed.

It appears that Ribbentrop, who also talked a lot, dropped broad hints about growing tensions in Germany's relations with Russia. The signals were lost in translation, or misunderstood by the Japanese party. Assuming that an improvement in Japan's relations with Russia was still backed by Ribbentrop, Matsuoka left Berlin on 5 April, after a triumphant visit to Rome and the Vatican, and headed back to Moscow to seek a *rapprochement*.

In the early morning of 6 April, when Matsuoka and his entourage arrived at the border between Germany and Russia, they heard German radio announce that the *Wehrmacht* had marched into Yugoslavia. The Serbs had thrown out Prince Paul, who had taken his country into the Axis on 27 March, and had disowned the pact with Germany. Enraged by this act of defiance, Hitler launched a violent campaign to subjugate the Serbian army. This vindictive reaction proved Hitler's ultimate undoing. His Balkan campaign forced a five-week postponement of the invasion of Russia. 'If the invasion had started five weeks earlier, Hitler's armies might have reached Moscow before they were so acutely hampered by the winter snow,' says Kase Toshikazu, a diplomat who served as Matsuoka's secretary in 1941.[10] Of course, the Führer had no inkling at the time that he was cutting off his nose to spite his face.

The anti-Axis coup in Yugoslavia (engineered, it was widely believed, by Russian agents) and the German punitive expedition produced a more immediate effect. They reinforced Soviet leaders' doubts about Hitler's intentions and made them more receptive to Matsuoka's diplomacy when he returned to Moscow.

On 13 April Matsuoka and Molotov signed a neutrality pact, under which Russia and Japan would remain neutral if either were attacked by a third power. When the business was over, wine flowed liberally in the Kremlin, and toast after toast was proposed. Stalin toasted Emperor Hirohito, Matsuoka toasted Stalin. According to one version, Stalin told the Japanese foreign minister: 'You are an Asiatic, so am I.' To which Matsuoka, in elated mood, responded: 'We're all Asiatics. Let us drink to the Asiatics!'

The Russians had every reason to feel pleased. The neutrality pact appeared to drive a wedge into the Axis pact, and offered some insurance, however fragile, against an attack from the east. For its part, Japan had stabilized relations with the Soviet Union, and diminished the threat to its northern flank. It could now press forward with its southward advance with a guarantee of Soviet neutrality, in case its expansionist policy brought it into conflict with the United States and Britain.

§ On April 22, General Ott – who had arrived back from his journey two days earlier – and the Italian and Soviet ambassadors waited at Tachikawa airfield, west of Tokyo. A small twin-prop plane droned out of the overcast sky and brought the foreign minister down to earth at the end of his remarkable six-week tour. Matsuoka, dazzled by his international stardom, disembarked in raincoat and felt hat, carrying his distinctive bamboo cane. He exchanged what newspapers described as a 'warm handshake' with the prime minister, Prince Konoye and greeted the ambassadors; army officers welcomed him back; later the government gave a banquet in his honour.

Everywhere people gathered to shout 'banzai!' (hurrah!) as the returning hero rode into Tokyo to bow in homage before the palace, then reported to the prime minister, the emperor, and to a liaison conference between the government and the Imperial Headquarters. Haikus were composed to celebrate the auspicious occasion.

The foreign press was granted a five-minute press conference at Matsuoka's official residence. He was asked whether he had any plans for negotiations with the United States. 'No diplomat in the world tells the world beforehand what negotiations he contemplates or what measures he will employ,' he was reported as replying. To Richard Sorge, who was among the thirty foreign correspondents present, this was as good as official confirmation. In his report for the *Frankfurter Zeitung* an ultra-cautious Sorge quoted the Japanese press view that Matsuoka would now turn his attention to 'examining Japan-Anglo-American relations'.[11]

As he was in a great hurry, a press statement was handed out with

Matsuoka's thoughts: the neutrality pact was described as a reinforcement of the Three Powers Pact, and it was claimed that 'both Germany and Italy are sincerely welcoming the pact'. This was disingenuous, at the very least. Germany was surprised and confounded by the Russo-Japanese Pact. The pact was a reverse for Berlin's diplomacy. In Sorge's words: 'They [the Germans] never dreamed a Japan–Soviet neutrality agreement would be concluded.'[12]

As soon as Ambassador Ott returned to Tokyo, he related his misgivings to Sorge: 'I heard from the mouth of Ambassador Ott that Japan had tied itself too closely to the USSR by concluding the neutrality pact, and that Germany was not happy with it. From this I got the impression that relations between Japan and Germany had already worsened.'[13]

Sorge asked Ozaki to report on the reactions to the pact among the public and power-holders. This Ozaki accomplished without difficulty. Since June 1939, he had been employed by the Investigation Department of the South Manchurian Railway, *Mantetsu*, which had had vast economic interests in Manchuria, and was more like an empire than a railway company. His department collected and analysed data for the Kwantung Army, and was often commissioned by the military to carry out research projects. His job gave him access to political, economic and military information invaluable to the Sorge ring. Ozaki sounded out opinion in the *Mantetsu* and in the Breakfast Society, and heard Saionji's account of the mission. In the second half of April he met Sorge several times to report his findings.

The pact was generally well received in political and military circles, and ordinary people were relieved that the danger of war with Russia had receded. There were divergent views, however, on the crucial point of whether the pact nullified Japan's alliance with Germany. On balance, the sages of the Breakfast Society were inclined to believe the new treaty was not in conflict with the Three Powers Pact, as it specifically excluded the Soviet Union as its target and underlined Japan's responsibility as a neutral nation, should conflict arise between Russia and Germany.

Ozaki remained dubious, however, reckoning that Japan's attitude would fluctuate according to changing circumstances, and that Russia should not assume that its eastern borders were now safe. 'We need to be on our guard for Japanese preparations to attack the Soviet Union' was his advice to Sorge.[14]

What Sorge heard at the embassy confirmed the wisdom of this scepticism. Matsuoka was hardly back in Tokyo when he offered the worried German ambassador assurances that in the event of hostilities between Germany and the Soviet Union, Japan would break the neutrality pact with Moscow. Ott was given to understand, as Sorge explained, that: 'If war broke out between Germany and the Soviet Union there was no cabinet in Japan that would shirk from participating in the war on Germany's side.'[15] The volatile foreign minister did not reflect the thinking of the cabinet, or the navy, or even most army leaders. But clearly Moscow would be ill-advised to place too much faith in any treaty concluded with Japan.

Sorge was also interested to know how Japan had responded to Germany's persistent pressure to attack Singapore. Very negatively, according to Ozaki, who had heard Prime Minister Konoye complain about Ambassador Ott's campaign to rally pro-Axis circles behind the 'strike-Singapore' plan. Konoye told Ozaki that 'it was only Ambassador Ott who had been toying with that [plan]'[16]

Some weeks went by before the embassy found out what Sorge knew already – that its protracted campaign had failed. Not until 10 June did the naval attaché, Rear-Admiral Wenneker, learn from his navy sources that Japan had absolutely no intention of attacking Singapore. The navy was worried that such an action would inevitably provoke a war with the United States, a war it was not at all confident of winning.

§ During Ambassador Ott's absence, Gestapo Colonel Josef Meisinger arrived in Tokyo to take up the post of police attaché at the embassy. His macabre reputation as the 'Butcher of Warsaw' had preceded him, and some of Ott's staff wondered what they had done to deserve such a man.

Meisinger's file at State Security Headquarters (RHSA) in Berlin showed him to be 'so unutterably bestial and corrupt as to be practically inhuman', according to Walter Schellenberg, head of the foreign intelligence section of RHSA. On his previous assignment to Warsaw, his sadistic atrocities had churned even the strong stomachs of his Gestapo superiors. Only the intervention of secret police chief Reinhard Heydrich had saved him from court-martial and execution. The posting to Tokyo was a means of keeping him at arms' length until the dust settled.[17]

Meisinger's physical appearance matched his notoriety. 'He was a frightening individual, a large, coarse-faced man with a bald head and an incredibly ugly face,' was Walter Schellenberg's description. A German woman who fell foul of the colonel recalls that: 'He was such a terrifying presence, my knees gave way when I went into his office.'[18]

Other German residents whispered that Meisinger was fond of taking a plate of raw meat from his refrigerator, and eating it with his fingers.[19]

As police attaché, Meisinger's role was to liaise with Japanese colleagues in criminal cases involving German nationals. More importantly, his duties entailed keeping watch on embassy staff and suspected enemies of the Third Reich within the German community, using a string of informants.

Among those Colonel Meisinger was ordered to place under surveillance was the correspondent of the *Frankfurter Zeitung*, Dr Sorge. German Security Headquarters had been alerted to doubts about Sorge's loyalties, and at some point in 1940 Walter Schellenberg was asked to investigate.

'At that time the Nazi Party, and above all the foreign organization of the Party, were creating difficulties for Sorge because of his political past,' Schellenberg wrote in his memoirs. He talked over the problem with Wilhelm von Ritgen, head of the German News Agency (DNB), for which Sorge did occasional work. Ritgen had no reason to complain about Sorge's reliability. Indeed, he had commissioned Sorge to provide a comprehensive rapportage on developments in Japan, which had been circulated among a small circle of senior officials, and proved how sound Sorge's judgement was. This service was so useful that Ritgen 'felt he could not dispense with Sorge's reports'.[20]

However, Ritgen suggested a check on Sorge's files in the Gestapo and Internal Security departments would be a wise precaution. When Schellenberg looked up the secret police dossiers, he found disturbing information. True, there was no hard evidence that Sorge had belonged to the German Communist Party. But he had been in contact with a large number of known Comintern agents: 'One could not help coming to the conclusion that he was at least a sympathizer ... but he had close ties with people in influential circles and had always been protected against rumours of this sort.'[21]

After some soul-searching Schellenberg decided on a compromise:

> even if we assumed that Sorge had connections with the Russian Secret Service, we must, after safeguarding our own interests, find ways of profiting from his profound knowledge. In the end, we agreed that I should protect Sorge from attacks by the Party, but only on condition that he included in his reports intelligence material on the Soviet Union, China and Japan.[22]

Henceforth, Sorge's reports to Ritgen were carefully vetted, but they always proved reliable, and even Schellenberg's foreign intelligence section made use of them.

The nature of Sorge's relationship with Germany's secret service is a matter of conjecture. Officially, he was still working for Ritgen's organization, but all the material was channelled to Schellenberg. Sorge had a good idea of the workings of German intelligence and must have been aware that the confidential information – most of which Ritgen did not publish – found its way to the intelligence services.

At the same time, it was decided that Sorge should be placed under close scrutiny, to try to find out if there was any basis for suspecting that he was in the service of the Soviet Union. The difficulty was to find someone to conduct the surveillance in faraway Tokyo, where the RHSA had only young, inexperienced agents who would easily be outfoxed by someone as clever as Sorge. 'I delayed doing anything – which was certainly very careless of me – until after Sorge had already begun to work for us,' Schellenberg wrote.[23]

The problem was solved by Heydrich's decision to dispatch Meisinger to the embassy in Tokyo. Schellenberg briefed the Gestapo man before he left. Meisinger was instructed to investigate Sorge's activities, and to keep German Security Headquarters informed on a regular basis by long-distance telephone.

Sorge assumed that the role of the Gestapo officer was to keep the embassy staff under close scrutiny, and that he too, as a part-time embassy employee, would be watched. The thought that the Gestapo may have unearthed incriminating details of his conspiratorial activities as a young man in Germany would no doubt have unsettled him. In Japan, he had made no secret of his antipathy for National Socialism, and he may have surmised that some ill-disposed Hitler devotee had reported his vitriolic comments to party headquarters in Berlin.

Sorge resolved to find out what Meisinger was really up to. Cultivating the newcomer proved easy. The colonel was delighted to find that the journalist was a hearty drinker, a lusty womanizer, and an entertaining raconteur.[24]

A boisterous, earthy relationship developed between the two men. A senior German diplomat who arrived in May discovered that Meisinger 'felt honoured ... that Sorge valiantly helped him devour his stock of whisky on many an occasion, even though he made great fun of the fat Meisinger while doing so.'[25]

CHAPTER ELEVEN

May 1941

IN EARLY May, Sorge's suspicions about a German invasion of the Soviet Union grew firmer. Many hours were spent discussing Hitler's intentions with the ambassador and the naval attaché, and it was apparent both had solid reasons for believing war was imminent. The two officials thought that Hitler was ready to take a massive gamble and open a second front in the east, without waiting for his armies to subjugate the English. Ott revealed that Hitler was absolutely determined to crush the Russians and seize the European region of the Soviet Union, which would give Germany the grain and raw materials it needed to achieve absolute supremacy throughout Europe.

On 2 May Richard summed up what he had discovered in a dispatch transmitted by Clausen to Moscow four days later:

> Possibility of outbreak of war at any moment is very high, because Hitler and his generals are confident that war with USSR will not hamper conduct of war against Britain in the least.
>
> German generals estimate the Red Army's fighting capacity is so low that they believe the Red Army will be destroyed in the course of a few weeks. They believe the defence system on the German–Soviet border zone is extremely weak.

Sorge learned that the ambassador was so sure that war was coming that he had urged Prince Urach – who was on an official mission to Tokyo and staying at the residence – to leave for home before the Trans-Siberian Railway link was cut.

> Decision on start of war against USSR will be taken by Hitler alone, either as early as May, or following the war with England.
>
> However, Ott, who is personally against such a war, feels so sceptical at the present time that he already advised Prince Urach to leave for Germany in May.[1]

At regular intervals, couriers from the German Foreign Ministry arrived in Tokyo with the diplomatic bag after a tedious two-week journey across Siberia. Escorting the couriers were officers from the three services – army, navy and airforce – and from General Staff Headquarters, selected on a rotation basis. Sorge went out of his way to befriend these officers, whom he found to be 'another extremely important source for my clandestine intelligence activities'.[2] Invariably they came to him with letters of introduction from highly placed officials in Berlin.[3]

Because of his war record, he established a rapport with these military men with the greatest ease. The middle-ranking officers were no doubt honoured by the attentions of such a well-respected authority on Japan. As lonely soldiers far from home, they particularly appreciated his guidance to the nocturnal pleasures that Tokyo and Yokohama offered, if you knew where to look.

These periodic visitors from home were valuable in two ways: first, they had access to Japanese military information. Their duties went beyond guarding the diplomatic bag. Each came to Tokyo with a specific mission, in pursuance of a bilateral accord on the exchange of military intelligence.

During their stay, they went to the Japanese army or navy head-quarters to liaise with officers handling relations with the Axis partners. Here they gave briefings on their specialization – which might be tanks, artillery or bombing techniques. Their Japanese counterparts recipro-cated with specialized information of their own. Displaying his own knowledge of the internal workings of the Japanese military, Sorge extracted information from his new friends without their noticing.

Second, Sorge gleaned reliable news about German troop concentra-tions in East Prussia and Poland, adjoining the Soviet Union's borders. In particular, General Staff officers on political assignments unwittingly gave useful pointers to Hitler's intentions. It was their duty, in the first months of 1941, to sound out their counterparts in Tokyo to determine what help Germany could expect if it invaded Russia.

Piecing the clues together, Sorge found his worst fears confirmed. The German build-up in the east was well advanced. Increasingly, a massive onslaught against Russia seemed inevitable.

Then, some time in May, Sorge received unsettling news. A German major named Niedermayer arrived from army headquarters in Berlin, armed with a letter of introduction from Dirksen, the former ambassador to Tokyo. Confident that Sorge could keep a secret, this officer lucidly laid out the Führer's strategy with the assurance of an insider. In Sorge's words: 'When we got talking, it turned out that a war between Germany and the USSR was already a certainty.'[4]

Niedermayer explained that Germany had three objectives in the East: first, to occupy the Ukraine, the granary of Europe; second, to force one to two million war prisoners to work in agriculture and industry, to make up for Germany's labour shortage; third, to eliminate once and for all the danger that existed on Germany's eastern border. In prison Sorge summed up what the major had said:

> Hitler thought that if he let this chance slip by, he wouldn't get another one. In other words, Hitler reckoned if he was going to fight a war it had to be now. He thought it would be impossible to force the German people to go to war with the Soviet Union again once the war with Britain was over.[5]

§ Japanese police had been alerted to the existence of a spy ring operating in Tokyo by the illegal radio traffic that government monitoring agencies had intercepted since 1937. Their direction-finding equipment was not equal to the task of tracing the transmitter, although the approximate location was known. To reduce the risk of detection, Clausen worked fast, operating the radio for as little time as possible, and sometimes breaking off and moving to another house before resuming transmission.

As a rule he worked between four p.m. and seven p.m, or in the early morning, when atmospheric conditions were at their best. The transmitter he had built from scratch had a range of 1,500 kilometres in daytime, and 4,000 kilometres at night. He was not told where the receiving station code-named 'Wiesbaden' was located, but thought it was probably in Vladivostok – although in the summer of 1941 he was given to understand that a new station had been set up, which he presumed was in Khabarovsk. Clausen's range was restricted because he was obliged to work without an outside aerial, which would have been too conspicuous.

As if to compensate for their meagre success in catching spies, frustrated police officials pressed for more and harsher legislation. In March 1941 the Peace Preservation Law was revised, with stiffer penalties and wider police powers of investigation. This law, enacted in 1925 to prosecute agents of the Comintern, was in practice the main instrument for bringing to heel communists and other 'thought criminals'.

In May 1941 the National Defence Security Law, designed to protect state secrets, went into effect. This law expanded the definition of state secrets to include diplomatic, economic and political matters. Military secrets were already covered by the Military Secrets Protection Law, passed at the turn of the century, and the Military Resources Protection Act of 1939. Offenders faced a possible death sentence.

To justify the battery of oppressive laws, the authorities fomented a spy hysteria with constant warnings that Japan was permeated by spies seeking to undermine the nation's fabric. There were periodic campaigns, such as the 'National Spy Prevention Week' between 11 May and 17 May. Senior police officials appealed for public co-operation in ferreting out the secret agents who lurked everywhere; foreign powers had eyes in the sky, and ears under every *tatami*. A rash of colourful posters in Tokyo exhorted soldiers and civilians alike to refrain from careless talk, with slogans such as 'Beware of spies!' and 'Spy prevention – something anybody can do!'

These campaigns were mere bluster, as far as Sorge was concerned, an irritation rather than a real threat. During 'National Spy Prevention Week', the chiefs of the neighbourhood associations, *tonarigumi*, were under orders to report to police on all visitors to foreigners' houses. Sorge took the precaution of cancelling all meetings with Ozaki and Miyagi until the brouhaha was over. For a few febrile days, it was wiser than ever for a Japanese to steer clear of foreigners.

In the past six years, Ozaki and Sorge had met in restaurants every month or so. Occasionally, they dined or lunched at the Ritz in Hibiya, Lohmeyer's in Nishi-ginza, or the Asia restaurant in the South Man-churian Railway building, where Ozaki worked. However, Sorge was fond of Japanese food, so his attentive host would reserve a room at one of his favourite *ryotei*, high-class restaurants like the Kagetsu in Tsukiji, the Izumi in Takanawa and the Saganoya in Atagoyama. These establishments offered a degree of privacy. But as the spy paranoia intensified, the serving-girls developed a worrying habit of querying Ozaki, in the politest manner, about the identity of his blue-eyed *gaijin* guest. Apparently, they were given orders by the police to report on meetings between Japanese and foreign clients.

At the end of 1940 Sorge and Ozaki decided the time had come to change their routine, in order to avoid this tiresome scrutiny. Sorge's house in Nagasaka-cho offered greater privacy, and they met here at intervals of two or three weeks. Soon after the outbreak of the war between Germany and Russia they began to meet each week, on Mondays at Sorge's home, with the Asia restaurant as an alternative rendezvous.

§ In the first light of morning on Thursday 15 May Sorge drove to the embassy as usual to compile the German community's newsletter,

Deutscher Dienst. The little blue Datsun groaned up the steep slope past the prime minister's official residence, then accelerated easily along the avenue behind the new Diet building, the empty shell of Japan's moribund democracy. At the embassy the gate-keeper, seeing the familiar face, waved him through, and he drove round to the parking area between the Old and New Chanceries. Here Sorge was completely at home. He knew every corner of the offices, the ambassador's residence, the out-buildings and the surrounding garden, those trim lawns and flower-beds shaded by maples, pines and cherry trees. Only the most senior diplomats were fortunate to have homes in the tranquil compound. Apart from the ambassador's grand mansion, two smaller houses were reserved for the minister and the head of Chancery.

The various departments of the embassy were divided among four buildings, mostly deserted at this hour. The economic section, headed by Dr Alois Tichy, was located in the west corner of the compound. From here a path ran behind the servants' quarter, which lay at the rear of the ambassador's residence, to the premises of the service attachés – military, navy, and airforce. Then came the New Chancery, which housed the political section under Hans Ulrich von Marchtaler, the administration section, and the first-floor cipher room, which handled the cable traffic.

A little way beyond, the path forked and widened. To one side lay the garages for the official cars and the rear entrance of the compound, a well-trodden route to the adjacent War Ministry. Straight ahead was the Old Chancery, a red-brick building that resembled a German post office in Kaiser Wilhelm's era.

This was where Sorge worked when he wore his official hat. It was the ambassador's idea to employ Sorge part-time in the press section. At first he resisted – everything bureacratic went against his grain. Then, in September 1939, when war broke out in Europe, he gave in to Ott's urging that he serve the fatherland by editing the *Deutscher Dienst.*

The post provided a number of advantages. It gave him official – though not diplomatic – status, a generous salary and useful perks such as a gasoline ration, when restrictions forced Japanese drivers to turn to inefficient substitutes like charcoal. In addition, the position gave him the formal imprimatur he lacked even as the ambassador's closest confidant, all-important from the bureaucratic standpoint, and an unassailable pretext to wander around the embassy at odd times of the day and night.

Sorge went up the gloomy staircase to the press section on the first floor. The ground floor, silent at this hour, was occupied by the library, the radio attachés and the cultural section – bailiwick of Reinhold Schulze, the most senior-ranking Nazi in Japan. (As principal regional leader, *Obergebietsführer*, of the Hitler Youth, he was only one rung beneath Baldur von Schirach, youth leader of the Reich.[6]) All the embassy staff were '*Pgs*' (*Parteigenossen*, members of the Nazi Party), either from conviction or necessity. Party membership was a condition of employment in the bureaucracy of the Third Reich.

Sorge went up the dimly lit staircase to the press section, the responsibility of Count Mirbach, sleek, haughty, and a keen Nazi who despised the 'riff-raff' that had flocked to join the party only after Hitler's rise to power. He was also scornful of Sorge, who, he told friends, lacked refinement, culture and talent as a journalist.

By the time Sorge arrived, Claus Lenz, the overnight news monitor, had gone off duty. His job was to watch the *Hellschreiber* (ticker-tape machine) in the *Funkraum* (radio room) and tear off the news items – the German Army Report, Italian Army Report and German News Service dispatches – as they trickled in. By dawn, there was a pile of these papers waiting for Sorge to cut and paste, a task that did not tax the intellect.

The material had to be condensed into the four-page *Deutscher Dienst,* which was intended for German nationals in Japan. The army report with news of the war against Britain (and, before long, Russia as well) went in unedited, and there was also home-town news about freak storms and railway accidents. However much Sorge disparaged it, this little bulletin filled a need: the German missionary in Hokkaido, the engineer in Nagoya, the shipping agent in Kobe eagerly awaited the arrival of this link to home.[7] After editing, which took only an hour or so, the pages were ready for photostatting when the Japanese staff arrived. Then it was time for breakfast with the ambassador, which had become almost a daily routine.

On this Thursday, the sky was blue, with a few clouds intermittently flushed away by a cool wind, and they took up their favourite position on the small lawn beside the ambassador's office. (In bad weather they would sit in the plant-filled conservatory, to the left as you came in through the main entrance of the residence.) As the house-boy served coffee and fresh rolls delivered by the German bakery, Sorge briefed Ott on the overnight news that had rolled in over the printer. This was followed by a discussion of the latest confidential messages from Berlin decoded by staff members in the cipher room.

At around nine o'clock, when the ambassador went off to the morning conference of department heads, Sorge passed by the residence for a word with the ambassador's wife. As he went into the entrance hall, a middle-aged woman, a stranger, emerged suddenly from one of the rooms. For a moment they stood, awkwardly, eyeing each other, but then Helma Ott came into view – she had been rummaging in the storage room under the staircase. 'Ah, you don't know one another. Sorge – Mrs Harich-Schneider.'[8]

Sorge did know the name. Margareta Harich-Schneider was an acclaimed harpsichordist in Europe, and her concerts earned high praise in the arts pages of the *Frankfurter Zeitung*. He studied her with curiosity, taking in the slender figure, glowing complexion, rose-bud lips and pert nose, the eyebrows that arched quizzically. Sorge, who wore an open-necked white shirt and crumpled trousers, bowed with exaggerated formality and a theatrical smile. 'Not a completely unknown name,' he said, elongating every syllable for effect. Then he turned to the door and hurried away.

Margareta – or Eta, as she preferred to be known – was puzzled by this odd behaviour. Even more intriguing were his looks: the sharp furrows between the nose and the corners of his mouth, the high cheekbones, the prominent forehead. A striking face, she thought, with something demoniacal about it. She was also impressed by the infinite depth of his blue eyes, noting that they darted restlessly from side to side, perpetually vigilant.

'Who's that interesting man?' Eta asked Mrs Ott.

'A journalist – *Frankfurter Zeitung*,' said the ambassador's wife, adding sharply, 'He doesn't have any interest in women.'

Why ever did Helma think to impart this information about a complete stranger? Eta thought to herself. The curious remark stuck in her mind and coloured her opinion of Sorge, until it eventually dawned on her that the ambassador's wife had stood the truth on its head.

§ Erich Kordt, who had just arrived in Japan, would not easily forget his first encounter with Richard Sorge, which happened in the middle of National Spy Prevention Week. The newly appointed minister at the German Embassy bumped into Sorge at around midnight in the Imperial Hotel, as he was about to take his leave of a fellow German diplomat and retire to bed.

'I want to introduce you to Dr Sorge,' Kordt's companion said, spotting the journalist at his usual table in the lobby bar.[9] Kordt knew the name and something of the man's reputation already: Sorge was said to be a man who loved women and drink and despised convention. Even so, he was taken aback to find that the leading German journalist in Tokyo was an unkempt figure, reeking of alcohol, and, tonight at least, in a fiercely combative frame of mind.

Almost at once Sorge tried to provoke an argument, pouring scorn on Foreign Minister Ribbentrop's attempts to embroil Japan in Germany's war with Britain. Sorge had discovered that Ribbentrop had sent his subordinate to Tokyo with instructions to incite Japan to strike against the British Empire in Singapore, an endeavour in which Ott and his staff had failed completely. Barely were they introduced than Sorge expressed the view that Kordt would have no more success than the ambassador. 'The Japanese are not going to move against Singapore just to please you people in Berlin. They may be pirates, but they're not going to do you the favour.' Then he had a word of advice for Kordt, as a newcomer to Japan. 'The Japanese are not so simple to fathom, my friend, but I know one thing for sure. Next week will decide whether they get back together with the Americans or not.'

Matsuoka, the foreign minister, had nailed his flag to the mast of the Axis. He was firmly committed to Germany. Prime Minister Konoye was not, and wanted above all to avoid trouble with the United States.

Sorge told Kordt that Tokyo's recently appointed ambassador to Washington, Admiral Nomura, was engaged in talks with the US State Department in an attempt to steer relations away from their present collision course. At the moment this was a higher priority for Japan than its alliance with Germany.

Kordt was astonished. This was the first he had heard about the Japan–US dialogue, and the idea that the Japanese were secretly trying to do a deal with the Americans struck him as absurd.[10]

'Allow me to suggest, Herr Doktor Sorge, that you are completely mistaken. I cannot believe that the Japanese government is negotiating with the Americans behind our back! That would make nonsense of the Three Powers Pact.'

'Yes, this is beyond you, I know!' said Sorge, rudely.

That he took an instant dislike to the diplomat we know from Sorge's remarks to friends. Kordt was everything that Sorge despised – a sleek, cautious, career-minded bureaucrat, Foreign Minister Ribbentrop's boy, an unquestioning servant of the Thousand-Year Reich.

Kordt refused to believe that Japan would stray from the Three Powers Pact, the cornerstone of its foreign policy. At this stage he assumed that Dr Sorge's talk about Japan and America seeking a settlement was a groundless rumour – and he said as much. Sorge replied:

Just wait, *Herr Gesandte* [envoy]! I can give you all the details the week after next. Not this week – this is spy-week, and every *tonarigumi* (neighbourhood association) is obliged to report to the police on the movements of foreigners, and the people they meet.

   Because of that my friends will wait until next week to come to see me. When spy-week is over, nobody will bother in the least who comes to my house. You see, the Japanese are even bigger bureaucrats than you people in Germany!

If Sorge was trying to give offence that night, he was wholly successful. He came over as a 'proper braggart', Kordt recorded later, noting that Sorge's intake of cognac may have made him more argumentative than usual. Yet Sorge's blue eyes were still fresh and alert after hours of drinking, a fact that the diplomat could not help but admire.[11]

That first, negative impression would linger until the very end, but Kordt soon came to accept that Sorge was indeed a first-rate authority on Japan, as colleagues had assured him. Soon after that first meeting Sorge, true to his word, came to the minister's office and offered useful insights into Japan's secret talks with America. The ambassador too obtained much of his information about the secret Japan–US talks from Sorge, confirming Ott's opinion of him as 'the man who knows everything'.

The risk that Japan and America might improve their tense relations greatly unsettled Ott. He discovered (almost certainly through Sorge) that America was applying pressure on Japan to withdraw from the Axis. Suspicions of skulduggery by the Japanese were reinforced by their attempt to keep the Germans in the dark about the negotiations in Washington. Mortified by this turn of events, Ott asked Foreign Minister Matsuoka for assurances that Japan still stood firmly by the Three Powers Pact.[12]

Unknowingly, Ozaki was a German informant at one remove, providing the intelligence that Sorge used to enhance his standing among German officials. His inside knowledge of the Japanese government's America policy stood Sorge in good stead. For some months in 1941, Germany's intelligence on the progress of the Japan–US dialogue was refracted through the medium of a Soviet spy. By alerting Ott and Kordt to secret deals between the Japanese and the Americans, Sorge also helped to poison the atmosphere in the Axis. The shakier the basis of trust between Tokyo and Berlin, the less effectively their alliance could work against Soviet interests.

A diplomat serving at the German Embassy in 1941 confirms that Sorge kept the German side informed about the negotiations, which were held principally in Washington: 'We learnt a little about them from the American press, something from our ambassador in Washington, and a good deal too from Richard Sorge.'[13]

§ The Russians had their own reasons for following the development of Japan's relations with America. Sorge and Ozaki kept a close watch, though not until September were they free to devote their full attention to this subject. It was Ozaki's opinion that – whether Tokyo and Washington patched up their differences or came to blows – the Soviet Union could only benefit. He explained:

> If Japan and the US reach an accord, this will distance Japan from Germany. And then Japan will be careful not to antagonize the Soviet Union. On the other hand, if the talks break down, it follows as a matter of course that Japanese forces will advance towards the South. And if this brings Japan into conflict with America and Britain, then the Soviet Union will be spared from a Japanese attack.[14]

In Sorge's view, this analysis was overly optimistic.

> That may be so. But relations between Tokyo and Washington can only improve if the Japanese agree to at least a gradual troop withdrawal from China. Let's say that to satisfy the Americans, Japan succeeds in making peace with the Chungking government. In that case, the Japanese army could scale down its troop strength, and might turn northwards, against the Soviet Union.

This was the nub of Moscow's concern in the Japan–US negotiations. As long as half the Japanese army was tied down by fighting in China, the danger of an attack on Russia was much reduced. In this sense, a settlement of the protracted 'China Incident' was not desirable for Russia. Consequently, along with his other duties, Sorge was obliged to pay close attention to every blow in the shadow-boxing between Japan and America.

§ Sorge also reported on the Japan–US talks to Berlin, to the head of the German News Agency, Wilhelm von Ritgen. In turn, the reports were read by the German Intelligence Service. Walter Schellenberg, director of the foreign intelligence section of the German Security Headquarters set great store by this material:

> Sorge's intelligence material grew more and more important to us, for in 1941, we were very keen to know more about Japan's plans concerning the United States. Already Sorge had predicted that the Three Powers

Pact would prove of little real – meaning military – value to Germany. And after the beginning of our campaign in Russia he warned us that in no circumstances would Japan renounce her non-aggression pact with the Soviet Union.[15]

Sorge's relationship with German Intelligence is intriguing. Beyond Schellenberg's account, and some suggestive clues, there is only supposition. But if we have no certain knowledge, a plausible case can be made out that Sorge was gradually drawn into the web of German espionage by dint of the official assignments he accepted. What little evidence there is indicates that he received payments from the German Security Service, High Command, and the German News Agency (which by 1941 was effectively a branch of German Military Intelligence), as well as the German Foreign Ministry.

It is ironic to reflect that German army and security officials were warmer in their appreciation of Sorge's services than his masters in Moscow; and reluctant to dispense with him even when suspicions about his true loyalties surfaced.[16]

§ The ambassador was afraid that Sorge was going off the rails. A number of car accidents, when he drove drunkenly into walls and telegraph poles, had come to the attention of the embassy. Ott was told of shouting matches between Sorge and staunch Nazis, which sometimes led to fisticuffs, when politics were discussed. The ambassador was terrified that the higher authorities in Berlin might get wind of the wild antics of the journalist who held a position of trust in the embassy. Ott reckoned that Sorge's increasingly erratic behaviour stemmed from a brain addled by alcohol, aggravated by a nervous condition attributable to the devastating motorcyle accident in 1938. Whatever the cause, he had to protect his own position. There were two senior Nazi functionaries on his staff, in addition to the Gestapo man Meisinger, and Kordt, who he suspected was Ribbentrop's spy in Tokyo. Fretful and insecure, Ott felt they were all waiting for him to put a foot wrong.

Some time in May, he made a half-hearted attempt to get Sorge out of the way before a really serious scandal erupted. Prince Albert von Urach, a family friend, was staying at the residence, and the ambassador asked him into his study and sought his help:

Something has to be done about Sorge. The man's drinking harder than ever, and he seems like a nervous wreck these days. This not only reflects badly on the embassy; I worry that something unpleasant might occur. It goes without saying that one's first concern is for the good name of the embassy.

What I propose is this: when you go home, you take Sorge with you.
I will do what I can to see that he is given a good press position in
Berlin. You and he are good friends, and I suggest you travel home
together.[17]

Urach was about to leave Japan. Ott, alerted to the approaching hostilities between Germany and the Soviet Union, had insisted that he make
haste to return home.

The prince was on excellent terms with Sorge: on a previous visit he
had slept on his sofa, and had taken the hospitality to include the right
to fondle Hanako, to his host's annoyance. But he knew of Sorge's
violent antipathy towards Nazism, and saw little chance of persuading
him to exchange his unfettered existence in Tokyo for the harsh restrictions of wartime Germany. Reluctantly, he agreed to try.

The result was as expected. Sorge drank the whisky provided by the
ambassador, and sent Urach back to Ott with his answer: No thank
you, nothing would tempt him back to that great concentration camp,
Germany![18]

The ambassador looked dismayed. The Prince asked, politely, why
he had not approached Sorge himself.

'Mr Ambassador, you and Sorge are always together, I would respect-
fully suggest that you could argue the case more convincingly than
someone like myself who knows just how bad things are in Germany
in wartime. Could you not talk to him yourself?'

Ott shook his head.

'I can't do that! I'm his friend!'[19]

This was the dilemma. The ambassador feared that his good friend
and trusted adviser was becoming a liability, but he lacked the will and
rigour to make a clean break, as duty and good sense dictated. Time
would tell that had he handled the problem more determinedly in May
1941, a great calamity would have been averted.

After the abortive attempt to send him home, Ott went on as before,
pretending all was well. His concern about Sorge's mental equilibrium
in no way undermined his faith in his friend's loyalty. This is clear from
subsequent events. Soon after the awkward episode, he dispatched Sorge
as his personal envoy to Shanghai, and entrusted him with the embassy's
highly confidential code-book.

Like the ambassador, Hanako also witnessed wild swings in Sorge's
moods. One night in May, she heard muffled sobbing and found him
curled up on the sofa in the study, clasping his head in his hands. She
was taken aback. Never before had she seen him in such a state; it
astonished her to see a grown man weeping. She went over, knelt beside

him, and he rested his head in her lap, writhing as if in agony. 'Be like a *"mama-san"*' he begged. Perplexed, Hanako caressed his arms and back soothingly, until he grew calmer. After a while he lifted his head, and looked up at her, appealingly like a child. What was wrong? she asked.

'*Sabishii* [lonely],' Sorge said in a pathetic voice.

'Why lonely? I don't understand.'

'I have no friends.'

'What do you mean? You have Ott-san, Weise-san, Clausen-san. You do have friends,' she said. In fact, she suspected that he had other women friends as well – she had once found a photo of Mrs Ott lying around the house – but this was not the time to bring *that* up.

Sorge refused to be consoled.

'No real friends,' he persisted. 'I have no real friends in this world.'[20]

In these episodes we find clues to Sorge's mental state in the spring of 1941; the conclusion must be that the strains of flitting between light and shadow, as spy, journalist and embassy auxiliary for over seven years, are affecting his stability. The dashing, confident, self-sufficient operator of the early 1930s is no more. In his place, we see evidence of a self-pitying, neurotic, solitary man.

There is a self-destructive urge in his fierce drinking bouts. No doubt the anguish is compounded by disturbing hints that his superiors in Russia distrust what he is sending them, and are ignoring his warnings of an impending German invasion. There is a shrill tone to some of the messages arriving from the Fourth Department. If his stock is so low in Moscow, what does the future hold for him? Germany is like a huge concentration camp, Japan an island of solitude, and Russia a dubious prospect for a spy who has fallen from favour.

As the summer wore on, he was to seriously consider escaping to Shanghai, perhaps the best bolt-hole of all. In May, when he was sent to China on embassy business, he had an opportunity to flee, but did not seize it.

§ On 17 May – a Saturday – Richard drove to the Foreign Ministry to pick up a temporary diplomatic pass. He was travelling to Shanghai on embassy business, at the urgent bidding of Ambassador Ott.

Ott was worried. He knew that Japan and the United States were seeking a diplomatic solution to the growing crisis in their relations. The main source of friction was Japan's military grip on China; if Japan agreed to withdraw its troops from China, much of the tension between Tokyo and Washington would dissolve. Despite assurances to the contrary from Matsuoka, Ott feared that Japan would indeed loosen its links to the Axis – even pull out of the alliance – to appease the Americans.

The ambassador had learnt that Japan was asking the United States to use its influence with the Chungking government to mediate in the conflict in China. This was highly disturbing news, though it seemed unlikely that the Japanese army in China – however much it wanted to end the war – would agree to any move by the Konoye government to bring the Americans into the peace process.

All in all, Ott was perplexed by the latest developments, and turned, as usual, to the man he always relied on when he was in a fix. 'I would be grateful if you would make a quick trip to Shanghai to report to me on the mood in various Japanese circles in China,' Ott said. 'Try to find out what they think about these rumours that the Americans will be invited to act as peace mediators.'[21]

§ Before leaving, Richard completed two dispatches for Moscow. Both are dated 19 June, and from the original telegrams we see that they were transmitted by Clausen two days later. In the first message, he warned that the German invasion might begin before the end of the month:

> New representatives who arrived here from Berlin said the war between Germany and USSR may start at the end of May, because they are under orders to return to Berlin by then. However, they also said that it is possible the danger may blow over in this year. They reported that Germany has nine army corps composed of 150 divisions.[22]

The second message dealt with the Japan–US negotiations and their implications for Germany:

> According to Otto [Ozaki] and German ambassador Ott's sources, USA proposed, through [US ambassador] Grew, to Japan that they establish a new friendly relationship. USA offered to mediate between Japan and Chungking on basis of Japan's troop withdrawal, to recognize Japan's special position in China, and grant favoured commercial status.
>
> USA also offered to give special treatment to Japanese economic demands in South Pacific. However USA demanded Japan stop encroachment in South Pacific and effectively renounce Three Powers Pact.

Sorge also told Moscow that the Japan–US talks had gone ahead during Matsuoka's absence in Europe, and that, much as he might have wanted to, he could do nothing to reverse the process. Nor was Matsuoka able to help when Ambassador Ott approached him yet again with a German request that Japan attack Singapore. The foreign minister would have liked to oblige his German friends, but he was powerless to do so in the face of opposition from his fierce rival, Baron Kiichiro Hiranuma, the home minister, and the navy:

> Agitation for Japan–USA negotiations was widespread by the time Matsuoka returned home. Thus it was too late for Matsuoka to take firm stance against USA, and comply with German request concerning attack on Singapore.
>
> Intense struggle taking place between the active faction and faction advocating wait-and-see. Leaders of latter group are Hiranuma and navy. Navy will only begin to move after capture of Suez Canal, but likely to delay taking action.
>
> Matsuoka was optimistic when he spoke to Ambassador Ott about this internal struggle.

Sorge concluded the dispatch by relaying how the ambassador expected Japan to react in the event of hostilities. Ott thought that Japan might indeed intervene, but only if Russia were defeated, and Soviet strength in the Far East diluted by troop transfers from Siberia to the western front:

> Ott learnt that Japan will remain neutral for first few weeks in case of German–Soviet war. However Japan is likely to begin military action against Vladivostok in case of Soviet defeat.
>
> Japanese and German military attachés are maintaining watch on westward transfer of Soviet troops from the Far East.[23]

§ Japan Air Transport operated a daily service from Tokyo to Shanghai, via Osaka and Fukuoka. The flight left Haneda Airport, weather permitting, at 6.30 a.m. and was scheduled to arrive at 2.50 p.m. A leaflet attached to the ticket advised passengers: 'Please go to the toilet prior to flight as some aircraft do not have toilets. Sandwiches will be served.'

Shanghai held many fond memories for Richard. It was here, in 1930, that he had first fallen under the spell of the Orient. Here lay the roots of his compulsion to grasp the mysteries of an ancient and complex civilization. And it was here, in these teeming, clattering streets, that he sensed the exhilaration of developing his own espionage operation and exercising his own judgement, relatively free from Moscow's interference.

With friends and press colleagues in Tokyo, Richard made no secret of his sympathy and affection for the Chinese, and the deep revulsion he felt at Japanese aggression. But his true feelings were not allowed to intrude when he wrote newspaper articles or dealt with the bureaucracy.

In Shanghai he assumed the 'sincere' demeanour appreciated by the Japanese and, armed with recommendations from the German consul-general, made the rounds of the Nipponese establishment – the Consulate-General, army and navy commands, and business community.

Sorge found the Japanese in a defiant mood, as anticipated:

> About ninety per cent of them were categorically opposed to peace mediation, and said that if Prime Minister Konoye and Foreign Minister Matsuoka tried to push it through, they would meet with fierce opposition. I got the impression from this that the Japan–US negotiations were doomed to fail.[24]

Sorge's feet could hardly have touched the ground on that brief trip to Shanghai, so full was his schedule of official calls. Of his other engagements, we know only that the visiting *Frankfurter Zeitung* man was the guest of honour at a dinner offered by the German News Agency chief, and that he was invited for tiffin at the house of a young diplomat, Erwin Wickert – who recalls that Sorge flirted outrageously with his new bride.[25]

Sorge did not have to wait until returning to Tokyo to relay his findings to Ott. He sent Ott a coded telegram describing the atmosphere, and giving his analysis – which Ott must have read with a feeling of relief. The ambassador relayed this report to the German government 'without altering a single letter'.[26]

It will be recalled that Sorge was familiar with German embassy and army codes since at least 1936, when Senior Military Attaché Ott sought clarification from German Army Headquarters about the secret talks that led to the anti-Comintern pact. On that occasion he entrusted Sorge, rather than any of his embassy colleagues, with the drafting of the message, using the army code. Now, as the ambassador's personal emissary in Shanghai, Sorge was authorized to communicate with the Tokyo embassy in code.

Code-books and cipher tables – the keys to protected communications – were kept locked up in the embassy's cipher room in the New Chancery building, which was supposedly as secure as a bank vault. But Sorge was allowed to use these materials for official assignments. It stretches the imagination to suppose that these coveted keys were not spirited out of Japan and passed on to Moscow's code-breakers.

That Sorge was given a sensitive mission, and access to the codes, in May 1941 raises an intriguing question. The inference must be that the ambassador was unaware of the German Security Service's suspicions about Sorge's true allegiance, which dated back to 1940. If Ott was being kept in the dark, then we may conjecture that it was because the Gestapo, in the shape of Colonel Meisinger, had instructions to maintain close watch on the head of mission – just as Ott feared.[27]

§ The daily flight from Shanghai, the 1941 timetable of Japan Air Transport shows, stopped at Fukuoka and Osaka, before arriving at Haneda at 4.30 p.m. We believe that Sorge took that flight on Tuesday 27 May; it is certain that he dined that evening at the German ambassador's residence.

At the dinner table with the Otts and Sorge were Eta Harich-Schneider, who was the ambassador's house-guest, and the German consul-general in Kobe, Herr von Balzer. Something about the harpsichordist had sparked his interest, and before leaving that evening he discreetly invited Eta to come for a drive the following afternoon.

This was the night when the stunning news about the loss of the *Bismarck* reached the embassy. British naval aircraft had crippled the 35,000-ton warship – which Chancellor Hitler had launched only a few months earlier – with aerial torpedoes; the pride of the German fleet had been finished off by British naval guns. The naval attaché, Paul Wenneker, would have passed on the bulletin, which arrived at 8 p.m., to Ambassador Ott without delay. It came as a shock to everyone. The mood in the embassy the next day was dark, as Wenneker recorded in his war diary.[28]

Japanese newspapers headlined the dramatic naval battle in the North Atlantic. The reports emphasized that the Germans had faced an overwhelming British naval force, and that the loss of the *Bismarck* was outbalanced by the sinking of the British battle-cruiser *Hood* – 'the largest warship in the world'. In any event, it was a significant dent in Germany's armour; perceptive Japanese took note that Hitler was taking an awfully long time to make good his boast of bringing Britain to its knees. We can imagine that Sorge cheered inwardly: any setback for Hitler was heartening news.

Wednesday brought condolences from the Japanese navy, and by the end of the week the embassy's mail-bag was full of letters of sympathy from Japanese citizens and schoolchildren, some enclosing donations for German sailors' families. 'Put into the petty cash box,' the naval attaché noted in the diary.[29]

§ The afternoon of Wednesday 28 May, when Richard took Eta on a whirlwind tour of Tokyo, was warm and sunny. Since arriving in mid-May, Eta had seen little of Tokyo beyond the embassy compound. The

Otts' residence depressed her – the endless gossip, the intrigues, and the family rows that she could not help hearing. So she was delighted by Richard's offer of an excursion – so pleased that the warning about his madcap driving could not deter her.

'Are you sure you want to put your life in Sorge's hands?' Anita Mohr had asked over lunch. Anita, a striking, flirtatious blonde in her early thirties, was Helma's constant companion, and Eugen Ott was head-over-heels in love with her. Eta had learnt this from Helma, and, much to her distaste, was then forced to listen to the sorry story of the breakdown of the Otts' marriage. For the past six years, the couple had slept in separate bedrooms. It was the sort of intimate confession that Eta preferred to be spared.

'It's heavenly to be out of the embassy compound, and actually get close to people,' she said, as Richard sped through the streets, swerving among the bicycles and slithering over the tramlines. 'You feel so remote from the real world when you're driven in the ambassador's car.'[30]

'You've been here two weeks, and they haven't shown you anything, have they?' Richard said. 'That's because they know nothing about this place themselves. What an unimaginative bunch! They kept you playing music for them all the time, I suppose?'

'I don't mind that. The Otts are charming towards me.'

Richard, taking his eyes off the road, leant towards Eta and stared at her fiercely. 'Charming? Charming, unimaginative, unprincipled people.'

He braked suddenly, and they jumped out, at the foot of the steep flight of stone steps below Atago Park. Noticing that Eta was short-sighted, he placed a protective arm on her shoulder as they climbed.

His limp was very noticeable, and he made fun of it. 'The Kaiser took two centimetres from my leg, and gave me an Iron Cross,' he told her. Yet she was struck by how nimbly he moved his body. They counted out each step in chorus until they reached the park, a good vantage point to view the city. Beneath them, a dense mass of little houses, broken by a handful of higher structures, stretched monotonously to a muddy flatland bordering Tokyo Bay.

'Ugly!' Eta exclaimed. 'It does look a mess. Uglier than Naples, even.'

They caught their breath, drank cups of weak green tea at a tiny stall, then made their way back down the steps. As they drove across Tokyo, Sorge pointed out temples and monuments and displayed his knowledge of Japanese history. Eventually they arrived at a cemetery – Eta did not catch the name – and strolled over to a little enclave where foreigners were buried, segregated from Japanese in death as in life. There was a pleasant grove of cherry trees, which had lost their blossoms by now, and a grassy area, and here they rested for a while in the warm sunshine. Richard nodded towards the foreigners' tombstones.

'The first Europeans butchered by the Japanese are buried here,' he said. 'Now they don't kill us with their swords, but in their hearts they hate us just as much. They smile, and behave politely, but don't be fooled! Their most ardent wish is that we all go home. But they can't drive us out, because they need European techniques to develop their industries and our markets to sell their wares.

'They wear a mask of courtesy, but even that is wearing thin. When I came to Japan eight years ago, they were much more tolerant of foreigners. But now – the malevolence towards whites! We Germans are supposed to be on the same side, but the fact is most Japanese make no distinction, and they don't like us any more than they do the English and Americans. Not long ago there was quite a fuss over a German woman who was slapped by someone in a train – not because she was German, but because she was white.

'It's not surprising really. They're breast-fed on chauvinism, and conditioned to think of themselves as a divine race, from which it follows that Japan has a holy duty to rule Asia – and the rest of the world as well if we let them get their hands on it.

'In place of the Nazis' ideology, the Japanese rulers have the "Way of the Gods" to bolster their ineffable superiority. All policies have a divine sanction from a sacred throne inherited from the first emperor, Jimmu, who began to rule 2,601 years and three months ago. Not even the Nazis have this kind of holy authority for their master-race super-state. It must make Hitler green with envy!'

Eta listened like a good pupil. When Richard, didactic as always, paused for breath, she inserted just one question, about the emperor of Japan. What sort of man – or god – was he?

'The emperor? The biggest brothel-owner in the country! But the Japanese are infinitely patient. More than half are farmers with a rice-field the size of your garden in Berlin! They have debts twice as much as what they make in a year. And many of them are so poor they have to sell their daughters to brothel-keepers.'

When Richard tired of lecturing, he wanted to know about her past. Eta gave little away. She told him she had married the well-known writer, Dr Walter Harich, straight after high school, but the marriage was over. Walter had been good to her. Thanks to him she went on to study music – something her father had opposed. They had two daughters, then the marriage went sour, and suddenly she found herself in Berlin, with no job, hardly any musical experience, and two girls to support.[31]

Then – a stroke of fortune – she was asked to play at piano evenings at the International Association for New Music in Berlin. That led to further engagements, and eventually she was in demand. In the past ten years, she'd built a reputation, giving recitals in nearly every major European city.

She did not tell him the full story, how she had escaped from Germany – only to end up as resident musician at the German Embassy in Tokyo. This could wait for another day, when she knew Sorge better. In Hitler's Germany, she had learned to lock up her true feelings, and to assume that even people she knew well might be Gestapo informers. In the German Embassy in Tokyo, she had found the same nervous watchfulness and distrust.

Richard proposed dinner, and it was past sunset by the time Eta returned to the embassy. There was an unmistakeable frostiness in the air. It did not take much imagination to work out the reason for the Otts' grumpiness. By spending an afternoon with Sorge, she realized, she had encroached on a jealously guarded personal domain.

Eta tried to make amends by offering a little concert for Helma, as 28 May happened to be her *Namenstag* (saint's day). Harmony was restored with the help of Bach and Cabezon, and the harpsichord that had just arrived from Germany. But she could not escape an ominous sensation that if she continued to meet 'their' Sorge privately, the Otts would not always be so easy to mollify.[32]

§ Among the guests registered at the Imperial Hotel at the end of May was Lieutenant-Colonel Erwin Scholl, who was stopping in Tokyo en route to a new posting at the German Embassy in Bangkok. He arrived while Sorge was in Shanghai, and would have keenly anticipated the reunion with a friend he had last seen two years before.

As soon as Sorge returned to Tokyo, they went to dinner at the Imperial Hotel. The most likely date is Saturday 31 May. It was a crucial meeting. Sorge was anxious to tease out of his friend the answer to the problem uppermost in his mind. When would Germany move against Russia? By that Saturday he was sure that Scholl had come to Tokyo with instructions to brief the ambassador on the imminent invasion. This was Sorge's dry summary of the dramatic events that weekend: 'Lieutenant-Colonel Scholl conveyed clearly to Ambassador Ott, in total secrecy, that Germany and the USSR were finally to go to war and he should take the necessary measures; and he told me various details about it.'[33]

It was most likely to have been the Friday when the ambassador revealed to Sorge the gist of what Scholl had told him. Although he did not oblige by giving Sorge the precise date, there could be no remaining doubt that the German invasion was only two to three weeks away.

On Friday 30 May Sorge had drafted this urgent message for his controllers:

> Berlin informed Ott that German attack will commence in latter part of June. Ott 95 percent certain war will commence. Following is indirect evidence which I see at the present time:
>
> The technical department of German Air Force in my city [by this Sorge meant Tokyo] received orders to return home without delay.
>
> Ott instructed military attaché not to send any important reports via USSR.
>
> Shipment of rubber through USSR reduced to minimum.
>
> The motives for the German action: because of existence of powerful Red Army, Germany has no possibility to widen the sphere of war in Africa, and has to maintain large army in eastern Europe. In order to eliminate all dangers from USSR side, Germany has to drive off the Red Army as soon as possible. This is what Ott said.[34]

It was in 'a corner of the lobby' of the Imperial – as Sorge said after his arrest – that Hitler's greatest secret was passed by an unsuspecting German officer to a Soviet agent.[35]

Scholl had no reason to doubt Sorge, a fellow veteran of the student battalions of the First World War, and a friend who had obliged on so many occasions by drafting his reports to Berlin. Possibly the two men strolled over to the rear of the lobby to the terrace where tea was served, which would be empty at this hour and out of earshot. Here there was a corner by the windows overlooking the Japanese garden composed of ponds, stone lanterns and bamboo. At a weekend, the Hatano Orchestra would have been in its usual position in the gallery, and Viennese waltzes would have filled the lobby as Scholl gave Sorge details of the coming cataclysm:

'The operation begins on 20 June,' Scholl said. 'There might be a few days' delay, but preparations are now complete. We have 170 to 190 divisions massed on the eastern border. These are all armoured or mechanized divisions. The attack will take place along the entire front, and the main thrust will be directed towards Moscow, Leningrad and, after that, the Ukraine.

'We have sufficient armed forces to smash the Red Army at one blow, and take prisoners. There will be no ultimatum. The declaration of war will come after the start of hostilities. We're confident the Red Army will collapse within two months. The Soviet regime is likely to fall as well. By the time winter comes, the Trans-Siberian Railway will be running and we can link up with Japan.'[36]

One can imagine the emotions this recital must have stirred in Stalin's spy. Hitler was poised to unleash a tide of barbarism, to destroy the Soviet system and crush the Russian people beneath the heel of Nazism. It was a matter no longer of guesswork but of fact, and Sorge had discovered when it would all begin. If he felt a sense of triumph in this moment, it is understandable. If he believed that he alone had the power to save the Soviet Union from disaster, it is surely forgiveable.

Suppressing his excitement, Sorge carried out his promise to give Scholl a 'night on the town'. First the two had dinner at the hotel – possibly in the New Grill, where Sorge liked the Beef Steak à la Chaliapine, a creation of the Imperial's own chefs. Later they did the rounds in Ginza and got outrageously drunk. Whether he had time to sleep that night we do not know. But next morning he was up with the dawn, as usual, and drafted what he believed was the most important dispatch of his intelligence career.[37]

CHAPTER TWELVE

June 1941

EARLY ON the morning of 1 June, Sorge telephoned Clausen's house. The utmost discretion was called for; they had to assume that telephone lines were tapped. Clausen was to come over at once. Nagasaka-cho was close by, so Max could have driven over in a matter of minutes to pick up the draft containing Scholl's information. Sorge undoubtedly impressed on Clausen the extreme urgency of the dispatch, which he hoped would galvanize Russia's leaders to boost massively the nation's border defences.

> Expected start of German-Soviet war around June 15 is based exclusively on information which Lieutenant-Colonel Scholl brought with him from Berlin, which he left on May 6 heading for Bangkok. He is taking up post of attaché in Bangkok.
> Ott stated he could not receive information on this subject directly from Berlin, and only has Scholl's information.[1]

The telegrams released from Russian archives raise an intriguing question. Sorge told police that the invasion date given to him by Scholl was 20 June – just two days out. But in the actual telegram, we see that the date is given as 15 June. (The latter date – one week before the actual outbreak of war – would appear to have reflected Hitler's planning at the time that Scholl set out from Berlin in early May.) When Sorge was interrogated, did he suffer a lapse of memory? Or was he, with the benefit of hindsight, trying to impress his inquisitors by enhancing the accuracy of his report to Moscow?[1]

Obediently, Max encoded the material and transmitted it to Vladivostok later that day. At around the same time he also radioed the 30 May message, conveying the vaguer time-frame for the invasion that the ambassador had given Sorge.

Sorge sometimes called at the Clausens' home, but Max did his best to discourage such visits. His wife Anna wanted as little to do with the chief as possible. Sorge was a dissolute character, in her mind, and she was convinced he would lead her Max into temptation. 'You keep away from women! It will only lead to trouble!' she warned.[2] No doubt she was also concerned that Sorge's wantonness could one day lead to disaster: a jealous woman could lead to the downfall of the ring if Sorge gave something away when his mind was clouded by drink or passion.

There was a more fundamental problem – Max's work for the Tokyo ring. The gradual deterioration in his physical and mental state was causing Anna sleepless nights. The calm, self-disciplined man she had married was growing irritable and edgy, drinking constantly to calm his nerves, and his once robust health was badly undermined. In the spring of 1940 he had suffered a serious heart attack, from which he had recovered, and she was terrified that the strain of his work would cause a relapse. She kept prodding him to tell Sorge that he really needed a rest; what she wanted most was for him to abandon his clandestine activity for Moscow altogether and spend his time running the business instead.

Anna did not bother to conceal her heartfelt dislike of communism and the Soviet Union. When she found out from Edith that Vukelic was trying to persuade his divorced wife to leave Japan for the Soviet Union, Anna urged her to refuse. Life in Russia was hellish, she told Edith, on no account should she and her son settle in that miserable country. Vukelic was not well pleased by Anna's intervention, which Sorge also came to hear about.

To Anna's satisfaction, Max, once a staunch communist, was undergoing a change of heart. He was doing well as a businessman. They lived in a big house, drove around in a Mercedes, and were never short of money. When he mixed with other German merchants who spoke in glowing terms of Hitler's revolution, something rubbed off on him. To use Clausen's own words, 'I was becoming more sympathetic to Hitler's policies.' As his belief in communism was eroded, his enthusiasm for his perilous mission waned. This was reflected in the obstructionism that, unbeknown to Sorge, was grievously affecting the network's communications with the Centre.

§ While Sorge was accomplishing his intelligence coup in Tokyo, Ambassador Ott was spending a restful Whitsun weekend with his family at their seaside house at Akiya. Eta accompanied them, but went her own way, taking long, solitary walks along the deserted sandy beaches. The weather was warm and cloudy, the sea-water still too cool for bathing. Richard, a regular visitor to the Otts' villa, was invited, but pleaded a heavy work-load that obliged him to remain in Tokyo.

Eta's embassy concert on Tuesday 10 June was long remembered as a glittering social event. Senior Japanese politicians, business leaders and military officers, in dinner-jackets or bemedalled uniforms, with their kimonoed wives, turned up in strength. Diplomats from Axis and neutral nations and a sprinkling of prominent German residents were also invited. The proud hosts, the German ambassador and Mrs. Ott, shook hands with the cream of society flowing into the ballroom on the ground floor of the residence.

Soviet Ambassador Constantin Smetanin and several of his staff were among the guests. Sorge, in a white tuxedo, watched the guests filter in to take their seats, and no doubt marvelled at the German ambassador's gall in inviting the Russians on the eve of Hitler's planned invasion of their country. Clearly, Ott's intention was to preserve an air of business-as-usual, for rumours were already circulating of German troop manoeuvres along Russia's borders.

§ On that Tuesday, Rear-Admiral Wenneker, the naval attaché, had sent an important cipher to the Navy High Command in Berlin stating confidently that: 'the Japanese army will not take part in a German–Russian conflict for the foreseeable future because it is evidently not prepared for this. The navy approves such a decision.'[3]

The ambassador had already vouchsafed his view that Japan would remain neutral in a German–Russian conflict for the first few weeks, and this Sorge had duly relayed to Moscow. Possibly, he was given the same analysis by Wenneker, who often passed on confidential information from his Japanese navy sources. From now on, Sorge would be preoccupied by the crucial question of how Japan would react to such a conflagration.

§ One of the works on the programme that evening was Bach's Concerto for Harpsichord and Two Flutes. Eta Harich-Schneider conducted from the harpsichord, grappling with an enthusiastic but largely amateur orchestra. However, an audience starved of musicians of Eta's calibre seemed prepared to overlook any minor imperfections, and the performance was judged a tremendous success.

After the concert, a sumptuous buffet dinner awaited the guests in the adjoining salon. Helma Ott, who had thought up the season of concerts, basked in the praise of her guests. Eta found herself surrounded by admirers, oozing compliments. The portly Soviet ambassador pushed forward to kiss Eta's hand. 'You were wonderful, absolutely wonderful!' said Smetanin. 'I want to thank you for making such beautiful music!' Then she heard someone behind her say: 'You need a brandy!'[4]

Eta turned. Richard Sorge held out a glass for her. She had looked for him in the audience in vain, and was delighted to discover he had come. It was their first meeting since dinner on Whit Sunday, although she had glimpsed him from her window, early some mornings, at the breakfast-table in front of the ambassador's study.

The days had passed in a whirl of rehearsals for embassy concerts, recordings for gramophone records, and more rehearsals for a radio recital. But sometimes she had found herself thinking about Richard, and wondering if he would invite her out again.

At first, she had to admit, the *Frankfurter Zeitung* journalist had not impressed her greatly. His tastes in literature and films seemed to be low-brow, his appreciation of music left much to be desired. Moreover, their outlooks on life were fundamentally opposed. She belonged to the Roman Catholic middle class, which made her, in Richard's scornful terms, a 'pious petty bourgeois'. While she believed in God and an after-life, and in doing good works, Richard was a nihilist who held nothing sacred, and enjoyed life like a glutton because this was all there was.

As she got to know him better, she revised her initial opinion. The nihilism, she decided, was an outer shell shielding a core of humanism. Though his constant sarcasm and scepticism often grated, she preferred to dismiss it as sound and fury. Most remarkable, there was no trace of malice in the man.

What struck her from the outset was the sharp contrast between Richard and the people around him – the German diplomats and businessmen, most of them self-servers and careerists, *Geldmenschen* interested only in money.[5] Among these slippery, smug and stilted Germans, he shone, in her words, 'like a true aristocrat, pure and uncorrupted, natural and spontaneous'.[6] When he confided to her, in unprintable language, how painful it was to associate with such people, she felt an instant rapport. That was exactly how she felt, too.

After one or two drinks, Richard took her arm, drew her to one side, and proposed a nocturnal expedition into the city. 'Let's get away from here,' he said. 'There's a flower festival I want to take you to. You have to relax sometimes, you know!'[7]

Richard quickly wearied of these official receptions, larded with counterfeit smiles and fake flattery. As expected, the Otts did not take kindly to the departure of the star of their gala. Helma looked aggrieved when she spotted Sorge leave at the same time. By around 9 p.m., Eta had changed out of her floor-length gown into something more practical, and came running out to Richard's car. The couple drove away, laughing conspiratorially.

After fifteen minutes or so, they arrived in a quarter of Tokyo where the streets, lit by long chains of paper lanterns, teemed with crowds so dense that they could drive no further. Leaving the car in a quiet, dark alley, Richard took Eta by the arm and, as they walked, made an unexpected confession. 'I am a lonely fellow,' he said, earnestly. 'I have no friends, no one. And the way the political situation is developing – it's so depressing. But your music tonight – that really lifted me up.'

They emerged into a crowded street and edged their way through the throng to a temple precinct where they heard a deep booming noise. Visitors were taking turns to strike a large bell, and throwing coins into a big wooden chest. Richard pushed through the crowd around the bell, clinging to Eta's hand. Swinging a wooden clapper against the bell, he tossed a coin, and she saw his lips move in silent prayer.

'Come on, everybody comes here to pray they'll get rich. Now it's your turn.'

Before leaving the temple, Richard led the way into the main hall, where Buddhist monks were sitting. They both knelt down, and Richard, with a good deal of bowing in the Japanese fashion, proudly introduced Eta to the monks he knew from earlier visits. 'She's a famous musician from Germany. Now she is in Japan to give concerts,' he said in his imperfect Japanese.

They plunged into the mass of people swarming around the stalls laden with flowers, plants and shrubs. Wizened old men and their wives, young women with babies on their backs, soldiers in uniform peered at the wares on offer, haggled earnestly with the stall-holders, or simply looked on and enjoyed the hubbub. Everyone, it seemed to Eta, took pleasure in a festival that provided a short respite from the drabness of wartime conditions.

They examined a number of stalls with bonsai trees. 'They fascinate me, these dwarf trees,' said Richard. 'They are like a metaphor for the Japanese themselves, rigidly trained to suppress their own nature, and turned into artificial, disciplined creatures. Look, I'm going to buy you this wicked little pine.'

They carried their purchases to the car, and Richard suggested that, as it was such a glorious night, they walk for a while. Eta asked if he would like to hear why she had left everything behind in Germany, including two daughters, and set out on a journey that brought her to Tokyo, where she was stranded, without any clear idea what to do next. 'Quite frankly, I'm in a mess,' she said. 'In autumn 1933, I took up teaching at the State Academy for Music, and in two years I was given a full professorship. That's when the problems started. Naturally, my director and the other top people were proper Nazis, and of course, they expected all the teachers to join the Party. I was a state employee, and state employees have an obligation to support the Party, though then it wasn't yet a legal requirement.

'Time and time again the director or someone said, "When are you going to stop being so selfish and causing us so much trouble?" I was considered especially awkward because I stood up for the rights of some of the non-Aryan teaching staff and students who were being given a very hard time.

'Naturally, it was forbidden for Jews to give public recitals. That's where I came a cropper. One of my students was graduating, a Jewish girl, and as usual I put her in a concert, and we had all kinds of people come. She gave a beautiful performance of Rameau and Couperin. As a musical event, it was a resounding success. But naturally, that sort of thing was seen as a sign I was becoming a real *Volksschädling* [someone harmful to the German people].

'Two years ago the Culture Ministry threw me out of the Academy without notice. I kicked up a fuss, even went to court, and the Berlin district court recognized that my dismissal was illegal. But in Germany naked power rules, not the law.

'That wasn't the end. I was designated an 'enemy of the Party, a Roman-casuistic political Catholic, in thrall to Jewry'. There's a mouthful for you! It would be funny, except that enemies of the party have a tendency to disappear and never be heard of again.

'I'm lucky to have dear, dear friends who feel like I do, that the whole German *Volk* community is diseased, and who still have some influence. They decided it was time for me to leave, and made the necessary arrangements for me to come here, and I'm supposed to travel on to South America, if I can get a berth on a ship.

'And for that I need the ambassador's help. The thing is this: he doesn't know the real reason I'm here. He thinks I came to Japan to give my concerts and harpsichord course at the Musashino Music Academy, and when that's over, that I'm going back to Germany on July 11th. I don't know how to approach Ott about this. What do you think I ought to do?'[8]

Richard went over what she had told him, point by point, arriving at a conclusion that brooked no disagreement.

'There's no way you can go back to Germany, even if you wanted to. You'll have to stay here. By July 11th, we'll be in the middle of a war with Russia, so the Trans-Siberian Route is not an option. Besides, it would be far too risky.'

'But I feel such an impostor playing along with all the Nazi palaver at the embassy. I can't be myself.'

Richard squeezed her shoulder.

'An impostor indeed! Look, there are other kinds of impostors there, believe me. Impostoring can sometimes be a merit. For goodness' sake, don't tell Ott about your problem. Ott's a frightened man. He thinks someone is watching him all the time, and that he's finished as ambassador if he puts a foot wrong. Believe me, he won't lift a finger to help you.

'Once he was all right. He was against the Nazis. When he heard he was being appointed ambassador, he asked me whether he ought to accept. I warned him against it. You'll lose your integrity in this post, I told him. And that's what happened. He's become a time-server and careerist. Whatever principles he started out with have gone out of the window long ago.

'Look what he's up to now. He's trying to drag Japan into the war, into Germany's war, to improve Hitler's chances against Britain. It's not that he likes the Nazis or wants them to rule the world. No! He's only doing it for the money. For filthy, despicable money and to advance his career!'[9]

As they walked back to the car, he told her that she could rely on him to sort out her problems, and that now they should simply enjoy the night. They were expected at a party, and it did not matter how late they arrived. A long drive across the deserted city, and they came to the elegant home of Kurt Ludde-Neurath, a secretary in the political department. Three other young German diplomats were among the guests. After red wine and sandwiches, the party moved to Richard's more modest lodgings in Nagasaka-cho, which Eta now saw for the first time.

A great deal of alcohol was consumed, a phenomenal quantity of whisky passing down Richard's throat. In the early hours of Wednesday 11 June, the party broke up and Eta was driven 'home' to the embassy. Their route passed the Soviet Embassy, and here Ludde-Neurath ventured a mischievous jest.

'Well, Sorge? Shall I drive in so we can see your friends?'

Eta was puzzled by the remark; but she would soon discover what prompted it. Sorge advertised his admiration for the Soviet Union with complete disregard for the effect it had on his listeners. In his eyes, Stalin could do no wrong, and the Soviet Union was the best partner Germany could have. Whenever Sorge mounted this hobby-horse, it was all Ambassador Ott could do to stifle a yawn.

An enjoyable night ended on a sour note. They reached the grey stone embassy residence, and then Sorge went out of control. To Eta's intense embarrassment, he began yelling at the top of his voice, 'Mrs Ambassador! Mrs Ambassador!' below their bedroom window, waking up the whole household. A sleepy-eyed houseboy opened the door of the residence, and Sorge gave Eta a good-night hug and staggered back to the car. Eta cringed. In the morning, she apologized for Sorge's rudeness.' He was completely drunk,' she said. That was no comfort to Helma, who was deeply wounded by Sorge's heartless behaviour.[10]

§ By June, Kawai Teikichi had decided that the time had come to start a new life. All his instincts told him that he was under police surveillance. It was impossible to conduct espionage when he was so 'hot'. He decided to ask Ozaki to relieve him of his duties until the danger was over.[11]

A brave man, Kawai had already suffered for his beliefs. His career as a spy began in the early 1930s, when he assisted Ozaki by travelling in northern China and Manchuria to collect information. On his return to Japan in spring 1935, Ozaki gave him a part to play in the Tokyo network, using him as an informant on ultra-nationalist organizations. But in January 1936 he was arrested on a tip-off from one of his former associates, and bundled off to Hsinking, capital of Manchuria, to be charged with passing secrets to the Chinese communists.

Luckily, police interrogators did not ask him about Ozaki and the Sorge ring; and despite severe torture, Kawai maintained a stoical silence about these connections. After his release, Kawai lay low in China for a while, before returning to Japan in autumn 1940 and offering his services to Ozaki once again.

Sorge and Ozaki decided that Miyagi should 'run' Kawai as one of his group of agents, and he was given a monthly payment of 60 to 100 yen a month. This arrangement did not work well. Miyagi was not impressed by the information Kawai brought, considered him something of a sponger, and discouraged him from calling at Ozaki's home. Kawai's stubborn refusal to betray the ring during his detention in Hsinking earned him precious little gratitude, although Ozaki was always supportive.

Around the middle of June, Kawai went to the Mantetsu Building in Toranomon to tell Ozaki that his apartment was being watched, which meant he could be of no more use to the ring. Though aware that he too was under surveillance, Ozaki seemed remarkably nonchalant. 'I don't think the danger has come that close yet. Even if we were to be arrested, it would only be for a year or so. It all depends on the political situation,' he said.

They talked in the New Grill of the Imperial Hotel, over glasses of draught beer, and even here Kawai had the distinct impression that a middle-aged, well-dressed man at the bar counter was showing an abnormal interest in the two of them. Was he the hotel's resident spy? Kawai wondered. Had things come to such a pass that nowhere in Japan could people meet without being observed by the secret police?[12]

That evening, Ozaki invited Kawai to dinner at one of his favourite restaurants in Shimbashi, where they could talk without fear of eaves-droppers. As they chatted and drank sake, Kawai could not help but think that Ozaki's cheerful exterior masked a deep anxiety. Some shadow seemed to have fallen over his ever-optimistic personality.

A few days later, Ozaki used his connections to arrange employment for Kawai at the Greater Japan Paper Recycling Company. From 1 July the cloak-and-dagger life of the *Shina Ronin* (China adventurer) ended, and he became an ordinary salary-man and commuter. Even so, a rabbity fellow with a moustache kept popping up near his home, and on the train to work. Kawai assumed the worst: the *Tokko* had not given up, and he was still being shadowed.[13]

§ Tokyo shimmered in a heatwave in mid-June. A fine, smoky dust rising from the streets made the eyes water and left the throat dry. Richard Sorge knew, with oppressive certitude, that this was the last week of peace. In the embassy, only Ott and the senior military attaché, Colonel Kretschmer, had been officially advised of the timing of the invasion. But the corridors of the German Embassy buzzed with specula-tion. Across the road, the Army General Staff was studying intelligence reports from Berlin and Moscow that indicated the imminence of war. The Japanese press spoke of growing tension between Russia and Germany and reported rumours of troop build-ups and mass evacuations from border areas.

On the sultry night of Tuesday 17 June the whisper of the approaching storm was still too faint to bother the revellers at the German Embassy in Tokyo. A hubbub of excited gossip and laughter filled the ballroom. An orchestra ensconced in the gallery played waltzes by Strauss, while strapping blondes and slender Japanese beauties whirled across the parquet in the arms of tuxedoed partners. Waiters in white livery cruised with trays of champagne and whisky.

Richard Sorge worked his way around the room, pausing at clusters of guests to exchange a few words, bending to kiss the hand of a woman here and there. When a waiter passed, he had a way of plucking a glass from the tray without diverting his eyes from whoever he happened to be chatting with. He drank, but within measure, not, as so often, to the point of melancholy and aggressiveness.

Nothing in his behaviour that night betrayed the tension that unwound in irate outbursts on so many occasions. The 'wild' Sorge was unusually restrained. His energy was released on the dance-floor, and he partnered Eta for the tango 'At the Balalaika'. But for much of the evening they sat in the embrasure of a window opening on to the garden, breathing the sweet fragrance of the *tobera* blossoms as they watched the dancers.

'I've rehearsed six Bach concertos and the Goldberg, and I'm utterly worn out!' said Eta. 'And you're making me tipsy with all this champagne.'

'And Her Excellency is watching us!' said Sorge. Indeed, Helma Ott, wherever she was in the room, had a clear view across the bobbing heads on the dance-floor, and kept glancing in their direction.

'I know. I have a feeling she's always watching me. The Otts have been very kind but – oh, I do wish I could get out of their house and find a place of my own to live! I mean, it's odd, we're both adults, and here I am creeping out through the back gate to meet you in secret as if I were their little daughter.'

'Just keep a distance from the Otts, and from everybody in the embassy. When the cards are down, you'll find you can't rely on any of them. Try to become as independent as possible. Learn Japanese, fluently enough to know how to bribe the police who handle foreigners!'

'Shall I tell you what Mrs Ott said to me, Richard? She said, there's something I ought to know about Sorge. *No* love affair with Sorge lasts very long. It always ends in tears. She said she just wanted to warn me, that was all. It was better I knew *before* I got involved with you.'[14]

§ Three days later, over breakfast, Ambassador Ott told Sorge what he already knew. Hitler would carry the war to the east, to destroy Stalin's regime, and nothing could deflect him from that ambition. The German General Staff had assembled a massive field force for the attack.[15]

The two men were sitting in the conservatory overlooking the garden's bright clusters of blue and mauve hydrangeas. A steady rain was falling, and a faint mist rose from the warm foliage. This was Friday 20 June. Ott's revelation came as no surprise. If Scholl was right, then the German invasion of Russia was due to begin that day.

When Sorge arrived in the press section he would have anxiously scanned the news bulletins, braced for the announcement that hostilities had begun. But nothing of the kind had come in overnight. What he learnt at breakfast simply underlined the warnings already relayed to Moscow. These warnings, Sorge discovered to his horror, had been disbelieved and treated with contempt by his masters. A radio message casting doubt on the veracity of his information had come in not long before. It seemed that Stalin obstinately refused to believe that Hitler was about to tear up the non-aggression pact and march eastwards. As Clausen looked on, Sorge had read the message from Moscow and had flown into a rage.

Even so – and unsure whether it was not already too late – Sorge made one more try at rousing Stalin from his complacency. At some point on 20 June he reported on his breakfast meeting with Ott, adding that the Japanese military regarded war between Germany and Russia as a foregone conclusion.

> The German ambassador in Tokyo, Ott, told me that war between Germany and the USSR is inevitable. German military superiority affords opportunity to destroy the last great army in Europe ... The reason is that the strategic defences of the USSR up to now are even less fit for action than was the case in the defence of Poland.
>
> Invest [Ozaki] told me that the Japanese General Staff is already discussing what position to take in the event of war.[16]

This dispatch was in Clausen's hands by nightfall on Friday, and was transmitted to Vladivostok on Saturday 21 June.

Between 8 and 9 p.m. on Friday Sorge drove back to the embassy. Together with Eta he had hatched a plot to secure access to the Gestapo headquarters, located in the residence building. As he got out of his car, music floated from the open windows of the ballroom – probably Bach's Italian Concerto, which was on the programme that evening. Sorge crossed the foyer and entered the crowded ballroom. Eta, at the harpsichord, was dazzling in a pink evening-gown that draped the stool.

The previous Sunday they had attended a party together, and he had proposed 'one more whisky' at his house. Richard had danced around the hot little study in an exalted state. Drinking steadily, he had become carried away by a vision of himself as the slayer of the German Satan. 'If anyone destroys Hitler, it will be me!' he had shouted. Eta could not stop herself laughing at the megalomania of the *Frankfurter Zeitung* man. 'Yes, if only ...' she began.

It was on that Sunday, one month after their first meeting, that their affair started.[17]

The concert ended in tumultuous applause, and Sorge quickly slid away to avoid being dragged into the cocktail party the Otts had laid on for a few favoured guests. It was a still, warm night and he wandered through the garden, keeping to the shadows, waiting for Eta to emerge.

Inside the ballroom, Eta was being showered with bouquets and compliments. She had difficulty extricating herself – the Otts wanted to show her off to their important guests – and only got away by pleading a desperate need to sleep. She hurried to her room at the end of the corridor, locked the door behind her, and, careful not to switch on the light, changed out of her evening gown. Then she took the key out of the lock. Over the weekend the new police attaché, Colonel Meisinger, would be moving into Eta's suite. When Meisinger had complained that the police attaché's office was too cramped the ambassador, anxious to propitiate this dangerous man, had jumped to offer more spacious accommodation.

Eta would now have to move to a room on the upstairs floor, the Ott family's quarters, where she would enjoy even less privacy. When she told Sorge about the new arrangements, he recognized the heaven-sent opportunity.

'Can you bring me the key? I'll get it back to you in the morning. And don't worry about being upstairs next to the Otts. You can use the servants' staircase, so you can always go in and out the back door, without them seeing you.'

Clutching the precious key, Eta realized that the only way to leave the residence unnoticed was through the window, since the party was now in progress in the foyer. She opened the window and jumped.

She landed awkwardly on a flower-bed, soft and sticky after a day of rain. Picking herself up, she peered into the darkness. Sorge was coming across the lawn; she ran towards him and proudly held up the key between muddy fingers.

They got into his car and sped out of the embassy gate, where chauffeurs were waiting to ferry the guests home. Within minutes they were stopping at the end of the lane in Nagasaka-cho. Sorge, his arm round her shoulder, helped her into the house. He boiled a kettle of water, then wiped away the dirt from her knees, bathed the grazed skin and applied plasters.

'You see! This is what happens when you get mixed up with a gypsy like me!'[18]

The escapade, which thrilled Eta, brought them closer together. She felt now as if they were fellow conspirators pitted against a common enemy – the Nazi system of soulless conformity that spawned monsters like Meisinger, and turned decent people like Ott into unprincipled yes-men.

This was also the night Sorge related the nightmare of the trenches in the Great War, and revealed how the experience had turned him into a communist. He told her about his stint in a coal-mine in the Ruhr, how he had organized communist cells, about the years spent in Moscow, and about the Russian wife, who was 'not really his wife, but considered such', and to whom he was evidently deeply attached. He explained that he was working for the defeat of Hitler, and that he sat at the German ambassador's table only to get information that would serve this cause. This was the most he could reveal; his real reason for coming to Japan could not be explained to anyone.

Eta was a good Catholic who abhorred the godless despotism of Russia, but she shared with Sorge an abomination of Nazism. Much as she admired his courage, however, she found his hubris hard to bear.

'I, Richard Sorge, am going to deal with those pigs in Berlin,' he promised.

'That would be nice,' she said coolly, transparently unimpressed.

That night he let her into one more secret: Hitler was about to go to war with Stalin. It could begin at any moment.[19]

Early the following morning Sorge came to the residence and slipped Eta the key. He had lost no time in making a duplicate. It was Saturday 21 June, summer solstice – a holy day in the Third Reich calendar – and the ambassador was busy composing a eulogy to Hitler in order to edify the German community. In the afternoon a house-boy transferred Eta's luggage to her new room.

Once Meisinger was installed, Sorge could gain admittance with his key whenever he wished. After dinner with the Otts he would make occasional forays into the new Gestapo headquarters, and examine Meisinger's files on troublesome elements in the German community. He waited until the servants were off duty, and had to remember to tread gingerly around one very creaky floorboard on the lower corridor.

Meisinger kept his superiors in Berlin informed about Richard Sorge – their code-name for him was 'Post' – in regular telephone calls to either Walter Schellenberg, head of the overseas section of the Security Service, or Gestapo chief Josef Müller.

Sorge would quickly have worked out that the file labelled 'Post' dealt with his case. No doubt he was relieved and amused to find that Meisinger's reports on him were favourable: 'Post' enjoyed high standing in the German embassy, and also among Japanese government departments. 'Post' belonged to the overseas organization of the Nazi party, Japan section, Tokyo-Yokohama branch, and had volunteered his services as a lecturer at party seminars. Nothing had yet turned up to indicate that 'Post' was anything other than what he seemed: a leading journalist esteemed by everyone of consequence in Tokyo.[20]

§ On Sunday 22 June the summer rains lifted briefly, and Tokyo steamed in intense heat. Richard, smartly dressed in a white linen suit, drove into the embassy grounds shortly before 5 p.m. Eta, in flower-patterned frock and straw hat, came running across the garden, and sprang into the back seat. 'Let's go and booze at the Imperial,' he said. 'I need a drink.'

As they circumnavigated the moat of the emperor's palace, she told him that she had returned from church to find Helma Ott in her room, rummaging through her personal possessions, and about to march off with a bronze bowl and a bonsai tree, both presents from Richard. The ambassador had apologized for his wife's behaviour and had told her about Helma's affair with Sorge. She could not reconcile herself to the fact that it was over, he said, and that was the reason she so bitterly resented other women's relationships with Sorge. As for himself, Ott went on, he had overcome feelings of jealousy and formed a close friendship with Sorge. But unfortunately that had been destroyed, and now all they had in common were political interests.[21]

Richard clearly felt he was to blame for Eta's embarrassment. All he could do was urge her to find a house and live independently from the Otts.[22] They reached the Imperial Hotel at five o'clock, as the bar was opening. She ordered red wine, and Richard a double whisky – the first of many that evening.

Richard regretted Eta's problems with the Otts, but at that moment he was probably preoccupied with weightier matters. The German invasion was under way at last. Shortly after midnight, Hitler's troops had begun the long march east, on a 1,500-mile front extending from Finland in the north to the Black Sea in the south. At 4 a.m. Foreign Minister Ribbentrop notified Lieutenant-General Oshima Hiroshi, the Japanese ambassador in Berlin, that Germany and the Soviet Union had entered into a state of war.

At what point in the day Sorge heard of this is not known, but Tokyo resounded with the news by lunch-time, and when he arrived at the Imperial Hotel in the late afternoon newsboys were on the street with *gaigo* (special editions) that carried the screaming headline: 'Germany attacks Soviet Union!'

Sorge had known what was coming, but was none the less deeply affected by the actual event. Eta, now well aware of his emotional attachment to Russia, knew that nothing she said would console him.

1. Richard Sorge in the First World War, c.1915; aged 19.

2. Katya Maximova (middle, standing) with her two sisters, Tatiana (left) and Maria. Sorge's greatest love(?) Katya waited in vain for his return.

3. Sorge, c.1936.

4. Sorge was accepted everywhere – even at the Imperial Palace. Emperor Hirohito receives Ambassador Dirksen. Sorge looks on, c.1936.

5. Branko Vukelic and Yoshiko hiking, c.1937. (Courtesy of Mrs Yamazaki Yoshiko.)

6. Ozaki Hotsumi. (Kyodo News Agency)

7. Hanako pictured at Sorge's house.

8. Eta Harich-Schneider, c.1939.

9. ABOVE. **Sorge** (second from left) at Meissner's wedding in the German Embassy, 1937. Standing next to Sorge is Mirbach; Military attaché, Ott (fourth from left); Helma (sixth from left); Ambassador Dirksen (third from left, front row).

10. A happy moment as disaster neared ... The German ambassador with Ursula and Podwick. Summer 1941, Karuizawa. (Courtesy of Ursula Ott.)

11. Helma Ott in Karuizawa, 1941. (Courtesy of Ursula Ott.)

12. BELOW. Ambassador Ott with the dazzling Anita Mohr and his son Podwick, 1941. Not long afterwards Podwick volunteered for service on Germany's eastern front. He was killed in action. (Courtesy of Ursula Ott.)

13. ABOVE. German Embassy, c.1941. The ambassador lived on the first floor (Kyodo News Agency).

14. BELOW. Anti-Spy Week, May 1941. Sorge stayed away from his Japanese agents during this campaign, when the phobia about spies reached a peak (Kyodo News Agency).

15. ABOVE LEFT. Max Clausen, the wireless operator who, unbeknownst to Sorge, sabotaged the ring's operations.

16. ABOVE. Anna Clausen, the staunchly anti-communist wife of Max, who wanted her husband to give up his espionage activities.

17. LEFT. Miyagi Yotoku, photographed in prison, 1942.

18. BELOW. Hanako and Yoshiko at Sorge's grave in Tokyo. November 1976.

Wisely, she refrained from relaying Mrs Ott's opinion on the war, shared with Eta and a group of embassy wives over afternoon tea: 'We told the Russians that we need the products of the Ukraine, and if they're not willing to give them to us, we just have to take them for ourselves, that's all.'[23]

Soon after sunset, Eta returned to the embassy to dine with the Otts. Remaining behind at the Imperial Hotel bar, Sorge slid into a morose and aggressive state. Sometime between seven and eight o'clock he went to the public telephone in the lobby and dialled the embassy residence. 'This war is lost,' he shouted over the phone to the startled ambassador. Billy and Anita Mohr and other pillars of the German colony in Tokyo were shocked to receive phone calls from Sorge with the same doomsday message. The Mohrs called the Otts and they pooled their indignation: the man was drunk of course, but this really was going too far.[24]

§ The *Official Guide to Japan* (1933 edition) called the Imperial 'architecturally one of the most interesting hotels in the world', which hardly did justice to Frank Lloyd Wright's curious creation. Travellers compared the outside aspect to an Aztec temple; built in a porous, mustard-coloured stone, the hotel was dank and gloomy, as if hewn from a mountainside. One visitor felt as if he was stepping onto a stage set for the first act of *Aida* when he walked through the doors. And Sorge, so this observer commented, fitted in perfectly – the man was as bizarre as the setting.[25]

The Imperial was the focal point for foreign residents in Japan. Sorge occasionally ate at the New Grill, dozed in an armchair in the lobby, used the escritoire equipped with hotel stationery to write letters, or took up position in the bar, a few steps lower than the main lobby. A visitor entering the hotel remembers his surprise at hearing Sorge's stentorian voice rising from the lower level and echoing round the galleries of the lobby.[26] It was here that Sorge, explosively drunk, was spotted on the night of 22 June by a newcomer to the embassy, the young radio attaché, Erwin Wickert.

After a weekend in the cool uplands of Karuizawa, Wickert had reached Tokyo in the early evening with a companion, the air attaché, Walther von Gronau. On the train, the two had discussed the speculation about an imminent war between Russia and Germany.[27]

The news burst upon them as they passed through the gate to the crowded concourse at Ueno Station, where newspaper-boys were chasing around with the special editions. The two men parted and Wickert

made his way to the Imperial Hotel, his temporary home. He found
Sorge perched on a bar-stool, haranguing the barman and half a dozen
other people, who were staring into their glasses with embarrassment.

Wickert went over to try to calm the journalist.

'A fucking criminal!' Sorge was shouting, in English. 'A murderer!
Signs a friendship pact with Stalin. Then stabs him in the back. But
Stalin will teach the bastard a lesson. You just wait and see.'

The barman waved his hand, vainly signalling him to lower his
voice.

Sorge turned to the young diplomat and said in German: 'I tell you,
he's nothing but a common criminal. Why does nobody kill him? For
instance, some of the army officers?'

Wickert sought to impress on the irate journalist the risk he was
running by cursing 'Hitler and the other criminals' at the top of his
voice in a public place. Anyone might be listening – the English,
Americans, French, Japanese, Gestapo Colonel Meisinger. This did not
seem to worry Sorge, who only grew more excited.

'Meisinger is an arsehole! You're all arseholes!' he shouted.

Anxiously, the diplomat tried to pacify Sorge by drinking with him
for a while.

'And if you think the Japanese will attack Siberia, you all have another
think coming! There your ambassador is completely mistaken!'

When Sorge rose to go to the lavatory, his legs almost gave way.
Wickert decided that he was in no condition to drive home, and asked
at reception if a room was available. Sorge was too drunk and tired to
raise objections. Docile now, he shuffled along the corridor, supported
by Wickert and the lift-boy. He had to rush to the bathroom to vomit,
and then slumped on the bed without undressing. A few moments later,
he was fast asleep.[28]

§ The Soviet ambassador, hot and flustered, hurried to Matsuoka's
private residence in Sendagaya that evening, 22 June. Constantin Smetanin, a portly man, sweated copiously, and his rosy bald pate glistened
with damp. By contrast, Matsuoka appeared cool and composed even
if the truth was that the turn of events had caught him by surprise.

In the weeks before the invasion, Japanese intelligence agents in
Germany had reported a growing number of tell-tale signs, but the
Tokyo government shared the Russians' unwillingness to believe that
Hitler had the audacity to attempt to conquer the Soviet Union.[29]

'What has happened is quite intolerable, Mr Matsuoka! Germany
has a non-aggression treaty with the Soviet Union, and yet they have

attacked us without a declaration of war. Hitler's action violates every norm of civilized behaviour!'

The ambassador raged on for several minutes before he came to the point.

'Thanks to your efforts, Mr Matsuoka, the Soviet Union and Japan have a neutrality treaty. I have been asked to convey my government's request that both signatories faithfully abide by the terms of that agreement.'

In the words of a witness to this secret meeting, the Russian was 'practically begging' for assurances that Japan would stay neutral in the war.[30] The Soviet Union's greatest fear was that the Japanese would strike in the Far East, opening a second front to exploit German victories in the west. The foreign minister, eyes twinkling behind his wire-rimmed spectacles, appeared to relish his position of strength.

'I understand your concern. My government also is concerned about this unfortunate war. We wish to maintain friendly relations with the Soviet Union. But Japan is in a difficult position. The Three Powers Pact is the cornerstone of our foreign policy, and if the neutrality pact conflicts with the alliance with Germany, the alliance must prevail. Naturally we hope that this conflict will be brought to a speedy end, and you may rest assured my government's efforts will be directed to seeking an early termination of hostilities.'

Smetanin was visibly shaken by Matsuoka's implicit warning that Japan could involve itself in Hitler's treacherous war against the Soviet Union. There was no more to be said – the ambassador realized that at this point Japan had not had time to shape its policy. Smetanin calculated that the lack of unity in government circles might yet work to Russia's advantage.

But that meeting gave little reason to hope. It was a day of unremitting gloom for Smetanin and the Soviet leaders, who saw a high probability that German victories on the battlefield would tempt the Japanese army to intervene. Thoroughly dejected, the ambassador took his leave and hurried back to his embassy in Azabu to advise his government of Matsuoka's disturbing response.

§ Sorge had toiled in vain to alert his masters: Stalin was incredulous when the Germans invaded. Up to the last minute he believed that he had an eternal guarantee of peace with Hitler.

The Tokyo ring's warnings were disregarded, but so were those of other loyal agents in Europe who had heard about Germany's plan for a surprise attack. Stalin had been given a summary of these dispatches by Lieutenant-General Filipp Ivanovitch Golikov, the head of Red Army intelligence. Most were classified as derived from 'dubious sources', and all received short shrift. Servile underlings told him what he wanted to hear. 'Rumours and documents to the effect that war against the USSR is inevitable this spring should be regarded as misinformation coming from the English, or perhaps even the German intelligence service,' concluded Golikov in his assessment of the 'warnings' submitted to Stalin on 21 March.[31]

Stalin suspected an anti-Soviet plot by foreign powers and traitors in his own ranks. On 19 April, the British ambassador in Moscow passed on an urgent message about German preparations to invade Russia. Churchill's warnings – based on decrypted German signals, a source the British concealed – were dismissed by Stalin as a provocation. So too were the reports from his own agents in Japan and Europe, who Stalin believed had fallen for English propaganda.[32]

The dispatch dated 1 June – in which Sorge warned Russia to expect the invasion to begin on 15 June – serves as a graphic example of the prevailing paranoia. On the Fourth Department's copy of the telegram, decoded and translated into Russian, Sorge's superiors have scrawled their scathing comments: 'Suspicious. To be listed with telegrams intended as provocations.'[33]

An earlier warning from Sorge – the 19 May message indicating that the Germans might launch an invasion at the end of that month – is said to have prompted a coarse outburst from Stalin, who described him as 'a shit who has set himself up with some small factories and brothels in Japan'.[34]

A little later, as we have seen, the Fourth Department conveyed its scepticism to Sorge in no uncertain terms: 'We doubt the veracity of your information.' Sorge exploded when he read the stinging message, as Clausen recalled much later: 'Now I've had enough! How can those wretches ignore our message!'[35]

Possibly it was this, or a similar rebuff, that prompted Sorge to relay word of the impending German invasion to a wider audience – the readership of the *New York Herald Tribune*. We know that some time in May Vukelic was instructed to offer a tremendous 'scoop' to his American press colleagues. Vukelic approached the representatives of four American newspapers and news agencies.

Joseph Newman, the *Tribune*'s Tokyo correspondent, was the only one to show interest. Naturally he asked why Vukelic did not write it up himself. Vukelic explained that Havas, the French news agency for which he worked, could not run such a story because it was under Nazi control. Without mentioning Sorge's name, he assured Newman that his sources were utterly reliable.

After weighing the risks, Newman went ahead and filed the story to his office at the end of May. (To his surprise it was passed by the Japanese censors). The article was published on 31 May – buried deep inside the paper – under the headline 'Tokyo Expects Hitler to Move Against Russia'.[36] Newman believed that Sorge was motivated by a desire to let the world know in advance what Hitler was plotting. Ironically, the editors of the *New York Herald Tribune* lent more credence to information derived from Stalin's man in Tokyo than Stalin did himself.

Russia paid the price for Stalin's scornful dismissal of Sorge's reports. In the first hours of the war, the Luftwaffe pounded Russian aeroplanes sitting on the ground, and wiped out scores of tanks. German armoured divisions advanced at an amazing rate of fifty miles a day. For the Russians, taken unawares, only a titanic effort would reverse a desperate situation.

§ In Moscow on that Sunday, the Fourth Department was a scene of frenzied activity. Fully expecting the Japanese army to move out of Manchuria and seize part of Siberia, the Red Army General Staff tried as a matter of urgency to fathom Japanese reactions to the German invasion. Directives were hurriedly radioed to the Red Army's 'legal' and 'illegal' organizations in Tokyo. One was a curt order dated 23 June to Gushenko, the Soviet military attaché: 'Report on the Japanese government's stance on the German war against the Soviet Union.'

The director sent an identical wireless message to Richard Sorge, who was in no fit state to provide a report on Sunday evening. On Monday morning he was spotted in the lobby of the Imperial Hotel, dishevelled and wearing the rumpled linen suit he had slept in.

The fact that events had proved Sorge right did not endear him to the Great Leader. Indeed, it may have eventually sealed his fate: Stalin was not anxious to have living witnesses to his criminal blunder in failing to prepare Soviet defences against a German attack, despite the series of warnings. But now, in its darkest hour, the Soviet Union's salvation hinged on the capabilities of the Tokyo unit's intelligence. The Kremlin was forced to revise its opinion of Richard Sorge. From now on, Stalin depended on Sorge and his group to tell him whether, and when, the Japanese were going to attack in the East.

§ On Monday 23 June at 9 a.m. Foreign Minister Matsuoka received the German ambassador at his private residence. Sitting where Smetanin had sat the day before, Ott explained why Chancellor Hitler had been compelled to go to war against Russia. Matsuoka gave Ott to understand that Japan would act like a 'trustworthy' ally, and would not remain neutral in the conflict. In other words, Japan would ignore its neutrality pact with the Soviet Union and remain loyal to the Axis.

This assurance, however, was merely wishful thinking by Hitler's greatest admirer in Japan. Matsuoka had no authority to commit Japan to support Germany's war against Russia, and was aware that the option of intervention in Siberia had lost favour in the military circles that mattered.

Ott drove back to the embassy, pondering the strategy he should adopt to embroil Japan in the war. He was under no illusions: despite Matsuoka's reassuring tone, it would not be an easy task convincing the Japanese cabinet that the national interest would be served by taking on the Russian bear.

The ambassador decided to mobilize his entire staff for a massive effort of propagandizing and persuasion. Germany had many friends in the Japanese army and bureaucracy, and these would be enlisted in the campaign. The strongest arguments for Japanese participation in the war, Ott believed, would be the battlefield triumphs of the *Wehrmacht* as it pushed ever deeper into Russia. The signs were good – early reports from Berlin told him that the Red Army had lost three divisions in a matter of hours, and that hundreds of Russian aircraft had been written off by the end of the first day of war.

§ Erich Kordt was struck by Sorge's intense emotional reaction to the Russo-German war – it 'appeared to move the scoffer and cynic Sorge more than any other event'.[37] Though the two men were not close, Sorge did not hide his feelings: 'He told me he felt a particular empathy with the Russian people, since he was born in Russia and his mother was Russian.'[38]

The strong Russian element in his personality was remarked upon by many friends, long before he was unmasked. Mrs Matzky, the wife of the former military attaché, had once asked, half-jokingly, 'Aren't you really Russian? There's something about you ...'. On that occasion Sorge, without faltering, replied that, no, he was from Thuringia.[39]

For the ambassador, the displays of emotion, the histrionics, the vehement idealism were manifestations of the Slav in Sorge. 'He's playing the Russian again,' Ott would say with a deep sigh.[40]

After his arrest, Sorge confided that – although he had German nationality and was brought up in Germany – he felt Russia to be his mother country. The remark was made during a conversation with one of his interrogators, and does not appear in the police record.[41]

Some authorities on the Sorge affair have contended that the spy did his best to conceal that he was born to a Russian mother. On the contrary, the available evidence indicates that he showed his pride in this bond to Russia. However, he was obliged to conceal his mother's nationality when he came up against Germany's race laws. In 1937 he applied for membership of the Nazi Press Association, a requirement for all German journalists. He was able to join only after satisfying the association that his forebears were of pure Aryan stock, as prescribed by Germany's race laws. Having a Russian mother would certainly have made it impossible for him to continue working for the *Frankfurter Zeitung*.

His ingenious solution was to misrepresent his (German) paternal relatives as forebears on his mother's side. A great-grandfather on his father's side became a relative of his mother's, while a certificate of baptism for another paternal relative was presented as that of his maternal grandfather. The documents he submitted to construct a good German lineage were found among Sorge's personal possessions, and police asked him about them. Although they knew his mother was Russian, they did not probe into why the papers showed his maternal forebears to be Germans. What is more surprising is that officials in Germany who processed his Aryan credentials failed to spot the deception, and gave Sorge the clearance he needed to join the Nazi Press Association.

§ As a matter of urgency, Ozaki visited Sorge on Monday evening to discuss how Japan might react to the war. That evening's *Japan Times and Advertiser*, which Sorge always read with great care, announced in front-page headlines that German armoured groups had advanced on a wide front, meeting feeble Soviet resistance, and that Minsk was expected to fall within a day or two. According to Ozaki, Japanese official circles were forecasting that the Red Army would collapse, and Russia would be defeated, in three months, or six months at the most. 'It is unlikely Japan will risk striking until Germany's victory is a certainty,' he said. 'But at that point the temptation to take a bite at Russia's posterior will be irresistible for our army. This is a case of *jukushishugi* – waiting for the persimmon to ripen and fall into your lap – a very pragmatic philosophy.'

'Yes, but if the *Wehrmacht* pushes beyond the Urals, Germany will feel all the persimmons are hers by right,' said Sorge. 'If Japan doesn't share the pain of war, Hitler won't share the fruits of victory. This is sure to be the line Ribbentrop takes towards Japan. Look, Ott went to sound out Matsuoka this morning, and I gather your foreign minister assured him Japan stands four-square behind Germany, and to hell with her neutrality pact with Russia!'

'It's just like Matsuoka to say that! He says whatever comes into his head,' said Ozaki. 'And even if *he* supports intervention, the government has taken no decision on whether to enter the war or remain neutral. That's the whole point. Konoye's circle is in a quandary. They can't make up their minds what course to take.

'Which means there is still scope for political manoeuvring. What I could do is try to persuade them that it's not in Japan's interests to fight the Soviet Union. I can impress on these people that it would be a grave mistake to underestimate the Soviet Union's military strength. And make them understand that even a military defeat won't destroy Russian unity or bring down the Stalin regime. My opinions carry some weight in Konoye's circle. There are many opportunities for me to exert influence. Will you let me try?'[42]

Ozaki would have been unsure how Sorge would react to this proposal. Two years earlier, he had suggested something similar – that he exploit his prestige as a recognized authority on China to sway opinion in favour of the Soviet Union. But Sorge had rejected the idea, arguing that the fundamental duty of the ring was intelligence and that political manoeuvring was a distraction from this primary task. The rules laid down by the Fourth Department were unambiguous: no one in the ring was allowed to go beyond their espionage duties. In Sorge's words, 'I was strictly forbidden by Moscow to engage in any activity unrelated to intelligence – that is, to undertake any organizational propaganda work of a political nature.'[43] However, when it suited him, he interpreted the rules of service in Red Army Intelligence rather broadly; this was the case with the ban on propaganda work.[44] 'We obeyed it faithfully, with the one exception that we worked actively on other people to influence their perceptions of Soviet national strength.'[45]

Now that the Soviet Union was locked in a life-and-death struggle, Sorge proved receptive to Ozaki's proposal. The situation was too grave to miss any chance to influence Japanese strategy. However, he told Ozaki that he had to clear the matter with Moscow first. He informed the Fourth Department that the opportunity existed for covert political activities to make Japan think twice before marching to the Germans' tune. The reply from the Centre was discouraging: extra-curricular activities of this kind were 'unnecessary'. However, the reply did not explicitly forbid them. As Sorge told his interrogators, 'I interpreted the word 'unnecessary' in its widest sense, and refused to construe it as an explicit ban on such activity.'[46]

Later in the week Sorge gave Ozaki the go-ahead, and they sat down to discuss tactics. It was Ozaki's idea to play on the fear of the Soviet military machine that had haunted Japan since her defeat in the 'Nomonhan Incident' in 1939, while at the same time stimulating the Japanese appetite for the raw materials found in abundance in Southeast Asia.

'I can take the line that it would be short-sighted and mistaken for Japan to attack Russia, because we won't gain much in the way of raw materials or other economic benefits in eastern Siberia. The point to make is that if Hitler smashes the Red Army as he has promised, Siberia will fall into Japan's lap anyway, without us having to lift a finger. Secondly, I can stress that Japan's political and economic interests lie in the south, where we can find the natural resources critical for the war economy. Thirdly, I can make the most of fears that the United States and Britain are looking for a chance to attack us. I can spread the word that if Japan becomes entangled in a war with Russia, the Americans and English may seize the opportunity to strike at us when our oil and iron reserves run out'

To Sorge, this seeemed like a sound approach. 'Yes,' he agreed, 'whenever anyone belittles Soviet strength, we should recall how the Russians wiped the floor with the Japanese army at Nomonhan. Whenever a chance arises, we should hammer home that Hitler has made a serious miscalculation. But we must avoid the impression of engaging in propaganda. That would defeat the whole purpose of the exercise, and it would jeopardize our principal mission.'

With this proviso, Sorge gave Ozaki a free hand to work on Prime Minister Konoye's advisers, while he concentrated on the German Embassy. As he explained, 'I did not restrict Ozaki's positive manoeuvres within the Konoye group, nor did I hesitate to work on the Germans.'[47]

A good opportunity for Ozaki to lobby discreetly for the Soviet Union arose when the Breakfast Society met on Wednesday (this was possibly before he obtained Sorge's approval). The talk, inevitably, was dominated by events in Europe. Yes, Ozaki said, it was true that a Russian military defeat was possible, as some members of Konoye's informal 'think-tank' believed. But he argued that it was highly unlikely this would bring about the collapse of the socialist system or Stalin's government. 'In this, Germany is making a big miscalculation,' he told the influential group. 'Besides, if Germany wins, we can take over Siberia without having to send our troops to fight in Russia's fearsome winters. And surely the important thing is that the natural resources we need are in the south, not in Siberia. If we're going to take such a risk, an advance to the south seems to make much more sense, doesn't it?'

Vukelic too was roped into the propaganda effort. 'We should try to promote a favourable mood towards Russia among US policy makers,' Sorge said, telling him to concentrate mainly on Joseph Newman, the *New York Herald Tribune* man. Buttonholing Newman and other American journalists, Vukelic played up the danger to the US posed by Japanese aggression in the Pacific. German diplomats and a German 'fifth column' in Tokyo were using every ruse to embroil Japan in a conflict with Britain and America, he said. Now that Russia had its hands full fighting Germany, the way was clear for Japan to expand into Southeast Asia and the Pacific. On 1 July a story appeared in the *Tribune* entitled: 'Japan Believed Still Aiming at South Seas Area'. The source of this story, Newman revealed many years later, was Branko Vukelic.

§ For the evening of 26 June Sorge's diary records the name 'Joe', followed by the word 'mail'. This denoted a meeting with Miyagi, who was to bring certain documents. From the weather reports for that Thursday, we know that Tokyo was hot, sticky and oppressive, typical *tsuyu* (rainy season) conditions. For Miyagi it was a time of growing disquiet. As he criss-crossed the steamy city on errands for Sorge, all his instincts told him he was being shadowed. It was no longer possible to shrug off the furtive presence in his wake as a figment of his imagination.

This was not the first time Miyagi had considered starting a new life, painting and farming in far-away Wakayama prefecture. From the start he had told Sorge he would only work for him until a replacement could be found. That was more than seven years ago, and a serene life in the countryside was still a dream. It was mainly from a sense of loyalty to Ozaki that he soldiered on. 'It's foolish for people like us to engage in this sort of thing!' Miyagi had told Kawai Teikichi. 'I never intended to do this on a permanent basis. Now I can't seem to get away from it.'[48]

Miyagi was in the habit of making wide detours, pausing at times to see if he had shaken off his 'tail'. This evening, as usual, he tried to assure himself that the coast was clear before turning into the lane to Sorge's house.

What was the document Miyagi took to Sorge that night, five days after the outbreak of the German–Russian war? It is on record that around this time he delivered a map of Hokkaido and Karafuto – Japanese territory close to the Soviet Union – on which he had carefully marked air bases and major ports, with notes on these installations.

One such map had already been sent by courier to Moscow, but as the danger of a Japanese attack increased, Sorge asked Miyagi to update the information. So he went again to the Seishido bookshop in Roppongi, bought an atlas of Japan, tore out the pages of the northernmost islands, and revised the data with the help of his Hokkaido agent, Taguchi Ugenta. The judicial records show that this material was handed to Sorge on an unspecified day in June.[49]

§ For several days, Sorge had focused on the intense activity in government and military circles. Hardly a day passed without a high-level conference of some kind. Ozaki had discovered that national policy on Japan's stance towards the Russo-German war had been shaped at a 'liaison conference' between the government and the High Command, held on 19 June and endorsed on 23 June at a meeting of senior army and navy strategists.

Shortly before Germany invaded Russia, the army's General Staff had formulated a cautious strategy to cope with that eventuality: Japan should improve military preparedness *vis-à-vis* the Soviet Union, but only intervene on Germany's side if a favourable opportunity arose. Navy chiefs had set their own agenda. They favoured expansion into Southeast Asia, wanted Japan to stay aloof from the Russo-German conflict, and opposed the squandering of military budgets on a build-up in the north.

After the outbreak of the war, the two services managed to find common ground, overcoming their traditional antagonism. The 23 June meeting of army and navy planners and other key officers agreed on a strategy of impeccable opportunism: to 'strike south' and at the same time reinforce army positions in the north, especially Manchuria, as a contingency measure. If Russia became ripe for plundering, they wanted to be prepared.

It was the military that held the controls of Japan's destiny. But the civilians were still ostensibly in charge, and *pro forma* liaison conferences between cabinet ministers and chiefs of the army and navy General Staffs were held, one after the other, until 1 July, with only one day of rest. These deliberations were strictly secret. The Domei News Agency coyly reported that the conferences were called to discuss a 'problem requiring immediate attention arising from the start of the German–Russian war'. The police issued a special warning that rumour-mongers faced severe penalties – and added pointedly that this applied also to 'big men in all walks of life, who, because of their special knowledge, are believed to be the source of the rumours'.[50]

Big men *were* the main source of rumours. Their propensity to gossip with others in their personal circles – automatically assumed to be reliable – ensured that the most confidential matters leaked out. As Sorge told his inquisitors, Japanese society was ill-suited to keeping secrets.

Saionji Kinkazu, the aristocrat employed as a consultant to the Foreign Ministry, was the source of a number of important leaks to the Sorge ring. Ozaki approached him some time between Monday 23 June and Wednesday 25 June and, as a close and trusted friend, elicited without difficulty the crux of the decision taken by military and government leaders at the 19 June liaison conference. Saionji conveyed that Japan would take a neutral course in the eventuality of war between Germany and the USSR.[51]

Ozaki then talked to another friend, Tanaka Shinjiro, the head of the *Asahi Shimbun*'s political and economic desk. Tanaka revealed what he knew about the pivotal Army–Navy talks on 23 June which had resulted in the 'unified strategy' for striking at Southeast Asia while refraining, for the time being, from intervention in the Russo-German conflict.

By his own account, Ozaki briefed Miyagi on his findings on the 'morning of the 26th', which formed the basis of the report drafted for Sorge. Miyagi included snippets of information from his agent, Taguchi Ugenta, and from his own sources. The next step was to put this material into English, a task he entrusted to the ring's translator, Akiyama Koji. Given the large amount of work involved, it is unlikely that this was completed by 26 June or that this was the document Miyagi brought to Sorge's house that night.

§ On 28 June, a wet Saturday, Sorge lunched at the embassy with Ambassador Ott and was told something of how Japan was responding to German efforts to lure it into the week-old war. After a final cognac, Sorge left the embassy and drove the short stretch to the Tameike crossing. A ceramics shop stood on one corner, and here he waited in his car for Eta to come. She arrived at 3.15 p.m. and they went at once to Richard's house in Nagasaka-cho. Richard was tense, railing against the 'pigs' in the embassy. Eta was becoming used to these outbursts, tolerating them because she understood how oppressed he was by the invasion of 'his' country.[52] A little before six o'clock he drove her back to the embassy, returning in time for a further appointment with Miyagi at 7.30 p.m. Possibly he had already begun to draft the following telegram to the Fourth Department, based on what Ambassador Ott told him over lunch, and on information received earlier from Ozaki.

The decision to send troops to Saigon was adopted under pressure from radical elements who demand action, but with the condition first, that conflict with America is to be avoided and, second, that Japan will play for time while the German–Soviet war is being fought.

Invest [Ozaki] maintains that Japan will attack to the North [Russia] as soon as the Red Army is defeated, and also pointed out that Japan intends to purchase Sakhalin in a peaceful manner ...

German Ambassador Ott corroborated the first part of the above. But with respect to the second part, Matsuoka, queried by Ott, replied that Japan will fight against the USSR, as he has always assured him she would.

Matsuoka told Ott that the Emperor has given his approval to the movement to Saigon some time ago, and this cannot be changed at the present time. Thus Ott understood that Japan will not attack to the north [Russia] for the time being.[53]

From the content of this dispatch, we can gauge that it was drafted before he saw Miyagi's report. But less than a week after the German onslaught started the Tokyo ring outlined to Moscow the course Japan would take. Sorge's tone is confident. He reports that the danger of a Japanese attack on Russia still exists, but is not expected to materialize immediately. All depends on how the Red Army acquits itself on the battlefield.

From the material at our disposal, it seems that this is Sorge's first post-invasion report on Japanese intentions. No doubt it was read with close attention in Moscow. Stalin's signature is on the telegram, indicating that it was seen in its entirety by the Soviet leader rather than summarized in the daily intelligence digest. However, the telegram, dated 28 June, did not reach the Fourth Department until 4 July. Max Clausen sat on this vital message for almost a week before transmitting it. Poor atmospheric conditions might have prevented radio contact with Vladivostok, but it seems more likely that Clausen deliberately delayed this dispatch – and many others, too, if his prison testimony is to be believed.

§ While Sorge composed his dispatch, Japanese government and military leaders were huddling in conferences in the centre of the capital. Resolutions decided by the military had been adopted by the civilian government. The 'Imperial Policy Outline Responding to the Changing Situation' had been hammered out, and was now awaiting the sanction of the emperor. From that point on, it would stand as Japanese policy – and determine the fate of the nation. The essence of the Imperial Policy was lucidly conveyed in Miyagi's report, based on the briefing by Ozaki, his own sources and his own opinions:

The Japanese government and senior military officials, being in possession of firm information about Germany's attack on the USSR, decided Japan's policy towards Germany and the USSR at a conference held on June 19, 1941.

The Japanese government decided to adhere to the Three Powers Pact with Germany and Italy while strictly observing its neutrality treaty with the Soviet Union.[54]

Miyagi then outlined the strategy decided at the Army–Navy summit on 23 June. Two or three Japanese army divisions were already on their way to Indochina as part of the plan to expand into Southeast Asia. At the same time the army would build up forces in Hokkaido, Sakhalin and Manchuria in line with policy for the northern front.

Army circles were quoted as predicting the defeat of the Soviet army within three months. The document also included an interview with a general – Araki Sadao – which demonstrated how eagerly hawkish elements in the Japanese army yearned to strike at the Russians, and how contemptuous they were of Japan's civilian leaders. General Araki, a former war minister, was quoted as remarking that 'our national policy is based on advancing to the north. Now the opportunity to destroy the USSR has arrived.' Matsuoka was 'a fool', said Araki, and he hoped the foreign minister and the whole Konoye cabinet would resign, so that the army could launch an attack on Russia.[55]

This document, written in pen, was impounded when police searched Sorge's home some four months later. Under questioning, Sorge told police he had received it from Miyagi 'two or three days' after the outbreak of the war.[56]

However, there is little trace of Miyagi's work in the 28 June telegram. This suggests that the report had still not reached Sorge by that Saturday.[57]

CHAPTER THIRTEEN

July 1941

ON 2 JULY, a sultry day of blue skies dashed with cloud, the emperor sat in council with his principal ministers and chiefs of staff. A rare *gozenkaigi* – Conference in the August Presence – was taking place in the Imperial Palace to 'decide crucial national policy'. That was all the morning newspapers gave away of the momentous conference that would determine the fate of the nation, and a large slice of humanity. Across the moat, on the hot pebbles of the great plaza, loyal subjects bowed deeply in the direction of god-on-earth.

Emperor Hirohito, who was also commander-in-chief of the armed forces, presided, wearing naval uniform. He was seated in front of a gold screen with incense burners on either side. Before him stretched two tables draped with brocade, lined with cabinet ministers and army and navy leaders.[1]

A terse communiqué issued later in the day illuminated nothing: 'A crucial national policy to be adopted in meeting the prevailing situation has been decided on.' But what policy? The mystique of the throne forbade profane speculation, and the National Defence Security Law forbade public discussion.

The *New York Times* Tokyo correspondent, Otto Tolischus, deduced that the emperor had sanctioned the policy agreed upon the previous day at a cabinet meeting that followed a series of conferences and audiences at the palace. 'What the policy was, no outsider knew. The press pleaded with the public to be patient.'[2]

The mystery deepened when Matsuoka stated, opaquely, that the government was 'making preparations in which we can place confidence' to meet the 'supreme emergency'. The foreign minister exhorted the public to 'adopt a cool, composed attitude, unifying all classes, and, in response to the August Will of his Majesty, the Emperor, endeavour not to make the slightest mistake in the direction of the path of our country'.

Foreign correspondents, diplomats and spies in Tokyo were groping to discern the direction Japan would take. Sorge, especially, was impatient to find out. If the *gozenkaigi* had firmly ruled out an attack on the Soviet Union, Red Army chiefs could safely transfer more forces to the western front to help repel the invaders. It was a matter of the utmost urgency. In fact, four Soviet Far East infantry divisions had been transferred westward in the first few days of the German onslaught, although Sorge was probably unaware of this.[3] But the Russians could not significantly dilute their strength in the Far East unless they were absolutely sure that the Japanese did not plan to intervene.

Marshalling his resources, Sorge set about piercing the wall of official secrecy. On Thursday 3 July Miyagi visited Sorge's house, but he could provide no insights. Informants such as Taguchi Ugenta had been of no help.

Fortunately, Ozaki lost no time in making his own enquiries. On either 3 or 4 July, he met Saionji Kinkazu, the talkative Oxford-educated aristocrat. Circumspect as always, he refrained from posing leading questions. Casually, he put it to Saionji that Japan had decided on a neutral course in the Russo-German war. This was a confident deduction, as Ozaki was already in the picture about the policy shaped at the conferences that took place on 19 and 23 June. Without hesitation, Saionji confirmed that Ozaki's assumption was absolutely correct. He had every confidence in his friend, and happily told him everything. As he explained many years later: 'That was the sort of relationship I had with Ozaki. I had no secrets from Ozaki.'[4]

Then, at the weekend – 5 or 6 July – Miyagi called on Ozaki for a briefing. This formed the basis of the report he completed and took to Sorge 'around July 10'.[5] Ozaki's information – the gist conveyed directly, the details via Miyagi – was that the imperial conference had adopted three main resolutions.

First, Japan must prepare itself to respond to all eventualities and developments in the international situation. Second, Japan would adhere to the neutrality pact with the Soviet Union, so long as the international situation remained unchanged. Third, Japan would carry out its policy of expansion in the south whatever the obstacles, and make the necessary military preparations to follow this course. Ozaki had also learnt that the Supreme Command had decided on 5 or 6 July to station troops in Saigon at the end of the month.[6]

Before finalizing his report to Moscow Sorge sounded out Ambassador Ott, and found that he saw things in a different light. Early on the morning of the imperial conference, the ambassador had received urgent instructions in a coded message from Berlin. Foreign Minister Ribbentrop had told Ott that he should press Japan to occupy Vladivostok as quickly as possible, then advance westwards to link up, before winter, with the German invasion force on Soviet territory. The two allies would thus establish direct communication and settle the Russian question once and for all by eliminating the Bolshevik menace. The way would then be clear for Japan's southward advance.

Ott had arranged an urgent meeting with Foreign Minister Matsuoka on the evening of 2 July and conveyed Ribbentrop's request for Japanese participation in the war. Matsuoka's response was not encouraging, recalls Kase Toshikazu, who was then the foreign minister's personal secretary. Ott was told that Japan's basic policy on this question had been decided earlier in the day at the imperial conference, at which Matsuoka himself was present, and that it was impossible to deviate from it. It had been decided that Japan would not enter the Russo-German conflict at this stage. However, Japan would proceed with military preparations so as to be ready to deal with the 'Russian question'.

According to Kase, Matsuoka 'pointed out that Japan's effort to restrain the United States and Great Britain in the Pacific constituted a no less vital contribution towards the common cause than an intervention in the Soviet–German War.'[7] The signals Ott picked up in his talk with Matsuoka were somewhat different. Perhaps he heard only what he wanted to hear. In any event, he went away convinced that Japan was prepared to do Germany's bidding. The following day, in a telegram to Berlin, Ott gave an up-beat assessment of the progress of his war promotion effort: 'Everything indicates that Japan will enter the war against Russia.'

This was the optimistic prognosis the ambassador conveyed to Sorge on 9 July. Japan, he believed, would go to war against Russia within two months; the military attaché, Colonel Kretschmer, shared this view, although the naval attaché thought otherwise. In Sorge's words, 'Naval attaché Wenneker and I myself took the contrary view that Japan would not enter the war this year. And when Japan launched its large-scale mobilization, Ott became ever more confident that Japan would join the war.'[8]

On 10 July – eight days after the imperial conference – Sorge prepared his report for the Fourth Department. The conclusions of the ambassador and Ozaki diverged in one vital respect. The German ambassador placed more weight on the imperial resolution that Japan would improve military preparedness in the northern area; Ozaki, however, stressed that Japan's expansion was being directed to the south, and that Japan would take a wait-and-see stance towards joining the Russo-German conflict. 'I too thought this and radioed it urgently to Moscow Centre,' Sorge told his interrogators.[9]

It was his firm impression that Japan had decided 'to take steps to assure security in the north, but begin actual military action in the south, that is French Indochina.'[10]

In the 10 July telegram – apparently the first concerning the *gozenkaigi* – he reported both versions to Moscow, but gave greater weight to Ozaki's information:

> Invest said that at the conference in the presence of the Emperor it was decided not to alter the plan for action against Saigon [Indo-China], but it was decided at the same time to prepare for action against the USSR in case of the defeat of the Red Army.
>
> German Ambassador Ott said, in similar vein, that Japan would begin the attack if the Germans reach Sverdlovsk.
>
> The German military attaché telegraphed to Berlin that he is convinced that Japan will enter the war by the end of July or the beginning of August, and as soon as she has completed preparations.[11]

The dispatch also mentions that Matsuoka had expressed fears to Ott that the Soviet Union might sent bombers over Japan if the latter joined the war. Ott sought to allay these fears by asserting that: 'the USSR has only 1,500 first-class aircraft in the Far East, only 300 of these are heavy bombers with a capability to reach Japan, and two new types of plane suited for such a missions are not yet stationed in the Far East.'[12]

The ambassador was under intense pressure to achieve quick results; on 5 and 10 July, Ribbentrop sent further urgent orders to Ott to coax the Japanese government into attacking Russia from the east. Perhaps Sorge nodded sympathetically as Ott grumbled that Berlin failed to grasp how difficult it was to persuade the Japanese to act. But inwardly he was seething: the ambassador, Sorge believed, was more concerned with furthering his career than with the morality of war-mongering on Hitler's behalf.

In a second telegram to the Fourth Department, also dated July 10, Sorge reported: 'Ott was very surprised by Ribbentrop's haste, saying he ought to be aware that Japan is not yet ready, and is only making an outward show of [going to] war.'[13]

Two days later, he advised Moscow that Ott sounded somewhat less confident about his chances of persuading Japan to intervene. 'German ambassador Ott told Inson [Sorge] that he proposed to Japan that she enter the war, but for the time being Japan wishes to remain neutral.'[14] He went on to explain that there were elements agitating forcefully for the advance to the south, but younger officers of the Kwantung army were in favour of taking on the Russians. In conclusion, Sorge gave his own estimate of how Japan would respond to German requests to join the war.

> Preparations for war will last some six weeks, while Japan watches the course of the Russo-German war.
> If the Red Army suffers defeat, then there is no doubt the Japanese will join the war, and if there is no defeat, then they will maintain neutrality.[15]

It is clear from this that Sorge still saw a strong likelihood of Japanese intervention, depending on the military situation. At this stage he could not offer the Red Army a clear-cut estimate that would permit a sizeable transfer of troops to the western front. His long summer vigil was just beginning. Over the following weeks the painstaking investigation would continue, as he struggled to make sense of the confusing signals Japan was putting out.

Soviet leaders paid close attention to his dispatches, at least in the first weeks of the war with Germany. His 28 June telegram was read by both Stalin and Foreign Minister Molotov. Two telegrams, one dated 10 July and one 12 July, bear the signatures of Stalin and his war cabinet – Molotov, Lavrenty Beria, Georgi Malenkov and Kliment Voroshilov – attesting that they were read and evaluated at the top.

At the end of a dispatch dated 10 July, there is a note in the handwriting of the deputy head of Red Army General Staff Intelligence: 'In consideration of the high reliability and accuracy of previous information and the competence of the information sources, this information can be trusted.' After Sorge's warnings of the German invasion proved correct, the Fourth Department acknowledged the value of the Tokyo ring and belatedly placed its trust in Sorge.

§ As a professional journalist, Robert Guillain also wished to discover what transpired at the *gozenkaigi* on 2 July. The Havas News Agency bureau chief was more fortunate than his colleagues in the foreign press corps. He simply turned to his assistant, Vukelic – 'Vuki', as his friends knew him – for help.

'At noon I said, Vuki, you'd better go and see Mr X and see what you can find out about the conference,' Guillain recalls. Dr Sorge – 'Mr X' – had proved a valuable source of information on delicate matters in the past. 'We called him Mr X between ourselves, just in case someone overheard our conversation. It was a necessary precaution when ordinary Japanese were forced by the police to report on foreigners' activities.'

France was under German occupation, and Guillain had no direct relations with Sorge, whom he assumed to be a Nazi. But he had encouraged Vukelic to maintain discreet contact with Sorge, even after the outbreak of war in Europe, and when there was some important event in Japan or Europe he made a habit of asking Vuki to go and see what Mr X knew about it. 'At 3 o'clock, as far as I can remember, he was back, with the news that Japan would not enter the war against Russia and would occupy French Indochina.'[16]

That evening Guillain, at a dinner party, passed on this news to the French ambassador, Charles Arsène-Henry, who was incredulous. 'He thought it was absurd, and said, Guillain, if you know the secrets of an imperial conference and the Japanese find out about it, you realize that tomorrow morning you'll be hanging from the end of a rope?'

Irritated by the rebuff, Guillain approached a guest at the dinner party, Eugene Dooman, the counsellor at the US Embassy, though he had few contacts among American diplomats. 'He listened, and then asked me, how long had I been in Japan? Three years, I said. Dooman said he had been there fifteen years, and started talking about the importance of Japanese *kimochi* (feeling) and said his *kimochi* told him there would be no landing in southern Indochina.'

The next day Guillain repeated his information to Colonel Thiebault, the military attaché at the French embassy, who sounded more interested. But as far as Guillain could ascertain, his report went no further. The embassy was in the service of the Vichy government, a puppet of the Nazis, and totally impotent when it came to stopping the Japanese from marching into France's colonies in Asia.

Between 1938 and 1941, Guillain was given a series of important 'scoops' by Vukelic: the Japanese débâcle at Nomonhan, the talks that led to an alliance between Germany and Japan, and negotiations on a non-aggression pact between Hitler and Stalin. Japanese censorship, and – after the German invasion of France in June 1940 – Nazi control of Havas restricted Guillain's freedom to file stories, but he was in the habit of feeding the French ambassador with some of the information from Vukelic.

'Between February and June 1941 I sought to persuade my ambassador that a war would break out between Germany and the Soviet Union,' Guillain recalls. 'He steadfastly refused to believe it. Then, fourteen hours before the event, I told him Hitler would attack the following day. That was a leak planted by Vuki and Sorge, twenty-four hours in advance.'

Guillain was assured by Vukelic that Sorge was not the died-in-the-wool Nazi he seemed, that he was profoundly devoted to peace and the avoidance of war, and this motivated him to pass along selected information.

> I never had the slightest suspicion, of course, that Vukelic and Sorge were spies. Later I understood that they believed these leaks would serve their cause, which was the fight against Hitler and Nazism, and the defense of the Soviet Union. Their aim was that certain information should reach the enemies of Hitler in Paris, London, or elsewhere. For three years I served, without knowing it, as a channel for the organized leak of secrets by the Sorge spy ring.[17]

§ On 7 July, the fourth anniversary of the 'China Incident', Sorge reminded readers of the *Frankfurter Zeitung* of a forgotten war that had claimed millions of lives. Japan's armies were floundering in the Chinese quagmire. The generals long realized that they could not win a decisive battlefield victory, and were resigned to fighting a brutal, demoralizing war of attrition. Sorge's article quoted a declaration by the High Command that settling the 'China question' was the highest priority of Japan's national policy, and gave the army's figures on the cost of the war in lives: 3.8 million Chinese and slightly more than 100,000 Japanese dead. (The China conflict was also draining the Japanese exchequer, absorbing a third of government expenditure.)

As Sorge pointed out, the war affected every sphere of the economy, which was now a controlled war economy; one of the repercussions was the abolition of political parties and their replacement by a 'movement of national unity'.

Under the headline 'Four Years of war in China. Japan's determination to resolve the China conflict', Sorge wrote:

> The Japan–China conflict broke out exactly four years ago, on 7 July 1937. The Japanese action, generally considered at first to be a short-term punitive campaign against Chinese troops in North China, developed into the protracted, still unfinished war ... For Japan, pursuing and ending the war in China transcends all the other problems thrown up by the war in Europe.
>
> From the first battles in the north, the war in China has led to the Japanese occupation of all North China, and Inner Mongolia, then to the hard battles for Shanghai and Nanking with the subsequent occupation of the whole Yangtze basin up to Ichang; in southern China, too, large areas were occupied, encompassing the entire coast; and finally, the ocupation of the northern part of French Indochina. If the border of Manchukuo is included, the Japanese army is now spread along a front some 1,300 kilometres in length.

The unexpected expansion of the conflict with China brought Japan from the first mobilization measures to the full mobilization of a 1,000,000-strong army, to the constant war readiness of the navy, and to the development of a considerable air strike-capacity.

The account of the prolonged agony in China, by-lined 'S', was dry and factual. Even the most chauvinistic Japanese could not take exception to what Sorge had written (although some believed that the military was understating the number of Japanese casualties). No one reading the article could ever have suspected that the writer was pro-Chinese, and committed to the struggle to defeat Japanese aggression.

§ Eta wrote at the time that she was gripped by a 'Richard Sorge fever'. It was a condition that must afflict numerous other women, she thought. Richard loved to conquer, and there was no shortage of tittle-tattle around the embassy on the subject of his sexual adventures. Sorge told her that he had no other attachments, while admitting that various women still claimed proprietorial rights. The affair with Helma Ott was long in the past, but she was eager to sabotage his romance with Eta. According to Richard his affair with Anita Mohr was no more than an amusing memory, but she made no effort to disguise her jealousy.

As for the 'little Japanese woman' who had lived with him 'at times', he had sent her away at the beginning of May. 'It was too dangerous,' Richard said, explaining tersely why he had decided to end that affair. It was less than the whole truth about the romance with Hanako, with whom he had spent half of each week for the better part of the past five years. As Hanako recalls events, she did not move out of Nagasaka-cho until October, shortly before Sorge's arrest. According to Eta, however, the house bore no trace of a female presence during the summer months when she paid regular visits to the house. She wanted to take him at his word when he said he was now free of attachments, including that to Helma Ott. In her eyes, his sexual appetites, the subject of much rumour, were of no consequence. The important thing was that his devotion to her seemed total and exclusive.

Arriving in Tokyo with no friends – although she had known Helma Ott fleetingly in Berlin – Eta felt acutely the isolation of the foreigner in Japan. The strange, teeming life beyond the embassy walls was incomprehensible and impenetrable. In the German colony, too, she felt an outsider. She was too intelligent, forceful and independent to go along with the Heil Hitler-chanting and the toadying that was required for smooth relations with the Otts and their coterie.

In return for hospitality, Eta obliged the Otts by performing at the embassy concerts and grand soirées that Helma was fond of arranging. For a lucky few, the German Embassy was a mecca of culture and elegance, of frothing champagne and breathless waltzing under sparkling chandeliers. As Richard often remarked, the German diplomats and business executives had too much money and too little work, but they did work hard at their pleasures. They were fortunate in being stranded in Japan, far from the war raging in Europe, but most realized this dream-like limbo would not last indefinitely. It was wiser to live for the moment, without thought for the future. It was in the same spirit that Eta and Richard met nearly every day.

'You've got to get out of the embassy,' said Richard one afternoon in early July. 'Otherwise the Otts will control you completely, as they do the rest of the Germans here. Now the war with the Soviet Union has cut communications, the only contact with home is via the embassy – and that makes Ott all the more powerful, like the prince of the German community. The trouble is, Ott is secretly anti-Nazi, and desperately anxious to prove the opposite. The result is he goes to the other extreme and is worse than a proper Nazi.

'Leave the embassy as soon as you can. Find your own place. I'll help you. Make yourself independent from these wretched people. Learn Japanese, concentrate on your music and have as little to do with the embassy people as possible. The thing is this: I won't be around all that much longer. One of these days you'll be on your own here. We've got to start thinking of your future.'

'You're going away? I didn't realize,' said Eta, dazed by this revelation. It was the first time since they met that Sorge had talked of leaving Japan.

'Not immediately,' Richard said. 'But I want you to know that I may have to leave the country suddenly. I may have no choice. I can't explain the reason. But if it happens, and if some people at the embassy tell you I've run off with another woman – promise you won't believe them!'[18]

§ Under moonlight, on the warm, fragrant night of 10 July, Ambassador Ott hosted a small cocktail party on the lawn beside the residence. Insects rasped and chirped noisily, but the hum of conversation was more subdued than usual. Germany was now fighting on two fronts, and with the cutting of the Trans-Siberian Railway link, the sense of isolation in the small German community was intense. But life had to go on, and fortunately the ambassador had taken the precaution of stockpiling whisky, champagne, caviar and good-quality *Wurst* to ease the pain.

The party was held in Eta Harich-Schneider's honour, following a triumphant concert success at Tokyo's Nihon Seinen Kaikan hall that evening. The ambassador did the honours: Helma had left for Karuizawa earlier that day to open the family's summer villa.

Richard arrived, apologetic about missing the concert due to an important deadline. Eta assumed that this meant an urgent news story for the *Frankfurter Zeitung*, but the dispatch that went out that day was for the eyes of Stalin and Molotov – crucial intelligence concerning a state secret, the policy of advancing to the south rather than the north which Emperor Hirohito had endorsed only a few days earlier.

It is reasonable to assume that this was a great load off Sorge's mind – he had responded to the Centre's impatient demands for an estimate of Japan's intentions, although he knew this was only the beginning of his quest. The achievement could be savoured only privately, such was the lonely nature of the spy's trade, but no doubt he enjoyed the satisfaction of outwitting the Nazi diplomats and businessmen on the embassy lawn.

On that night Sorge was seen to be in high spirits. Although he drank copiously, he took care to avoid a repeat of his recent intemperate behaviour. The outrageous telephone calls to the ambassador and his circle on 22 June had been forgiven, if not forgotten. They had all agreed that the less said about the incident the better; if Meisinger or the Nazi organization in Tokyo got wind of it, the consequences for all concerned could be serious.

Nevertheless, Sorge's tantrums were taxing the ambassador's patience. As Ott confided to Eta, their long and close friendship was fraying, although he still valued Sorge as a political oracle and reliable fixer in tricky situations. It seems to be the case that Sorge was granted more licence than anyone so troublesome could reasonably expect. The Otts, and some other friends, tried to protect Sorge from his own self-destructive tendencies. He was a cross to be borne with sighs of resignation.[19]

§ 'Mrs Eugen Ott, wife of the German Ambassador, arrived at Karuizawa Thursday, and opened her summer house at No. 1415,' readers of the *Japan Times and Advertiser* were told on Friday 11 July. By now, if they had not left for the sea or mountains already, the majority of foreign residents in Tokyo were plotting their escape from the furnace. When the rains lifted, the heat in the city would become intense, and the ordeal was made worse by persistent rain – the summer of 1941 would go down as the wettest on record so far.

'Vacation Days Are Here Again!' announced the *Japan Times and Advertiser* at the end of June, as it did every year. Europe was engulfed in war and, remote as the turmoil was, it cast its shadow over expatriates in Japan. No one could feel confident about the future, but that seemed all the more reason to make the most of the holidays. The social column of the *Japan Times and Advertiser* recorded who went where. Fewer American and British names made the column this summer: many felt there was no longer a place for them in the xenophobic New Order.

The British and French who remained gravitated to Lake Chuzenji, high in the mountains beyond Nikko; the Germans and Americans made for Karuizawa, in cool upland below a live volcano. Hakone, at the foot of Mount Fuji, was also popular with Germans. Near Hakone was the hot-spring spa of Miyanoshita, with Japan's oldest Western-style hotel, the Fujiya, a year-round favourite with all nationalities. The guest registers show that Sorge, Wenneker, Kretschmer and indeed most of the staff of the German Embassy were regular visitors.

A new attraction was the Kawana Hotel in Izu, advertising itself as the 'most up-to-date hostelry in the Empire'. An English-language guide-book to Japan in the late 1930s carries a photograph of two men playing chess in the newly opened hotel; they are sitting in the solarium that looks across the golf-course to the sea. Wolfgang Galinsky, a German diplomat who bought the guidebook soon after arriving in Japan, would later put names to these faces – Richard Sorge and Eugen Ott.

§ A few days after Mrs Ott's arrival, a certain Mr K. Baumfeld was reported to have joined his wife and family in the mountain resort. 'His potato plants, which he has been going up to take care of from time to time during the spring, are now full grown.' It was a sure sign that foreign residents could no longer count on the comfortable life-style to which they had become accustomed. By 1941 a number of foreign residents were cultivating a potato patch in their leisure time; fresh vegetables were disappearing from the shops along with many other commodities in Japan's war economy.

The Japanese muttered about the poor quality of rice, the dwindling supplies of tofu, matches and cigarettes. Foreigners grumbled, usually more vocally, about the lack of sugar, vegetables and butter, and, with good reason, about the racial discrimination of shopkeepers who refused to serve them. In July, their lack of fortitude brought a sharp rebuke from a correspondent to the *Japan Times and Advertiser*. Signing himself 'A True Japanese', the letter-writer bluntly advised these moaning minnies to go home if they weren't satisfied:

Wartime upsets everything normal, and I trust that no foreigners will
howl over the sugar ration as they did last summer in a port city [Kobe]
… We are under no obligation to furnish them with bread, sugar, butter
or anything else. They should be prepared to eat rice and misoshiru
[bean-paste soup] the same as we do. Or else, if things here do not meet
their whims in any way, they are cordially requested to get the hell out
of here. We have enough mouths of our own to feed.[20]

In response, an aggrieved foreign resident of twenty years' standing
fired off a letter from Kobe, agreeing that foreigners should not expect
special treatment. But, he went on, Japanese rice dealers had simply
refused to sell to foreigners before ration coupons were introduced.
True, Japan had plenty of mouths to feed. The population had indeed
doubled since the era when Japan was sealed off from the outside
world: this was entirely due to benign foreigners who had brought
trade and industrialization to these shores. 'But apparently there are still
some people who would like to have foreign trade, and all the benefits
of the never ceasing development of the whole world, however, without
foreigners. About as reasonable a proposition as wanting to have the
cake and eat it.'[21]

§ Since the start of July, Ambassador Ott had harnessed the entire
German Embassy to his campaign to coax Japan to move against Russia.
He and his staff endeavoured to convince War Minister Tojo, Army
Chief of Staff Sugiyama Gen, pro-German politicians like Matsuoka
and sympathetic newspaper editors that the *Wehrmacht* would take Moscow in six weeks. They contrasted German military prowess with the
dismal morale of the Red Army, the Soviet government and the Russian
people, and hammered home the message that the feeble Soviet military
machine in the Far East would distintegrate as soon as the Imperial
Army marched in. The response was not encouraging: Matsuoka and
top military leaders told Ott that the troop mobilization would not be
completed for another two months. Japan would join the war when the
German army had occupied Moscow and advanced at least to the Volga
river line. Ott gloomily briefed Sorge on the Japanese wait-and-see policy.
   Sorge heard more about the attempt to rally the Japanese behind
Germany's war from the senior military attaché, Colonel Kretschmer.
Berlin had instructed Kretschmer to trumpet German military victories
to the Japanese army's General Staff. Kretschmer even drew up a plan
of how the army might go about taking Vladivostok and Siberia – just
as Wenneker had done for the navy in February when Germany was
prodding the Japanese navy to attack Singapore.

The military attaché also gave Japanese army officers a German intelligence report that large units of Soviet troops were being moved from Siberia to the western front, a report based on the fact that soldiers who belonged to Soviet Far East units had fallen into German hands. In this way Kretschmer tried to lead the Japanese to believe that Russia's eastern defences were much weakened, and Siberia ripe for plucking.

Sorge did not sit idly by while all this was going on. For weeks he waged an intensive psychological warfare campaign aimed at contradicting and undermining the embassy's endeavours. While the diplomats painted a rosy picture of the advance across Russia, Sorge spread gloom and doom by the bucketful. His part-time job editing the German news bulletin proved helpful: 'As I was then working in the embassy information and propaganda section, I saw different propaganda material sent from Germany, and so I knew how hard Germany was trying to secure Japanese intervention.'[22]

Buttonholing Japanese press and official acquaintances, Sorge declared that Hitler's timetable for defeating the Soviet Union was as unrealistic as Napoleon's in 1812, and equally doomed to fail. In an extraordinary gesture, he called together the German press corps and lectured them on why the Reich was heading for disaster. This was a few days after the outbreak of war.

Wherever possible Sorge neutralized the efforts of the embassy staff, with which he was completely familiar. In one instance, Lieutenant-Colonel Nehmitz, the assistant air attaché, told him that at Ott's instructions he had produced a report designed to reassure Japan that it need not fear Russian air-raids if it joined the war. Sorge was shown the report and, to his undoubted satisfaction, found the tone utterly unconvincing: 'Nehmitz gave me this report to read, and you could see at a glance it was just too phoney to be effective.'[23]

Sorge tried to outflank the air attaché by telling contacts in the General Staff headquarters and in the Foreign Ministry that the Soviet Union's airforce capability was far superior to Japan's. They were warned not to take everything the German Embassy put out as the gospel truth: most of it was propaganda. His Japanese listeners may well have been impressed by this show of candour: for was not Sorge himself in the embassy press section, editing a daily newsletter filled with official bulletins on German war victories?

None the less, it must have seemed odd, to Japanese in official positions, that a man on the payroll of the German Embassy took such a pessimistic line in private.

§ On the wet, cool night of Wednesday 16 July, a black Ford swept out of the back gate of the prime minister's official residence at Nagata-cho. With the inside lights extinguished, it sped towards Hayama, on the shoreline sixty miles southeast of Tokyo, arriving at the seaside villa of Emperor Hirohito shortly before 9 p.m. Here Prince Konoye, the effete and ineffective prime minister, ceremoniously tendered his resignation, and those of his cabinet. Exactly one year ago Konoye had been driven from his summer house in Karuizawa, in the same car, to Tokyo, to receive the imperial command to form a cabinet.

At 11.15 p.m. the government spokesman – Dr Ito Nobumi, president of the Board of Information – announced that the cabinet had resigned *en bloc* earlier that evening. The emperor had accepted the resignations. His Imperial Majesty would return to Tokyo the next day. Until a new cabinet was formed, Konoye would continue to oversee state affairs. No satisfactory explanation for this change was given.

Ozaki had been aware for some days that the Konoye cabinet faced a crisis and might be forced to resign, and passed on what he knew to Sorge. Konoye's dilemma was this: if his government's negotiations with America failed, the cabinet would fall; yet if Konoye compromised with the US – which meant agreeing to a troop pull-out from China – that would be unpalatable to hardliners. Either way, Konoye would be in trouble.[24]

The following evening, 17 July, Sorge telephoned a brief story on the event to his newspaper, which ran it the next day. The article gave absolutely no hint that Sorge had been forewarned. Konoye's resignation, the report said, 'came as a big surprise even for very well informed political circles'.

The new cabinet, announced on 18 July, was identical to the previous one, except that the headstrong Matsuoka had been replaced as foreign minister by Admiral Toyoda Teijiro. This was a transparent face-saving ploy to eject an opponent of the talks between Japan and the United States. The removal of Matsuoka was a serious setback for Ambassador Ott, and Sorge found him in a despondent mood on the day the ministerial line-up was made public. 'This is bad news for us,' Ott told him gloomily on that Friday, when the press reported that 'Mr Matsuoka has not been feeling very well for the past few days' – which was undoubtedly true. 'Matsuoka was a good friend of Germany, though he had peculiar ways. Now that he's gone, the government may try to settle the crisis with America even if means giving Germany the cold shoulder. Matsuoka was the one man I could rely on to put the case for Japanese intervention in the war against the Russians. He failed to win over the civilian or the military leaders, but I know that he tried. He always told me how much he admired the Führer.'

In more than one cable, Ott had assured Foreign Minister Ribbentrop that 'everything points to Japan's intervention in the war against Russia'. Now he was afraid he might have to eat his words. 'The new fellow, Toyoda, takes a very cool attitude towards Germany,' the ambassador said.[25]

Sorge was not sympathetic. Any reverse for German diplomacy filled him with barely concealed satisfaction. No doubt his persistent harping on the inevitability of Germany's defeat, and Japan's good sense in remaining aloof from the fray, irritated Ott intensely. Back home in the Reich, of course, such a *Miesmacher* (defeatist) would be quickly silenced.

On many mornings Sorge was in a combative frame of mind, engaging in vehement debate with the ambassador until the breakfast crockery rattled under his pounding fist.

'This war is criminal! We have no chance of winning! The Japanese laugh when we put out the line that we'll be in Moscow by the end of August! Their army intelligence people know better than to believe this propaganda. The *Wehrmacht* is still advancing, but we're taking heavy losses. The Red Army is contesting every kilometre!'

A day or two after the ousting of Matsuoka, they sat on the lawn outside the ambassador's study, drinking coffee in the early morning freshness of the garden. 'In three years – at the outside – we'll have lost this war. If the Japanese join in, it may take a bit longer. But in the long run, we'll be destroyed, you mark my word!'

The ambassador could hardly squeeze a word in edgeways, and these days he seldom tried. There was little point in entering into argument with Sorge about the rights and wrongs of Hitler's Russian campaign: he had lost all sense of proportion and went wild when contradicted. 'You're not the only one with misgivings about the war,' Ott interjected, feebly. 'But what can I do?'

'Well, you could stop selling the line to the Japanese that the *Wehrmacht* will shake hands with their army in Siberia if they join in the war,' said Sorge, with mounting irritation. 'Don't think for a moment Japan will intervene just to please us, *Herr Botschafter* [Ambassador]! From what my sources tell me, you're wasting your time trying to drag these people into the war.

'First, because we are trying to make them believe that we're going to win this war and destroy Stalin. Naturally, the Japanese ask themselves why they should spend good money to go to war when they can take as much Russian territory as they want without fighting once Germany has crushed the Red Army. This is the ripe persimmons strategy – you just wait for the persimmons to ripen and fall into your lap.

'And second, why should Japan become a cat's paw of Germany and get involved in a hazardous winter war against the Soviet Union, and expose herself to the danger that America and Britain might seize the chance to strike at Japan. It just doesn't make sense!

'And another thing. We both know that Japan's economic interests lie in the south, where she can simply grab the rubber and tin and oil she needs for her war machine. Not in Siberia, where there are no resources that can be easily exploited. Just think about it for a moment, *Herr Botschafter*. If you were the Japanese War Minister, would you send hundreds of thousands of men into Siberia just to keep Joachim von Ribbentrop happy?'[26]

There were many occasions in these weeks when Sorge's anger overflowed, as he watched Ott pursue his war diplomacy with a will. He flung discretion to the winds, airing pro-Soviet views that had been acceptable almost up to the eve of the war (for Hitler and Stalin had been partners in a non-aggression pact, and Ribbentrop was contemplating an expanded Axis embracing Russia) but which now rang like propaganda for the enemy.

For nearly three years Sorge had made allowances for the ardour with which Ott adapted to the role of Nazi ambassador, ready to believe that he was a decent man, who in his heart opposed the Hitler clique. He was untroubled by Ott's gestures of loyalty to the Reich – such as his abstention from church, except at Christmas, although he had been a practising Catholic. As he explained: 'If the Foreign Office finds out I go to mass, that's the end of me as ambassador.'[27]

What sickened Sorge most was the way Ott clicked his heels and followed to the letter every order from Hitler and Ribbentrop, however loathsome, when he could safely have acted with less zeal at this distance from Berlin. As Ott's mission came to revolve around inciting Japan to fight Germany's enemies, he sank ever lower in Sorge's esteem. He now saw the ambassador as morally corrupt, prizing his privileges – a handsome salary, the fawning respect of the Japanese, extraordinary power over the German community – more than his principles.[28]

It is evident that Sorge did little to hide his feelings. Their friendship was clearly under strain by the spring of 1941, when Ott made his feeble attempt to engineer Sorge's return home. In July, Ott revealed to Eta that his personal relations with Sorge were in a parlous state. The ambassador was sensitive to the opinions of others. In conversation with Eta he revealed that 'Sorge advised me not to take this post. He thought it would cost me my integrity.' Worried about what Eta had been told by Sorge, he was anxious to correct any false impressions. 'But I like to think I still have a little integrity – don't you think so?' he said. 'The trouble with Sorge is his lack of realism. He just doesn't understand the way the world works.'[29]

§ The birth of a new cabinet barely different from the old one was greeted with widespread cynicism. Alert Japanese suspected that the whole thing was stage-managed by the military, who appeared to have the Konoye government on a leash that was getting gradually shorter. Bleakly, Nagai Kafu told his diary on 18 July:

> The newspapers say Konoye will remain, while everyone else will be reshuffled, as if the whole game was pre-arranged. From now on, the tyranny of the military circles will get worse, and the social situation bleaker. I am too old to care about such mimicry of the Nazis' politics.
>
> The quality of rice is bad, sugar is in ever shorter supply. But I can put up with anything if I imagine I am in exile, watching the moon with a clear conscience.[30]

§ On that same Friday the ambassador telephoned Mrs Ott, asking her to interrupt her vacation in Karuizawa and join him in Tokyo for official functions surrounding the advent of the new cabinet. The break was not unwelcome: it had rained without respite since Helma arrived in Karuizawa the previous week, and the wooden house was damp and chilly.

Mount Asama had rumbled eerily on Sunday, like a prolonged clap of thunder. Vapour poured from the mouth of the volcano, but was lost in the dense cloud cover that hovered over the mountains and the town. The German community that had taken up residence in Karuizawa for the summer grumbled loudly about the miserable weather, the shortages of essentials, and the deteriorating manners of the Japanese, in that order.

§ Each fresh German victory in Russia wounded Sorge. 'Stalin Line Reported Pierced at Great Depth by Nazis', announced the *Japan Times and Advertiser*'s front page on 17 July, and he sank into a morose spell for a day or two. German armoured groups had advanced more than 400 miles since the war began, and were now only 200 miles from Moscow. Smolensk had fallen the day before, although this was not yet in the newspapers.

We may surmise that the darker the war news, the harder Sorge pushed himself to discover the broad strategic intentions of the Japanese. His information was unsettling. In the first part of July, a large mobilization had begun. The whole thing was supposed to be strictly secret but in practice it was impossible to conceal the call-up of reserves, the billeting of soldiers, and the transport of men, equipment, provisions and horses through railway stations and ports on such a scale.

These were fraught weeks for Sorge. He had accepted Ozaki's interpretation of the decisions of the imperial conference of 2 July, namely that Japanese military expansion would be directed southwards, and not against the Soviet Union. But doubts crept in that the reinforcement of the Kwantung Army in Manchuria was, as Ambassador Ott said, the prelude to an offensive against the Soviet Union. As Sorge wrote, 'At the start, the large-scale nature of the mobilization and the fact that some reinforcements were sent northward gave us cause for anxiety.'[31] Henceforth, the analysis of Japanese mobilization plans consumed all the energies of Sorge and his collaborators. From the middle of July Sorge and Ozaki arranged to meet every Monday, instead of every two weeks or so as before.

Ozaki picked up important clues at the South Manchurian Railway, which was contracted to transport Japanese troops, at the Breakfast Society, and from contacts in the business world. Long experience as a journalist had taught him the art of fishing for information in a deceptively casual fashion. When he met an executive of Mitsui Bussan, the leading trading house, in late July, Ozaki remarked that it looked as if the army intended to strike somewhere in the north. Oda Shintaro, the deputy chief of Mitsui's shipping department, rose to the bait: 'From the news I'm getting, more units are going south than are going north,' he said.[32] He went on to volunteer highly confidential figures on the troop movements obtained by his department: '250,000 to the north, 350,000 to the south, 40,000 remaining in Japan.'

Ozaki passed this information on to Sorge, but expressed his personal opinion that the mobilization was targeted mainly at the north. This was alarmingly at odds with his earlier verdict that the Japanese strategy of striking into Southeast Asia had triumphed over hostility towards the Soviet Union. Sorge was confused and anxious; in his testimony, he mentioned his dissatisfaction with the intelligence on the mobilization supplied by Ozaki.

His superiors were breathing down his neck with queries about what Japan was plotting. To the Soviet leadership, the transfer of men and equipment to areas of Manchuria close to Russia's borders seemed to foreshadow a war, and the extension of Japan's Greater East Asia Co-

Prosperity Sphere sanctioned by the emperor on 2 July to include Siberia and the Maritime Provinces. Soviet forces were tied down and could not be shipped westwards, where they were desperately needed to deal with the Germans.

Sorge had no shortage of information; the problem lay in interpreting it decisively enough to convince Red Army strategists of the correct course of action.

§ Most of the individual pieces of the mobilization puzzle were collected by the tireless Miyagi. Braving rain, clinging heat and humidity averaging 94 per cent, he trekked through mud one day and whirlwinds of dust another to reconnoitre the movements of army units. Countless hours were spent in dingy bars and restaurants coaxing minutiae out of casual acquaintances or strangers, at great personal risk. Often he sensed the presence of the police 'shadow'.[33]

His investigation depended heavily on help from Corporal Odai Yoshinobu of the Imperial Japanese Army. As anticipated, Odai was called to the colours once again in late July. His unit was stationed at Utsunomiya, seventy miles north of Tokyo, home of the 14th division. Miyagi had no choice but to travel to this dreary town, in sticky, overcrowded trains, and pray that his meetings with the soldier did not attract unwonted attention.[34] At one of these meetings Odai told Miyagi that the 14th division planned to call out the reserve and send it to the continent, possibly Manchuria, and that new training grounds for tanks and infantry had been laid out near Utsonomiya.

Miyagi found out that the mobilization in Tokyo was being conducted in three phases. He provided Sorge with details about the sort of troops being called up – their age groups and their degree of battlefield experience. His survey showed that many of the units being shipped to Manchuria were made up of inexperienced soldiers and reserves, who would be of little use if the army really intended to launch combat operations against Russia.

To assess how many troops were being deployed to the south and how many to the north, Miyagi observed the types of uniforms that were being issued. Soldiers given lightweight uniforms were clearly being sent to the warm climes of the south, while those with winter gear were destined for cold places like the frontier with Siberia. This was the sort of tell-tale detail that soldiers gossiped about among themselves, and with the civilians they mingled with. The army threatened severe punishment for careless talk, but it proved impossible to prevent leakages, as can be seen from Nagai Kafu's diary entry for 24 July:

Soldiers waiting to be shipped out are said to be billeted these days in private homes around Shitaya and Sotokanda. They have winter dress so they think they will be sent not to the south but to Mongolia or Siberia. They are all in their thirties and include those who have been retired from active duty after seeing combat. Shortages of merchandise and food in this city have become so acute that people are truly alarmed by a call-up on this scale.[35]

§ In July, irksome new rules made life more miserable for English-speaking foreigners living in Japan. Henceforth only Japanese could be used in telephone conversations between cities in Japan, and only Japanese or German in telephone conversations between Japan and Europe. Not surprisingly, Anglo-Saxon expatriates – few of whom spoke Japanese – were indignant. The *Japan Times and Advertiser* reported a case where a finance house telephoned a foreign customer in Yokohama on some urgent business. The foreigner could not speak Japanese; use of English was forbidden; the business had to be deferred. The paper commented, self-righteously, 'The fault, of course, lies with the customer for not speaking the language. Shortness of residence, like intoxication, is no excuse.'[36]

With this petty regulation – ostensibly an anti-espionage measure – Japan punished its foreign residents for the actions of their governments. Rancour towards the US and Britain grew more venomous day by day. In July, the press launched an officially inspired propaganda campaign to denounce the encirclement of Japan by the ABCD powers – America, Britain, China and the Dutch East Indies. In a chorus of rage, the newspapers cried out against the encircling alliance that was 'squeezing the life-blood out of Japan', and demanded government action, without specifying what form it should take. The US and the British Empire – the principal backers of the Chungking government, which was thwarting Japan's efforts to 'bring peace and prosperity to China' – were identified as enemies number one and two.

Otto Tolischus, an American journalist, was struck by the even-handed coverage of the war between Germany and Russia in Japanese newspapers. This 'show of scrupulous neutrality', he recorded in his diary on 13 July 1941, 'suggested that any immediate move would not be to the north.'[37]

§ Police agents resembled flies buzzing around a cow, thought Kawai Teikichi as he made his way to the Meguro ward of Tokyo, where Ozaki lived. Although he had retired from the business of espionage, there were days when Kawai *knew* they were still on his tail. Such was the sensation on 27 July, a Sunday of searing heat. To test his hunch he deliberately dropped a magazine, with a newspaper folded inside, on the crowded footbridge at Uguisudani Railway Station. He turned and watched. A middle-aged man treading close behind him picked up the magazine and glanced at the newspaper. Then he approached, flushing with embarrassment, handed over the items and disappeared into the crowd. It was the 'rabbit' he had seen so many times before.[38]

Hoping he had driven off his pursuer for a while, Kawai continued on his way. Out of his first month's paypacket he bought a box of *sushi* for Ozaki, as thanks for helping him find a job. Arriving at the house, however, he found that Ozaki was out, and that his wife, Eiko, was with a guest. Kawai recognized the man as Ito Ritsu.

Ito was a friend and former classmate of Ozaki, and now worked with him in the Investigation Department of the South Manchurian Railway. To the police he was a shady character with a long record of harbouring 'dangerous thoughts'. His membership of the Japanese Communist Youth League had earned him two years in prison; he had recanted, but before long returned to his old ways, helping to reconstruct the outlawed Japan Communist Party. This had led to his re-arrest in a crackdown on suspected communists in November 1939, and he had been held in police custody until the following summer.

During this period in detention, Ito Ritsu endured a severe interrogation. The confession he made to his captors would later become a focus of controversy. Much would be made of the fact that, upon his release on probation in August 1940, he returned to his old job at the South Manchurian Railway. Was he installed there as a police informer? If so, whom was he assigned to watch?

Ozaki made no attempt to distance himself from him when he was let out. Ito continued to serve as an able assistant, and the two men met socially as well. They had much in common, apart from similar political views. They were both intellectually gifted, sociable, and indefatigable womanizers. Rightly or wrongly, Ozaki believed that his intimacy with a man who been on the wrong side of the law posed no threat to his own position.[39]

On this Sunday, when he visited Ozaki's home, Kawai found no reason to suspect that Ito was anything other than he seemed – a sharp-witted and amusing companion whom Ozaki trusted completely. But some years later, after dark questions were raised about Ito's role in the exposure of the Sorge network, Kawai claimed to have felt all along that there was something odd, duplicitous even, about this man who had insinuated himself into Ozaki's affections.

§ Without firing a shot, Japanese forces marched into French bases in southern Indo-China on 28 July, in pursuance of a 'joint defence agreement' announced that day between Tokyo and the Vichy government of France. The Japanese army and navy were already well established in the northern part of Indo-China, a French colony. Now they seized the coveted rice-lands of the south, gaining a rich food supply and a strategic base from which to expand the frontiers of their sphere of 'peace and prosperity'.

As the Japanese navy took over the French naval base at Camranh Bay, the press in Tokyo reminded readers that the Russians, nearly forty years earlier, had sailed from this harbour to their destruction at the hands of Admiral Togo's fleet. That, as every schoolboy knew, was the first great Japanese naval victory over the white man.

This new stage in the enlargement of the Greater East Asia Co-Prosperity Sphere provoked an immediate and firm response from the Western powers. The US, Britain, Australia and the Dutch East Indies froze Japanese assets, paralysing trade with Japan. President Roosevelt ordered tighter controls on sales of US oil, Japan's main source of energy. America's swing from appeasement to confrontation provoked a grave political crisis in Japan. It came as a sharp shock to the Konoye government, which had not anticipated such a tough reaction while talks with the US were still pending – a point Ozaki made to Sorge.

The press in Tokyo foamed indignantly at the churlish attitude of the Western democracies. 'There are nations that are calling this peaceful southern expansion of Japan a military invasion, attempting thus to prevent the establishment of the East Asia Co-Prosperity Sphere,' the *Hochi Shimbun* seethed. On 29 July the front page of the *Japan Times and Advertiser* carried photos of Japanese sailors 'giving their autographs to Indo-China natives' and being pedalled in tricyles through the streets of Saigon. 'Japanese sailors see Indo-China Sights', read the caption. The advance by the Japanese – 'the foremost exponents of peace and prosperity in Asia' – must have appeared completely benign to the unsuspecting newspaper reader.

On 28 July and again the next day, Sorge filed two brief news stories on events for the *Frankfurter Zeitung*. The 'peaceful occupation of Indo-China and the surrounding seas by the Japanese army and navy' had been carried out 'speedily and smoothly with the full co-operation of the French and native forces,' he wrote, quoting the '*Japan Times*, which is close to the Foreign Ministry'. The articles are devoid of even a trace of irony, although it goes without saying that Sorge toed the official line with tongue in cheek.

Sorge calculated that the move into southern Indo-China had relieved the strategic pressure on the Soviet Union's eastern borders, he said later. The Japanese advance would work to Russia's advantage by deepening the rift with the US, 'and so I thought at the time that the risk of Japan going to war against Russia had lessened'.[40]

Patently, the 'Advance South' option had triumphed. The navy was absolutely opposed to war against Russia, as were the war minister and the majority of army leaders – although a hard core at General Staff headquarters continued to bay for war against the Bolsheviks.

In retrospect, all this was clear enough. But at the time Sorge was prey to uncertainty – more so than he cared to admit to interrogators. The great mobilization continued for several weeks and poured tens of thousands of troops into Manchuria, close to Russia's borders. From evidence that has become available recently, it is clear that this led Sorge to suspect Japan of waiting for a favourable opportunity to attack.[41]

On Wednesday 30 July Sorge told Moscow that Japanese war preparations would be completed by the second half of August. Japan might launch an offensive if Soviet defences in the Far East were weakened by troop transfers to the western front. He wondered how long the rabidly anti-Soviet elements on the army General Staff were prepared to wait once they scented blood.

> Invest and Intari [Ozaki and Miyagi] said more than 200,000 men will be called up under the new mobilization in Japan. Thus about two million men will be under arms in Japan by the middle of August.
>
> Japan will be able to begin war from the second half of August, but will only do so should the Red Army actually be defeated by the Germans, resulting in a weakening of defence capabilities in the Far East.
>
> This is the viewpoint of the Konoye group, but how long the Japanese General Staff will bide their time is difficult to say at the moment.
>
> Invest is convinced that if the Red Army stops the Germans in front of Moscow, Japan will not make a move.[42]

So Japan was still hedging its bets, according to Sorge. He could not believe that the Japanese had given up plans to strike against Russia in favour of the 'Advance South' option. Japan's dual strategy towards the south and north baffled him. Ozaki's intelligence was equivocal, as we see from this telegram. Possibly Sorge, who was intent on influencing Ott, had instead been influenced by Ott – who was confidently predicting that the Japanese would intervene when they were ready.

§ Common sense demands that a secret agent avoid emotional involvements that might compromise his covert role. In Sorge's own words, there must be 'no attachments, no strings, no sentimentalities'. The life of an *apparatchik*, he told his friend Hede Massing, was by definition 'lonely and ascetic'. Sorge himself did not live up to the high standards he set for his profession. During his service in Tokyo, there was nothing ascetic about his dedication to drink and women. Both, no doubt, provided a necessary release from the pressures of life on the sharpest of edges, but they were no antidote to loneliness. Neither the company of women nor alcohol could cure the pain of solitude, which became almost unbearable in the final years of his mission in Japan.

A legend has grown up on the subject of Sorge's tumultuous love life. The report on the Sorge espionage case compiled by US Military Intelligence (G-2) in 1949 gave a lurid account of his philandering. It alleged that he was 'intimate with some 30 women in Tokyo during his years of service, including the wife of his good friend, the German ambassador, the wife of his chief foreign assistant and the mistress of this same assistant'.

US army investigators obtained their information from Japanese police and prosecutors involved in the Sorge case, and enshrined it in their report. From that moment, the image of Sorge as a tireless fornicator was cast in stone: he would forever be remembered as the spy who cuckolded both his friend Ott and his collaborator, Vukelic.

It is certain that Helma Ott was among the women who shared Sorge's bed. There is hearsay evidence that Sorge and Edith Vukelic were paramours. Ohashi Hideo, the assistant inspector who interrogated Sorge, spoke meaningfully of their 'special relationship'. However, it appears that this began either after Edith and Branko separated, or after their divorce in 1939. According to Ohashi, Sorge feared that Edith was resentful at the break-up of the marriage, and posed a security risk; he believed she would be less likely to betray the ring if they were lovers. The claim by US army intelligence that Sorge was intimate with Vukelic's 'mistress', however, was unfounded and mischievous. Yoshiko Vukelic swears that she was not the mistress of Branko before their marriage, or of Sorge at any period, and there is no reason to disbelieve her.

Sorge's affair with Helma's bosom friend, the glamorous Anita Mohr, was short-lived, and in the end Sorge treated her with undisguised contempt. Not all his relationships with women were so brief and shallow. For the five years he consorted with Hanako, he showed himself to be tender and scrupulously considerate.

The liaison with Eta was cut short by his arrest; her account of him as a devoted and caring lover during their few shared months is utterly convincing. In contrast to the vacuous women he sometimes fell for, Eta sparkled with intellect and artistry. She fulfilled his need for a sympathetic and loyal companion in whom he could confide; and while he never revealed himself completely to anyone, he apparently bared more of his soul to Eta than to any of the women he loved in Tokyo.

Possibly his deepest attachment was to Katya. It was Eta's impression that he was very fond of the woman he described as 'not really his wife, but considered as such'. Sorge's letters to Katya resonate with a heartfelt longing to share his life with her. Poignantly, they tell of a great love that was doomed to end in grief.

CHAPTER FOURTEEN

August 1941

ON 2 AUGUST Sorge travelled to Karuizawa with his old friend Colonel Scholl, now stationed as military attaché in Bangkok, and Ott. In the tranquillity of the ambassador's summer villa, the three men spent the weekend conferring on political matters. We do not know for certain what was discussed. Scholl's visit to Tokyo apparently included meetings with Japanese army intelligence officers, and it is likely that in Karuizawa the group reviewed official German efforts to embroil Japan in war. No doubt Sorge's store of information on Germany's manoeuvrings in the Far East was much enriched that weekend, and no opportunity missed to exploit contradictions in the alliance between Tokyo and Berlin.[1]

Not long after Germany's early stunning triumph on the battlefield, Hitler's plans for a lightning conquest of the Soviet Union began to go awry. It was soon apparent that the Führer had underestimated the troop reserves that Stalin could bring up from the depths of the USSR; above all he had failed to appreciate the sheer grit of the Russian soldiers defending their motherland.

The Germans continued to penetrate deeper into Russia, but they were incurring heavy losses. Japanese army leaders pored over reports from their intelligence agents, waiting, like vultures, to move in for the kill when the prey was totally enfeebled. However, they quickly realized that the invasion was not going according to plan, and that the forecast that the *Wehrmacht* would occupy Moscow in six weeks was an empty boast. In the second week of August, Sorge reported to the Fourth Department that Japan's appetite for war with Russia was diminishing.

The fact that Moscow was not occupied last Sunday, contrary to what the German Supreme Command promised Oshima [Japan's ambassador in Berlin] has cooled Japanese enthusiasm. Even Green Box [Japanese Army] had the impression that that the White–Red [German–Soviet] War may develop into a second China Incident, because White [Germany] is repeating the same mistakes as Green [Japan] in China.[2]

This was a telegram that could be expected to lift morale in Moscow, but apparently it got no further than Max Clausen's hands. If Clausen's account is to be believed, he received the dispatch from Sorge but failed to transmit it.[3]

There is no such telegram to be found in the material released recently by the Russians – although this does not rule out the possibility that it could be lurking in a corner of some still hidden archive. It is probable that Clausen was telling his interrogators the truth when he said that he failed to send the report, the English text of which was confiscated two months later when police searched his home.[4] Once again the radio man had thrown a spanner into the operations of the Sorge ring, without it being detected. Sorge continued to give him material to encode and transmit, untroubled by fears about his integrity and loyalty.

§ A few days into August, Ozaki gave Sorge disturbing news. According to a rumour circulating in Tokyo, war between Japan and the Soviet Union would start on 15 August, once the big mobilization was completed. 'That's what Ott thinks, as well,' Sorge said, despondently. 'How do *you* see the situation?'

'It's hard to say,' said Ozaki. 'But I sense a change in attitude in government circles. They supported the mobilization at first, because the German army was expected to bring the USSR to its knees once and for all. But I gather the unexpected checkmate in the war is making them more hesitant.'

'The German advance has slowed down,' said Sorge. 'The Red Army is contesting every centimetre of Russian soil. That should make the Japanese think twice before making any move.'

'Yes, and on top of that, we may not even be in a position to go to war in the north,' said Ozaki. 'There is a lot of pessimism about the effects of the freeze on Japanese assets by America and Britain. It means that shortages of war materials like iron, petrol and so on are going to get more severe. To make matters worse, the bad weather this year has cut supplies of farm produce.'

'But what about this rumour?' Sorge asked. 'Do you think there's anything in it?'

'In my view, if there is an attack, it would have to begin at the latest by the last ten days of August,' said Ozaki. 'Japan has to complete the main offensive in Siberia within the three months of September, October and November, on account of the Siberian winter.'

This was true: combat operations could not be delayed beyond the beginning of September. Snow would hamper transportation, even with horses, and large-scale action would be impossible after November.

Ozaki could not give a clear-cut answer to Sorge's question. From the talk in the South Manchurian Railway, it appeared that the issue of whether to fight the Soviet Union had not been resolved. Hot-heads in the War Ministry and General Staff headquarters were still arguing that the time was ripe to launch their longed-for crusade against the Bolsheviks.[5]

§ Ambassador Ott's campaign to persuade Japan to fulfil its duties as a true ally was like climbing an icy slope, and the going became even more treacherous after Matsuoka's forced exit from politics deprived Germany of its best friend in the cabinet. So it came as a surprise to Sorge that Ott, in the first week of August, remained cautiously optimistic that the Japanese could be coaxed onto the battlefield.

Sorge was sceptical. There was no doubt that when Ott met senior officials they briefed him more thoroughly than any other foreign ambassador. As a consequence, Sorge was privy to the thinking of the Japanese civilian and military leadership, percolated through Ott. But he knew that the Japanese did not trust even their German allies fully; they had a tendency to give Ott only a corner of the truth, and by and large what they thought he wanted to hear.[6]

On Wednesday 7 August in a message to Moscow, Sorge reported what the ambassador had told him, with a caveat.

> Ott expressed the view that although the general political stance is unchanged, the pace of joining the war will be very slow. At the same time, Ott expressed complete confidence that the new cabinet supports joining the war.
>
> In any event, it is decidedly more difficult for Ott now in view of the fact that the new cabinet is considerably more indifferent towards relations with Germany than the previous cabinet with Matsuoka.[7]

On 11 August, Sorge drafted a dispatch for Moscow that reflected the intense uncertainty in his mind about which course Japan would take.

> During the first days of the Germany–USSR war, the Japanese government and General Staff decided on major mobilization to prepare for war. But after six weeks of war, Japanese leaders are watching the German offensive being held up, and significant German forces being destroyed, by the Red Army.
>
> The American position is becoming more anti-Japanese, the economic blockade against Japan is intensifying and the Japanese General Staff has no intention of terminating mobilization. There is a firm belief in the

General Staff that they should take the final decision in the immediate future, especially as winter is already approaching. In the coming two to three weeks, Japan's decision will be finally made. It is possible that the General Staff will take the decision to intervene without prior consultation.'[8]

The final sentence has an ominous ring. Sorge was still agonizing over the risk that anti-Bolsheviks in the army might take matters into their own hands, defying the spineless Konoye government.

It is clear from this that neither Sorge nor Ozaki were aware at this point that the hawks in the army General Staff had already bowed to the will of the War Ministry. On 9 August – two days before Sorge drafted this message – the Japanese High Command reached an overall decision not to fight the Soviet Union within the year, although they did not rule out an attack in 1942. Japan was now irreversibly committed to pressing ahead with the advance southwards, and preparations for the inevitable conflict with the US in the southern region would be accelerated. Japan was heading deeper into Southeast Asia, intending to drive the white man out of his colonies there, once and for all.[9]

§ On the evening of 8 August the ambassador, with Colonel Kretschmer, the military attaché, in tow, arrived late for dinner. Consul-General Balser, visiting from Kobe, and Eta were in the drawing-room chatting and drinking aperitifs to while away the time. Helma Ott was in Karuizawa. 'I do apologize for keeping you waiting,' Ott said. 'There were some very important matters to discuss.' The ambassador glanced meaningfully at Eta. 'Sorge was with us, but unfortunately he cannot stay for dinner.'

'I must thank you, Mr Ambassador,' said Kretschmer effusively, as he took his seat at the dinner table. 'I am indebted to you for the opportunity to obtain such splendid information. Sorge's connections are really incredible!'

The ambassador took this as a personal compliment and nodded with satisfaction. 'Yes, absolutely right. That's exactly why we keep the chap here.'[10] It is not known what 'splendid information' Sorge imparted that evening. Possibly he passed on what Ozaki had told him about how hesitant the Konoye coterie was to get involved in a war with Russia, and told them about the shortages of war materials that limited the options. Or perhaps he relayed the rumour – again from Ozaki – about Japan going to war on 15 August when the mobilization was completed.

The following day, 9 August, Ott and Kretschmer dispatched separate cables to their superiors in Berlin. The content of these messages was virtually identical: they both reported that Japan had not yet reached a decision to fight against the Soviet Union, but could be expected to strike when circumstances were favourable.

Sorge knew what the cables told Berlin. The ambassador and the military attaché gave him their gist, if not the actual contents, as is clear from a dispatch he drafted three days later, on 12 August. By then Kretschmer had briefed Sorge on his inspection tour of Manchuria, conducted in early August to assess Japan's war readiness. In the game of trading information, Sorge always came out well. In the first part of his report, Sorge summarized what Kretschmer (referred to by the code-name 'Marta') had given him.

> Six divisions have already arrived in Korea and may stay there in prepara-
> tion for a possible attack on Vladivostok. Four extra divisions have arrived
> in Manchuria as reinforcements. Marta cabled White [Germany] that as
> yet no decision has been taken to launch offensive even when preparations
> are completed. In Marta's opinion, the first target of a Japanese attack
> will be Vladivostok.[11]

Kretschmer clung to his faith in Japanese intervention, but clearly had no idea when it would materialize. The same was true of the ambassador, who was still unable to give his superiors a timetable.

> Ribbentrop is sending telegrams daily in effort to influence Japan to take
> action. Talks were held on this with Generals Doihara and Okamura.
> Ambassador Ott believes the Japanese are waiting for the moment when
> they see the Red Army weakening, as though entry into the war in any
> other conditions would be unsafe, especially as their fuel reserves are
> very low.[12]

Sorge had not yet reached his own conclusions, but at least he was able to tell the Russians how the Germans sized up Japanese intentions.

Moscow, however, received only half of this valuable report. From Russian archive material, it is possible to compare what the Fourth Department saw with the actual text drafted by Sorge (which Japanese police impounded in October 1941.) We see that Clausen radioed only the second portion of the manuscript – 'Ribbentrop is sending ... ' – on 15 August omitting a few words, but without altering the sense. He suppressed the whole of the first part of Sorge's text, which summed up Kretschmer's briefing.[13]

It was one of numerous occasions in 1941 when Clausen compressed Sorge's intelligence reports. At other times, it will be recalled, he simply cast them aside or delayed transmission. Explaining his behaviour to interrogators, Clausen said that by this time he was fast losing his faith in communism. While there may be some truth in this, what we know of Clausen's disposition suggests that the sabotage was motivated primarily by personal grievances.

§ Hanako recalls that one night when she and Sorge were alone he made a startling announcement. It was his mission, he declared, to put an end to the war in Europe – to all wars, in fact. 'Sorge is a big man. He does good things all the time. Do you know what? Sorge is a god. God is always a man. People need more gods. Sorge will become a god.'[14] A gramophone recording of Beethoven's *Fantasia* filled the little study, appropriate background music to Sorge's bombast. Clutching a bottle of vermouth, he was in an exalted mood – not for the first time, and Hanako was never quite sure how to react at these moments. How does one respond to someone proclaiming his own divinity? Once again, Sorge was possessed by a fantasy that the war in Russia could be won, and Japan spared the agony of war, by his single-handed intervention. As we have seen, Eta witnessed a similar display.

Even when not riding the crest of an alcoholic binge, Sorge that summer was filled with a belief that the fate of the world ultimately hinged on his performance in Tokyo. Such self-delusion bordering on megalomania may be common among a certain type of secret agent. In the words of one expert on intelligence, 'Many [agents] seem to overestimate the influence of clandestine activity – and particularly any in which they participated – on historical events.'[15]

§ The virulence of Japanese xenophobia was brought home to Sorge by a nasty incident that month involving Hanako. She was called into the Toriisaka police station for questioning, and humiliated by Superintendent Matsunaga, chief of the foreigners section.

'Why does a woman with your education consort with a foreigner?' Matsunaga demanded roughly. 'Aren't there enough men in Japan?'

He more or less ordered her to separate from Sorge, out of respect for 'the national quintessence of Japan'. When Hanako balked, the policeman was furious. Ordinary citizens – and women as a matter of course – were expected to show a more humble and compliant manner to the guardians of the law.

'A Japanese woman who lives with a *keto* (hairy barbarian) is not a true Japanese! We know what goes on in that house. From this window I can even see when you're in bed – exposing your white buttocks!'

Hanako was dumbfounded. The idea that the goings-on inside the bedroom were visible from the police station appalled her: did this man spend his afternoons with a pair of binoculars at his window, observing their love-making?

'These *keto* are good are they, these guys really treat women well, eh?' the inspector mocked. 'We Japanese men can't compete, is that it, eh?'

When she recounted this incident to Sorge, his face turned red with rage.

'So the police want to take you away from Sorge do they? Well just let them try! Japanese boys are enjoying themselves with German girls, and Germany doesn't say that's bad! 'If Japan takes you from Sorge, I will take all the German girls away from Japanese boys. Yes, all of them. I can do it. I only have to send a telegram to Germany!'[16]

§ While Ott and Kretschmer worked on their cables to Berlin, Sorge attempted to relax in Karuizawa with Eta. They spent 9 and 10 August at the ambassador's summer house, under the watchful eyes of Helma Ott. When he left, with some relief, to return to Tokyo early Monday morning, Eta stayed behind to rehearse for her Karuizawa concert.

Saturday started well. They travelled in a comfortable American car with Franz Krapf, an elegant young German diplomat, and his Swedish girlfriend. It was a long journey through narrow, winding roads, but the time passed quickly. They listened to Sorge's anecdotes about the First World War and the German folk-songs he sang from the soul, sentimental verses about country boys who go to fight for king and country, in which he found a political meaning. Eta and Krapf followed with operatic arias, which they sang as a duet.

In tiny villages along the way, children waiting for German Embassy cars to pass shouted raucously and lifted their arms in mock Nazi salutes. When the road began to climb into hill country, a chill crept into the car. At four o'clock they turned the last bend on the steep ascent, and the first houses came into sight. Beyond, a panorama of volcanic mountains and dark cool forest greeted the eyes. They had travelled only ninety miles, but while Tokyo blistered in heat that evaporated thoughts, Karuizawa, at 3,000 feet above sea level, invigorated the most sluggish spirit.

The flavour of this little town, a summer resort for foreigners since the turn of the century, was distinctly cosmopolitan, at least during the 'season'. But the flavour was no longer Anglo-Saxon. Since the large exodus from Japan of Americans and Britons, Karuizawa had become a *Deutsches Dorf,* a German village. German was the language heard on all sides in the *machi*, as everyone called the little high street. A bakery sold pumpernickel bread and *Apfelkuchen,* and sometimes rare luxuries like honey. Fujiya's restaurant, with a resident German cook, advertised a 'good solid German lunch' and a *gemütliche* coffee hour to 'fortify you before you climb Mount Asama'. The customers buying vanilla ice-cream at Brett's Pharmacy, near the tennis courts, were, for the most part, German. The one cinema offered recent films from Berlin – *Verklungene Melodie* (Fading Melody), with Brigitte Horney, was showing this particular weekend.

For many Japanese the name Karuizawa conjured up a mixture of foreignness and olympian high society. Rare was the prominent Japanese politician or businessmen who did not own a summer villa there, hidden behind a curtain of trees. The rich and powerful migrated north in July and August and consorted in their own little cliques, insulated from the hoi-polloi.[17] Decorum and discretion were less in evidence among younger members of the smart set. The provincial newspaper, *Shinano Mainichi*, noted disapprovingly in July 1941 that Karuizawa was 'a favourite resort of worldlings, vanity is everywhere. Daughters of wealthy families with permanent waves and young wives on bicycles attract the sight of promenaders.'

This summer, the Karuizawa season began later than usual. July had been exceptionally cool and wet, and international tensions delayed the arrival of many important men involved in politics and diplomacy. General Ott certainly had few chances to enjoy his villa during these weeks. His aristocratic chief, von Ribbentrop, had placed a heavy burden on his shoulders, and was now waiting impatiently for the *samurai* to take up their swords.

§ Franz Krapf's car bumped along the dirt road that led from the town, passing the tennis courts, and within a few minutes they turned in at the open gate of a two-storey clapboard house. It offered few of the comforts of the ambassador's residence in Tokyo. There was a chilly, damp feel to the house, which was closed up for most of the year. The furnishings were simple, mostly of the rattan and wickerwork variety. Partitions between rooms were paper-thin, and conversations – and the Otts' conjugal rows – carried into adjoining rooms. Eta found the whole atmosphere depressing, and was relieved when an excuse to cut short her stay came up. However, there was one great saving grace: an enchanting garden with a large sweep of lawn, where a profusion of wild flowers grew. There were cedars and cypresses, and a venerable willow that provided a great pool of shade, where Eta liked to sit with a book when she was not rehearsing or exercising Helma's two Afghan hounds.

Mrs Ott was delighted to see Sorge again, only a week after his last visit in the company of her husband and Colonel Scholl. She would have been happier if he had come without Eta, but the virtuoso was due to keep her company for a few days and give a concert locally. Since the day in June when she had removed an antique bowl and a bonsai tree from her rival's room, Helma had acted with restraint. But every little sign of intimacy that passed between Eta and Sorge wounded her.

At dinner that evening, Sorge wore an unhappy expression. Hans Ulrich von Marchtaler, chief of the political section, who was vacationing in Karuizawa, gossiped with Helma about disagreeable incidents between German and English families in the town. They discussed the ambassador's plan to settle German women refugees from the Dutch East Indies in Karuizawa.

After dinner, when Eta and Sorge strolled in the garden, he seemed tense and edgy. 'I must get back to Tokyo. I have a lot of things to write. And these people get me down with their petty gossip,' he said irritably. 'They're all so smug and self-satisfied. Germany is sliding towards total destruction, and they worry about how to wangle a bigger petrol ration.'

Sorge's concern was the situation on the eastern front, and the human suffering on both sides. He recounted the latest developments with the passion of someone who had known the horrors of the battlefield, and who could never consider war in the abstract. 'The *Wehrmacht* is gaining on Odessa. Kiev may not be able to hold out much longer. But the Red Army is stronger than it looks. Look at the way it's absorbing even the heaviest attacks! There's absolutely no way we can win this war. That's what I've been telling Ott and Kretschmer all along. And, do you know, I think they're beginning to believe me.'

§ The next day, Sunday 10 August, was overcast at first, although the sun broke through in the afternoon. Eta made her way to the Catholic Church, along the dirt road veined with the root systems of ancient pines. Sorge was seen walking out of the gate later in the morning. Nearby was the Mampei Hotel, filled with diplomats' families at this time of the year. The weekend before, Sorge, Ott and Scholl had spent an evening in the Mampei's crepuscular bar, oak-panelled and furnished with leather armchairs in the style of a London club.

Sorge's route that morning is not known. If he had turned right at the gate, he would soon have arrived at a wooded hill that sweeps up to the horizon. A path through the dark forest follows a stream that tumbles over rocks and leads to a spring overgrown with wild flowers. Eta often came this way with Helma's dogs, filling her lungs with the cool, crisp air fragrant with the sweet scent of pines. In the afternoon he was back at the house, sitting reading on a wicker sofa on the verandah looking on to the garden.

At dinner Sorge came to life, provoking laughter with amusing tales of his student years. Wine flowed freely, and the little party sparkled. Helma was moved to recount episodes from what she called 'the happiest time of my life'. This was Munich in 1919, the year of a short-lived uprising engineered by socialists and intellectuals. She was already divorced from her first husband, who, like her, was a communist. She was young, free and idealistic, and left-wing politics was a passing phase. It was all a long time ago, and remembered in a rosy glow.

Helma and Sorge shared many friends involved in the events of 1919, and the two grew animated as they traded reminiscences of this or that person, names that meant nothing to Eta. She sat in silence, completely shut out of the conversation.

It would not have been the first time they harked back to that era. They would have discovered as soon as they met in Japan that they had both left-wing friends and causes in common. As their intimacy deepened, Helma could hardly have failed to notice that *his* political loyalties had not changed since his younger days.[18] In this case, it would be surprising if she did not alert her husband to the fact that his inseparable companion remained a staunch communist, and that their association could well prove harmful to his career – unless, that is, she was too deeply in love to take any action that would put a distance between her and Sorge.

The tantalizing question is how much Eugen Ott knew, with or without the prompting of his wife. Looking back, Eta Harich-Schneider reflected that he was far too perceptive to miss the signals that pointed to his friend's true allegiance. 'I am absolutely convinced that Ott suspected Sorge to be a communist,' she said. 'Sorge did not have to spell it out – it was the only conclusion to be drawn from the extreme positions he took in every political discussion they had, and not only his attacks on the Nazis.

'The two spent hours and hours in political polemics, over chess, at breakfast, after dinner. Sorge did most of the talking, or the shouting, while Ott listened. I was sometimes there on these occasions, and it was impossible not to be struck by Sorge's outspokenness. But how much

Helma Ott revealed to her husband about Sorge's convictions I do not know.'[19]

His well-advertised fondness for everything Russian did not trouble Ott until war loomed, and it became heresy to voice such sympathies. Eta Harich-Schneider theorizes that Sorge had actually told Ott that he had stayed for a while in Russia, and that the ambassador would not have been unduly perturbed.[20]

Certainly Sorge's attacks on the National Socialist credo and organization would have sent shivers down the spine of anyone in Ott's position. But Ott was less worried by his friend's philosophy than by the risk that he would be overheard and reported to the Gestapo, landing them both in hot water. 'Some of the political opinions he expresses I prefer to take with a pinch of salt,' Ott said, in a revealing remark. From the ambassador's comments to friends, we see that he regarded Sorge as a good patriot, with his heart in the right place, but a hopeless idealist – unlike himself, who had accommodated himself to the Hitler regime because there was no other choice.

No doubt Sorge's unvarnished candour disarmed Ott, and others too. The more radical the opinions he voiced, the less imaginable it was that he could be an impostor. No one who wore his heart on his sleeve like Sorge could be anything else than what he appeared.

§ 'Four Divisions Wiped out by Nazis around Nikolaev as Reds retreat en masse.' Back in Tokyo, Sorge was growing accustomed to heart-sinking headlines in his *Japan Times and Advertiser,* like this one on Wednesday 20 August. Much as he would have liked to, he could not dismiss it simply as Axis propaganda. Day by day, news bulletins from more credible sources spoke of a bloodbath on a terrifying scale. United Press in London had estimated that, in the first two months of war, the Red Army had lost over half a million men.

In his own battle behind the German lines in Tokyo, success was eluding him. Japan's true intentions were still a mystery. He could not rule out an attack on Siberia, nor could he forecast it with certitude. It was perplexing and frustrating. Mercifully, the rumour that an offensive would begin on 15 August proved false. And then the fog gradually began to lift. Miyagi brought fragments of information that shed light on the drift of the great mobilization. He had discovered, first, that a large number of the troops bound for Manchuria were attached to small auxiliary units intended to supplement existing divisions, and did not represent the transfer of major components. And second, it turned out that the greater part of the troops mobilized were being held in Japan, and transferred gradually to the southern region – Southeast Asia – or to China.[21]

Miyagi provided another heartening item of information. In the first half of August, he found that his friend and informant Corporal Odai was no longer at the army base in Utsonomiya. Odai's relatives in Maebashi had no news of his whereabouts. Then, a little later, a short message arrived from Manchuria. Miyagi passed it on to Sorge, who recalled the gist: 'He [Odai] was optimistic that there would be no war against the Soviet Union before the year was out, and that before long he would be able to return to Japan.'[22]

All of this gave cause for hope, but fell well short of proof that the danger was past. Sorge and Ozaki agreed that 20 August was a critical juncture. If there were to be a large-scale Japanese offensive it would have to begin some time between then and the end of August, so as to be completed before the Siberian winter paralysed operations. But Red Army chiefs would have worked that out for themselves; Sorge's duty was to anticipate events, not wait for them to happen.

The Red Army desperately needed reinforcements from the Far East Command to throw against the Germans. But, after nine weeks of probing, Sorge was unable to assess the status of the Japanese threat. From what we know, his sense of failure was acute.

On the night of 20 August Sorge's anguish melted away, if only briefly. It was nine p.m. Richard and Eta entered the darkened ballroom, their footsteps echoing as they crossed the marble floor. She lit a candle, and placed it on the grand piano. The residence was deeply silent. Ambassador Ott was attending a social engagement, Mrs Ott was miles away in the hills of Karuizawa.[23]

Eta played first the Waldstein, to Richard's delight, then the Moonlight. The doors of the ballroom were open to the night garden, and insects darted in and out. As she played Eta glanced at Sorge, who was leaning against the piano, the furrowed face thrown into dramatic relief by the candle-light. He shook his head from side to side in rapture, captivated by the music.

It may have been on such an evening – with Bach ringing in his ears – that he slipped along the corridor to Meisinger's office, opening the door with the duplicate key he possessed, to skim through the Gestapo colonel's files. The residence was deserted, and Meisinger was absent on a trip. We know that Sorge kept up to date with Meisinger's investigation. By creeping into the office on a number of occasions in August he was able to satisfy himself that, so far, the Gestapo man had been unable to uncover anything incriminating to report to his superiors in Berlin.

§ On 22 August – or perhaps one or two days later – Sorge's spirits were lifted by interesting news provided by Paul Wenneker. The naval attaché had held a fruitful discussion with the Japanese naval staff that Friday. We know that Sorge did not have to wait long for a full briefing. 'You and I were right, Sorge. Japan is not going to fight the Soviet Union, after all,' the rear-admiral began. Ott and Kretschmer, who counted on Japanese intervention, had misjudged the situation.[25]

'The Japanese have weighed the risks, and don't think they'll gain anything by getting involved,' Wenneker went on. 'There's no guarantee of success before the winter, and in case of a German victory over Russia, Japan will take a share of the spoils at no cost to herself. And the other consideration is that a takeover of Siberia would do nothing to ease the acute problem of securing raw materials.'

This was crucial intelligence, from well-placed Japanese navy officers prepared to speak their minds to their German colleague. 'That means they will push ahead with their advance to the south?' Sorge asked.

'That's right! They plan to expand their naval air bases in Indochina, and when they've put in more army units, they'll move in to occupy Thailand before the year is out. They'll control the Gulf of Siam, and the eastern side of the isthmus. Get their hands on rice, rubber and tin, as well as an excellent base to move against Singapore and Burma.'

'Even though they may collide head-on with America, as well as Britain?'

'The Japanese are worried about a conflict with America. But what they're most afraid of is having to fight on two fronts, in both the north and the south. The navy is doing its utmost to discourage an offensive against the Soviet Union, which some elements in the army still ardently desire.'

'What you heard is the navy's view, of course, not that of the two General Staffs?' asked Sorge.

'Right. This is the navy's thinking. Whether the army and government will go along with it is open to question. As you can imagine, the young officer group in the army are none too happy. But it's unlikely that the army will dare flout both the civilian government and the navy and launch its own offensive against the Russkies.'

'No final decision has been taken yet, then?'

'They expect an official decision in a day or two, some time between now and the 25th,' Wenneker replied.

'So the question now is whether the Americans will stand by with folded arms and let all this happen – allow the Japanese to take the leadership in Asia.'

'The Japanese seem to believe they'll get away with it!' said Wenneker. 'They've taken account of the risk of conflict with America in their planning.'[26]

§ Wenneker sent a summary of his discussions with the navy officers in a long cable to Berlin that Friday, and briefed the ambassador on the contents. When Sorge spoke to Ott, he found him reluctant to agree with the naval attaché's conclusions that the Advance North option was now dead. The ambassador had obtained no satisfaction in talks with Admiral Toyoda, the foreign minister, but could not bring himself to admit defeat.

Within a day or two, Sorge drafted a lengthy report for Moscow, based on Wenneker's disclosures. It opened with an important statement:

Paula [Wenneker] told Vix [Sorge] secret information he was given by Green Bottle [Japanese navy] that the navy and government have decided not to launch a war in the course of this year. Japan is expected to begin occupying key points in Thailand in October.

Sorge no doubt composed the message with a song in his heart, expecting that it would go some way to allaying Soviet fears. Then he handed the text to his wireless operator – and that, apparently, was as far as it got. In prison, Clausen said he had failed to transmit the manuscript. If he was telling the truth, as the evidence at our disposal suggests, this is among the most heinous examples of Clausen's perfidy.[27]

§ Between 20 and 23 August, army chiefs in Tokyo held a conference with the top brass of the Kwantung Army. Ozaki heard about it at the South Manchurian Railway office. A colleague told him that senior officers had arrived from Manchuria for talks that would formalize a policy decision worked out earlier in the month, to the effect that Japan would avoid a war with Russia. Ozaki quickly reported this auspicious development to Sorge, who saw it as corroborating what Wenneker had said. But before radioing the information to Moscow, he wanted to be sure of the outcome of the conference. What could Ozaki find out?

While he waited expectantly, Sorge drafted two messages on Saturday 23 August. One contained Miyagi's figures on Japanese troop deployments, and a clue he had picked up that suggested that the Japanese army was planning an expedition to the tropics, rather than the frozen wastes of Siberia.

In the first and second mobilizations, 200,000 soldiers were shipped to Manchuria and northern Korea.

There are now altogether 25 to 30 infantry divisions including 14 old divisions in Manchuria. 350,000 soldiers will be dispatched to China, and 400,000 remain in the islands [Japan].

Many soldiers have been issued with shorts – short sharovary [wide trousers] especially for the tropics – and from this it can be assumed that large numbers will be shipped to the south.[28]

Sorge expanded on this in his second message, which conveyed Japan's reluctance to move against Russia.

Invest [Ozaki] reported that [Inspector-General of Aviation] Doihara and [War Minister] Tojo believe the time is still not ripe for Japan to enter the war.

The Germans are very dissatisfied with this attitude of the Japanese. Konoye ordered Umezu [Commander-in-chief of the Kwantung Army] to avoid all provocative acts. At the same time, government circles are discussing the question of occupying Thailand and Borneo more seriously than before.[29]

On either Monday or Tuesday – 24 or 25 August – Ozaki invited Saionji Kinkazu to the South Manchurian Railway Building for a chat. Saionji was working nearby at the prime minister's official residence as a temporary consultant, a post he had taken up on 14 August.

Ozaki traded gossip with Saionji – presumably enquiring how he was getting on in the new job – before guiding the conversation to the matter that preoccupied him. 'I've heard that people from the Kwantung Army have come to Tokyo to discuss whether to go to war with the Soviet Union or not. Is that right?' Ozaki ventured.

'Well no, the thing is this,' said Saionji at once. 'The army and the government have already made the decision not to go to war.'[30]

This was the verification Ozaki and Sorge wanted. It dovetailed with what they had learnt from their other sources, and could be communicated to Moscow with confidence. The report – which appears to have been drafted on either 25 or 26 August – is emphatic, the tone hinting at the excitement he must have felt.

Invest was able to learn the following from circles nearest to Konoye. From 20 to 23 August, the High Command and officers representing the Kwantung Army discussed whether they should go to war with the USSR. They decided not to launch the war within this year, repeat, not to launch the war this year.[31]

Even so, Ozaki preferred to err on the side of caution, hesitating to affirm that the threat was one hundred per cent eliminated. In his view, Japanese policy could veer again if there was an unexpected turn in

Germany's war with Russia, and internal troubles in Siberia. Moreover, he thought a war with Russia in the following spring could not be ruled out. But on balance, he considered that – barring some unforeseen development before 15 September, the absolute deadline for launching an offensive – Russia was safe from attack until winter was over. After including these caveats, Sorge continued:

> Invest learnt from military sources that the army would start hostilities when two conditions obtain. First, the Kwantung Army's troop strength becomes three times that of the Red Army. Second, there are visible signs of internal collapse in the Siberian Army.
> Further, Invest said that reinforcements dispatched to Manchuria have been withdrawn from the front line [close to the Russian frontier] to the rear.

Sorge had beamed happily as he listened to the information and analysis supplied by his indispensable collaborator. In prison, Ozaki recalled his reaction with perceptible satisfaction: 'Sorge looked delighted, as if a heavy burden had fallen from his shoulders.'[32]

Two months had gone by since the German invasion – a summer of disquiet when both men were led astray by a massive mobilization that appeared to portend a Japanese offensive. As we have seen, only Miyagi, from an early stage, had thought there was little likelihood of a Japanese strike against the Soviet Union. In his judgement, Singapore was the natural target for Japan, and Thailand a stepping-stone to Singapore, and he had compiled a report on the various indications that pointed to a 'Strike South' strategy.

Sorge appears to have dismissed Miyagi's assessment out of hand. For some time, his pessimism was unshakeable. Energetically though he and Ozaki propagandized about the utter folly of a Japanese attack on Russia, both men thought in private that it could well come to that.

Eventually, their painstaking enquiries, combined with Miyagi's un-flagging leg-work, brought the picture into sharper focus, and their fears about a Japanese attack began to fade. But not until the third week of August, when Ozaki brought the final piece of the mosaic, did Sorge feel confident about the course Japan would take.

On this occasion, Clausen carried out his duties and transmitted the text, or part of it. (Possibly he feared that the Fourth Department would become suspicious if the cable traffic from Tokyo declined too drastic-ally.) In the course of his interrogation, Clausen pointed to the document – seized by police when they searched his house – and said: 'The manuscript I actually sent was shorter than this.'[33]

§ A short while after her ordeal at Toriizaka Police Station, Hanako was summoned a second time. Again she was told to break up with Sorge, but Superintendent Matsunaga was calmer and less threatening than before.

'Look here,' he said, 'if you separate from Sorge you can do well for yourself. You can get a handsome financial settlement [*tegireikin*] from him. He's got enough money. We'll work it out for you. You see these files' – he pointed to a sheaf of documents on his desk – 'all these are Japanese women who broke off their relationships with Chinese and Koreans for a decent cash settlement. It would make a nice little nest-egg for your marriage. These women got 3,000, 5,000 even 10,000 yen. Be sensible.'

'It's not money I'm after,' Hanako said. 'He's always been kind and generous. Please don't bring this matter up with him.'

'Well, we can't force you to be sensible. Are you going to leave him? You've got to decide one way or the other. You realize I have to submit a report on your conduct to the Ministry of the Interior.'

With a sigh, Matsunaga took out a sheet of paper, and the questions began. As on the previous occasion, he pried into every aspect of her relationship with Sorge. Wearily Hanako recited the answers, and at the end signed the document without protest.[34]

'That was the way it was then,' she recalls. 'The police meddled in your private life as they pleased. And this was before Japan went to war with the United States. *Iranu oseiwa* – what nosy parkers!' In old age Hanako reminisces about the painful events of August 1941 in a matter-of-fact way, with no trace of rancour towards the arrogant police officials who abused and humiliated her. 'That was the second time I was summoned to the police station. I discovered that in the meantime Sorge had struck a young officer called Aoyama who had gone to the house to find out where I was living. Hit him on the chin and knocked him to the floor! That was how mad he was!'[35]

When Sorge found out about the second interrogation, he made no attempt to disguise his concern. After a moment's thought, he suggested it would be better for her to leave Japan. 'You can go to Shanghai,' he said. 'Shanghai is better – I've got money there, so you'll be all right.'

'You're coming too, aren't you?' Hanako asked anxiously.

'Yes, but not at once. My work here is nearly finished, and then I can join you in Shanghai. Does that make you happy?'

'Yes, I'm happy,' she said.

But as she lay on the sofa, a deep sense of unease possessed her, a premonition of darkness closing in. Listening to him typing, she wept silently, and fell asleep. She was still there when Clausen came round in the evening, and noticed that she had been crying.

'The police made her cry,' said Sorge, when he saw the look in Clausen's eyes. 'I'm worried. Do you have any ideas?'

The two men then held an earnest discussion in German. Hanako caught only the odd word; it seemed that they were talking about passports. Frowning, Sorge turned to her and explained.

'You don't have a passport, so it's going to be hard for you to go to Shanghai. I don't know what we're going to do. I think it's all right to stay in Tokyo together. Are you worried?'

'I'm not worried. As long as I'm with you, it's all right'

'Probably we can go to Shanghai together later. Are you happy now?'

The next day, Sorge pressed her to accept $2,000, a very princely sum in 1941. In this fashion, he set the seal on their separation. He told her not to worry about the police, and indicated that he would find some way to stop them bothering her again. The following week, he invited Matsunaga and Aoyama, the young officer he had punched on the chin, to a 'peace conference' at a restaurant in Nihombashi. An interpreter from the German Embassy, Tsunajima, joined them at Sorge's request. Hanako came as well, looking demure in a kimono, and maintained a discreet silence for most of the evening. Sorge pressed sake and beer on the two policemen, and then conferred at length with Matsunaga, while Tsunajima interpreted. Hanako could not hear what they were saying, and never discovered exactly how Sorge managed to sort out the problem.[36]

'I don't know whether he paid them anything or not,' she said, many years later. 'But it was not all that long afterward that the *shunin* [head of department] came to my house, carrying the report he was supposed to submit to the Ministry of the Interior about my disgraceful conduct. Look, he said, let's forget about this matter. No one need ever know. And he burnt the document in the *hibachi* [charcoal brazier], there and then.'[37]

§ There were mornings when Ozaki awoke to a chilling premonition that the police were on their way, and in a few moments would storm in and arrest him. The gnawing anxiety grew more acute as the summer wore on, although friends and colleagues apparently noticed nothing: outwardly he was cheerful, garrulous and self-possessed, as always. With much effort, he concealed his secret fears from his wife. But he confided in a fellow conspirator, Kawai Teikichi, when they met by accident towards the end of August. The encounter occurred in a crowded carriage on the Ginza line of the underground railway system. Ozaki was on his way to Ueno station to catch a train to Hokkaido. There was just time for a drink, so they made for a beer-hall at the station.[38]

When they had found a seat in the crowded tavern, Kawai whispered that he was probably still under surveillance – it made him feel trapped 'like a rat in a bag'. This prompted Ozaki to confess that he felt much the same. 'They're after me too. I feel as if I'm living all the time with a police spy at my back. The other day when I was drinking in a bar there was this fellow who came and sat by me and said something. I thought he seemed like a spy, and I shouted at him.'

This admission was deeply disquieting for Kawai. It was not in character for Ozaki, always courteous and unruffled, to shout at anybody. Was he, too, beginning to lose his nerve? If Ozaki was worried, their situation must really be serious. After a brief, disturbing conversation, the time came for Ozaki to catch his train, so they drank up and walked over to the gate. Many years later, Kawai described the parting. 'He looked back, a figure in the crowd on the platform, and then disappeared with a wave of the hand. It was my last image of him as a free man.'[39]

CHAPTER FIFTEEN

September 1941

THE TOKYO ring's assurance in August that there would be no Japanese attack that year did little to calm Stalin's fears. The Soviet Far East Command remained in a high state of alert, anticipating an offensive. Sorge, knowing his superiors' intense distrust, realized they would want harder evidence that he had read Japanese intentions correctly. By his own account, Moscow persisted until September in suspecting that the Japanese militarists would invade, and only then did they have 'complete trust in my reports'.

By that stage, sigint (signals intelligence) would have corroborated Sorge's prognosis. Japanese army communications monitored by Red Army listening posts along the borders with Manchuria would have confirmed that the danger was past. Moreover, Sorge soon provided factual evidence that reinforced his initial conclusion.

At the end of August, he advised the Fourth Department that he was sending Ozaki to Manchuria to investigate the situation on the ground.[1] In reality, his right-hand man was making the journey to participate in a major conference of the Investigation Department of the South Manchurian Railway headquarters in Dairen, as a representative of the Tokyo office. He would meet colleagues who handled military transportation and logistics, with accurate knowledge of Kwantung Army movements at their fingertips. The trip was a chance to ascertain at first hand whether the Kwantung Army was abiding by the decisions reached in Tokyo in late August.

Before leaving for the continent Ozaki furnished Sorge with statistics on Japan's oil stocks, fulfilling an urgent request from the Fourth Department. The Western powers' economic blockade had slashed the oil supplies reaching Japan, and the Russians were keen to know the level of existing stockpiles. If they knew how long the stores would last, the Russians could estimate how long Japan would be able to fight a war. Furthermore, the tighter the oil reserves, the greater the imperative to advance south, to the oil-fields of the Dutch East Indies, rather than advance to the north.

Ozaki had to invent a plausible excuse for requesting a junior colleague in the Investigation Department to dig up the information: like
all industrial statistics, oil reserves were strictly secret, and especially
sensitive because they were military related. 'Can you give me the
overall picture, and also a breakdown on army and navy oil stocks?' he
asked Miyanishi Yoshio, a fellow researcher. It was a justifiable request,
as the two were engaged in compiling a report on the economic situation.
But to allay suspicion, Ozaki delivered a little homily on the pointlessness
of any study of the national economy that failed to take account of the
autonomous economic power of the army and navy.[2]

Obediently, Miyanishi made enquiries and came up with the figures:
2 million tons of oil in civilian hands, 8 million tons held by the navy,
2 million tons in army storage. Checking through other sources, Ozaki
heard that the actual figure for the navy was nearer 11 million tons.

Ozaki then talked the matter over with Miyagi and Sorge, and gave
his conclusion. 'Normal non-military consumption is four million tons
a year, so there wouldn't be a drop left after half a year, going by these
figures. The oil situation alone shows that Japan has two alternatives –
pushing south to secure Dutch East Indies oil, or getting oil by bowing
to the United States.'[3]

The question of whether Japan would bow to the United States took
centre stage for the Tokyo ring in early September. The Fourth Department was taking a keen interest in developments. If Japan and the
United States came to blows, Japanese strategic pressure on the Soviet
Union in the Far East would cease. The Red Army could throw all its
resources against the Germans, and the Americans would be drawn into
Britain's war against Hitler. A Japan–US conflict would directly benefit
the Soviet Union.

Sorge sensed that no headway had been made in the quest for a
diplomatic settlement, and enlisted Ozaki's help to keep watch on the
negotiations (the main venue was Washington). Secret though the talks
were, they were briefly illuminated at the end of August. It emerged
from a news leak in Washington that Prime Minister Konoye had sent
a personal message to President Roosevelt; the prince was forced to
summon an emergency cabinet session to explain his initiative. Although
the contents of his message were not revealed, the Japanese public
learned for the first time about government moves to find a way out of
the crisis with America.

Ozaki assumed – correctly – that Konoye had proposed a meeting
with the US president in order to break the deadlock. But even personal
talks at this level were bound to fail, he said, because the Americans

refused to yield on their demand for the complete withdrawal of Japanese troops from China and Indochina. This was totally unacceptable to the Japanese military. The Supreme Command was already preparing for the anticipated collapse of the 'peace negotiations' with the US.

As army and navy strategists saw matters, the campaign to secure new oil supplies had to start before oil stocks dwindled to a point where fighting a war became impossible. If it waited too long, Japan would find itself in the humiliating position of having to swallow America's demands. The General Staffs had been working on the blueprints for mobilizing and deploying more than four million troops and for requisitioning and equipping at least 400,000 tons of merchant shipping.

After heated debate, the Konoye cabinet bowed to the Supreme Command, and agreed to a policy of preparing for war with Britain and the United States. The policy was formally sanctioned by Emperor Hirohito at an imperial conference on 6 September. Japan was committed to commencing war against the United States, Britain and the Netherlands if negotiations failed to produce a satisfactory settlement by the first ten days of October. The nation would complete preparations for hostilities by the latter part of October.[4]

This decision was known only to a tiny handful of top military and government leaders at the time, but Tokyo's rumour-mills were already humming with dire predictions of a conflict with the United States. Nagai Kafu recorded in his diary on 3 September: 'Fine weather. There are frequent rumours about a possible outbreak of war with the US.'[5]

Two days earlier he had grumbled about the burdensome war economy, and guessed that there was worse to come:

Camera films are sold out. Cigarettes also sold out for the past two or three days. Rumour in the city has it that domestic iron and copper utensils will be confiscated [for military use] so quite a few people have sold them to second-hand dealers. We're now in a society where we even have to hide the metal pipes we smoke.[6]

§ In the first days of September, amid the embers of summer – the lingering heat that the Japanese know as *zansho* – Eta settled happily into her new home in the Aoba-cho district. With intense relief she left the Otts' residence, where petty jealousies, mischievous gossip and furtive watchfulness poisoned the atmosphere. She had regained her privacy and even had her own little garden, now softly coloured with cosmos flowers. With a full schedule of concerts, radio recitals and recording sessions, she was content to remain a little longer in Japan.

On 1 September, the day she moved house, Richard came round for an inspection, and that very same afternoon sent over a huge bouquet of orchids. Two days later he called again, and sat with a bottle of whisky as she played Scarlatti sonatas on the harpsichord. On several occasions around this time he spoke of leaving Japan, of going to Shanghai or possibly Berlin. He spoke too of the possibility of arrest, although it did not then occur to Eta that he was referring to the Japanese police: she assumed it was the Gestapo that worried him.[7]

Without fail, they noticed policemen loitering near the house when she saw him off, and these were not officers from the local station. 'I know that face!' Richard exclaimed one night, flinging the window open. 'O-yasumi-nasai! [good-night!]' he shouted at a lurking policeman.[8]

Only later did it strike her that Richard – despite the nonchalant pose – realized that he was under close surveillance by the Japanese police, and knew that his days of freedom were numbered. 'How do you think Ott's good-time club will react when I'm in prison?' he said one evening, grimacing. 'You can be sure they'll go on having fun, drinking and whoring just the same, and nobody will spare a thought for poor Sorge.'[9]

Time and time again she was forced to listen to tirades against the Otts, the Nazis and their collaborators in the embassy. Although she agreed with his sentiments, the vehemence of his manner was excessive. There were only extremes in Richard's life, she reflected wearily, only black and white. If she challenged a point, he flew into a rage. He would brook no contradiction. The sharp swings in his mood also tested her patience. The transition from enthusiasm and laughter to melancholia or anger might be quite sudden, or he might veer from self-deprecating humility to intolerable arrogance. His sheer unpredictability began to frighten her.

One day in early September Richard stormed in unexpectedly. He was noisy, triumphant, and the worse for drink in the middle of the afternoon. 'It's cut-and-dried! The matter is completely cut-and-dried!' he exulted. 'I don't need Ott any more! He can go to hell as far as I'm concerned, and so can all the other Nazis in the embassy!'

All this meant nothing to Eta. She stared blankly, waiting for an explanation. 'The draft is finished! All finished!' he cried. She tried to calm him, but he was too exhilarated. He paced around the living-room, scattering cushions and magazines, disturbing the meticulous order of the furnishings.

'What's got into you? Do you mind explaining?'

'I've beaten them, I'm telling you. I've beaten them, and nobody knows but you. I think you might congratulate me ...'

'Richard! How can I congratulate you if I don't know what you're talking about?'

He could not tell her just yet, of course, but she would understand soon enough. Now he had pressing business and had to leave, he said, swollen with hubris. With that, he stalked out of the house, shirt-tails hanging over his trousers. But the next moment he was back, took her by the hand, and yanked her out of the door with him.

'Into the car! We're going for a spin!'

Anaesthetized by alcohol, he drove at full speed, chortling at the rocking motion as the wheels slid over tramlines. An empty whisky bottle rolled wildly in the well of the car. Eta, heart pumping, saw Hibiya Park, the Imperial Hotel, the Teikoku Theatre fly past. She said nothing, fearing that an admonition to slow down would have the reverse effect. After what seemed an eternity he tired of the aimless driving, and they raced back to her house. Then he sped off on what he said was 'urgent business'.

The incident left her shaken and upset. The devil-may-care manner that had attracted her in the early days of their friendship had become more like a demonic urge to destroy himself and antagonize everyone who cared about him; it was only much later that she understood the emotions that had convulsed him during these fraught weeks.[10]

On the morning after this episode the telephone rang; it was Richard. 'Did I really offend you yesterday? Forgive me! Can I come and see you this afternoon?' Reluctantly, she agreed. When he arrived – as usual, with a bouquet of flowers – he was humble and contrite.

'Please, play "Soeur Monique",' he entreated her. She went over to the harpsichord, sat in a shaft of sunlight by the open window and filled the air with the Couperin piece Sorge adored. She remembers she must have played it ten times in all, while he sat on the floor at her feet.[11]

What was the draft that had caused Sorge to gloat and exult and indulge in his wild antics the previous day? We know that in early September he learned that the embassy had given up the attempt to entice Japan to join the war against Russia.

Ambassador Ott, in low spirits, confessed that his efforts were to no avail. To his chagrin, a German victory was not rated highly by Japanese army staff officers; they also believed that winter, which would rule out operational activity in the Soviet Far East, might prove no less of a formidable obstacle to the German advance on Moscow.

After checking the views of the military attachés, Sorge reported to Moscow that Ott (code-name 'Anna'), Kretschmer, ('Marta') and Wenneker ('Paula') now recognized that Japan would not intervene; he asserted categorically that no attack would materialize within the year.

> In the careful judgement of all us here, and Marta, Paula and Anna, the
> possibility of Green [Japan] launching an attack, which existed until
> recently, has disappeared at least until the end of winter. There can be
> absolutely no doubt about this.[12]

Sorge went on to remind his masters that Japan might make a move if
the USSR transferred divisions from the Far East Command on a large
scale, and if there was unrest in Siberia. However, the Japanese military
was embroiled in a major internal row about who was responsible for
the big mobilization. The cost of maintaining the greatly enlarged
Kwantung Army was causing economic and political difficulties.

Clausen told interrogators that he transmitted this dispatch, one of
several sent on 14 September. As proof, we have the telegram received
by the Fourth Department. A comparison with Sorge's actual manuscript,
confiscated by police, reveals that Clausen simplified the text to reduce
his work. What Russian Military Intelligence officers actually saw runs
as follows:

> In the opinion of Ambassador Ott, Japanese attack against USSR is now
> out of the question. Japan might attack only if the USSR transfers troops
> on a large scale from the Far East.
>
> Bitter arguments began in various circles about responsbility for the
> large-scale mobilization, and the cost of maintaining the expanded Kwan-
> tung Army, which indubitably created major economic and political
> difficulties in the nation.[13]

Another message radioed the same day summarized what Ozaki
('Invest') had reported prior to his departure for Manchuria on the line
taken by the Japanese government.

> Invest left for Manchuria. He said that the Japanese government had
> decided not to go to war against the USSR, but that armed forces will
> stay in Manchuria for a possible offensive next spring in case USSR is
> defeated by that time.
>
> Invest noted that the USSR will be absolutely freed [word illegible]
> after 15 September.
>
> Iteri [Miyagi] reported that one battalion of the 14th division which
> was to be dispatched to the north has been kept in the Guard Division
> barracks in Tokyo.'[14]

The second paragraph was garbled in transmission, but there could be
no doubt about its import. As Sorge had radioed at the end of August,
15 September was the army's absolute deadline for taking military action.

These two messages underlined his estimate that Russia need no longer concern itself with the Japanese threat – an assurance that would allow the Red Army to concentrate on defeating Hitler's armies. Drafted some time between Ozaki's departure on 4 September and Clausen's transmission date, 14 September, they gave Moscow cause for cheer, and Sorge every reason to feel pleased at the progress he was making.[15]

§ An entry in Sorge's diary for 21 September records an appointment with 'O' (for 'Otto'). This referes to Ozaki, who returned from Manchuria on 19 September and may have briefed Sorge in outline: he took nearly a fortnight to complete a full report.

As expected, the journey had proved extremely fruitful. At the Dairen conference, Ozaki had picked the brains of the Investigation Department's best experts. He had then taken the train to the capital, Hsinking, and to Mukden, meeting South Manchurian Railway executives and observing rail movements of troops and material. He returned with a clear picture of the Kwantung Army's troop dispositions and war preparedness.

With satisfaction, Ozaki confirmed their assessment of Japan's intentions. 'The danger's passed,' he said. 'The mobilization during summer brought the total strength of the Kwantung Army up to 700,000. But already a few units have been shipped back to Japan. Others have been moved back from forward positions to winter in southern Manchuria. In fact, the *Mantetsu* had orders to lay on trains to ship a great many troops from the northern area to the south of the country. What's more, the army has not transferred forces from North China.

'However, the danger was very real for a while, as we suspected. In the first week of the mobilization the Kwantung Army ordered the railway company to have 3,000 experienced workers on standby to take over the Siberian railway, in readiness for an invasion. Then the number was brought down to 1,500. Now the Kwantung Army can make do with fifty workers to handle the military transport network.'[16]

Subsequently, Ozaki wrote up his findings and gave the manuscript to Miyagi, who arranged a translation. It appears that this was handed over when he met Sorge – according to the latter's diary – on 1 October.

Sorge's dispatch containing Ozaki's information is dated 3 October, and was radioed the following day.[17] It contains a warning that vigilance was still essential: the Japanese army had postponed, but not abandoned, its aggressive schemes.

In September, the railway company was ordered to construct a new railway in secret between Tsitsihar and Sonu facing the Soviet town of

Ushumun. Japan intends to develop this region for offensive purposes, in the event of hostilities, which could commence in March next year. That is, if the war between USSR and Germany develops in such a way that this is possible.[18]

§ Very early one morning Sorge was spotted examining the badly damaged car he had parked in front of the Old Chancery; he wore the sheepish expression of someone surprised to discover that he had been driving around Tokyo with a flat tyre. The night before, he had been too intoxicated to notice such details.[19] The vehicle had been loaned by a diplomat who now regretted his generosity. Sorge's little Datsun was in the garage for repairs, after a drunken collision with a lamp-post.

These escapades, which provoked a good deal of comment in the embassy, all but exhausted Ott's reserves of patience and understanding. 'Sorge's erratic behaviour is getting out of hand,' he said, when he called Minister Erich Kordt into his study for a few words. 'If matters are allowed to continue, there is a real risk that the embassy will be brought into disrepute.'

§ The deterioration in Richard's mental state was all too evident to Eta. Wild fits of temper alternated with spells of melancholia; sometimes she believed him to be possessed by a neurotic compulsion to destroy her affection, and every other good thing in his life. On 28 September, a Sunday, he arrived nursing a secret rage, and primed to explode. This time the irritant was Eta's church attendance. She had gone to mass that morning, as usual, with Count Mirbach, the head of the press section and one of the few practising Christians among the Nazi diplomats.

'Why on earth do you go to church with Mirbach every Sunday?' Richard fumed. 'You have got to stop this! How can an intelligent woman like yourself accept the teaching of a church that dictates what you do with your own body? The church has reduced women to servitude! By forbidding birth-control, they rob a woman of freedom to give herself to whom she pleases, when she pleases, without being chained to a marriage!'

'Like cows in the meadow!' interjected Eta.

Sorge ignored the comment. 'Stay away from the priests! Don't go there any more!'

'You don't have to come, handsome Richard. I always say a good few prayers for you!'

The words were no sooner out than she realized her mistake. Richard's fury reached a new peak. The idea of someone praying for his soul was anathema.

'Don't you dare!' he shouted. 'I forbid you ever to pray for me! If there were a God, I, Richard Sorge, would revolt against this monster, the creator of an awful world where the big eat the small, and the powerful trample the poor people underfoot. ...'

'You don't have to shout – shouting doesn't make your thoughts sound any more original.'

Sorge stared at her in wonderment. Long afterwards, Eta remembered the scene in the little drawing room: the cushions neatly arranged on the sofa, the bottle of red wine and half-filled glasses, the faint breeze from the open window flapping the music scores on the harpsichord. She would never forget the expression on his face, the eyes like stone, as if he was seeing her for the first time. And it was like a stranger that he intoned, in a cold, mechanical voice, 'Communism is something great and beautiful.'

With that he turned on his heels, limped out of the door to his car, and was gone. Eta stood, staring out of the window, frozen by grief, certain that this was the end. After little more than four months together, she had lost him. She looked at the two glasses of wine, almost untouched. They were like a silent reproach, as she sat down at her desk to share her despondency with her diary. 'Why ever did I have to contradict him?' she asked. 'Why, when at other times I always let him rattle on just as he pleased?'[20]

If only, she told herself, she had run out and called him back, sat him down with the wine, and played the Scarlatti or the Couperin he loved, and soothed the internal strife that ravaged him. It seemed to her that the man she had thought of as a 'bird of paradise among the sparrows' in the corrupt Nazi embassy had finally flown away – just as he had warned her he must some day.

§ It was on this unhappy Sunday that the first stitches in the fabric of Sorge's *apparat* were unravelling. Cold-eyed men from the Tokko, the Special Higher Police, pounced on Kitabayashi Tomo, one of the least significant agents recruited by Miyagi. The repercussions were overwhelming, and out of all proportion to her contribution.

Kitabayashi, a well-preserved woman of 57, had supplied Miyagi with a few crumbs of information on air-raid exercises, rice rationing, and on families where a man had been called to the colours. Her importance to the Sorge group was in inverse proportion to the damage she inflicted.

The dressmaker was arrested with her husband in Kokawa, a country town in Wakayama prefecture. When she was brought to Roppongi Police Station in Tokyo and questioned about her contacts with the Japanese section of the Communist Party of America, she involuntarily gave away Miyagi's name. After exhausting her as a source of information, police believed they were hot on the trail of a group of subversives linked to communists in the United States, involved in spying and other nefarious activities designed to undermine the state.

What led the police to Kitabayashi in the first place? In post-war Japan, it was held as truth that the tip-off came from Ito Ritsu. Ito, it will be recalled, was Ozaki's assistant in the Tokyo office of the South Manchurian Railway. Arrested in November 1940, he was questioned about his part in reconstructing the shattered Japan Communist Party.

At some point in a prolonged, brutal interrogation, Ito may have revealed that a certain Kitabayashi was a former member of the Communist Party of America. She was watched closely at first, but led an irreproachable, vegetarian lifestyle – the most suspicious thing about her was membership of the Seventh Day Adventist church. After a while the surveillance was reduced, until her name surfaced during the interrogation of her niece, Aoyagi Kikuyo, in connection with an underground left-wing group.

Aoyagi was arrested in June and told police about Kitabayashi's communist connections. However, there is persuasive evidence that members of the Sorge ring had been under scrutiny for many months, at least, and that neither Ito nor Aoyagi furnished police with any names that were not already blacklisted.

In the end, the communist links of Miyagi and most of his sub-agents – like Kitabayashi – proved fatal to Sorge. Fourth Department agents were under strict instructions not to contact local communist parties or associate with known left-wingers. Sorge knew the rule but found it hard to enforce. Espionage in an impenetrable society like Japan's could be conducted only with the help of local people. Amid the rabid spy-mania of the 1930s, the only Japanese liable to agree to work for the Soviet Union were committed communists, and most of these had a police record.

§ On Monday, when Ozaki visited Nagasaka-cho, he found Sorge in an aggressive mood. In fact he must have been insufferable, for Ozaki makes a rare reference to his chief's odd behaviour in his prison testimony. As the bearer of up-to-date information on the secret Japan–US talks, he probably anticipated a warmer welcome.

'I succeeded in getting a look at a draft of the government's proposals to the United States,' Ozaki said, no doubt well pleased with himself, as Sorge led him upstairs to the study. 'What's in it?' Sorge demanded, gruffly. Whereupon Ozaki recited, from memory, the main points in the draft – Japan had proposed to the US that they conclude a comprehensive peace treaty and a new commercial treaty and, most important of all, had offered concessions that included some troop withdrawals from China.

Sorge was an exacting taskmaster, but in Ozaki's experience unfailingly correct and respectful. However, that evening something in the German's manner put him off his stroke. In prison he would express doubts whether he had rendered the meaning of the draft in terms that Sorge understood.

'Who showed it to you?' Sorge asked in the same brusque tone of voice.

'An aide to Konoye,' Ozaki answered.[21]

The aide – whose identity he did not disclose – was his good friend Saionji Kinkazu. They had met at the Kuwana Machiai, a house of assignation in Kyobashi.[22] Saionji pulled out a document from his briefcase – two or three pages of foolscap paper written in fountain pen, with six main items, and littered with additions and corrections.

This was his work – a raw draft of the latest set of proposals that Japan hoped would stave off a conflict with the United States. Saionji, while still a consultant (*shokutaku*) at the Foreign Ministry, had recently begun to work in a similar capacity for the cabinet. Prime Minister Konoye had taken him on to assist with the drafting of all the position papers for the Japanese negotiators.

Saionji was expecting dinner guests, and Ozaki had no wish to be seen with a sensitive document in his hands. With little time to skim through the document, he tried to memorize the main points, and returned it to Saionji a moment before the guests arrived.[23]

This is what he relayed to Sorge, along with his own reading of the situation. 'Japan and the US could settle their differences – so Konoye believes – providing the Americans accept his compromise plan. The plan calls for us to pull out some troops in central and southern China, and in French Indo-China.

'But there's still a big gulf between the two sides. The Americans are inflexible, demanding a complete withdrawal of Japanese troops from China and Indo-China: a halt to expansion in Southeast Asia, and withdrawal from the Three Powers Pact. You know, we Japanese seem to be much more anxious than the US to reach an agreement.'

Ozaki's briefing enabled Sorge to inform Moscow that the Japanese side had presented no concrete proposals, and that hopes for a successful Japanese–American conference were slender. By 3 October he had prepared a report predicting that if the talks produced no results before mid-October, Japan would begin a military campaign in Southeast Asia. Clausen radioed the text to 'Wiesbaden' on 4 October:

> If US side does not compromise with Green [Japan] by end of September or middle of October, Green will first move against Thailand, and after that begin to move against Malaysia, Singapore and Sumatra. ... However it appears Green [Japan] is exerting every effort to achieve a compromise, even at the expense of Germany.[24]

Examining Sorge's diary, we see that he met Ozaki on this Monday and paid out 200 yen for his collaborator's expenses. From Eta, we know that at some point that day he visited her house. The day before, he had raged and ranted and marched off. She was convinced that he would not return. But on Monday morning he had telephoned, serene and conciliatory, to tell her that he planned to come round later, bringing some friends. 'Clear skies follow a typhoon,' she told herself, much relieved.

CHAPTER SIXTEEN

October 1941

WEDNESDAY I OCTOBER   Not far from the German embassy lay the Sanno Shrine, a temple complex where soldiers had been labouring at a construction site in recent weeks. Following a directive from the Fourth Department, Sorge decided to take a closer look. Passing under the *Torii* archway, he climbed a long flight of stone steps towards the shrine, which sat astride Hoshiga hill.

It rained in Tokyo that Wednesday and the shrine, which on a fine day attracted many strollers, would probably have been deserted. Sorge made his way to the top and saw the new concrete anti-aircraft emplacements of Tokyo Air Defence nestling in the shadows of the ancient cryptomeria and cypress trees. As he circled the complex he would have made a mental picture of the layout of the defences, which testified to growing concerns about the capital's vulnerability to enemy bombers.

The construction of these gun platforms was supposed to be secret, but, as Sorge told interrogators, he could hardly miss them. On many a day, after wrapping up the embassy newsletter, he walked the paths that meander around the hillside, threading through scores of garish red arches.

Some time in September, the Fourth Department had requested details of the locations of anti-aircraft commands in Tokyo and elsewhere. Sorge himself discreetly surveyed the positions at Sanno Shrine, at the Outer Gardens of the Meiji Shrine, and near the Imperial Palace. Miyagi pinpointed many other emplacements, and came up with the answers to a series of routine requests for military data: 'how many new tank units had been formed? How many 18-ton tanks did Japan possess? How many government measures had been taken to increase production of new equipment?'

On I October Miyagi visited Sorge, bringing information collected from Odai and other agents in his sub-ring. The War Ministry, he reported, had completed a third large-scale mobilization, this time netting low-grade recruits for home defence units stationed in Japan. Anti-aircraft exercises, which had been rescheduled, would begin on 12 October and would last for ten days.

Along with the strengthening of home defences, anti-aircraft drills were held to prepare the population mentally for the perils that confronted the nation. Newspaper editors and army men had whipped up a mood of crisis, yelping that the US and Britain were strangling Japan with the economic blockade. Colonel Mabuchi of the army press section had denounced this squeeze as a 'crime against humanity'. In a violent radio broadcast, he warned that Japan intended to break out of the encirclement and secure sources of raw materials – by diplomacy if possible, or else by force. Japan, he promised, planned to forge ahead with the building of the 'Greater East Asia Co-prosperity Sphere'.[1]

Time was not on the side of the peace-makers. The inexorable countdown had begun on 6 September, when the imperial conference decided to declare war on the United States and Britain if the talks produced no prospect of an amicable settlement by the beginning of October. On 25 September army and navy chiefs, fearful of missing an opportunity to strike, had pressed the government to make a decision on peace or war by 15 October. The patience of the generals and admirals was running out. Japan now had to choose between swallowing its pride or advancing boldly to secure the raw materials it needed.

The emperor had not expressed his desire for peace in the forthright terms Konoye apparently hoped for.[2] If the emperor was passive, the prince was supine. As his whole political career had shown, he lacked the will to stand up to strong personalities. Moreover he had been a frightened man ever since four would-be assassins armed with swords and daggers had leaped onto the running-board of his car in early September. His driver had sped away, shaking them off, but it had brought home to him the fact that war-hungry nationalist zealots would stop at nothing to achieve their aims.

When October arrived, hopes of averting a conflict withered. The army and navy had virtually completed war plans for the conquest of Malaya, the Philippines, the Dutch East Indies and Borneo, and for a surprise attack on the American Fleet at Pearl Harbor. The negotiations with the Americans had produced nothing to justify Konoye's pleas that military leaders give him more time.[3]

The tempo of peace moves was *molto adagio*; that of the preparations for war was *vivace*.

THURSDAY 2 OCTOBER   A concert party was held at Eta's house. Richard arrived shortly before 5 p.m., poured himself a gin, and went into the kitchen to mix cocktails before the guests arrived. He was his old self, in perfect self-command, gracious and diverting.

Read-Admiral Paul Wenneker, the unwitting source of so many secrets read by the Russians, was there with his wife. Count Mirbach sat next to Araki Mitsuko, an attractive socialite and a member of the Otts' clique. Everyone knew, or thought they knew, that Mrs Araki – married to a university professor who remained invisible – was Mirbach's lover. She turned up at Eta's house looking dazzling in a pale blue kimono of the highest cost and refinement.

After the concert, when most of the guests had left, Sorge, brimming with bonhomie, played master of ceremonies. 'Come! Come!' he announced, 'I want you to hear my favourite piece of music one more time – if the *maestra* will oblige, of course.' Drink in hand, he ushered Count Mirbach and Mrs Araki over to the harpsichord and insisted that they all listen to Eta's performance of Couperin's 'Soeur Monique'.

'Sublime! Sublime!' he exclaimed when the last chord died away, 'The *maestra*'s playing is sublime – for a few minutes she held my soul in her hands! Did you not feel it too?' Richard pulled Eta to her feet. 'A toast, ladies and gentlemen!' he called out. 'To my little Prussian genius!'[4]

FRIDAY 3 OCTOBER   For three weeks, the Tokyo ring's wireless transmitter was silent. According to Clausen's notebook, nothing was sent between 14 September and 4 October. Apparently he tried on 27 September, but he told Sorge that transmission was impossible, blaming adverse atmospheric conditions.

Directives from Moscow did get through, however, perhaps via the Soviet Embassy. Clausen received a visit from 'Serge', the liaison man, on 18 September; the titular consul used Max's typewriter to write out instructions, possibly Moscow's requests for information on Tokyo's anti-aircraft command, tanks and army units. (All Clausen could recall under interrogation was that they were written in poor English.)

On Friday, Sorge summarized Ozaki's findings on the military situation in Manchuria. It appears that he had waited for Ozaki's written report, which had to be translated and may well have been among the material Miyagi delivered on the first of the month.

Clausen promised Sorge that he would try once again to contact 'Wiesbaden' – Vladivostok – the following day, 4 October.

In the evening Minister Erich Kordt held a cocktail party in his house in the embassy compound. Count Mirbach and Mrs Araki showed up again, and Rudolf Weise, the chief of the German News Agency,

Mrs Weise, and Sorge and Eta were invited. Although he lambasted the German diplomats as Nazis, money-grubbers and careerists, Sorge cheerfully consumed their tax-free liquor while extracting information. If he found Kordt, a favourite of Foreign Minister Ribbentrop, a useful man to know, the reverse was also true. The number two man in the embassy had reason to thank Sorge for valuable *aperçus* on sensitive issues the Japanese tried to conceal from their German allies.

While the party bubbled merrily, Kordt teasingly proposed a toast to 'Professor Sorge' – a fitting title, he thought, for an expert who took a didactic delight in 'explaining' Japan to all comers. Richard managed a weak smile. Amidst all the jollity, he was taciturn, flat and languid – a complete contrast to the previous night.[5]

SATURDAY 4 OCTOBER   At last Max Clausen succeeded in establishing radio contact with 'Wiesbaden' from an upstairs room *chez* Vukelic. Between four p.m. and six p.m. he tapped out, in Morse code, six messages Sorge had given him. He fortified himself with hot sake; without alcohol to steady his nerves, Vukelic noticed, Max seemed unable to work.

It had not always been like this. Arriving full of enthusiasm, he had carried out his duties in Japan with the intrepidity and resourcefulness that had so impressed Sorge in China. But six stressful years had gnawed away his physical and mental reserves. Stiffer penalties awaited the spy who was caught, and police surveillance had tightened. The deterioration in his well-being had been observed by Sorge, and the previous autumn he had urged the Fourth Department to find replacements for Max and himself. If the director had heeded these entreaties, things would have turned out very differently.

Sheer terror at being arrested compounded Clausen's breach of trust. Discarding some messages and shortening others, he cut down the risk of being caught red-handed with the radio equipment. On 4 October, he again cut corners, abbreviating several of the dispatches – including Sorge's summary of Ozaki's observations in Manchuria, and his forecast of a Japanese advance into Southeast Asia if no diplomatic solution were found.

At six o'clock Max came downstairs and seemed inclined to stay on to drink and chat, but Vukelic made it clear it was time for him to leave. Vukelic took his family responsibilities seriously, and wanted the wireless equipment removed from the house before Yoshiko and the baby returned.

They cleared up, and because of Clausen's heart condition Vukelic carried the heavy bag to Clausen's car and drove with him to Hiroo-cho. It was the last time he had to perform the chore. There was to be no further wireless contact between Moscow and the Tokyo ring.[6]

§ That Saturday was Sorge's forty-sixth birthday. Perhaps this was the day that he and Hanako arranged to meet at Lohmeyer's restaurant, close to the Rheingold where fate had brought them together exactly six years earlier.[7]

At some point in the summer, Sorge decided to ask her to move out of his house completely. Perhaps he made the decision because he was making plans to leave Japan. After her interrogation at Toriizaka police station, which alerted him to the closeness of police scrutiny, he would have been convinced of the wisdom of letting her go.

He broke the news gently. She should find a clever Japanese boy to marry and make a new life, otherwise she would end up alone – 'Japan will kill me, I will die,' he had declared dramatically. The next day he told her that she should take all her things with her when she went home in the evening. 'It's dangerous keeping your stuff here. It's better this way.' And so, when he went out, she packed her clothes, cosmetics, her toothbrush and combs. Carrying a small suitcase, she left the house where she had spent five years and returned, with a heavy heart, to her mother's house in the Higashi Nakano district of Tokyo.

When they met at Lohmeyer's, Sorge surveyed the restaurant from the door, and his trained eye spotted the police presence at once. 'Miyako, there are a lot of police here today. Are you afraid?' he said, choosing a table in the centre. She shook her head, and Sorge studied her with concentration.

'It's all right if you're a little afraid. I am not foolish. I won't cause you danger. Tell me, did the police come to your house?'

Yes, she said, she'd had a visitor from Toriizaka police station, and the problem was settled. The report on her relationship with Sorge would not be submitted to higher authority after all – it had gone up in flames in her mother's *hibachi*. 'I feel so relieved,' said Hanako.

'Sorge is always good to you. I am glad,' he said.

They drank cocktails, and ordered dinner, and Sorge asked her what her brother thought about the crisis in relations between America and Japan.

'My brother said the Japanese government won't lose, it always wins, and Ambassador Nomura is a great man. But *I* don't believe things will get better. The China Incident has gone on so long. So many people have been killed. War is no good. The Japanese government likes war.'

'That's right. The Japanese government is always a robber,' said Sorge. 'The people are to be pitied. And I am even more to be pitied. War is bad. I know America is strong. If Japan fights with America she can't ever win, she will lose, lose. And then Japan will be in a truly pitiable condition.'

Hanako recalls that the lights were just coming on in the Ginza when they left the restaurant. She expected Sorge to suggest they return to his house, but he had other plans. They stood there, stared at by passers-by who resented Japanese women who associated with foreigners.

'I think it's dangerous to be together today. The police are watching. Go back to your mother. I will contact you by telegram. You won't be lonely with your mother.'

'Aren't you lonely?'

'It doesn't matter if I'm lonely! You go back home. Give my best wishes to your mother.'

She held his hand tightly for a moment, let it fall away, and said goodbye.

Many years later, Hanako recollected this parting. 'We had eaten early. It was just starting to get dark. He said he had to go to the Domei News Agency. So he went off in one direction, and I went in the other. We never met again.'[8]

§ We have certain knowledge of Sorge's movements later that night. He showed up at a birthday dinner at the Otts' residence, which went sour. All the ambassador's friends were there, but Eta had not been invited.

This was Helma's doing. Why should she invite someone she saw as a rival for Sorge's affections? And how could she know he would he take the exclusion of Eta as a personal affront, and sulk through dinner, nod perfunctorily when she toasted him in champagne, rise after the coffee, and fling his napkin on the table? 'I have an appointment,' he announced. 'Good-night, everybody.' With that, he stormed out of the room. The other guests stared open-mouthed. Helma looked crushed: she could be in no doubt where his appointment took him.

Eta was surprised and delighted when Richard knocked on her door at nine o'clock. While he recounted the episode at the embassy, with a certain relish, she opened a opened a bottle of wine and lit candles. She played sonatas by Couperin and Bach, as he kneeled on the floor beside the harpsichord, leaning his head against her body. His annoyance over the Otts' pettiness seeped away.

'Thank you a thousand times, ' he said, when she paused, 'That was the best birthday present anyone could give. When I arrived here tonight

I felt every bit of forty-six. A lot more, in fact. But when I hear you play it makes me feel – well, ageless. Is that why you have no wrinkles?'

The rest of his forty-sixth birthday was spent happily; it would be his last in freedom.[9]

SUNDAY 5 OCTOBER   The European members of the ring gathered at Sorge's house for a luncheon party. Vukelic brought a bottle of French wine, and wished 'the boss' a happy birthday. Clausen contributed some eggs, a luxury by virtue of their scarcity. For an hour or two they ate omelettes and guzzled a superior brandy, obtained by Sorge through Paul Wenneker at the embassy. The talk was mostly about the war in Europe.

On that cool, cloudy Sunday, Sorge dashed off a short article for his newspaper. Under the title 'A Challenge', it recorded that Japan had lodged a sharp protest at the removal of diplomatic privileges for its embassy in Tehran – 'for which the governments of Britain and Soviet Russia are held responsible by the Japanese Government'. The article, telephoned through to Germany, appeared in print in the *Frankfurter Zeitung* on Monday 6 October – the last contribution from the Tokyo correspondent with the by-line 'S'.

That evening there was yet another birthday celebration. Sorge was guest of honour at an amusing party hosted by a German newspaper correspondent who admired him as an able colleague. He enjoyed himself immensely and was at his best – the raconteur who reduced an audience to stitches, the *Salonlöwe* who made women swoon, the dynamo who danced the night away. To enthusiastic applause, he partnered Eta in a tango, and improvised a daring fandango with the decorative wife of Rudolf Weise. Eta excused herself early – she had slept little the previous night – and the host of the party offered to walk her home. When she left, Sorge was still dancing, with an air of intense concentration, immersed in the music.

MONDAY 6 OCTOBER   The prospects for an accommodation between Japan and the United States were fading, and there was a rumour that the Konoye government might resign *en masse*. The prime minister had no more room to manoeuvre, squeezed between American inflexibility on one side, and obdurate army and navy chiefs on the other. This was Ozaki's assessment of the situation when he met Sorge that evening. 'What I hear is that if the negotiations break down he will have to go; and if they succeed, the military will force him out because that means we are bowing to the United States and giving up our gains in China.

My view is that the negotiations are likely to fail. But the outcome is still up in the air – there will be more twists and turns before the breakdown.'[10]

The discussion with Ozaki convinced Sorge that the talks between Japan and the US were doomed. The Japanese answers were vague, but this much was clear – Japan was not prepared to give up control of China, painfully won over the past decade, or abandon the prospect of further expansion in Southeast Asia.

Within a day or two, Sorge compiled a dispatch in which he unambiguously forecast that war between Japan and the United States was now inevitable, and not far off.

> According to information from various Green [Japanese] official sources, if no satisfactory reply to Japan's request for negotiations is received from the US by the 15th or 16th of this month, there will either be a mass resignation or a thorough reshuffle of the Japanese Government. In either event, it means that war with the United States will begin in the near future, this month or next.[11]

With regard to the USSR, he added, Japanese leaders were adopting a wait-and-see attitude. If the Germans won, the fruits of war in the Far East would be there for the taking. 'In any case, the American problem, and the problem of the southward advance, are far more important than the northern problem.'[12]

This dispatch had not been transmitted by 16 October, when the Konoye cabinet resigned, so Sorge retrieved it from Clausen, intending to make changes. He never got round to this task, however, and the report was never sent. Police found the text when they searched his house on 18 October.[13]

In prison, following the Japanese attack on Pearl Harbour, Sorge expressed regret at being prevented from completing his intelligence work on the Japan–US crisis. As he wrote in his memoirs, 'In December the crisis finally resulted in war, but we were only able to study the first phase. We were unfortunately deprived of the opportunity to accomplish this mission.'[14]

On Monday, as Ozaki and Sorge parted, they arranged another rendezvous, apparently for 13 October, at the Asia Restaurant in the Mantetsu Building. Neither man suspected that they were never to meet again.

TUESDAY 7 OCTOBER   Sorge came down with a raging fever that sent his head into a spin. He was too unwell to drive to the embassy, so the German community was deprived of its newsletter, to the regret of missionaries in a remote part of Japan.[15] There was nothing for it but to stay in bed. Autumn sunshine poured through the big windows into the upstairs corridor, in big shafts speckled with dust.

Being alone depressed him terribly; without companionship, he would sink into morose introspection. On such occasions, when there was no one else to talk to, he turned to Clausen. Today was no exception. He telephoned Max and asked him to come round and help out, as he was unwell. In prison, Max grumbled that whenever his chief was slightly sick, he had to stay with him constantly: 'This was because he was afraid to be by himself.' Sorge informed the embassy that he would not be coming in that day. The ambassador and his wife, whom he had slighted three days earlier, were full of solicitude. Miss Berger, the embassy nurse, was sent over at once in an official car, with a box of medicaments and orders to stay at his side for the duration of his illness. When Clausen arrived he found Sorge sitting up in bed, with a poultice applied to his forehead. Miss Berger, young and pretty, was dancing attendance, brandishing a thermometer and dispensing medicines.

True to form, Sorge dictated a message, which Clausen took down dutifully but never sent. Presumably Miss Berger was out of earshot at this moment. In the evening, Clausen was chatting with the nurse when the doorbell rang. Max recognized the visitor as 'Joe', the rather sickly-looking Japanese man he had occasionally seen before at the house.[16]

If Miyagi sensed that he was being shadowed (as he told Kawai Teikichi), his frequent visits to Nagasaka-cho in this period verged on recklessness. Invariably he brought explosive documents which – had he been stopped by police and searched – would have detonated the entire ring. On that Tuesday, he delivered a map of Tokyo on which he had marked the anti-aircraft emplacements, and we believe that he also brought a report – in the form of handwritten notes – on the Japan–US negotiations, based on a briefing by Ozaki.[17] His package of documents also included part of a report from Ozaki's office, classified *gokuhi* (top secret), which analysed Japan's war-making capabilities.[18]

Miyagi was ushered into the shabby ground-floor parlour, and offered some of the sake Max had heated up. It appears that he was not invited upstairs to see the patient; Clausen took delivery of the documents.

WEDNESDAY 8 OCTOBER Weak and groggy, with a burning temperature, Sorge was in no fit state to leave the house. However, he insisted on rushing over to Aoba-cho to lend Eta money when he heard that a fee due for a concert had been delayed. Miss Berger had arrived early to minister to his needs. She forbade him to go out; Sorge ignored her.

The autumn sky was blue, the heat tempered by a gentle breeze, but the glorious weather did not raise Sorge's spirits or dispel his nervous irritability. Eta was dismayed when he launched into one of his diatribes against the Otts.

'Why do you think they sent me this nurse?' he raged. 'I'll tell you why. They think I'll make advances to her, and that's what they want – to get us into bed together. Can you imagine what sort of people they are to try something like this?'

'I think it was very kind of them to make sure you get proper medical attention. Very considerate,' Eta said.

'No! No! They're happiest when I'm dependent on them. It was just the same after the motorbike accident. I was a helpless invalid, completely at their mercy, and Mrs Ott was delighted! They want to have total control! Their scheme now is to get me hitched to this nurse. They hope I'll forget about you – it's you and me being together that Helma cannot tolerate. Well, they'd better think again. I wouldn't lay a finger on this woman – she's only a child!'[19]

Eta listened wearily. These tirades against the Otts were like a cracked record, and she was not unhappy when he stood up to leave. He said he felt a bit dizzy and wanted to rest. She kissed him goodbye, for what turned out to be the last time. Later on feelings of guilt overpowered her. Displaying his usual loyalty and devotion, he had left his sick-bed because she was short of money – and she had felt relief to see him go.

That evening Sorge had his last meeting with Miyagi, who – conscientious as ever – had made some revisions to his report on Japan–US relations. It appears they talked briefly. Miyagi conveyed Ozaki's best wishes for a speedy recovery, and added his own. According to Sorge's diary, he took receipt of the sum of 100 yen in expenses.

THURSDAY 9 OCTOBER   Vukelic visited his ailing boss with a 'scoop'. Joseph Grew, the US ambassador, had said in a speech two nights ago that the chances of Japan and America settling their differences through diplomacy were bleak. This, at least, was Vukelic's version of what the ambassador had told a select audience at the American Club. He had not been there, but had been given a briefing by Joseph Newman, the *Herald Tribune* correspondent, and gathered that negotiations between the two countries were not proceeding smoothly.[20]

Sorge, still confined to bed, listened to Vukelic's report without great excitement. It was interesting, but hardly earth-shattering. Sorge reckoned that the Americans intended the ideas contained in the speech, which was not made public, to filter out to the Japanese government. No doubt the Soviet Embassy had got wind of it as well. There seemed no point in relaying Vukelic's 'scoop' to Moscow Centre.

Perhaps this was the day Sorge made his astonishing confession. Hardly believing his ears, Vukelic listened as the 'boss' admitted that he had been scared to return to his chosen motherland. The Communist Party's brilliant theoretician, Nikolai Bukharin, and other great Bolshevik leaders had been wiped out. At one point, his own life had been in danger too. Even now, he was hesitant about venturing back. About two months later, Vukelic summarized what Sorge had said:

> He told me he would like to go back to Moscow if permitted to do so. But he would feel lonely because now no one was left of the old 'Lenin group' in Moscow. If he went back he would be the last of this 'Lenin group'. And he said that it was his being in Japan that had saved him from becoming a victim of the purges.[21]

We can imagine the impact that this admission had on Vukelic. In the seven years they had worked together, Sorge's faith in his Soviet masters had seemed unshakable. In their frequent political discussions Sorge always came across as the true believer stoutly defending the good and the bad in the Soviet Union, even the excesses of the Terror. He had even rationalized the execution, in 1938, of Bukharin – a grand old man Sorge had known personally and admired. Stalin was not a wicked man and there must have been some really exceptional circumstances behind it, he had once told Vukelic. Now it emerged that he too had been classed, like Bukharin, as a Trotskyist and Enemy of the People.

As we have seen, he had expressed fears for his safety to a friend in the summer of 1935, and two years on had refused orders (which may have been signed by Stalin) to return to Moscow. The reward for devoted service to the Soviet Union would have been a firing-squad at dawn. But Sorge soldiered on in his dangerous calling, clinging, in the words of his fellow Soviet agent Kim Philby, to a 'confident faith that the principles of the Revolution would outlive the aberrations of individuals, however enormous'.

If he had ever wavered in his commitment, the German invasion of the Soviet Union would have provided up the moral justification for serving a dubious regime. But prior to that fortuitous event, a degree of self-deception would have been needed to sustain the faith without which Sorge could not have continued to operate. As a writer on espionage matters has observed, 'an intelligence officer must remain absolutely fixed in the attitudes that made him decide on his career in the first place. The tiniest crack in his ideological motivation and he risks collapse.'[22]

Vukelic caught his first, disturbing glimpse of cracks in Sorge's previously seamless ideological armour on this day. He talked frankly of the bottled-up fears and forebodings, which must have been an important element in his frequent bouts of depression. There was no further point in concealing how precarious his position with the Russians had been, and how uncertain his future looked. Now Vukelic was told of Sorge's decision to fold up the espionage ring and leave Japan for good. He and Vukelic would soon go their separate ways. Sorge's path might one day take him back to Moscow, but clearly he was actively considering other, safer options.

FRIDAY 10 OCTOBER   The police had in their hands a statement from Kitabayashi Tomo. She had named a Japanese member of the Communist Party of America, Miyagi Yotoku, presently residing in Tokyo's Roppongi district. The statement said that Miyagi had boarded in her home in Los Angeles fourteen years ago, and they had renewed their friendship in Japan.

The police already had Miyagi in their sights – there is evidence that he had been on a Tokyo Metropolitan Police blacklist since 1935 – but Kitabayashi's confession served as a detonator.[23] Shortly after dawn on Friday, three officers from the *Tokko*'s First Section stormed into a lodging house in Roppongi and dragged Miyagi out of his *futon*. While he dressed, they riffled through documents on his desk and found parts of a top-secret South Manchurian Railway report.

The painter was taken to Tsujiki police station, where a brutal interrogation began. Miyagi refused to talk. At the weekend – on 11 or 12 October – there was an electrifying incident. Seizing a moment when his captors' attention was distracted, he hurled himelf from a second-storey window. In the process he injured a leg; he was hauled back into the police station, bleeding profusely, but alive. The interrogation resumed.

His brave attempt to protect the others by taking his secrets to the grave had failed. He could do no more. He began to talk freely about his information-gathering activities for the Comintern, and he named Richard Sorge and Ozaki Hotsumi as comrades and fellow spies. The interrogators were startled; up to this point, they had had no certain idea whether they had picked up the trail of a spy ring, or (their initial supposition) a subversive group smuggling American Communist Party anti-war literature into Japan.

Only now did the *Tokko* officers realize that they had stumbled on something big – an espionage case involving at least one well-connected Japanese, and a prominent foreigner – and would have to tread very carefully indeed. Cautiously they decided to consult higher authority. At this juncture Yoshikawa Mitsusada, a prosecutor attached to the Tokyo District Court, made his entry. From now on he would occupy centre stage in the Sorge drama.

§ On Friday evening 'Serge', the Russian liaison man, visited Clausen's business office in Shimbashi, as arranged. The map of anti-aircraft emplacements and other material compiled by Miyagi was handed over. 'Serge' reimbursed the $500 Clausen had already paid out for Edith Vukelic's travel expenses. Edith had set sail for Australia with her son Paul on 25 September. Weary of Japan, she had finally opted to join her younger sister in Perth. Sorge had had to obtain Moscow's approval. Since her divorce from Branko in 1939, she had allowed Clausen to use her home as a wireless station, receiving a generous monthly allowance of 400 yen from Sorge – twice as much as he gave Vukelic. 'Serge', alias Soviet Consul Viktor Sergevitch Zaitsev, set 20 November as the date for the next meeting. Events outside his control would prevent Clausen from keeping this appointment.[24]

SATURDAY 11 OCTOBER   Sorge was still feverish when Ambassador Ott arrived at the house with a bottle of brandy. But he had recovered much of his strength, and was itching to escape from the house-arrest prescribed by Miss Berger. From what we know of the encounter, it seems that the ambassador engaged in some gentle ribbing on the subject of the patient–nurse relationship. This only deepened Richard's suspicion of Helma's ulterior motive in lending him the decorative 22-year-old. Indeed, it turned out that Helma had told her bluntly that she should marry Sorge, and 'put some sense into his head'. The advice, quite uncalled for, caused Miss Berger much distress.

Sorge's illness had deprived Ott of the one man in the embassy with whom he could discuss political matters freely, without fear that an indiscreet remark might be reported to higher authority in Berlin. The house visit gave him a chance to ask Sorge how he saw the future of relations between Japan and the United States. Would they go to war, or – a prospect that filled him with gloom – would cooler heads prevail and the two nations patch up their quarrel?

'Konoye and Toyoda are so keen to reach an agreement that they'll sacrifice the Three Powers Pact if need be,' the ambassador said. 'Even if they don't abrogate it formally, surely it will exist in name only if America makes any significant concession to Japan at this point? I've only one hope left now – that America is so stupid it fails to see how serious Japan is about coming to a settlement. In that case, war between the two is very likely.'[25]

Ott held out the hope that the United States would provoke Japan to fight. Sorge's response is not recorded. He no longer felt obliged to trade information with Ott to conserve their relationship; as we have seen, in early September he had exulted that he no longer needed Ott or the German Embassy. With his assessment that a Japanese attack was unlikely, he regarded his core mission for Moscow as completed. However, out of habit or pride in his reputation he shared with Ott his view that if no diplomatic solution were found by 15 or 16 October, the Konoye government was finished, and a Japan–US war inevitable.

Ott would have been greatly cheered by such a forecast. Now that there was no prospect of Japanese intervention in Siberia, his instructions were to encourage Tokyo's leaders to strike a blow against American domination of Asia. Since September this was Germany's priority with regard to Japan. Hitler calculated that if America's military capabilities were absorbed in Asia, it would no longer be in a position to divert appreciable resources to help Britain.

Ott had begun the year by prodding Japan to attack the British Empire; in summer he had urged Japanese intervention in Siberia; and now he was trying to demonstrate to the Japanese that they had most to gain by fighting the United States. In fact, for months he had done little else but try to engineer a conflict that would serve the interests of the Reich. Sorge's mission was the mirror image of Ott's: the preservation of peace. From his knowledge of the barbarism and folly of war had grown his conviction that the only worthwhile goal of intelligence activity was to *prevent* armed conflict.

SUNDAY 12 OCTOBER Air-raid sirens blasted in Tokyo at the start of a fortnight of air defence drills (ten days elsewhere in Japan). Every neighbourhood organization across the land was mobilized to practise blackout drills and fire-fighting exercises. Earlier in the year there had been similar manoeuvres, but now there was a sharper edge to the government's call for citizens to prepare for bombing raids by an unnamed enemy. By no means every Japanese took the danger seriously: 'While women were busily engaged in air-raid drills, many men were standing aside, it was noted with regret in some regions,' the *Japan Times and Advertiser* lamented.

Each Sunday Miyagi visited Ozaki's house to give painting lessons to his daughter Yoko, a legitimate pretext for the two men to meet and discuss their covert business. On this day, Miyagi failed to turn up. Ozaki thought this 'a little strange', but was blissfully unaware that the artist was at that moment giving police a complete account of their relationship.[26]

MONDAY 13 OCTOBER A feeling of disquiet crept over Ozaki when Sorge failed to turn up as arranged at the Asia restaurant on the sixth floor of the Mantetsu Building.[27] It happened that there was a perfectly innocent explanation, although Ozaki would never find this out. For some reason, Sorge thought the appointment with Ozaki was for Wednesday, and was expecting Miyagi to come round on Monday. Of course, the painter did not come.

In the final days, Sorge's faculties were clouded by fever when they were not fogged by alcohol. Undoubtedly his once formidable powers of concentration were weakening. Descriptions of his behaviour that autumn give us some clue to his state of mind. It was remarked on a number of occasions that he was inattentive, deep in reverie. We know too of his neurotic spells, the loss of mental balance, the unprovoked rages that caused his friends great distress. Possibly the debilitating fever in October should be seen as a physical symptom of a great psychological upheaval. For years he had experienced the hunted life of working under cover; he had pleaded in vain with his masters to be released from the extreme duress of his circumstances. All the evidence suggests that by October 1941 Sorge was burned out, and knew it. We can easily imagine that the uncertainties of his existence were intensified by anxiety about the fate that awaited him in Russia. So many of his old friends and mentors had fallen victim to Stalin's paranoia; and as we have seen, he did not cherish any illusion that he would be spared.

§ On that Monday, police picked up two members of Miyagi's peripheral ring, Kuzumi Fusako and Akiyama Koji. Like most of the Japanese recruited by Miyagi, Kuzumi – the divorced wife of a Christian minister – was a communist. Akiyama, the translator of so many secret documents, was the only member of the Sorge ring who was not ideologically motivated, although he was fully aware that the man who gave him assignments was a communist.[28]

TUESDAY 14 OCTOBER War Minister Hideki Tojo was in an irascible mood at the morning cabinet meeting. He categorically demanded that the government abandon negotiations with the US. Prince Konoye's attempt to arrange a summit meeting with President Roosevelt had failed, and Tojo believed that it was foolish to continue with this hopeless dialogue. The Americans, he suspected, were trying to protract the negotiations in order to gain time until they were ready to strike at Japan.

On 12 October, his fiftieth birthday, the prime minister told Tojo that he, Konoye, had been responsible for leading Japan into the conflict in China, and could not take responsibility for another war. Surely Japan could make some 'temporary' concessions to the Americans, and withdraw some troops from China? Tojo was unyielding, openly contemptuous of Konoye's weakness. To bow to American pressure would nullify the enormous sacrifices made in four years of fighting, and depress the army's morale.

On this Tuesday, the cabinet decided that the final preparations for war should be allowed to take their course. Konoye's position had become untenable; he lacked the nerve to swim against the tide of militarism, or to ride it any longer. The next morning, he went to the palace and explained his feelings to the emperor. His relations with the war minister were extremely tense, he said: indeed, Tojo had declared that he no longer wished even to talk to him. Regrettably, he had to recommend that His Majesty appoint a new cabinet, headed by one of the imperial princes.[29]

WEDNESDAY 15 OCTOBER   By six a.m. Ozaki had finished breakfast, and was relaxing in his study, which caught the morning sunshine, engrossed in reading. It was a moving book, the last testament of a veteran journalist who had died in China.

Suddenly he heard a trampling of heavy feet and a great commotion in the hallway. He knew at once who the visitors were. With remarkable composure, he put down the book and went to greet the *Tokko* agents under the command of Inspector Takahashi Yosuke. In a letter from prison he described his feelings that morning:

> I had had an uneasy premonition for several days and on that morning I knew that the final hour of reckoning had come. Making sure that Yoko had left for school, for I was anxious my daughter should not be present, I left the house without looking at my wife and without any farewell speech.[30]

He was taken to Meguro Police Station, which was not far from his house. The interrogation began. Japan's great China expert soon discovered that the police knew a good deal about his espionage activities. Miyagi had been arrested, and evidently he had talked. The inquisitors homed in on Ozaki's relationship with Sorge: 'I realized that the whole network was being exposed, and I said to myself that everything had ended.'[31] At first he categorically denied any knowledge of a spy ring, but he knew resistance was futile. At around midnight, he agreed to make a statement.

§ On this same day, Joseph Newman, the *Herald Tribune*'s correspondent, was heading for the sea and sunshine of Hawaii. At forty-eight hours' notice, he had been granted the precious permit allowing him to sail on the *Tatsuta Maru*, one of only three Japanese ships permitted to enter US waters since the embargo against Japan took effect. Newman planned to meet up with his wife and enjoy a three-week vacation.

Hardly had the ship left Yokohama than Japanese police raided his office in the Domei Building in Tokyo, waving a warrant for his arrest. Only by making a scene were press colleagues able to persuade the US ambassador to use his embassy's communications to alert *Herald Tribune* editors in New York. Just in time, Newman was contacted in Honolulu and warned not to return to Japan.

It is a matter of conjecture as to what would have happened to Branko Vukelic's friend and associate if the warning had not got through. The police probably had sufficient evidence to charge Newman under the National Defence Security Law. By leaving Japan when he did, the journalist had saved himself a good deal of unpleasantness.[32]

§ In the evening, Clausen came to Nagasaka-cho. Sorge had recovered from his illness, though he still looked pale and out of sorts. The chief wore a worried expression. 'Something is wrong,' he said. '"Joe" did not turn up Monday as we'd arranged. He's usually so reliable and careful about keeping appointments. I wonder what this can mean. Has he been caught, do you think?'[33] Clausen was unnerved. If 'Joe' had been caught, they were all in danger. He would recall that Wednesday as the day when he 'had a presentiment that the time of arrest was approaching.'

The two men left the house together at around 6 p.m., and caught an *entaku* (one-yen taxi) to the Mantetsu Building. There they went their own ways. This was the evening Sorge mistakenly believed he had an appointment with Ozaki at the Asia restaurant. He waited around for a while, but there was no sign of his Japanese associate.[34]

§ It is likely that this was the day that Sorge tried once again to persuade his controllers to allow him to leave Japan. He had fulfilled his mission, and could now be of much greater use elsewhere. Would the director please arrange for himself and Clausen to be redeployed?

Over the years, his masters had made it quite plain that they would not recall Sorge just to suit *his* convenience. They were unmoved by his laments that the strain of working in Japan was unbearable. One concession they did make, however: in 1940 they sent money, with a suggestion that he take a holiday in Hawaii. But, Sorge told his interrogators, he had not found the time to avail himself of this generosity.[35] Besides, what he wanted was not a sun-tan, but a complete reassignment. Drafting the umpteenth request he took a different tack, suggesting that it was in the Fourth Department's interest to make better use of two highly experienced officers like Clausen and himself:

> With profound sympathy, we follow closely your country's heroic struggle against White [Germany] and greatly regret being in this place where we can be of no use or assistance whatsoever.
>
> Fritz [Clausen] and Vix [Sorge] would like to ask whether we should return home or go to White [Germany] to start new work. Fritz and Vix realize that both these moves are extremely difficult under present circumstances, but we are familiar with our work and believe we can do something of use, either by crossing the border to serve under you, or by going to Germany to engage in new work. We await your reply.[36]

When Clausen came to see Sorge, he was shown this message, which Sorge wanted him to radio, along with two other items typed on the same sheet. One was the important message predicting the likelihood of hostilities between Japan and the US following Konoye's anticipated resignation. The other recorded Ott's anxiety – conveyed when he called on Sorge at the weekend – that Japan was sidelining its Axis allies in her desire to do a deal with Washington.

Clausen skimmed through what Sorge had written. 'It's a little too early to send this. I'd like you to keep it for the moment', he said, handing back the sheet. By his own account, Clausen declined to accept Sorge's messages because he had lost his taste for communism and clandestine work. His mind was made up: he would not co-operate further.

Sorge's recollection was rather different. He said that Clausen *had* taken them home on either the 15th or 16th, promising to transmit at the first opportunity. But then came news that the Konoye cabinet had resigned; naturally, he wanted to update one of the messages, so he asked Max to return the draft. This explanation of how the manuscript came to be found in Sorge's house after his arrest rings truer than Clausen's tale of bravado. Open defiance was out of character for Clausen; there is no evidence that he ever openly disobeyed an order or risked a confrontation. For many months he had simply ignored orders when it suited him, in stealthy acts of betrayal that would not be detected.[37]

Examining Sorge's final request to Moscow, we may conclude that he never questioned the wireless operator's loyalty. If he had any doubts, it is hardly likely he would have proposed that he and Max be transferred to wartime Germany to resume their clandestine work as a team. The chief's trust in Clausen, and his respect for his professional abilities, held up to the end.

Max doubtless had his own sound reasons for ensuring that this message was never seen in Moscow. We may assume that he had weighed the options and calculated that wartime Germany was as disagreeable a prospect as the Soviet Union. Until a sense of foreboding seized him that Wednesday, the overt sphere of his life in Japan had been happy. He had found contentment running a business – what had begun as a cover had become his pride and joy. Like Vukelic, but unlike the rootless Sorge, Max had a real stake in Japan.

THURSDAY 16 OCTOBER Max knew something was seriously amiss when Sorge reported that both his principal Japanese collaborators had missed appointments. There was a certain lack of urgency in Sorge's manner that unsettled the radio man. 'I'd telephone Ozaki and check why he didn't come,' he said, 'if I knew the number.' Clausen realized that he was referring to the informant 'Otto', whose code-name had been changed in summer to 'Invest'. This was the first time Max heard Sorge refer to this informant – whom he had never met – by his real name.[38] 'Anyway, let's wait two or three days, and if Ozaki doesn't come, I'll telephone then.'[39]

If Ozaki and Miyagi really had been caught, Sorge had to assume that they would eventually talk, and lead the police to himself and the other two European members of the ring. As a sensible first step, he might have contacted Ozaki's wife or made enquiries at his office, if only to put his mind at rest. Displaying amazing nonchalance, he took no action.[40]

The conclusion is inescapable: in these final days, he felt in no personal danger – despite his awareness of close police surveillance and his occasional musings about losing his freedom. By his own account, he did not expect to be caught. Were the alarm bells muffled by the effect of illness, stress or alcohol – or all three? Or was it hubris that made him neglect the most elementary of precautions, at a time when there was still some faint hope of saving himself and some of his colleagues?

§ While Sorge waited for word from Ozaki, the latter was giving his interrogators at Meguro Police Station a breathtaking account of his life as an agent for the Comintern and his relationship with Sorge. These revelations, lending substance to Miyagi's earlier confession, prompted a police decision to put the house in Nagasaka-cho under round-the-clock surveillance, which began either Wednesday or Thursday.

But the prosecutors were not yet ready to draw in the net. They wanted statements from both main suspects convincing enough for the minister of justice to authorize the arrest of a prominent German national – so close to the ambassador that Ott came calling at his house when he was sick. A serious diplomatic incident could not be ruled out, but at least the authorities could claim to have irrefutable proof of Sorge's involvement. The statements were needed quickly: the prosecutors fretted that they would be robbed of their quarry if Sorge realized what had happened and sought asylum in the German Embassy.

At 5 p.m. prince Konoye went to the palace to submit the resignations of the entire cabinet. Three months earlier, when the second Konoye cabinet was immediately succeeded by the third, Sorge had filed several articles for the *Frankfurter Zeitung*. His editors were no doubt expecting a piece about Konoye's fall, announced officially late on Thursday evening. This was a very big story indeed. However, they waited in vain for something. Sorge doubtless thought his career as a Tokyo correspondent was at an end, as he considered how to get out. Uppermost in his mind was a yearning to fly away for ever from these infinitely sad and lonely islands. Soon he would have no more use for his professional cover.

FRIDAY 17 OCTOBER   'On Thursday when Miyagi did not come I became uneasy, and on Friday I was really worried.'[41] Sorge was at last seized by an intuition that the situation had become serious, yet his behaviour that day does not suggest a man peering into the abyss. He did not make haste to radio the message asking to be transferred – as he explained later, it was drafted not because he suspected that the police were on his heels, but because he felt his mission to be completed. So there was no sense of urgency in his movements, no frantic compulsion to enjoy the freedom that was about to slip away.[42]

The morning was spent mundanely. Max Clausen, equally worried, came over and they walked to a nearby garage to retrieve Sorge's ill-used car, after the latest repairs. It was a mild day, sunny, with blue skies lightly patched with cloud. Lunch was taken at the *Minoru* restaurant in Shimbashi, one of Max's favourite haunts. They turned over the problem of the vanished Japanese associates, looked at every angle and found rays of hope – perhaps Ozaki was tied up by some urgent business, perhaps the sickly Miyagi had fallen ill?

They sat there long into the afternoon over comforting quantities of alcohol. Not until 4 p.m. did they finally leave the restaurant to go their separate ways. For the next two hours we lose track of Sorge. As for Clausen, he felt no urge to tend to business; no doubt his office in the Karasumori Building near Shimbashi station was closed for the Shinto festival *Kan-name-sai*, a national holiday.

He looked elsewhere for distraction: first some shopping in the Ginza area, and then a film. Two cinemas close in the neighbourhood had American films, which Max and Anna liked best. Anti-American sentiment was on the boil, but the government had not yet denied its citizens the magic of Hollywood. The choice for Clausen was between the Hibiya Film Theatre, showing Myrna Loy and Tyrone Power in *The Rains Came*, or the Hogakuza, where Frank Capra's *Mr. Smith Goes to Washington*, starring James Stewart, had just opened. From the cinema, Clausen headed back to the bar of the Minoru restaurant for more beers to deaden his aching apprehension.

§ Because his company was closed for the holiday, Kawai Teikichi, the retired adventurer-spy, had time on his hands this Friday. He made for Ozaki's house in Meguro. As soon as the door opened, and he glimpsed the expression on Eiko's face, he knew that his worst fears had come true. 'He was taken to Meguro Police Station the day before yesterday,' she said. Kawai's heart sank. What could he say to console her? 'Is this going to be long-drawn out, do you think?' he asked, struggling to hide his emotions. 'It could take time. We have to be be ready for that eventuality. Winter is coming, so please, if you could send in a padded coat, it would be kind. If he has to sit on the hard floor for a long period it will give him haemorrhoids.'[43]

§ Vukelic followed his usual routine at Havas. Domei News Agency copy was rewritten into brief news stories for the French news service. As it was a holiday, there were no evening papers to sift through.

The Domei News Agency carried a story from Berlin which Vukelic

believed would interest Sorge. The news item was profoundly depressing: Romanian and German ground troops, with *Luftwaffe* air
support, had captured the Black Sea port of Odessa. He went out to a
public telephone and dialled Sorge's number – Akasaka 118; as there
was no answer, Vukelic tried Clausen's home, again without success. It
was now around 6 p.m. After tidying up his desk he took the underground train to Akasaka-Mitsuke, and telephoned Sorge a second time.
The boss was home, and invited him to come over. As they talked,
Vukelic noticed that someone close by was eavesdropping; he asked
himself whether he was being shadowed.

When Vukelic reached Nagasaka-cho, at about 7 p.m., darkness had
fallen. The Special Higher Police officers staking out the house were
invisible. Clausen was there already, and with Vukelic's arrival, the
watchers became convinced that the suspected spies could only be
plotting one thing – how to make good their escape.

In the downstairs parlour, Sorge and Clausen sat at the little dining
table with an *isshobin* (half-gallon bottle) of sake. The mood was sombre
as Sorge explained the situation. '"Joe" hasn't shown up recently,' he
told Vukelic. 'He didn't keep his appointment, and we've heard nothing.
We're afraid something may have happened to him.'

'Is this the first time something like this has happened?' Branko
asked, perturbed.

'There was one time before when he couldn't come. But never for
this long.'

'Maybe he's ill?' suggested Vukelic. Sorge and Clausen had considered
that possibility. 'That's true. "Joe" did look sickly when I saw him last.
It would be awkward if he's fallen ill. We really have to do something.
There's a danger he might die.'

Bleakly, they considered possible courses of action. No decisions were
made, and the conversation drifted to Germany's stunning victories.
The *Japan Times and Advertiser* that morning had carried reports of
German forces closing in on Moscow: 'Great Moscow Battle Reaching
its Crisis; Reds in Last Stand' screamed the headline.

Now Vukelic added to the gloom by announcing that Odessa had
fallen, Leningrad was under attack from the air, and – according to an
unconfirmed Domei report – German troops were only thirty-seven
miles down the road from Moscow. The city's population was being
armed to take part in the final, desperate defence of the city.

More sake was consumed, and they sank into numbing despondency.
Vukelic moved on to the latest news about the new cabinet, which was
being formed that night. But Sorge, who had followed political matters

so intently in the past, could muster little interest, so absorbed was he in his private concerns.

As the three men moped over their sake cups, Tojo Hideki, the new prime minister, was picking his new team, retaining Justice Minister Michiyo Iwamura, the only survivor from the previous cabinet. And in the course of that evening, Iwamura gave the green light for the arrest of Sorge and the two other Europeans. The confessions of Ozaki and Miyagi had implicated Sorge in an espionage affair, and Iwamura, in good humour, was easily persuaded by the Prosecution Bureau of Tokyo District Criminal Court that it had impeccable grounds for detaining the German journalist.

A vignette left by Vukelic conveys the poignant mood of that last encounter. Sorge and Clausen discussed how to get out of Japan and go to Germany – if they could choose, it was clear that Germany, not the Soviet Union, was the preferred destination of these two Soviet agents. Vukelic, whose own motherland was under German occupation, poured cold water on the scheme, pointing out that war had severed travel routes between Japan and Europe.

'There's no way to get back there from Japan,' he said.

'Not at all! If we want to return, it's easy!' they both retorted. If the Centre told them to go to Germany, by whatever means, then they would find a way out of Japan – Sorge and Clausen talked as if they were absolutely confident of this.

'We can get out as crew members on a ship,' they said.

Sorge may have had in mind the blockade-breakers that ferried precious cargos of rubber and other war materials from the Far East to Germany, via the port of Bordeaux. The sea route was hazardous, a deadly cat-and-mouse game with the British submarines and destroyers that patrolled the Indian Ocean. Only a few days earlier – 14 October – the *Elsa Essberger* had set sail for Germany loaded with raw materials and thirty Japanese torpedoes. No doubt Sorge expected that his friend Paul Wenneker, the naval attaché (whose support role in the blockade-running operations was crucial) could easily arrange for him and Clausen to be taken on as crew. We can gauge that Sorge felt confident he had nothing to fear by returning to Germany – a view possibly supported by his stealthy peeking into Colonel Meisinger's files.

Vukelic understood that Sorge had set his heart on leaving for new pastures, and was now ready to fold up his espionage *apparat*. 'There's no more work for us here in Japan,' the boss told him.

§ Before long, Clausen got up to leave the dismal party, valiantly

resisting all Sorge's attempts to refill his sake cup. Possibly he feared
Anna's nagging – she was wont to make a scene when he came back
late, with alcohol on his breath, from Sorge's house.

Vukelic, who normally trotted off early to his Japanese wife, agreed
to stay a little longer, to keep his dispirited boss company. More sake
was heated up.

'Do you know where "Joe's" house is?' asked Sorge. Vukelic did not
know – how could he? He did not even know 'Joe's' real name, as
Sorge would have realized if he had had his wits about him.

'But you know "Otto", don't you?'

'No,' said Vukelic. Sorge had mentioned 'Otto' on occasions as the
source of certain items of intelligence.

'But you must know Ozaki, the famous journalist?'

The name meant nothing to Vukelic. Sorge had deliberately limited
contacts between the Japanese and European segments of the ring. He
had never met anyone called 'Otto' or Ozaki. Sorge was breaking the
cast-iron rule that agents should only be known by their code-names,
for the sake of security. Had he given up caring? From Vukelic's
testimony we know that Sorge was inebriated that night. Possibly he
was more drunk than usual. There was no rhyme or reason in his
discourse.

'Please telephone Ozaki at the South Manchurian Railway,' Sorge
told Vukelic.

It may have struck Vukelic as odd that Sorge had no way to contact
important associates like 'Otto' and 'Joe' in emergencies like this. The
boss knew the telephone number of neither Ozaki's house nor his office.

'Look, how can I call Ozaki if I don't know his proper name and
what section he works in?'

'But he's a famous journalist, always writing articles, so you must
know. You'll find out his name if you look in *Contemporary Japan* for his
article. Call the publishers of *Contemporary Japan* and say you want to
know Ozaki's address.'

Patiently, Vukelic leafed through back issues of the magazine at
Sorge's house, found a subcription form, and promised to contact the
publishers first thing in the morning. Eager to return to his wife and
baby son, he took his leave. Outside the air was chilly, and a light rain
began to fall as he made his way home.

Sorge, left to brood alone, was soon in bed. Police posted near the
house noted that the lights went off at eleven o'clock, unusually early.
There were to be no more nights of dissipation. There would be no
more burning the midnight oil as he laboured over his book and erudite

essays. A few hours more, and he would lose all control over his own fate.

SATURDAY 18 OCTOBER   At 5.50 a.m. the Special Higher Police squad surrounding Sorge's house stood by for final orders. It was still dark; only a few pale slivers of grey pierced the black sky. At an upstairs window in Toriizaka Police Station, Yoshikawa Mitsusada shivered as he tried to make out what was happening. He was directing the operation, and it was his responsibility to see that everything went according to plan.[44]

The arrest of Sorge was planned for 6 a.m., when other teams of police would pick up Clausen and Vukelic at their homes. But a hitch had developed. At this early hour, Sorge had a visitor, who had arrived in a car with diplomatic plates. Lights were burning on the upper floor. As the minutes ticked away, Yoshikawa fretted that someone might alert Sorge about the other arrests. What if he tried to make his escape, or – an even more alarming possibility – attempted suicide? The tension was unbearable.

Around 6.30 a.m., the visitor came out of the house, alone, and drove away. Morning light seeped into the sky, heavy with cloud, and rain tapped at the window. From his vantage point, Yoshikawa could see the arresting officers steal into the little front garden.

Assistant Inspector Ohashi Hideo – the Comintern expert in the Tokko's foreign section – lead the team. At his signal, Sergeant Saito Harutsugu, flanked by two other police officers, rang the doorbell. Ohashi hovered in the background. The door opened. Sorge was still in pyjamas, but wide awake, shaved and washed.

Saito, who was also attached to the foreign section, recited the lines he had carefully rehearsed. 'Good morning. I have come about the car accident the other day.' Sorge's expression betrayed no emotion, no flicker of surprise at the sight of these early callers. Yet a little later he would tell his captors: 'I was absolutely astonished when the police arrested me. It was never part of my calculation that I would be arrested.'[45]

With a sweep of his arm, the German newspaperman invited the trio into the downstairs parlour. It was at this moment that Ohashi, tense and impatient, burst in and barked out commands. The other three seized hold of Sorge, pinned his arms to his back, and manoeuvred him out of the door. He went quietly. There was no resistance. Someone found an overcoat and flung it over his shoulders. Lashed by rain, they marched down the narrow lane to the police station two hundred yards away.

Yoshikawa, waiting in an office with Ogata Shinichi, the chief of the foreign affairs section, introduced himself.

'I am Yoshikawa, prosecutor,' he said in halting German.

'Why am I under arrest?' Sorge demanded angrily.

'We capture you on suspicion of espionage activities in violation of the National Peace Preservation Law.'

'That is preposterous! I am the correspondent of the *Frankfurter Zeitung*. My job is to send news to the paper, and this is totally legitimate. What's more, I am an information officer in the German Embassy, and I am a Nazi!' Sorge shouted.

'Are you not guilty of spying for the Comintern?' Yoshikawa had brushed up his German in advance, but in the excitement of the moment the words came out awkwardly.

'No!' Sorge shouted, 'I am a Nazi. I insist that you call Ambassador Ott at once!'

'Sie sind ein Kommunist, nicht ein Nazi. As a communist, you cannot be a Nazi,' said Yoshikawa, mixing German and English.

'It's outrageous to arrest someone from the embassy of Germany, an allied nation, as a spy. There will be a strong protest, you may be sure, and it will have serious repercussions on relations between Japan and Germany!'

After the initial fraught exchanges, Yoshikawa decided that he would wait for the suspect to cool down. Sorge was taken to a cell to undergo a body search. The aim of this routine was to check for hidden weapons or poison, but it also had the intended effect of demoralizing a suspect. Humiliation was a means of control. Sorge, not easily cowed, growled angrily, but had to strip down and submit to the search. Later in the day, he was told he was being moved. By then, he had quietened down. 'It was as if he knew the game was up,' remarked Yoshikawa many years later as he recalled the drama.

§ That morning, shortly before Sorge's arrest, a policeman marched into Max Clausen's house in Hiroo-cho. Waking with a start, Clausen saw the familiar face of Sergeant Aoyama Shigeru at his bedroom door.

The previous evening, on his way home from Sorge's house, Max had bumped into two policemen from Toriizaka police station. One was Aoyama, an officer with whom he had established an amicable relationship. Where was he going? they had asked, and something told Clausen that they were taking more than a routine interest in his movements: 'I somehow sensed that the time of my arrest had drawn near, and caught the tram home with growing disquiet.'[46]

He had pondered whether to burn the manuscripts and code work-sheets and other evidence of espionage, and to bury the radio equipment in the garden. 'But after all I did nothing and decided to leave things as they were, and went to bed at 10 or 11 o'clock.'[47] Now he bitterly regretted his inaction. Aoyama told him he was wanted at the police station to assist with enquiries into a traffic accident, but Clausen knew this was a subterfuge. Another policeman in uniform stood downstairs, and two more plainclothes men waited in a car outside the house.[48] He dressed, ate a hurried breakfast and tried to calm Anna, who was frantic. 'I'm just going to the police station. It's about the car accident,' he said, as he was led away. 'I won't be long.'

§ Meanwhile a third detachment from the *Tokko* foreign section pounced on Vukelic. He was dragged from his bed, made to dress and hustled downstairs, before the eyes of his terrified wife.

'They didn't give him time to put on his shoes, so he slipped on sandals as they pushed him out of the door,' Yoshiko remembers. 'Some officers remained behind to search the house. They were especially interested in his darkroom. To my horror, one of them spotted two boxes with Clausen's wireless equipment.

'"What's this?" he wanted to know. I tried to answer in a casual way: "I've no idea. I don't know the first thing about these gadgets."

'Two policemen stayed behind to guard the house, but I managed to smuggle the radio out and got an old school friend to dispose of it. Then the policeman who had found it came back and asked, "You remember that strange gadget which I asked you about? Where is it?"

'I said I didn't know, and cried, and cried, and the policeman gave up. But then Clausen went and confessed he'd left the radio at our house, and the police kept coming back and asking what I'd done with it.'[49]

§ Eta had been busy with rehearsals, and had not seen Sorge all week. At 5 a.m. on Saturday she woke from a nightmare, filled with foreboding. She recorded the terrible dream in her diary:

> First I heard the garden gate open, and then I heard the hurried, limping walk. The door was opened with force, and then he came up the stairs, quickly, as if in great anger. He swung round on the landing and came towards me, and from the bed I saw his face. It was the face of someone who had been strangled, with eyes bulging horribly.[50]

She told herself that this awful vision was the product of a guilty conscience – she had neglected to visit Sorge, although she knew he was unwell. She rushed to the telephone and dialled Akasaka 118. A grumpy voice answered, that of a Japanese man. No, Sorge was not there. 'Please leave your name and telephone number,' the man said. On Saturday afternoon, she tried again. The same ill-tempered voice answered.

Almost certainly, the voice belonged to Assistant Inspector Ohashi, who spent all that day in Sorge's house confiscating evidence. It was an irksome task that left him exhausted. Files, notebooks and manuscripts filled the study, and there were maps, cameras, photographic gear, equipment for developing, and in the region of a thousand books. Every item was examined, catalogued, packed in boxes, then loaded onto a one-ton truck and, at midnight, finally transported to Tokyo Metropolitan Police headquarters.[51]

In the mountain of material was a typed manuscript, some three hundred pages long. This was the book, entitled *On the Origin of the Japanese*, that Sorge had been working on intermittently for many years. Only two months earlier a well-known German scholar on Japan, Dr Otto Karow, had been shown this work by a third party. His verdict was scathing: the manuscript was superficial, unoriginal, and not worth the trouble of editing.

We can well imagine what a blow this was to Sorge's pride. Although he modestly described his research as a 'hobby', he regarded it as of great practical importance to his espionage work. In his prison memoir he wrote that his expertise on Japan had won him the respect of the embassy; in different circumstances, he would have liked to have been a scholar – certainly not an espionage agent.

§ In the evening, Sorge was moved from Toriizaka Police Station to Tokyo Detention House. This mournful concrete fortress, located in the northern suburb of Sugamo, housed both suspects and convicted prisoners. Its facilities included a well-used execution chamber.

After admission formalities, Sorge was issued with a thin mattress and quilt and marched to Cell 11 on the first floor of Wing 5. Six feet wide and eleven feet long, the cell was equipped with a wash-basin with running water, and a flush toilet. The wash-basin lid could be lowered to serve as a table, and the cover of the toilet provided a seat. The window was composed of small squares of frosted glass set in an iron framework, with a tiny opening at the bottom that admitted air but no view of the outside. There were no bars.[52]

A ceiling light burned all night, and guards could scrutinize their charges through a peep-hole in the metal door. Sorge was woken at 6 a.m. by a blast on a bugle and a clanging bell. Half an hour later, a warder flung open the door for morning inspection. Then came the regulation prison breakfast, soup with a nauseating taste and smell, cold rice and some lukewarm tea.

This was to be his home for the next three years.

Part Four

CHAPTER SEVENTEEN

Paying the Price

AMBASSADOR OTT was notified of Sorge's arrest by the Japanese Foreign Ministry on Saturday afternoon. A brief memo said that Richard Sorge had been arrested 'on suspicion of espionage', together with a second German national, Max Clausen. Ott was startled by the police action, and filled with outrage. There was no doubt in his mind that it was a 'typical case of Japanese espionage hysteria'. His first thought was that they had discovered that Sorge had passed confidential information on the Japan–US negotiations to the German Embassy.

He did not rule out an intrigue by anti-German elements in the bureaucracy. The new prime minister, Tojo Hideki, whose cabinet had been sworn in that Saturday, stood squarely behind the Axis. But the new foreign minister, Togo Shigenori, was more suspect. The embassy was in possession of information that Togo was unsympathetic towards Nazi Germany and that his views were influenced by his German-born wife Edita, who was Jewish. Ott had no clear idea who was behind the arrest of his friend. All he knew was that it was a terrible mistake.

'Sorge a spy? For whom, then? What twaddle! [*Gewasch*]. I would put my hand in the fire for the man,' Ott told people around him. On Saturday evening Ott confided in Heinrich Loy, general manager of Agfa Japan, who served as the Tokyo area *Ortsgruppenführer* (regional group leader) of the Nazi organization in Japan. Loy echoed the ambassador's amazement and outrage. Sorge was sometimes flippant, even rude, about Nazi personalities, but he had been considered sound enough to be offered the post of regional group leader in 1937.

A few months later, when the Japanese authorities announced that Sorge had been indicted as a Soviet spy, Loy would admit to a sneaking admiration for his skilful charade:

> I've known Sorge personally for a long time, but this news surprised me and made me realize he was very different from other people. Normally people you've known a long time will make a careless slip on some occasion. Particularly when someone drinks like a fish, as Sorge did, you

expect that he will reveal his true self when he's in his cups. But Sorge never gave any hint of his true self. Considering that he managed to conceal his identity up until now, I have to say he was an exceptional man.[1]

Erwin Wickert, the young radio attaché, heard the news on Sunday at Shimbashi Station. The rain had lifted, and he and a friend were planning an excursion to Kamakura to photograph the huge bronze Buddha, Daibutsu. His friend Fritz Cordt, press attaché at the German mission in Shanghai, arrived late at the station, breathless, and excited. 'Sorge has been arrested! They're saying he's a spy!' Cordt exclaimed.

Wickert was dumbfounded. He assumed it was a blunder by the secret police, who imagined spies lurking under every tatami. What would they do to Sorge? He recalled the case of Jimmy Cox, the Reuters correspondent arrested on spy charges, who had died during interrogation by the *Kempei* (military police). But Wickert was confident that the ambassador would do everything in his power to clear up the matter and get Sorge freed.[2]

No one was more upset than Helma Ott. For days she fulminated against the Japanese and nagged her husband to lodge a protest in the strongest possible language. It was all he could do to stop her storming the Foreign Ministry to demand Sorge's immediate release.

A US Military Intelligence report on the case summed up the reaction of those most affected by the event:

> Sorge's arrest was a great shock to his close friends, Ambassador Ott and the Gestapo chief, Colonel Joseph Meisinger. They could only believe that the Japanese had committed another of the blunders for which they were legendary, and they worked hard to get their friend out of jail. There was also a disturbing question: if by some chance, good Nazi Sorge actually was a Soviet spy, where did that leave two highly placed Nazi officials who had trusted and confided in him for so long?[3]

The small circle of Germans who learned about Sorge's arrest immediately after the event heatedly denounced the Japanese. On Sunday, indignant German correspondents hurried to the embassy to discuss their colleague's plight with Rudolf Weise, head of the German News Bureau.

They all agreed that Sorge had offended the authorities by writing critical newspaper articles, and was now paying for his lack of discretion. Weise drafted a ringing declaration attesting to Sorge's absolute political reliability and personal integrity, which all the correspondents signed. A day or two later it began to dawn on them that they had acted rather hastily, without checking the facts. What if there was something to the accusations after all? Mysteriously, the petition went missing before it could be submitted to the Japanese authorities.

On Monday, on Ott's instructions, the counsellor, Erich Kordt, lodged a protest with the Foreign Ministry. On Thursday 23 October, the ambassador cabled his first report to Berlin on the arrests of the two German nationals.

The Japanese public was kept in the dark about the smashing of a dangerous spy ring. Nothing about the arrests could be reported by the government-controlled press. The ambassador shared the news with only a few select members of the German colony. Discussion of the matter was forbidden, a taboo enforced by the menacing Gestapo colonel, Josef Meisinger. If asked about Sorge, embassy staff were under strict orders to say only that he was 'away'.

From the outset Ott must have understood that if, by some remote chance, his trusted friend really was a Soviet spy, his career was finished. Rather than face reality, he insisted that the whole thing was a grotesque mistake. That was what he wanted to believe, and years after the dust had settled, that was the illusion he clung to.

§ For weeks, Eta puzzled over Sorge's sudden disappearance. 'I thought incessantly about Sorge, believed him to be in Shanghai or Berlin,' she wrote later. She was told nothing by the embassy. At her concert on 29 October, the Otts appeared relaxed and cheerful. On 15 November Eta plucked up courage to ask what had become of him. Helma replied, with a certain malicious satisfaction, that if one befriended Sorge one just had to expect that he would suddenly take off for a few weeks or years.[4]

Another month passed before she discovered the terrible truth. The source was the Otts' friend, Mrs Araki. 'Isn't it awful, the Sorge thing?' the pretty socialite lamented. She then proceeded to pour out everything she knew: Sorge was in Sugamo prison, he had betrayed to Stalin vital information given to him by Ott, he had confessed to spying for Russia, he was in league with Japanese, American and other nations' communists.

Eta was badly shaken. She knew there was a death penalty for spying. Would they send the man she loved to the gallows? She asked Mrs Araki what could be done. 'Nothing. There's nothing anybody can do. He will serve a long term. But of course they can't hang a white man.' She added: 'Whatever you do, don't breathe a word to anybody. All the Germans are strictly forbidden to talk about it!'[5]

Lily Abegg, an aggressive journalist for the *Frankfurter Zeitung* who covered Asia, lost no time in taking over the job of Tokyo correspondent and blackening Sorge's name. He was conceited, boastful, uncultivated, and unbalanced.[6] 'You watch, when he's out of prison he'll grumble that we had an easier time than he did. And won't he brag about the experience!' Lily said to Eta two months after the arrest. Furious, Eta retorted that he was the most noble and selfless human she had ever met.[7]

§ The interrogation of Richard Sorge began on Sunday 19 October at 9 a.m. The prosecutor in charge was Yoshikawa Mitsusada, a bright and ambitious 34-year-old and the special favourite of Nakamura Toneo, head of the Thought Division of Tokyo District Court Prosecution Bureau.

Yoshikawa's immediate and urgent task was to obtain a confession. The pressure was intense. Ambassador Ott was demanding to see Sorge without delay, and the Prosecution Bureau wanted to obtain a confession before the meeting, which had been approved by Prime Minister Tojo. There was much concern that the detention of this well-connected German national might develop into a serious diplomatic incident. Japan could not risk offending its Axis partner, least of all at a time when a conflict with the US appeared inevitable.

In later years, Yoshikawa reminisced about the most dramatic case of his entire career: 'There were great political and diplomatic pressures, and a great fuss with Mrs Ott. I had to get at the truth quickly. With the change of cabinet, and Tojo taking office, we could keep the lid on the Sorge events, which was fortunate.'[8]

But Sorge would not be budged. He proclaimed his loyalty to the Third Reich, which paid his salary, and the Nazi Party. He acknowledged only that he sometimes collected confidential information for the ambassador, whom he served as advisor. The accusations were preposterous.

'I am a Nazi!' he persisted.

'Stop lying! You are a communist, not a Nazi. I suggest you confess immediately,' said Yoshikawa.

'I am a Nazi. I demand that you contact Ambassador Ott this minute. He will be able to clear this matter up.'[9]

Yoshikawa was absolutely convinced he was face to face with a spy. The question was, *whose spy*?

We were wondering whether Sorge was really a spy for Germany, and using communists in Japan, but actually spying for the Nazi regime in Germany. That was one question. The second question was whether Sorge was a double spy for both Berlin and Moscow. The third question was whether he was really a spy for Moscow, pretending to be a Nazi. Therefore, we examined Sorge without preconceived opinion. We took a very cautious attitude.[10]

Assistant Inspector Ohashi Hideo, of the Special Higher Police's foreign section, was the principal police interrogator in the Sorge case. Ohashi, thirty-nine, a sturdy man with a plump, jolly face, also came under pressure to obtain an admission from Sorge that he was a spy for the Soviet Union or the Comintern. With Yoshikawa breathing down his neck, Ohashi hectored and wheedled relentlessly and tried to demonstrate the futility of resistance.

'What is the point of denying it? Your subordinates Miyagi and Ozaki have both confessed to being spies. We found material in your house that was not the sort of information a journalist possesses. It was quite clearly transmitted to the Soviet Union. At Clausen's house we impounded the same sort of typewritten manuscripts, and work-sheets for encoding, and the wireless equipment. All this is irrefutable evidence of espionage activity.'

One of the suspicious papers Ohashi placed before Sorge was the typewritten draft of that final solicitation that he and Clausen be withdrawn from Japan. This was discovered in the house search at Nagasaka-cho. It contained no mention of the Soviet Union, but the style and use of code-names were suspicious: it was not the way a journalist would address his editor.

Within a day or two, Ohashi told Sorge that Clausen had confessed and revealed the nature of the Tokyo ring. 'It is so patently obvious you and the others are engaged in espionage that the Japanese government won't release you even if Ambassador Ott does lodge an official protest,' Ohashi warned.

The government, he went on, had imposed a news blackout, so the newspapers could print nothing about the case. The reason – which Ohashi did not explain – was that public confidence would be undermined by news that a spy ring had penetrated high official circles.

'So there has been no public announcement about this case?' Sorge appeared surprised.

'All reporting is prohibited,' Ohashi replied.

'I don't wish this affair to be known, so if it is not being made public, I don't mind admitting my spy activities and talking about them.'

Out of the blue, Sorge's acknowledged his espionage role for the first time. Ohashi felt a surge of relief and triumph when the suspect began to waver. This was on the afternoon of Thursday 23 October.[11]

According to Ohashi, Sorge made a formal confession on Friday 24 October. The witnesses, apart from himself, were two senior *Tokko* officers, Yoshikawa and two other prosecutors, and an interpreter, all packed into the tiny Buddhist chaplain's office where the interrogation was conducted.

But according to Yoshikawa, the breakthrough came on Saturday 25 October, a moment of high drama:

> Sorge asked for a piece of paper and a pencil, and wrote down, in German, I have been an International Communist since 1925, and then burst into tears, hiding his face on the table. He was in despair. He screwed the paper into a ball and threw it across the room, got to his feet and paced up and down. 'This is the first time I've been defeated!' he shouted. It was quite a drama. [Prosecutor] Tamazawa was also surprised. Other prosecutors came into the room to watch. Then he quietened down.[12]

Yoshikawa felt intense satisfaction. Sorge had cracked sooner than anticipated: 'I was expecting that it would take a longer time, and if it had taken a longer time I would be pushed in a difficult position because of pressure from the German Embassy as well as from the Japanese Army.'[13]

The inquisitors saw before them a pathetic figure, physically and emotionally drained. When he was arrested Sorge was physically below par, and possibly on the verge of a breakdown. The interrogators caught him at his lowest ebb, and after five or six days of relentless questioning – and almost certainly sleep deprivation – he had no more energy to resist. His fighting spirit was dead. He was so utterly exhausted that he pleaded with Yoshikawa to be allowed to rest before the formal investigation began.

But for some students of the Sorge case, such an early surrender was utterly out of character: a man of such immense willpower would have resisted longer – unless, perhaps, torture was used to break him.

§ In pre-war Japan, a suspect – particularly one accused of political crimes – could expect rough treatment in police hands. Treatment of foreigners was more gentle, though there were well-authenticated instances of Europeans suffering severe abuse in custody.

We have no certain knowledge that the three Europeans in the Sorge ring were tortured into confessing, but it cannot be ruled out. Immediately after the war, Japanese judicial officials denied that coercion had been used. Yoshikawa and Ohashi claimed that they behaved like gentlemen from start to finish. But in later years, Ohashi revealed that

– although he did not witness the episode with his own eyes – Vukelic had been subjected to torture immediately after his arrest: 'It seems that Suzuki [Inspector Suzuki Tomiki] was beating Vukelic. I did not see it in person, though. I was conducting the investigation in a different room at the time.' In defence of his former colleagues, Ohashi said that individual police officers acted only on orders from the prosecutors who supervised the investigation.[14]

Clausen – the only one of the trio who lived to tell the tale – may have avoided unpleasantness by giving his captors what they wanted. According to Yoshikawa, both Vukelic and Clausen confessed 'within two or three days. Clausen was quick. He complained about his heart condition. He was the first to talk, without a moment's hesitation [*guzuguzu sezu*]'.[15]

Whether Sorge was tortured, or at least deprived of sleep to hasten his collapse, remains a matter of conjecture. All we know for sure is that he was subject to rigorous questioning which, in Yoshikawa's words, 'went on from early morning till late at night'.[16]

Ishii Hanako is among those who believes that violence was used in the early days of his detention. She claims certain knowledge that the three police–prosecutor teams engaged in a no-holds-barred contest to make the suspects talk: 'There was a fierce competition to see who would get the first confession. The reward was promotion.'[17]

The experience of an American journalist lends weight to her view. Otto D. Tolischus, Tokyo correspondent of the *New York Times*, was arrested as a suspected spy on the day that Japan attacked Pearl Harbor. Like Sorge, Tolischus was held in the Tokyo House of Detention and questioned for over two months, beginning on 3 January 1942. The early interrogations, in which third degree was used to extract a confession, give an idea of what Sorge too may have suffered. *Tokko* officers, screaming and cursing in broken English, accused Tolischus of disclosing Japan's national secrets. 'You have come here on a secret mission, haven't you? I am now going to put a question to you, and you are going to answer Yes! And God help you if you don't! You are a spy. Confess! You are a spy! You are a spy! Say, I am a spy!'

Tolischus was made to remain in a kneeling position, Japanese-style, while two interrogators slapped him repeatedly, stamped their feet on his knees and ankles, and banged his head against the wall. They gripped his head in a ju-jitsu hold as if to strangle him. They pushed a pen between his fingers and pressed until they almost broke.

This was was not exceptionally harsh treatment for a recalcitrant suspect. No doubt much worse was meted out to Miyagi at Tsukiji

Police Station, and Kawai Teikichi had suffered fearful torture in police cells in Hsinking in 1936. Tolischus had reason to believe that Sorge was ill-treated. During questioning on 15 January 1942, the interrogators – whom Tolischus dubbed the Snake and the Hyena – referred to a German journalist held in the same prison.

> 'I asked the *Frankfurter Zeitung* man,' said the Snake, 'and he told me you were a spy. Everybody says so. Your own American colleagues say so. Why deny it?'
>
> When he mentioned the *Frankfurter Zeitung* man, which meant Richard Sorge, I could almost credit it, as Sorge was probably undergoing tortures similar to mine. But when he mentioned other American correspondents, I knew he was lying.[18]

§ After the traumatic admission of guilt, Sorge braced himself for a new ordeal. When the time came for his meeting with General Ott – which he had vociferously demanded – Sorge had second thoughts. To Yoshikawa, it seemed almost as if he had an attack of scruples, and shied away from looking the ambassador in the eye.

By Sorge's lights the exploitation of friendship was a trifle, when set against the noble cause of preserving the Soviet Union and averting war. But Yoshikawa had a distinct impression that Sorge experienced twinges of conscience, and it took all his powers of persuasion to bring him round.

> He said nothing for a while, he seemed deep in thought. He told me then that their political opinions differed, but they were personally good friends. So I said that if I were him I would meet [Ott] because it was a normal, human thing to say a last farewell. Finally, he said, I'll meet him, and I passed the message to the Foreign Ministry.[19]

When the moment arrived, Sorge was marched into the interview room. The *amigasa*, the straw basket prisoners had to wear over their faces, was tucked under his arm.[20]

Ott was seated at a conference table, with one or two of his staff and an array of Japanese officials. Sorge, grim-faced, remained standing. Ott stared intently, seeking clues in his friend's eyes. 'Sorge was badly shaved. He made a shattering impression', the ambassador said later.[21] Both men appeared ill at ease. The interview was mercifully brief. Ott asked three questions, agreed beforehand with the prosecutors.

'How is your health?'

'I am well,' Sorge replied.

'How is the food you are receiving?'

'It is satisfactory.'

'Do you have any request?'

'I need nothing, thank you.'

Sorge looked thoroughly miserable. 'This is our last farewell, Mr Ambassador,' he said in a low voice.[22]

The significance of that remark could hardly escape the ambassador. He adamantly refused to accept that Sorge was a spy – woe betide any German who dared to express such a view in his presence. But in this moment, his pained expression seemed to tell a different story. Sorge also appeared to be struggling with his emotions. Ohashi observed him closely. 'Sorge must have felt distress at having deceived Ambassador Ott, who had relied on him,' he wrote later.

No man had been closer to Ott in Tokyo than Sorge. Together they had deciphered Japanese riddles, and weathered one political crisis after another. He had entrusted Sorge with the most sensitive assignments because there was no one as knowledgeable, reliable and steadfast. Sorge was part of the family, like an uncle to Ott's daughter Ulli, his chess partner and companion on travels, whether to Manchuria, Akiya or Nishi-izu. Sorge had borrowed his wife for a while, and teased him about his infatuation with Anita Mohr. There was hardly a corner of Ott's life unaffected by Sorge.

By all accounts, this encounter, which would be their last, affected both men deeply. Sorge seemed so shaken that Yoshikawa – fearing a suicide attempt – decided to ask the chief warden to place him under close watch. Prison guards kept up a vigil, regularly checking at the peep-hole in the door. Sorge, they reported next day, had slept fitfully, tossing and turning throughout the night.[23]

§ In Sugamo prison, Max Clausen's brittle composure quickly fell to pieces. For a day or two he wept and babbled hysterically. With almost no prodding, he volunteered complete co-operation with the investigators. When the impounded wireless equipment was brought to Sugamo, Clausen assembled it in front of police, demonstrating how he communicated with 'Wiesbaden', and explaining all the technicalities in exhaustive detail.

The remorse poured out of Clausen, who impressed upon his captors that he had undergone a thorough change of heart many months ago, since when he had fumbled through his work as an unwilling accomplice. Indeed, he had done much damage to the ring by his stealthy actions, transmitting to the Centre only a fraction of Sorge's intelligence reports. To support his claim, he gave a detailed breakdown of what material he transmitted, and failed to transmit, and showed that in 1941 the latter outweighed the former.

For decades, it has been a matter of conjecture whether this was a fiction to mitigate his crime in the hope of lenient treatment, an under-standable ruse for a prisoner a few blocks away from the execution chamber. Now that the Russians have released copies of telegrams that *did* reach the Fourth Department, it is time to re-examine Clausen's role. The new evidence provides at least a tentative answer to the question of whether he toiled heroically for Sorge, or double-crossed him.

Max Clausen started out in Japan as a dedicated and audacious operator, and served Sorge and his masters in Moscow well for over four years. But by 1941, as we have seen, his personal circumstances had transformed his world view, and prompted doubts and misgivings about his subterranean work. In his testimony, he offered a wide range of reasons for not carrying out his duties conscientiously:

> If I had transmitted all the cable drafts which Sorge gave me they would probably have come to 40,000 word groups, but in fact I only transmitted just over 13,000 word groups. The reason I didn't send everything is, firstly, because Sorge gave me too many texts to send and it would have been really hard work to transmit them all. On top of that I had heart trouble and I didn't want to ruin my health. Secondly, I had become sick of spy work. Recently my belief in Communism began to waver, and I lost the will to pursue spy work really seriously.[24]

Referring to notebooks impounded by the police, Clausen listed twenty-one occasions on which he transmitted a total of 13,103 'word-groups' (*gogun*) between January and October 1941. This was the most vital phase in the ring's history, a peak in Sorge's activity, yet Clausen's output was well below the average of previous years. By comparison, the notebooks showed that Clausen sent 29,179 word-groups on sixty occasions in 1940, and 23,139 on fifty occasions in 1939.[25]

The prosecutor then asked Clausen for the 'most recent transmission dates and number of words'. The wireless operator again referred to the notebooks, which gave a breakdown of work on fourteen dates between 6 May and 4 October. According to his figures, a total of 7,118 word-groups was transmitted in these six months – a surprisingly small volume in an absolutely critical time, when Sorge was working at full stretch.

How do Clausen's figures – drawn from his notebooks, which the police seized as evidence – compare with what we now *know* he trans-mitted to the Fourth Department? Examining copies of cables obtained from the Russians, we find eighteen transmission dates in 1941, between 6 May and 4 October (including five occasions when two cables were sent on the same day).

Certain discrepancies emerge. Where Clausen said he transmitted on fourteen occasions, our evidence shows that there were eighteen occasions. Clausen's notebook does not record that he transmitted on 17 June, 21 June, 11 July, 12 August and 24 August, yet we know that Sorge's reports were sent on these days. On the other hand, his notebook showed that he transmitted on 5 September, and 11 June, but we have been unable to obtain the telegrams radioed on these days.

Clausen's notebook was clearly an unreliable *aide-mémoire* (on two dates he did not bother to record how many word-groups were sent). Some material that he claims to have destroyed did in fact reach Moscow. For instance, Sorge's report on the 2 July Imperial Conference was sent, although Clausen testified that he could not recall transmitting it. On the other hand, he owned up to sending a number of messages that we have been unable to locate; if they were sent, they presumably still lie buried in Russian archives. It is possible that when the archives are opened wider, some of these may surface. However, with the evidence at our disposal, we find a broad correlation between what Clausen confessed to transmitting – dates, length of text and content of messages – and the telegrams we know were received by the Centre in the final six months of operations. Many of the details tally. For instance, Clausen told interrogators he was sure his last transmission was on 4 October, and the penultimate one on '14 or 24 September'. Sure enough, we have in our hands a cable for the former date, and the Russian Defence Ministry tells us that 4 October is the last date on which the Sorge ring was in contact with the Centre.

Clausen's testimony contains inconsistencies, but these were more likely to be lapses of memory than attempts to deceive police and prosecutors. Fearful that a long spell in prison would make his poor health even worse, Clausen bent over backwards to co-operate, and would have had every reason to lie about his role. But the available evidence strongly suggests that Clausen told the truth: he was a disaffected Soviet agent who had duped Sorge.

There can be little doubt that Clausen's perfidy diluted the impact of Sorge's intelligence in 1941. If Moscow had received all the dispatches drafted by Sorge, and the texts in their entirety, Sorge might have commanded more serious attention from the Soviet leadership.

Clausen described his duplicity in the days prior to the German invasion of Russia. On 17 June 1941 Moscow urgently instructed Sorge to report on Japan's intentions, and on troop movements along the border between Manchuria and the USSR.

> Sorge drafted and gave me numerous messages, but I transmitted just a few and tore up most of them. The reason I transmitted these few is because I was sure that the home country would cable an enquiry to its embassy in Japan and Serge would come and demand to know why I hadn't sent the information. So I sent just a few that were not so important.[26]

Suspicions were not aroused, because Clausen kept up a minimal but regular flow of traffic. Sorge was blind to what was happening. Much vital intelligence never got through, in the Soviet Union's hour of greatest need. Even the shipment of large quantities of material via the Russian Embassy could not compensate for the wireless operator's dereliction of duty.

Sorge paid a heavy price for the reckless motorbike escapade that had led him, in 1938, to give his wireless operator the network's secret code. When Clausen was tapping out, in Morse code, the five-digit groups of figures without knowing what these stood for, tampering was impossible. But once he knew the code, he also understood how far he could go in destroying and abbreviating messages with impunity.

§ Early in the investigation Ohashi revealed something that disturbed Sorge deeply: the police knew all about the code used for the ring's radio communications. Clausen, said Ohashi, had explained exactly how the code worked, and deciphered the illegal traffic which Japanese monitoring agencies had intercepted but failed to decrypt. The earliest intercept was dated 24 December 1937.

Hearing this, Sorge went pale. Usually, he was cool and composed during questioning, but on this occasion he could not conceal his emotions.

'How could he do this?' he exclaimed angrily. 'A code must never be betrayed! It is the life-blood of a spy ring. An intelligence agent guards his code with his life. I vowed that if I were captured I would never give away this secret.

'I did all the code work myself for several years. Clausen simply radioed the messages. I also decoded the messages that came in. It was after I had a motorcycle accident and was laid up in hospital that I changed the procedure. It seemed more practical if Clausen could handle the whole operation. So I decided to teach Clausen the code. I asked for, and got, Moscow's approval, but it was my decision.'

Sorge reproached himself for the fateful decision, taken in St Luke's hospital in May 1938, to entrust Clausen with something so precious. And a terrible thought struck him. What if the Russians thought *he* had surrendered the code to his captors? The imputation of such dishonourable conduct would be unbearable. 'Please note for the record', he told Ohashi sternly, 'that it was Clausen, and not I, who revealed the secret of the code.'[27]

Sorge was intensely annoyed with his compatriot, but he bore no malice. At every opportunity in prison, he endeavoured to protect both Clausen and Vukelic, by portraying them as mere technical assistants. He would have felt less charitable had he found out how Clausen had used his knowledge of the code to engage in systematic sabotage, but the investigators apparently kept this to themselves. Thus Sorge was spared agonizing conjecture about which of his important dispatches may not have reached Moscow as a result of his careless decision and subsequent lack of oversight.

§ Hanako waited patiently for word from Sorge, but the promised telegram never came. When Superintendent Matsunaga turned up unexpectedly at her mother's house in late October, she realized why. Years afterwards, she recalled her anguish at hearing that Sorge had been arrested by the Tokyo Metropolitan Police.

> He said he didn't know the reason, but he thought it was something to do with illegal dollar transactions. I was so startled I reeled over onto the tatami. No! I said, Sorge wasn't the sort of person to deal on the black market. The superintendent said it must be true, because people said Sorge was a Jew, who prayed to the sun each morning. But that was absurd, I told him. Sorge didn't pray to the sun – that man didn't pray to anything.

Matsunaga had not come all the way from Toriizaka Police Station to Higashi-Nakano simply to pass on devastating news. What preyed on his mind was that he had done a deal with Sorge and burnt Hanako's statement about her affair with a foreigner. Now he was terrified that his superiors might find out. A week or two later he was back, looking even more sombre.

> Sorge was a spy for Russia, he said. The investigation hadn't finished, but it was more or less confirmed. Spies were normally shot, and there was no hope for him. You can imagine the state I was in. I was totally shattered. When the superintendent had gone, I dug out a photo of Sorge and pressed it to my lips, and said aloud: I don't care if the whole of

Japan thinks of you as an enemy, I'll love you always. I suppose a loyal
Japanese would have been horrified. But I didn't think it was an evil
thing to be a spy. What I regretted most of all was that he hadn't run
away to Shanghai, after all that talk. Why didn't he make a run for it?[28]

§ Each morning, a guard came to the cell to escort Sorge – face hidden
under the regulation straw basket – along gloomy, echoing corridors to
the Buddhist chaplain's office. Here, Sorge removed the contraption
from his head. The routine was that Assistant Inspector Ohashi conducted questioning in the morning, and Prosecutor Yoshikawa took
over from three o'clock, continuing until late in the evening.

After the initial ordeal Sorge collected himself, and his self-assurance
returned. He coped calmly with the formal interrogation, after laying
down his own ground-rules. First, the women in his life were not to be
discussed, and second, Hanako, having played no part in his espionage
work, must not be dragged into the police inquiries. On these conditions,
he promised his full co-operation.

The inquisitors set out to establish what secrets Sorge had betrayed,
his sources of information, and whether ring members and informants
were still at large. The priority of the Japanese government was to
assess the damage inflicted on national security. Twenty people, including
the three Europeans, were in custody by 25 October. A further fifteen
arrests directly connected to the case would be made by the end of
April 1942.

Sorge took care not to give his inquisitors any names they did not
have already. He played down the contribution of Vukelic, Miyagi, the
minor players and all the women involved, in the hope that they would
be spared the full rigour of the law. His intimate association with the
German Embassy was described in detail, and without exaggeration.
More questionable, surely, was his claim that Soviet leaders, as well as
his Fourth Department chiefs, held him in high esteem. But he no
doubt hoped to impress on his captors how valuable a role he could
play in Japan's effort to improve relations with Russia.

In the sessions with Yoshikawa, in whom he recognized his intellectual
peer, Sorge expounded on a wide range of subjects – international
communism, geopolitics, Japanese policy towards China, German–Japanese relations, the Russo-German war. The records of this part of the
investigation read like a potted history of the years 1933–41. Only the
dry translation of Sorge's answers survives today, but even so they
resonate like the lectures of a pedantic professor of political science at
a German university.

Japan, he told the prosecutor, appeared to be impenetrable, but it was really like a crab: once you got through the hard shell, it was soft inside, and information could be picked up easily. Insights like this intrigued Yoshikawa. In later life he said of Sorge: 'He had the air of a *sensei* [teacher] giving me instruction. It was fascinating listening to someone who knew so much about everything.'[29]

Sorge, however, knew little about what mattered most in his predicament – the Japanese legal system. And Yoshikawa, who spoke so warmly of the spy many years later, took part in a judicial deception that had fatal consequences for his prisoner. Police and prosecutors were intent on portraying the ring as an espionage group controlled by the Comintern, not the Red Army. Departmental rivalry lay behind this manoeuvre. If the true identity of the suspects emerged, the War Ministry might argue that its *Kempei* should be given jurisdiction over an affair of military espionage. The Justice Ministry was determined to keep the case in its own domain, even though it meant 'adjusting' the facts.

When prosecutors tried to establish which communist organization the spies were reporting to, they found that the stories of the principals did not tally. Clausen said he belonged to the Fourth Department of the Red Army. Ozaki and Miyagi both said they were working for the Comintern. Vukelic said he supposed he was working for the Comintern, but said he could never verify it.[30]

Sorge himself was evasive. At first he was reluctant to acknowledge being a Red Army spy, and the reason he gave some months later was dread of being turned over to the military police, renowned for their brutality. 'I had heard of an Englishman being handed over to the military police before in such a case,' he told the examining magistrate in July 1942.[31] (He was probably referring to the Reuters journalist Jimmy Cox, who had died in *Kempei* hands in 1940.)

Police and prosecutors played on this fear, and persuaded him that his best hope lay in being tried under the Peace Preservation Law. If the case were brought under this law, the War Ministry would be shut out, and the *Kempei* would not get their claws on him. But the Peace Preservation Law would only apply if Sorge identified himself as a member of a subversive organization like the Comintern (*kokusaikyosanto*).

What Sorge did not grasp until too late was that the prosecution intended to establish that he came to Japan to pursue the deadly aims of the Comintern – to overthrow capitalism and the imperial system, and turn Japan into a communist state. This was totally at variance with the facts, but an essential fiction in order to try the case under the Peace Preservation Law. For the Justice Ministry this law invariably offered the best chance of success in securing convictions, and the sternest penalties.[32]

Ohashi admitted many years later that he was under orders to misrepresent Sorge as an agent of the Comintern. Sorge hesitated in playing along with this distortion, but did agree, after some persuasion, to describe the organization he worked for as 'Moscow Centre'. To suit their purpose, the inquisitors interpreted this all-embracing term as meaning the Comintern. Ohashi Hideo later remorsefully confessed to his part in this perversion of justice. 'The fact is, Sorge was set up by the police. I have to say that I feel sorry for Sorge, for the way he was set up.'[33]

In the memoir he produced for Yoshikawa, Sorge began to hedge. 'From November 1929 on, my espionage groups and I were technically and organizationally a direct part of Red Army Intelligence, that is, the so-called Fourth Department,' he wrote. But a few paragraphs earlier he asserted: 'I do not know to this day whether or not I was attached to Comintern headquarters, or whether I was an agent of the so-called Fourth Department or some other agency, as, for example, the People's Commissariat for Foreign Affairs or the Soviet Communist Party's central committee.'[34]

Not until July 1942, in the pre-trial phase with the examining magistrate, did he finally set the record straight. 'That part is completely at variance with the facts,' he said, referring to his earlier testimony. 'I felt absolutely clear in my own mind that I belonged to the Fourth Department of the Red Army.'[35]

By this time he had access to legal counsel, and understood he had been duped. By obscuring his real affiliation, he had helped his inquisitors to create a fiction that the ring was operated by the Comintern. Out of ignorance he had contributed to the prosecution strategy, which was based on a lie. Nine months after his arrest, he tried to extricate himself from this blunder. It was too late: by then the die was cast.

§ The 'Comintern spy' charade had another grave consequence for Sorge: it allowed the Russians to disown him. The Soviet Union maintained the fiction that the Comintern was an international communist organization outside its control. When Sorge allowed himself to be designated a Comintern agent, he must have understood that it would be impossible for the Russians to acknowledge him as one of theirs. And so it was. When the Japanese approached the Soviet Union with a view to exchanging Sorge for one of their own spies, they were met with blank stares: 'The man called Richard Sorge is unknown to us.'

Sorge naïvely believed – for a while at least – that Stalin would order his rescue, in recognition of his valiant service to the Soviet Union. Soon after his arrest, Sorge asked Japanese officials to contact the Soviet Embassy with a view to initiating an exchange of prisoners. Assistant Inspector Ohashi recalls that the interpreter was out of the room at the time. 'Please let Serge at the Soviet Embassy know that Ramsay is being held at the Tokyo House of Detention,' Sorge urged. The request made Ohashi nervous. He ignored it, and decided to say nothing about it to his superiors.[36]

'Serge' – Viktor Sergevitch Zaitsev, a second secretary and consul at the Soviet Embassy – had served as 'mailbox' – the liaison between the ring and the embassy. A 'legal' intelligence agent, he enjoyed diplomatic immunity and was in no danger. A few weeks after the arrests, Zaitsev and another 'mailbox', Vutokevich, the chief of the consular division, quietly left Japan to avoid any embarrassment to the two governments.[37]

When Sorge heard, on 8 or 9 December, that Japan was at war with the United States and Britain, he must have felt that salvation was near at hand. In a swing of the tide of history, the Japanese were now at the mercy of the Russians. Six months earlier, when the Germans swept into Russia, the Soviet ambassador had begged the Japanese government for assurances that Japan would remain neutral. Now, embroiled in a hazardous war with America, it was Japan's turn to plead with the Soviet government to observe the neutrality pact.

After Pearl Harbor, Sorge must have calculated that it was in the interests of the Japanese to keep him safe and well. This was indeed the case. Precisely because the Japanese presumed he had some worth as a bargaining counter with Moscow, they declined to turn him over to the Germans. When Ribbentrop asked that Sorge be extradited to Berlin – where he would undoubtedly have faced a firing squad – the Japanese stalled.

During that first winter in prison, Sorge appeared optimistic that his return to the Soviet Union could somehow be arranged. According to Ohashi, Sorge believed that Rozovsky (the vice foreign commissar) would initiate contacts with the Japanese Embassy in Moscow to secure his release. Rozovsky was one of the Comintern delegates he had taken care of when they visited Frankfurt in 1924, and he had been instrumental in recruiting Sorge to work in Moscow.

The prisoner was confident that what happened to him mattered to high-level people in Moscow. At least, that was the impression he gave Ohashi: 'He would talk about a comrade involved in espionage who had been caught in Italy, or somewhere, and then released a few years later and returned to Moscow – he certainly didn't give up hope that they would get him out.'[38]

§ When autumn gave way to an icy winter, the little chaplain's room used for interrogations offered a welcome haven from the piercing cold of the cells. As soon as Ohashi arrived in the morning, he topped up the brazier with precious charcoal (rationed and hard to come by) provided by the Prosecution Bureau, and heated a kettle of water. The room was soon nicely steamed up, and they brewed up the English tea brought from Sorge's house.

At first Ohashi refused to allow Sorge to smoke – it was forbidden by prison rules. But Sorge made a fuss, claiming that his smoker's nose detected an aroma of tobacco in the room. After consulting with prison staff, Ohashi relented, and Sorge could relax with a cigarette until the supply – brought over from Nagasaka-cho – was exhausted.

Ohashi was given little more than four months to conduct his part of the interrogation and only managed to skim the surface of an affair of baffling complexity. As Sorge would have quickly perceived, he was completely out of his depth. Though he was the Tokko's specialist on Comintern affairs, Ohashi's grasp of the Soviet Union and communist structures was shallow. Moreover, the social and political background of a man like Sorge was utterly alien to him. He seemed greatly concerned with trivia – such as what languages Stalin and the Comintern leaders knew.

Much time was wasted on trying to make out what Sorge was telling them. Two interpreters, one who knew English, one who spoke German, were tried out, and Sorge opted for the first. Even so, it was uphill work: the interpreter was defeated by the jargon of socialism. The language barrier gave Sorge scope for blurring answers to awkward questions. The drawback was that he failed to grasp how his captors were twisting facts to suit their purposes.

The prosecutors, who were the key figures in any judicial investigation, at first ordered the police to complete their report by the end of the year. (It was customary for police to interrogate suspects first, and it was not unusual to take six months over a case of subversion.) The Special Higher Police fought to protect their turf, and after weeks of wrangling it was agreed that the prosecutors would interrogate Sorge for part of each day, while police continued with their own questioning.

In December Yoshikawa started putting flesh on Ohashi's superficial examination; his own enquiries were far advanced by the time the police took the last deposition from Sorge on 7 March 1942. As was customary on the last day, Ohashi put the question: 'What is the suspect's present state of mind and intentions for the future?'[39] Sorge replied that he hoped to be allowed to return to Moscow and continue his studies. 'If I cannot go back to Moscow I would like to make a living in Japan by writing or journalism.'

Then he made a plea for his Japanese associates to be treated with leniency: 'All the responsibility rests with me.' As for Clausen and Vukelic, they had simply followed orders, and were engaged in the technical, not the political side of the ring: 'Therefore when this case is over, I implore you to let them return to their families as soon as possible.'[40]

In later years, Ohashi claimed that he treated Sorge so considerately that he drew a stern rebuke from his *Tokko* superiors. His most prized possession is a handwritten letter of thanks Richard gave him on 7 March 1942:

> For Mr Ohashi. In memory of his most profound and most kindly investigation of my case during the winter 1941/42, I express my deep thankfulness to him as the leader of the investigation. I will never forget his kindness during the most difficult time of my eventful life.
>
> Richard Sorge

None the less, there is no hint of kindness in the report that Ohashi submitted at the end of his interrogation: he recommended that Sorge be sentenced to death. This inconsistency is hard to explain away. Ohashi, looking back after more than half a century, insisted that he had merely recommended 'an appropriate penalty', and that the head of the foreign affairs section later amended what he wrote to 'death penalty'.[41]

Something Sorge said when they parted in March made a lasting impression on the policeman: 'Mr Ohashi, if I am executed, my ghost will come back to haunt you.' At the time both men laughed, but Ohashi never forgot those words.

§ Prosecutor Yoshikawa, like Ohashi, professed to be a firm admirer of the accused in this, the most celebrated case he ever handled. By his account, he and Sorge enjoyed as smooth a working relationship as the trying circumstances allowed. He explained their *modus operandi* in these terms:

> We quickly reached an understanding. I outlined to Sorge what ground I wanted covered, and Sorge gave his own views on this. Later he typed out the points covered in the questioning. He was given the use of his

own typewriter, and he composed his statement, working late into the night. He was as hard a worker in prison as he had been as a free man.[42]

The result was a memoir (*shuki*) that was part autobiography, part discussion of his espionage activities. It skims over many important episodes in his career, and hides the names of most of those who had helped him. The workings of the Tokyo ring are described in a perfunctory way. The main interest of the memoir to the modern reader is what it reveals of Sorge's personality and motivation.

While the prosecutor and the prisoner appear to have respected the other's abilities, they were always adversaries in a deadly battle of wits, and neither would have lost sight of this. Yoshikawa, like Ohashi, was intent on sending Sorge to the execution chamber in Sugamo.

In June 1942, in one of his last sessions with Yoshikawa, Sorge argued that he should not be treated as an enemy of Japan, because he was not a spy in the normal sense of the word.

> The Soviet Union did not want political strife or military clashes with other countries, especially Japan, and would not invade Japan. Consequently, I and my group definitely did not come here as enemies of Japan. We were quite different from what is normally understood by a 'spy'. The 'spy' of England and America is someone who is searching out the weak points in Japan's politics, economy and military, as targets to attack. But we didn't collect information about Japan with that intention.[43]

§ One day early in the interrogation, Yoshikawa had placed a letter on the table in front of Sorge. 'Who is this from?' the prosecutor asked.[44] Sorge saw that it was one of Katya's letters. They had been stored, along with letters from his divorced wife Christiane and other private papers, by the naval attaché. They were the sort of things he absolutely did not want police to find if they searched his home while he was away. Wenneker had readily agreed to keep the locked suitcase in his own house.

'We recovered a suitcase with this and other letters. And a large sum of money as well,' said Yoshikawa. Wenneker had turned the suitcase over to the Foreign Ministry after Sorge's arrest (it had been forced open already – perhaps by someone worried that it might contain evidence of how close Sorge was to certain diplomats).

'It's my wife waiting in Russia,' Sorge explained. The prosecutor was surprised. To him it looked like carelessness on the part of this seasoned spy to hold on to papers that revealed Russian connections, and to store them with a German naval officer. Was it sentimentality that had kept him from destroying Katya's letters, Yoshikawa wondered.

Sorge was already making plans for when he got out of prison. 'I'm ticking off the days until I can return to Moscow and enjoy a peaceful life,' he volunteered. For the sake of his value as a bargaining-chip, he had to maintain that he was close to Russian leaders, and that he would be welcomed back with open arms. Whether he believed this himself is not clear, but all his illusions would have been shattered had he known of the ordeal that Katya underwent.

Although he had told Yoshikawa that Katya was waiting for him in Moscow, he had few grounds for hope. Indeed, contact appeared to have been lost after a letter he had written three years previously lamenting the cruel destiny that kept them apart: 'I will not be surprised if you give up the eternal waiting.'[45]

Katya's life ended in tragedy. While he was in prison, she was arrested – on 4 September 1942 – and accused of spying for German Intelligence. After a semblance of a trial, at which no evidence was presented, she was sentenced to five years' internal exile on the basis of her confession. The charges against Katya – so devoted to communism that she had given up drama studies to toil in a factory – were as spurious as those hurled against millions of other victims of Stalin's purge.

They had gone through the marriage formalities before Sorge set out for Japan in 1933. That was how he had wished it. As the wife of a Red Army officer serving overseas, Katya was entitled to draw an allowance and they could communicate through official channels. But in the end, the decision to become Sorge's legal wife had fatal consequences. In March 1943 she was banished to Krasnoyarsk, in Siberia. She died in a labour camp on 3 July 1943. The cause of death was given as a brain haemorrhage caused by paralysis of the respiratory system. She was thirty-eight years of age.

Katya's 'crime' was to be the wife of Sorge, and there can be little doubt that he would have paid the ultimate penalty had he ventured back. When she died in Siberia, Sorge was standing trial in Tokyo. Fortunately for his peace of mind, he could have had no knowledge of her fate. The agony would have been too much to bear, and would have destroyed the last remnants of his faith in the Soviet Union of Stalin.

§ On the morning of 17 May – almost exactly eight months after the principals were arrested – Japan's newspapers carried the first stories on the exposure of the Sorge ring. 'Richard Sorge was sent by the Comintern headquarters to form a Red spy organization in 1933,' the *Tokyo Asahi* reported.

The authorities could keep the lid on the affair no longer. For months, political gossip in Tokyo had linked the arrest of Ozaki to the collapse of the Konoye cabinet the following day. Speculation was rife that the army had framed Ozaki, who had worked for Konoye, in order to discredit the prince. This was Konoye's own belief until he recognized that a man he had trusted implicitly was indeed a spy. His political future looked even bleaker when two close associates, Saionji Kinkazu and Inukai Ken, were arrested in the spring of 1942. The prince, protected by his connections to the throne, escaped arrest, but he was required to testify in the case.

Word that high-ranking personalities had been arrested in an espionage affair spread fast. The nature of Japanese society, as Sorge pointed out in his defence, is not compatible with the keeping of secrets. The government decided that it was better to pre-empt the spread of wild rumours by providing a sanitized version of events. The Justice Ministry announcement (released to the press on 16 May) of the round-up of a Comintern spy ring was carefully worded. The significant fact that the spies' sources were high officials in the Japanese government and German Embassy was omitted. Use of the word 'important' to describe the intelligence gathered was nowhere to be found in the final draft.

There was no mention of the Fourth Department, or the Soviet government, in the account the press could print. The culprits were identified as agents of the Comintern, an international communist organization. At a time when Japan was locked in mortal combat with the United States, it made no sense to antagonize the Russians needlessly. Nor did Japan wish to disturb relations with Germany: there was no reference to Sorge's connections to the embassy, or his membership of the Nazi party. To play down the role of prominent figures, Inukai and Saionji were merely described as 'unwittingly leaking' secret information. Damage limitation was the aim.

However, the inescapable truth remained that foreign spies had penetrated to the heart of the Japanese establishment, and that was the most shocking aspect of the revelation. Government circles were concerned about the impact on the nation's morale. The police were instructed to sound out reactions to the news, and found ordinary people to be indignant that when Japan was at war, the highest social classes had jeopardized state security by reckless behaviour.

'It's inexcusable that high-class people like the Saionji family should be involved,' opined a reserve army captain in Gumma prefecture.[46] A farmer in Nagano prefecture remarked: 'It's really regrettable that this case should have been brought about by upper-class people.' Among the comments gathered by police, that of a war widow was bitterest of all: 'Its a fact that they shot our imperial troops in the back. And as they have been pursuing these activities since 1933 I feel, as one of those who suffered bereavement, that these plotters were to blame for the defeat in battle that caused the death of my husband.'[47]

Police also investigated the reactions of certain German residents. These registered shock, surprise, and obsequious admiration for police efforts in exposing the plotters. Lily Abegg, the journalist who was now Tokyo correspondent for the *Frankfurter Zeitung*, was among those interviewed by police on 17 May 1942.

> I have known Sorge since 1935, but had no idea he was a communist. He was always drinking and wasting time, but he wrote first-rate articles ... Most Germans here know that Ambassador Ott was on intimate terms with him, so the ambassador must be in a fix. But aren't all the members of the embassy staff in the same position as Ott? It's even more embarrassing for Meisinger, because the arrest was made by the Japanese authorities, and there is even a rumour that he was shot inside the embassy. But I think that was simply made up.[48]

All the embassy staff had been outwitted by Sorge, but no one looked quite as foolish as Meisinger. The Gestapo officer's duty was to hunt down dangerous elements, but he spent much of his time chasing Germans suspected of failing to greet with the *Heil Hitler* salute, and similar crimes. It was left to the Japanese police to unmask the Russian spy with whom Meisinger had spent rollicking evenings. His loss of face in Japanese circles was absolute and irrevesible.[49]

The service attachés were as imprudent and culpable as Ott. Apart from Scholl, none had been as close to Sorge, or as indiscreet, as Paul Wenneker. When the roof fell in, it was noticed that he was first to dissociate himself from his friend, and the most energetic in pushing the entire blame on to Ott. We know from his colleagues that Wenneker thought the post of ambassador might be his if Ott was brought down by the scandal. Wenneker, along with the army and air attachés, confronted Ott and demanded that he resign. The ambassador sent the three men packing: Sorge was completely innocent, he insisted.

For months, while he tried to hush up the affair in the German colony in Tokyo, Ott played down its significance in reports to Berlin. But his position had become untenable even before the scandal became public knowledge. An investigation ordered by Heinrich Himmler, head of internal security services, turned up evidence of Sorge's communist activities in the early 1920s that substantiated the Japanese charges in some degree. Then, in March 1942, a report to German Military

Intelligence from an agent in Manchuria revealed the alarming implications of the Sorge case. Because Ott and his staff had taken Sorge into their trust, vital information had been leaked to the Russians. The ambassador had lost his authority in Japanese eyes. Japanese faith in the embassy in Tokyo was seriously undermined.

Helmuth Wohlthat, at the time chief of the German economic delegation in Tokyo, also warned Berlin of the catastrophic effects on Germany's reputation in Japan. Many years later, he summed up the situation in these terms:

> The Japanese were of the opinion at first that the ambassador would resign of his own accord. When, to their surprise, nothing happened on the German side, they expressed their view of the situation in various quarters, and in Tokyo primarily, to the three service attachés and myself. I was personally approached by senior General Staff and Navy staff officers ... But it was a year before Ambassador Ott was relieved of his duties. Because of the circumstances, the ambassador's ability to influence the Japanese government on behalf of German interests was paralysed during that year.[50]

Ott tried to hold on to his post as long as possible. The axe fell on 23 November 1942, when a cable from Ribbentrop arrived with the instruction 'To be decoded by the ambassador personally'. It said that he was to be replaced, and should leave the embassy and 'rent an acceptable house in a quiet place' as a private person until further notice. But not until Christmas could he bring himself to announce this to the German community. Disregarding normal convention, Ott remained in Tokyo long after his successor, Dr Heinrich Stahmer, arrived. Finally, in May 1943, he withdrew to Peking, where he sat out the war with his wife and daughter. (His son Podwick had been killed in action on the eastern front.)

§ Stahmer took up his post in January 1943. He had played midwife to the Three Powers Pact in 1940, and now found his creation weak and sickly. The health of the alliance had indeed been gravely impaired by the Sorge affair. The Japanese drew their own conclusions about the deficient security in the embassy, the dilatory fashion in which the German government handled the aftermath of the affair, and the overall lack of judgement this demonstrated. Mistrust between the two allies was exacerbated by a lingering belief on the Japanese side that Sorge was a double agent, working for Germany as well as Russia.

The effects were soon felt by German nationals in Japan. They were scrutinized as never before – we know that the ambassador's movements were closely monitored – and denied travel permission, sometimes even for the short journey between Tokyo and Yokohama.

Official co-operation was even more grudging than it had been previously. After the Sorge affair, Japanese military agencies became more cautious about providing high-grade information to the service attachés in Tokyo, and this suspiciousness was reciprocated by Berlin. The souring of the atmosphere came as the Axis powers made common cause in the war against the Western democracies. Enthusiasm for pooling intelligence and material resources waned at the moment when it was most essential.

Sorge had derived satisfaction from reporting tensions between Germany and Japan; and endeavoured to aggravate them through his political manoeuvres at the embassy. Ironically, it was his being caught that gave the shaky Axis partnership its biggest jolt. It was a last, unintentional service to the Russians.

§ By all accounts, Sorge quickly adjusted to the prison regime. Hardships could be alleviated by money: Sugamo's demoralizing food barely sustained the penniless. With ample funds, Sorge could choose his own menu. Ohashi's search of his house had turned up $1,782 and 1,000 yen in cash, another $2,000 dollars was discovered in the suitcase he had given Wenneker for safe keeping, and he had money in the Mitsubishi Bank. This made him one of the wealthiest residents of Tokyo Detention House.

By contrast Ohashi, with his slender policeman's pay-packet, had to watch every sen. The captor lunched on *bento* (meals in boxes) costing between 50 sen and one yen. With envy, he watched Sorge tuck into the extravagant 5-yen *bento*. The captive's diet was supplemented by what Helma Ott sent in: most appreciated was a good supply of fresh fruit, including so many *mikan*, tangerines, that one inmate joked that Sorge's complexion turned an orange colour.

The real privation for a man like Sorge was the shortage of news about the outside world. The only permitted source was a weekly bulletin published by the government, which he struggled to read with the help of guards and an English-speaking inmate. His appetite for news about the Russo-German war was insatiable. As a special treat on some mornings, Ohashi read out to him the headlines from a newspaper he carried.

Sorge's joy was boundless on the day in November 1942 when he heard of the Soviet counter-offensive at Stalingrad. This, he perceived, put paid to Hitler's hopes of vanquishing Russia. His elation was witnessed by Kawai Teikichi (who had been arrested on 22 October 1941, and transferred to Sugamo in September after long confinement in a police station). Locked up in a cell close to Sorge's, Kawai happened to peer through the peep-hole and saw the German dance a little jig of joy in the corridor and pat the shoulder of a guard. No doubt Sorge gave himself some credit for his own contribution to the dramatic reversal in the Russians' fortunes at Stalingrad.[51]

We have one other vignette of Sorge in triumphant mood over a Red Army victory. Nakanishi Kou, whose espionage activities in China overlapped those of the Sorge ring, was awaiting trial in the Tokyo Detention House. One day, in the exercise yard, he had an opportunity to speak with Sorge. As he wrote later, 'Even now I can remember how his face lit up with pleasure when I told him the Soviet Army had reached Warsaw.'[52]

§ On 24 June 1942 the interminable investigation entered its third stage. After months of grilling by police and prosecutors, Sorge was forced to endure a long summer retracing the same ground, this time with an examining magistrate. The one benefit was that these sessions took place not at Sugamo, but at the Tokyo District Criminal Court – the trip to the centre of the city offered an agreeable respite from the perpetual gloom and stale odour of the prison. On the way to and from the court Sorge could glimpse, through the slits of his *amigasa* and the bars of the prison van, the bustle of the streets, and could savour briefly the greenery around the Imperial Palace moat.

This third round of questioning, however tedious, had another merit for Sorge. He was able to correct mistakes or falsehoods in his earlier testimony. Above all, he seized the chance to state unequivocally that he belonged to Red Army Intelligence, and not the Comintern.[53]

At one of the final sessions Nakamura Mitsuzo, the examining magistrate, asked if the accused understood the damage his network had caused to Japan's military and defence interests. Sorge begged to differ. An ordinary spy ring reports on the target country's vulnerable points, he said. But his group had a quite different purpose: to work for peace between Japan and the Soviet Union. Furthermore, he insisted that little of what he had relayed to Moscow could be classed as a state secret. Much of the material had already appeared in print in Japan, or was the sort of information circulating widely among knowledgeable Japanese.

> I think the indictment jumps to the conclusion too easily that our intelligence activities involved state secrets. As far as Vukelic was concerned, he provided neither state secrets nor important information. He collected

information from the Domei Agency that the foreign correspondents knew about. The same can be said about Miyagi. Miyagi was not able to gather important new information.

Political information in the real sense was obtained by Ozaki, and sometimes by me, in my case from the German Embassy, but it is doubtful to what degree even this can be called a state secret. Ozaki came with things he heard from the Breakfast Society, but the Breakfast Society was not an organ of the state, and what it did could not have been secret. There must be quite a lot of similar societies in Tokyo.[54]

In a democratic society, in a time of peace, such a defence might be valid. But it was naïve of Sorge to expect these arguments to carry weight in a totalitarian nation at war. On 15 December the examining magistrate reached his verdict: the accused had breached the Peace Preservation Law and the National Defence Security Law, and should be put on on trial.

Another winter passed before the trial began in the Tokyo District Criminal Court. Sorge was found guilty of violating four laws. In his summary the presiding judge, Takada Tadashi, said that the defendant had come to Japan to realize the objectives of the Comintern, which was intent on the overthrow of Japan's social system. The judge acknow-ledged that Sorge had left the Comintern in 1929 to set up his own spy network under instructions from the Fourth Bureau. But he maintained – this was essential for the judicial charade – that Sorge conducted espionage primarily to promote the Comintern's aim of international revolution.

Although perfectly aware that the Comintern was organized with the aim of realizing a world-wide communist society through the dictatorship of the proletariat, and in the case of Japan, of transforming the *kokutai* [national entity] and rejecting the private property system, he developed his own intelligence operations, centred on East Asia, under the control and leadership of the Fourth Department.[55]

This convoluted statement characterized Sorge as a military spy whose real purpose was to overthrow the emperor and impose a communist system in Japan. The logic was flawed to the point of absurdity, as Sorge realized. But courts in a totalitarian state are not bound by logic. What mattered was that this judgement ensured Sorge's conviction on the capital offence of violating Article One of the Peace Preservation Law.

On the morning of 29 September 1943, Sorge rose to make a final statement to the court: 'I had absolutely no thought or plan to start a communist revolution in Japan or spread communism in Japan,' he said.

He, and he alone, must bear full responsibility for the activities of the network. 'Please treat my Japanese colleagues as lightly as possible,' he requested.

The court rose to hear the judge pronounce sentence. We may well imagine the piercing loneliness of the accused at this moment, as the pitiless voice decreed his fate.

> In the case of the said accused, charged with violating the Peace Pre-servation Law, the National Defence Security Law, the Military Secrets Protection Law and the Military Resources Law, this court, with the participation of Prosecutors Nakamura Toneo and Hiramatsu Isamu, has reached a verdict as follows: the defendant shall be executed.

Sorge's bearing was erect and dignified, his composure absolute. There was no word or sign that indicated shock, or indignation that justice had been perverted to suit the Japanese state.

The next step was an appeal. Again, he returned to the theme that he and his group were not, for the most part, gathering 'secrets', but rather information that was already in circulation. Strictly speaking, although such leakages were illegal, 'in practice the Japanese social system is not amenable to the keeping of secrets.'

As for the information he had obtained from the German Embassy, Sorge maintained that little or any warranted the description 'state secret'. The appeal statement went on: 'It was given to me voluntarily. To obtain it I resorted to no strategy for which I should be punished. I never used deceit or force.'

Asanuma Sumiji, Sorge's defence counsel, submitted the appeal one day after the thirteen-day period prescribed by the legal procedures at the time. The deadline was 10 January. The appeal was submitted to the Supreme Court on 11 January (there was no intermediate stage between the first instance court and the Supreme Court for cases tried under the National Defence Security Law).

When Asanuma missed the deadline he was officially reprimanded by the court for negligence. However, even though a man's life was at stake, the judiciary refused to waive the rules. Asanuma was mortified at the unpardonable blunder, but his client was philosophical. He had not held out much hope for the appeal, he told the lawyer. It was Asanuma who needed consoling, and the condemned man did what he could to make him feel better. In any case, neither of them believed that legal man-oeuvres could have diverted the course of state-decreed justice, or rather injustice, at this stage. The only hope, frail though it was, was that political expediency might sway government leaders to spare Sorge's life.[56]

§ On the September morning that Sorge made his final statement, in the same court-room, Ozaki listened sombrely as Judge Takada pronounced the sentence of death. He was convicted of violating three laws, including the harsh Peace Preservation Law. Like Sorge, Ozaki was found guilty of espionage activities that were aimed at the overthrow of the social system and the emperor. The heinous felony for which he must pay with his life was his supposed attempt to 'transform the *kokutai*' – an untranslatable concept describing the mystical unity between the emperor and the people of Japan.

Ozaki's defence had centred on the *tenkosho*, or statement of conversion. The recanting of 'thought crimes' was part and parcel of the Japanese legal system up to 1945. A Japanese arrested for violating the *kokutai* could only begin to purge his or her guilt by a full recantation. A belief in communism was among the grave offences that a *mea culpa* – provided it was sufficiently abject – might mitigate.

But Ozaki's first statement, completed on 8 June 1943, failed to strike an appropriately repentant note. In the 30,000-word document addressed to Judge Takada, he sought to justify his left-wing beliefs and espionage activities: 'the political leaders of Japan have no coherent understanding of the direction in which the world is moving.'

The death sentence came as a stunning blow. Ozaki had thought that the severest penalty would be many years in prison – perhaps he could not conceive that someone of his social status, with friends in high places, would go to the gallows. At once, his loyal friend Matsumoto Shinichi, who had planned the defence strategy from the start, went into action, appointing new lawyers to work on the appeal. They agreed that Ozaki's only hope lay in composing a new and decidedly more 'sincere' *tenkosho*.

It pained Ozaki to beg for his life by disowning the beliefs and principles he cherished. Only after desperate entreaties from his wife, Eiko, did he agree to draft the statement. But in a letter to Eiko on 8 February 1944, he admitted that he was unable to write the confession of a true convert. The second statement was completed on 29 February; although it made a more favourable impression than the first, the court found that Ozaki's anti-state views were fundamentally unchanged.

On 5 April 1944, the appeal was denied. Ozaki appeared resigned to his fate and stoical, as a letter he wrote to Eiko two days later shows. He spent the remainder of his days in prison reading the many books brought to him by his wife – among them Goethe's works and Nehru's autobiography – and he composed essays on philosophy and religion, developing a particular interest in Zen Buddhism. Stamp-collecting had been a passion from his younger days, and one letter to his wife contains a request that Yoko should go to a certain shop and buy him some books on philately.

That he remained true to his convictions to the end is evident from remarks made to a prison visitor in early November. 'I would like to go and die splendidly as a communist,' Ozaki said. 'I have nothing to regret, and I am fully prepared.'

§ Max Clausen and Branko Vukelic both received life sentences. Anna Clausen, who had been arrested one month after her husband, was sentenced to three years in prison, one of the most lenient penalties meted out. She succeeded in convincing prosecutors that she had played only a minor role, as a reluctant accomplice, and this was corroborated by the stories of Clausen and Sorge. Subsequently, Max and Anna narrowly escaped death in the incendiary bombings of Japanese cities, and were among hundreds of political prisoners liberated by victorious American troops in October 1945.

Branko was less resilient. Life in Sugamo was made tolerable by the visits of his devoted wife Yoshiko, who brought clothes, books and money for food. But in July 1944 he was transferred to Abashiri prison, which lies in a bleak corner of Hokkaido notorious for its harsh winters. Before he left, Yoshiko was allowed to bring their three-year-old son Hiroshi to Tokyo Detention Centre for a brief reunion.

She found him thin and weak, and ill with dysentery, and could not stop herself crying. Vukelic tried to console her, with his usual optimistic smile, but firmly advised her against moving to Hokkaido – it was no place to bring a small child in winter. 'Perhaps you can come to see me in the spring' were his parting words.[57]

Vukelic did not survive the first winter in the coldest and most desolate part of Japan. On the night of 15 January 1945, Yoshiko received a curt telegram: 'Will you come to get his remains or shall we take the necessary steps? Abashiri Prison.' Procuring a ticket was immensely difficult in wartime, but Yoshiko appealed to the sympathy of station staff, and set out on the long, solitary trip to the frozen wastes of eastern Hokkaido. In a letter to Branko's mother written in December 1946, she described the scene in the dismal prison mortuary.

> At Abashiri I found him in a coffin wrapped in a white robe as was customary in Japan. He was so thin, frozen and stiff. I cried my heart out at the sight. I asked them to leave me alone with him. I don't know how long I stayed there, but finally somebody came to tell me I could not stay there forever.

The direct cause of death was given as pneumonia, but it was chronic diarrhoea and malnutrition that had sapped his strength and left him vulnerable. No doubt he had also suffered more than his fair share of physical abuse in the early stages of the interrogation.

Even General Willoughby, the US Military Intelligence chief who went to absurd lengths to portray the Japanese interrogators as gentlemen, had trouble explaining away Vukelic's death: 'His early death in prison raises the question of torture. He was only forty-one when he died, and the record does not show that he was physically below par before his arrest. It is very possible that he was firm in his refusal to talk, and was treated accordingly.'[58]

A letter reached Yoshiko long after the telegram. It was date-stamped 8 January 1945, though she assumed that it was written at the end of December, when he was already suffering from pneumonia: 'I can stand the cold much better than I expected. (Only my writing becomes worse than usual.) So our meeting next year may safely be realized according to the human calculation ...'

Miyagi Yotoku, racked by tuberculosis since his youth, was also too frail to cope with the stark prison regime.[59] He died in Sugamo, on 2 August 1943, while his trial was still under way. When the news reached Ozaki, whose trial was nearing its end, he was heartbroken. In a letter to his wife dated 11 September 1943, Ozaki wrote:

> The presiding judge told me that Miyagi died a month ago. I was well aware that he would be unable to stand prison life, but this news has shaken me. Miyagi was a splendid person ... in all his paintings, one feels this deep sadness, this terrible loneliness. Miyagi was a solitary man. Infinitely solitary. When he died, nobody came from his home place, Okinawa, to claim his body...[60]

§ During interrogation, Sorge presented himself as an analyst and interpreter of events rather than as a 'spy' – a label he rejected. In his testimony we sense his pride in the soundness of his judgement, although he acknowledged one or two occasions when he was wrong. When he came to explain the most crucial phase of his mission in 1941, he boasted of a quick and sure grasp of Japanese intentions towards Russia: the problem lay in overcoming the scepticism of his superiors in Moscow. As he told prosecutors on 11 March 1942,

> From the start I reported to Moscow that Japan would not participate in the war, but in the early period the Centre harboured doubts about my reports to that effect. However, from September they had complete trust in my reports, for which I received special cables expressing gratitude.[61]

This recollection, benefiting from hindsight, does not accord with the facts. As we have seen, he shared Soviet leaders' fears that they would have to fight on a second front, in the Far East.

As early as 28 June Sorge pointed out that the Japanese were biding their time, and would only move when the Germans had brought the Red Army to its knees. The Japanese were opportunists looking for easy pickings – and would stay away if the Red Army proved unbeatable. But assessing Japanese intentions with greater certitude proved a protracted, laborious process, as our examination of his reports during this period shows. There were many agonizing weeks of fumbling in the dark until Sorge finally established that the summer mobilization was not directed primarily against the USSR. Only late in the day could he assert with confidence that Japan was not planning to attack the Soviet Union that summer or autumn.

At the end of August Sorge relayed to Russia that the army had decided not to launch an attack in the course of the year. This was followed, in mid-September, by an even more categorical assurance. At the beginning of October, Ozaki's conclusions after a journey to Manchuria were transmitted: the army had relaxed its readiness stance, and cancelled a plan to take over the Trans-Siberian Railway. If Clausen had fulfilled his duties conscientiously, and Sorge's dispatches had not been compressed, delayed or even suppressed, Red Army strategic planning would no doubt have had the benefit of a fuller intelligence picture.

To what extent Sorge's reports influenced the Soviet leadership is not yet fully understood.[62] Most studies indicate that they were an important factor in Stalin's decision to shift resources from the Far East in order to strengthen defences on the western front. In this sense, Sorge's work in 1941 had a profound historical impact. His carefully researched estimates permitted Stalin to pull substantial forces out of the Far East to hurl against the German invaders in the west. The transfer of between eight and ten rifle divisions, together with 1,000 tanks and 1,000 aircraft, during October and November 1941 provided desperately needed reinforcements for the defence of Moscow.[63]

The German advance on Moscow began on 2 October for what Hitler called 'the last great decisive battle of the war'. At this moment the survival of Mother Russia hung in the balance, but Moscow never fell.[64]

The decline in Soviet strength in the Far East soon became evident to the Japanese army. According to General Staff intelligence estimates, the Russians had shifted to the west between nine and eleven infantry divisions, at least 1,000 tanks and more than 1,200 planes. By 24 October only 19 rifle divisions, 1,200 to 1,400 tanks and about 1,060 aircraft were left in Siberia.[65] By this stage, the Japanese decision to strike south was irreversible. Moreover, the onset of a rigorous winter ruled out a major offensive.

We may suspect that anti-Russian elements in the Japanese army gnashed their teeth in rage when their intelligence told them how greatly the Soviet Far East Command had been diluted by the transfers westwards. In October, it was learned, Soviet troop strength in the Far East had fallen to 'levels that might have invited IJA [Imperial Japanese Army] intervention earlier'.[66]

§ After Sorge's appeal was thrown out, he was told that there would be no advance warning of the execution date. According to Japanese custom, it would be announced to the condemned man when the day came, at dawn.

For a further ten months he would endure the anguish and uncertainty of a lonely prison cell. At night, from nearby cells, he could hear the delirious screams of other condemned men, tormented by the agony of not knowing if they would live another full day. In these circumstances, sleep could not have come easily, but Sorge bore the ordeal with fortitude. Whatever inner grief he went through, on the outside he was calm and unruffled, according to those who saw him in the final months. A prisoner on the same corridor, Nishizato Tatsuo, often came across Sorge in the exercise yard during this period: 'He always came out for exercise, and he did not look like someone waiting to be executed. Always he greeted me with a smile.'[67]

Sorge also appeared in good spirits to a visitor from the embassy, Karl Hamel. The Japanese authorities decided that he should be given a chance to bid farewell to his German friends. Meisinger was approached, but he thought the duty too 'distressing' and sent his young interpreter Hamel to Sugamo instead. Sorge appeared well-fed, and – Hamel observed with surprise – cleaner and neater than he had ever looked outside prison. Admiringly, the visitor noted how composed and collected the prisoner seemed. The impression was 'of a man proud of having achieved something great, and who is now preparing himself to leave the scene of his accomplishments'.[68]

Hamel had permission to receive Sorge's last will and testament. The condemned man's main concern was for his 80-year-old mother in Germany, the mother to whom he was so deeply attached all his life, whose birthdays he always remembered with a card or letter. Sorge pleaded that she should not be persecuted by the German police, as she had known nothing about his activities in the past twenty years. He asked for a letter to be forwarded to her. Japanese officials present at the interview promised to take care of this.

For himself, he asked for history books to be sent into prison – he wished to 'round out his picture of the world' in the time that was left.[69]

§ As the precious moments of life ticked away, the condemned man grasped at a frail straw of hope: that the Russians would negotiate to secure his freedom. During interrogation he had sedulously built himself up as a steadfastly loyal Red Army Intelligence officer, greatly prized by his superiors. Japanese police and prosecutors were given no hint that he was nagged by fear of the consequences of returning. His strategy was to convince them that he was so important they could extract a high price for surrendering him to Russia. If the Japanese believed this, there was little likelihood that the death sentence would be carried out.

The Japanese were quite willing to hand over their captive. After they had questioned Sorge at great length about the workings of his network, national interests would not be served by holding him in prison. A number of approaches were made to Soviet officials by Japanese diplomatic and military representatives, but these were met only with blank expressions and obdurate dismissals. 'Three times we proposed to the Soviet Embassy in Tokyo that Sorge be exchanged for a Japanese prisoner. Three times we got the same answer: "The man called Richard Sorge is unknown to us".' This was how Major-General Tominaga Kyoji recalled events in a conversation with Leopold Trepper, who had spied for the Fourth Department in Europe.[70]

For the Soviets, who never admitted to employing spies, Sorge had turned into an encumbrance by getting caught. Perhaps he was a liability in another sense as well: as an agent who had given warnings of the German invasion that went unheeded, Sorge was an embarrassment to Stalin. Certain others who knew about Stalin's grave blunder had been eliminated, or would be later. By a tragic twist of fate, Sorge's devotion to the duty of protecting the Soviet Union had made him a threat to the Great Leader, rather than a hero worthy of rescue from captivity.

Leopold Trepper, who knew and admired Sorge as a resourceful and courageous colleague, was in no doubt about why he was disowned: 'They preferred to let Richard Sorge be executed than have another troublesome witness on their hands after the war,' he wrote in his memoirs.[71] Owing to his association with imaginary 'enemies of the people', including his former Fourth Department chief, Sorge had long been considered an adversary by Stalin. 'Richard Sorge paid for his intimacy with General Berzin. After Berzin was eliminated, Sorge, in the eyes of Moscow, was nothing but a double agent, and a Trotskyite into the bargain!'[72]

The indifference of the Russians to Sorge's fate eventually persuaded the Japanese that there was no point in making further approaches, or showing mercy. On 4 November the justice minister put his seal on the execution order. Two days later Shigemitsu Mamoru, the foreign minister, attended a reception at the Soviet Embassy to mark the anniversary of the Bolshevik Revolution.

By this point, Japan was in dire straits. It had suffered a series of resounding defeats in the war against America. Fortunately the Soviet Union had respected the neutrality pact, and had not yielded to pressure to enter the war on the side of America against Japan. But then, on the eve of the anniversary, came a grim omen of Russia's real intentions. Stalin made a speech denouncing Japan as an aggressor, causing profound shock in Tokyo. The more percipient officials in the Foreign Ministry wondered aloud whether the Russians were biding their time and would attack Japan when it was thoroughly exhausted by the war in the Pacific. At the embassy reception on 6 November, the Russians wore smiles of welcome as usual. But a Japanese diplomat who attended the event, Kase Toshikazu, sensed a chill in the air: 'It was, I thought, like the sharp touch of the first frost that withers the late flowers.'[73]

In this delicate atmosphere, Foreign Minister Shigemitsu broached the question of the impending execution, recalled a Russian diplomat who was present. The intention was to discover whether the Soviet government had had an eleventh-hour change of heart. That was not the case. Shigemitsu met with a rebuff: Ambassador Malik had no wish to discuss the Sorge problem. The Russian witness's recollection, however, differs from that of Kase Toshikazu, who feels sure that his minister did not spoil the evening by bringing up the disagreeable matter at any point in the celebrations.

The assembled diplomats toasted the Emperor Hirohito and Generalissimo Stalin, and downed large quantities of vodka and whisky. 'The reception was a nice affair but there was none of the enthusiasm that had characterized the reception of a year before,' Kase noted.[74]

§ Tuesday 7 November was bright and wintry, the cells piercingly cold. Sugamo was awakened by a clanging bell at six, in the usual way. It was the 27th anniversary of the Revolution, a day when Sorge may least have expected the Japanese to take his life. He was now forty-nine years of age.

Shortly before ten he heard a guard's voice shouting 'Cell Eleven!' The call must have sent a chill through his heart, for it was much later than normal for morning inspection.

Then the prison governor, Ichijima Seiichi, entered the cell with a group of officials, among them the prison chaplain. He went through a solemn ritual, asking the name, age and domicile of the condemned man. He formally announced that by order of the minister of justice, Richard Sorge would be executed that day, and was expected to die calmly. Sorge, whose Japanese had improved in his three years of confinement, could not mistake the meaning.

'Do you understand?' the governor asked. He nodded. Did he wish to make any changes to his will? He did not. The governor then asked, 'Do you have anything to say?'

'No, nothing more,' said Sorge. Addressing the group of officials, he added, 'I would like to thank you for all your kindnesses.' Then he put on fresh clothes for the final journey.

The grim procession made its way along the corridor. Locked in a nearby cell, Nakanishi Kou heard the commotion and realized what was happening.

> As I recollect, Tokyo on November 7th 1944 was so cold that you felt ill. I couldn't see out from my cell, but once you got used to the dark in the detention centre, you became very sensitive to noises in the corridor. You developed a feeling for what was going on from the sound of keys, feet, voices, and so on, and from the atmosphere around people. Sorge's cell was just in front of the guard's desk in the centre of the corridor. I sensed from movements in the air that Sorge was being taken away that morning. I remember that, at the spot where the large key to the wing was kept, he seemed to nod in the direction of our cells, as if he was saying 'sayonara'.[75]

The group went out into the sunshine, crossed the courtyard, and entered a small building behind high walls. In an ante-room, incense tapers burned in front of a golden image of Buddha. Without pausing at the altar, he was escorted into a bare room.

He was led to the trapdoor set in the floor and stood calmly as his hands and legs were bound. He did not know that shortly after 9.30 that morning, Ozaki Hotsumi, his loyal helper, had stood on this same spot, and been hanged until he died at 9.51. Now the same noose was fitted around Sorge's neck, and the attendants left his side. The trapdoor snapped open under his feet at 10.20 a.m., and Sorge dangled in space at the end of the rope. Sixteen minutes later, at 10.36, the prison doctor pronounced him dead.

EPILOGUE

A Hero's Grave

MAX CLAUSEN walked free on 8 October 1945. Japan lay in ruins, occupied by the victorious Americans. 'The jails were opened with the casual good nature of the American conquerors,' wrote Major-General Willoughby, chief of military intelligence (G-2) in Tokyo, ruefully. The sick and emaciated Clausen and his wife Anna were among some five hundred detainees who emerged from prison cells into the daylight of a liberated Japan.

For several months they lived quietly in Urawa, near Tokyo, and then in the capital, paying a visit in December 1945 to Karuizawa, where they stayed with Frieda Weiss, Anna's German teacher. Early in the following year the Clausens, aware they were under surveillance by G-2, were spirited away on a plane to Vladivostok with the help of the Soviet Embassy.

Willoughby's ears pricked up when 'an excited Japanese official advised me that the release list of political prisoners contained foreign espionage agents, the remnants of the Sorge ring'.[1] On Willoughby's orders, a counter-intelligence officer compiled an initial report on the case based on Japanese Ministry of Justice materials. After the exposure of a Soviet spy ring in Canada in February 1945, the general had homed in on the Sorge story with a new passion. Now he became convinced the it was part of a global canvas of Soviet penetration and subversion: 'I decided that the Sorge Case, though 10,000 miles away, was a complete parallel and should be reported to demonstrate an existing world-wide pattern'.[2]

He instructed that a revised version of the Sorge report be sent to Washington, with a recommendation that it be used in military training schools for the study of Soviet intelligence techniques. At first Willoughby opposed publication, but he came to realize that the material had educational value for the American public: it would serve as a warning about what he saw as an international communist conspiracy directed against the Western democracies. Willoughby – affectionately described by General MacArthur as 'my lovable fascist' – intended to use the Sorge affair to demonstrate how Soviet espionage recruited and deployed an army of communist sympathizers and fellow travellers to sabotage free societies.

The Sorge report was released to the press in Tokyo on 10 February 1949. The effect was sensational.

The controversy in the US centred on allegations in the report that the American activist and journalist Agnes Smedley was a Soviet spy who assisted the Sorge ring in Shanghai. Another journalist, Gunther Stein, a naturalized Briton, was identified as a Soviet agent working for Sorge in Japan. The pugnacious Smedley immediately counter-attacked, vehemently denying that she had spied for any country. She called on General MacArthur to waive his official immunity, 'and I will sue you for libel'.

Smedley's defiance, and the threat of legal action, spurred Willoughby to launch an epic hunt for proof that she and Stein were indeed key figures in the ring. A protracted investigation failed to find firm evidence of guilt; none the less Willoughby continued his crusade against Smedley in a special report to the House Un-American Activities Committee in 1951, and in a book, *Shanghai Conspiracy*, the following year. By that time, there was no danger of a libel suit: Agnes Smedley died in the University Hospital in Oxford in May 1950.

To Cold War hawks like Willoughby, Smedley was the link between a bold and successful Soviet spy ring and the 'fellow travelers and prostituted liberals' in the United States who espoused left-wing causes. The Sorge material was used as ammunition to attack a broad spectrum of American liberals. The fact that Sorge spied for America's wartime ally, Russia, and that his targets were Japan and Germany, enemies of the United States, was conveniently forgotten or shunted aside by the Messianic red-baiter Willoughby.

Sorge's intelligence reports confirmed to Soviet tacticians that they could switch forces from Siberia to the west, for the defence of Moscow. These reinforcements, aided by a ferocious winter, saved Moscow and dealt the Germans a blow from which they never recovered. In this sense Sorge also helped save the Western democracies. Had Moscow fallen to Hitler's armies, the outcome of the war might have been very different. At the very least, the defeat of Germany would have cost countless more Allied soldiers' lives.

It was left to Agnes Smedley to remind the American public of the debt the Western democracies owed to the Soviet Union, and to men like Sorge. 'If 25 million Russians had not died in the war, would we be sitting here today?' she asked, in a speech in March 1949 in New York.

Far from acknowledging Sorge's contribution to the Allied victory over Nazism, Willoughby and others claimed that Sorge and Ozaki used their influence to steer Japanese aggression away from the Soviet Union and in the direction of Pearl Harbor. No proof has ever been found to support this mischievous theory; the evidence we have presented shows it to be a fallacy.

Certainly, Sorge's primary duty in Tokyo was to help the Soviet Union ward off a very real threat from Japan. However, he saw Nazi Germany as the most evil and dangerous foe, not only of Russia but of civilization itself. Japan's entry into a war with the Western democracies would relieve the pressure on Germany, according to Hitler's calculation. If the United States came to blows with Japan, its capacity to support Britain would be diminished. If Britain became vulnerable, Hitler hoped to finish off his war in the West and unleash all his destructive power against the Soviet Union.

Taking a broad strategic view, Sorge reckoned that it was imperative to alert the Western democracies to Japan's aggressive designs. For this reason, he organized leaks of information to Robert Guillain of the Havas News Agency and to the *Herald Tribune*'s Joseph Newman. He decided to feed selected information not only to Moscow, but to other adversaries of Nazi Germany who shared the aim of destroying Hitlerism.

§ 'Like a string of Chinese firecrackers, the release [of the Sorge report] set off a series of explosive reactions,' wrote Willoughby.[3] For the Japanese, the biggest firecracker in the report was the exposure of Ito Ritsu as the 'unwitting Judas' who led the police to the Sorge ring.

Interest in the case had been stimulated by a best-selling collection of Ozaki's letters to his wife from prison. Ozaki the traitor had been transformed by sympathetic media reports into a patriot and martyr who had fought against Japan's entry into a disastrous war; the publication of the moving letters revealed Ozaki to be a devoted husband and father, and a humanist rather than a hard-nosed communist.

In February 1949, the public was told that Ozaki had gone to the gallows as the result of a tip-off by one of his closest friends. 'A wretched fellow, today one of the four or five most influential leaders in the Japan Communist Party, betrayed them in pain and jealousy,' the Sorge report said of Ito Ritsu.

The sensational disclosure caused an upheaval in the Japan Communist Party, reborn after the war and becoming much too active for the liking of American and Japanese power-holders. Communist party officials declared that they had already investigated the allegation against Ito Ritsu and found it to be entirely false; they claimed there was a conspiracy of the occupation and pre-1945 police authorities to discredit the renascent party.

The discomfiture of the Communist Party was observed with satisfaction by Japanese police and prosecutors, on whose records the Sorge report was based. In America, Willoughby had milked the Sorge case to discredit liberals and left-wingers. In Japan the exposure of Ito Ritsu as the 'Judas' who betrayed the ring turned comrade against comrade, sowing the seeds of a bitter vendetta.

Ito, who has been described as 'the most enigmatic figure of the Showa era' suffered a tragic fate in the subsequent feuding among party factions. In the early 1950s he vanished from Japan, was purged from the party, and resurfaced in Peking in 1980, making a sensational 'return from the grave'. Attempting to clear his name, he completed a series of writings before his death in 1989. In reminiscences published posthumously, in 1994, he maintained that he was the victim of a frame-up. When he was being questioned in the summer of 1940, police were already watching Kitabayashi Tomo – whose arrest led to the unravelling of the Sorge ring. Ito made the startling claim that that Nosaka Sanzo, the party's former chairman (who died in 1993) was the real police spy who betrayed the Sorge ring and a number of communists of Japanese descent living in the United States.

The 'Judas' controversy, inseparably entwined with the Communist Party's bitter internal feuds, can still command headlines in the Japanese press after almost half a century. After the denunciation of Nosaka appeared in the January 1994 edition of the *Bungei Shunju*, rumours circulated that Ito's 'last testament' contains further disturbing revelations about Japan Communist Party leaders, alive and dead. This aspect of the Sorge affair – the row over who actually betrayed the spy network – smoulders like a live volcano.

§ Richard Sorge lies buried in Tama Cemetery, in a suburb of Tokyo, identified by a black marble tombstone bearing the Russian epitaph 'Hero of the Soviet Union'.

The impressive memorial dates from the rehabilitation of Sorge in 1964. Twenty years after his execution, the Russians finally claimed him as their own, in a rare official admission of the existence of Soviet espionage. Belatedly, the spy who died unrecognized and abandoned by his Moscow masters in a Japanese prison was proclaimed a national hero, and heaped with posthumous honours. A street and several schools were named after him in Moscow and other cities, a huge statue erected in the capital, and postage stamps issued with his likeness by the Soviet Union and what was then the German Democratic Republic.

This tardy act of justice became possible only when criticism of Stalin was permitted by the Kremlin. On 4 September 1964 *Pravda*, the newspaper of the Soviet Communist Party Central Committee, published an article describing Sorge as a hero who gave warning of German preparations for the invasion of the USSR. 'But Stalin paid no attention to these reports or to others.'

Today the Soviet Union no longer exists. In a vastly transformed Russia, a new generation is sceptical about everything connected with the old regime, including its heroes. But Sorge's name is likely to live on, as both a symbol of patriotism and a romantic figure whose exploits have a strong appeal even to young Russians who have more interest in Macdonald's than Marx.

Are the remains in Tama Cemetery really those of Sorge? An old theory that the spy was not hanged, but secretly returned to the Soviet Union – as he assumed he would be – occasionally flickers into life. Alas, there is no evidence to substantiate a yarn rooted in utter disbelief that the Russians could cold-bloodedly abandon one of their greatest agents.[4]

'There is no truth at all in the reports that Sorge was sent back to the Soviet Union,' says Ishii Hanako, adamantly. 'I know, because I saw the bones myself.'[5]

She had thought a good deal about Sorge during the dark days of war, and then, when peace returned, she learned from a newspaper article how he had met his end. Another three years elapsed before she read that Sorge's body was buried in Zoshigaya Cemetery, near the walls of Sugamo Prison, and went to investigate. But the grave could not be located – the simple wooden name-posts had been taken away for firewood. Hanako refused to give up the search for his remains. For more than a year this strong-willed woman battled with American occupation bureaucrats who now had jurisdiction over those records that had survived the wartime bombing of Tokyo. Sorge's coffin was finally traced in November 1949.

'It was in the section of the cemetery where they buried prisoners. It was a very desolate place,' she recalls. 'I went, on my own, to identify the remains with cemetery officials. The body had not been cremated because of the gasoline shortage.

'I looked carefully at the bones. On one leg was the mark of his wound from World War I. You could see the fracture had not set properly. I examined the teeth, which he had fitted after his motorbike acccident. I knew this was Sorge.'

Hanako had a ring fashioned from the gold bridge-work. She wears it always.

At her own expense, she arranged a cremation, and a burial plot in the verdant surroundings of Tama Cemetery. There Sorge's remains were interred, not far distant from those of his Japanese comrade, Ozaki Hotsumi.

Notes

PROLOGUE

1. Vol. 3, p. 5 of Obi, *Gendaishi Shiryo*. This indispensable four-volume work contains judicial records and other materials on the Sorge case. Hereafter referred to as *GS*.

2. *GS*, vol. 3, p. 5.

3. Ibid., p. 181.

4. Ibid.

5. Interview with Ishii Hanako. At the time of the events described in this book, Hanako used her mother's family name, Miyake; she later reverted to the surname of her father, Ishii.

6. *Der Spiegel*, series of articles on Sorge case, 13 June–3 October 1951.

7. Meissner, *The Man with Three Faces*.

8. Interview with Robert Guillain. In 1976 Guillain retraced his steps to the hospital, and the room where Sorge was treated, in the company of the author. This was before the complete rebuilding of the hospital.

9. *GS*, vol. 4, p. 192.

10. Interview with Eta Harich-Schneider; also *Der Spiegel*, 13 June–3 October 1951.

I. CHILD AND SOLDIER

1. The quotations in this chapter are taken from the statement (known in Japanese as *shuki*) that Sorge composed for the prosecutors in prison, reproduced in *GS*, vol. 1; hereafter referred to as Sorge memoir. This was the second statement attributed to Sorge: there also exists a first 'memoir', compiled by the Japanese police and based on their interrogation of Sorge.

2. Sorge told the Japanese authorities that his father had died in 1911. The date is given as 1 December 1907 by Julius Mader, citing official German records in Mader, Stuchlik and Pehnert, *Dr. Sorge funkt aus Tokyo*. The authors give the date of birth of Sorge's mother, Nina, as 20 April 1867.

2. STUDENT AND REVOLUTIONARY

1. *GS*, vol. 1, p. 218.

2. C. Sorge, *Die Weltwoche*, 11 December 1964.

3. *GS*, vol. 1, p. 220.

4. Poretsky, *Our Own People*. Here Poretsky is referring to the enthusiasm with which Sorge volunteered for military service in 1914.

5. C. Sorge, *Die Weltwoche*.

6. Mader, Stuchlik and Pehnert, *Dr. Sorge funkt aus Tokyo*.

7. Poretsky, *Our Own People*.

8. Massing, *This Deception*.
9. C. Sorge, *Die Weltwoche*.
10. Sorge memoir.
11. C. Sorge, *Die Weltwoche*.

3. MOSCOW, 1924–29

1. Agnes Smedley, quoted by J. R. and S. R. MacKinnon, *The Life and Times of an American Radical*, Berkeley, 1988.
2. Krivitsky, *In Stalin's Secret Service*.
3. C. Sorge, *Die Weltwoche*.
4. Ibid.
5. Ibid.
6. Wright, *Spycatcher*. Christiane, then living in a seminary near New York, was interviewed by a colleague of Wright's in 1966, in the course of an investigation into Soviet penetration of British intelligence agencies. Christiane was unable to help with the identity of the agent her husband had met in London. She was shown photographs, including one of Ellis – 'This man looks familiar,' she said. But after the lapse of so many years, she could not speak with certainty. Wright believes that Ellis was the important source that Sorge contacted in London.
7. Massing, *This Deception*. The meeting took place in Berlin at the end of 1929.
8. *GS*, vol. 1, p. 332.
9. Sorge memoir.

4. SHANGHAI DAYS

1. *GS*, vol. 1, p. 155.
2. This was Ruth Kuczynski's impression of Smedley. See Ruth Werner (Kuczynski's pen-name), *Sonjas Rapport*.
3. Chen Hansheng. It was Chen, head of the Institute for Social Science Research in Shanghai, who helped Smedley gain an understanding of the injustices in Chinese society. He was one of her most important contacts and helpers in Shanghai's dissident community. See MacKinnon, *The Life and Times of an American Radical*.
4. Ibid.
5. Sorge memoir.
6. Ibid.
7. Ibid.
8. *GS*, vol. 1 p. 338 (converted into direct speech).
9. See Takada Jiro, *Gendai Shiryo Geppo* (Materials on Modern History, monthly journal) October 1962. Also based on author's interviews with Kawai Teikichi, who recalled being regaled with Ozaki's amorous adventures, and Ishido Kiyotomo, who remembered his friend Ozaki's reputation for being a 'hormone tank'.
10. *GS*, vol. 2, p. 8.
11. See Guerin and Chatel, *Camarade Sorge*.
12. Pincher, *Too Secret too Long*.
13. This is Chapman Pincher's view of Ruth Kuczynski. Pincher was the first to print the allegation that Hollis was a Soviet mole and traitor (Pincher, *Their Trade is Treachery*). In a second work, *Too Secret too Long*, Pincher claimed that Hollis was controlled by Ruth Kuczynski – 'Sonia' – the eager recruit to Sorge's China spy ring

who operated as an undercover agent in Britain from 1940 to 1950. In *Spycatcher* Peter Wright, a retired MI5 officer, also cited the association with Smedley and Ewert in support of the thesis that Hollis served as a Soviet 'mole' and spy.

The public allegations, which provoked a sensation in Britain, came many years after Hollis was cleared by an internal investigation into possible Soviet infiltration of the secret services. In 1970 Hollis, then in retirement, had agreed to submit to questioning by former colleagues. According to Pincher's book, Hollis admitted to a friendship with Smedley, whom he knew to be a committed communist, but denied there was ever any attempt to recruit him. As for Sorge, he thought it 'probable that he had met him at various functions' but said that he could not remember him.

For reasons that are not clear, the investigators failed to question Hollis about Ruth Kuczynski. This was a surprising omission, according to Pincher, whose book alleges that the MI5 officer Hollis was a spy controlled by 'Sonia' during the period 1940–50 when she operated as an undercover agent in Britain.

The description of Hollis as a 'good bottle man' is Pincher's.

For an account of Sonia's adventures in Shanghai, see Werner, *Sonjas Rapport*. In 1993, Werner told the author in an interview that Pincher's allegations about a Hollis–Sonia connection were completely unfounded: she had definitely never met Roger Hollis.

14. *GS*, vol. 1, p. 123.
15. Ibid.

5. 'TOKYO WOULDN'T BE BAD'

1. *GS*, vol. 1, pp. 347–8.
2. Ibid, p. 180 (Sorge memoir) converted into direct speech without embellishment.
3. Ibid.
4. Official Russian archives.
5. *GS*, vol. 4, p. 116.
6. Neither man knew then that the liberal newspaper would die an early death under the Nazi regime. It was forced to close in December 1933.
7. *GS*, vol. 1, p. 229.
8. *Komsolovskaya Pravda*, 10 October 1964.

6. 'A MAN OF CONSEQUENCE'

1. Sieburg, *Die Stahlerne Blume*.
2. See Johnson, *A History of the Modern World*.
3. Ibid.
4. Grew, *Ten Years in Japan*.
5. Seth, *Secret Servants*.
6. *GS*, vol. 1, p. 227.
7. Ibid.
8. Ott had apparently been involved in hazardous intrigues inside the German army in the early 1930s. There is no firm evidence that he was among those officers who opposed the rise of Hitler, but when the Nazis seized power in January 1933 he was advised by friends in the German High Command to put as much distance as possible between himself and Berlin.

9. *GS*, vol. 1, p. 230.
10. Sorge memoir.
11. *GS*, vol. 4, p. 141.
12. *GS*, vol. 1, p. 227.
13. Sansom, *Sir George Sansom and Japan: A Memoir.*
14. Kordt, *Nicht aus den Akten.*
15. *GS*, vol. 1, p. 235.
16. Ibid.
17. Ibid.
18. Correspondence with Erwin Wickert.

7. THE RING TAKES SHAPE

1. Vukelic's statement, *GS*, vol. 3, p. 621. Parts of this testimony are rendered here as direct speech. Additional information was given to the author by Branko's widow, Mrs Yamasaki Yoshiko.

2. *GS*, vol. 3, p. 308.

3. Ibid p. 317.

4. Ibid.

5. *GS*, vol. 4, p. 173.

6. Ibid.

7. *Der Spiegel*, 13 June–3 October 1951.

8. Morin, *East Wind Rising.*

9. *GS*, vol. 2 p. 106.

10. Ibid, p. 327.

11. Interview with Kawai Teikichi.

12. Adapted from *GS*, vol 2, pp. 106 and 211.

13. *GS*, vol. 2, p. 211.

14. Ibid., p. 131.

15. Ibid.

16. Interview with Eta Harich-Schneider.

17. *Der Spiegel*, 13 June–3 Ocotber 1951.

18. See Kuusinen, *Der Gott Stürzt Seine Engel.*

19. In prison Sorge was questioned about an agent called 'Ingrid'. The judicial records show that he gave away little about their relationship, her work in Japan, or her true identity as the wife of the senior Comintern leader.

She came to Japan unannounced on a special mission from the Centre. But she was an old acquaintance whom I knew when she was in Scandinavia. I don't know what her mission was, but to the best of my knowledge she came on a mission that had something to do with the military. But she was under orders to have nothing to do with me or my group. Nevertheless she sent cables or letters through my group. Apart from that there was no relationship between us, but she did seek financial help from me because her financial situation in Tokyo was very bad. Later she came to see me at my home about money. This happened once a month during the five months she stayed here. Some five months later she was recalled to Europe by a cable addressed to me. But I don't think she was able to accomplish her mission. During her stay in Tokyo she spent two months in the Imperial Hotel and three months in the Nonomiya Apartments (*GS*, vol. 4, p. 136).

As for Clausen, when ordered by prosecutors to tell all about his comrades in the Tokyo ring, he characterized 'Ingrid' as one of the 'indirect' members assisting the group (*GS*, vol. 3, p. 105). At a later session he provided more details. 'Ingrid' was a Swedish woman he had met twice at Sorge's house, he said. She was collecting information for Sorge that seemed to be of little consequence: 'Once I saw a manuscript by her at Sorge's place. I don't know exactly when she came to Japan. I think she left Japan around 1938. I thought she was about forty at that time', *GS*, vol. 3, p. 157. All in all, police and prosecutors showed surprisingly little curiosity about 'Ingrid', and never suspected who she really was.

20. *GS*, vol. 1, p. 186.

21. The *Kempei* were supposed to handle military offences, but usually exceeded their designated functions. The *Tokko*, enlarged and reorganized in 1932, included sections that dealt with foreign nationals in Japan, censorship, and right-wing activities, but devoted most of its resources to sniffing out and suppressing left-wing and radical social movements. Between 1933 and 1936, no fewer than 59,013 left-wingers, liberals and others suspected of harbouring 'dangerous thoughts' (*kikenshiso*) were rounded up by the *Tokko*. Only about five thousand were brought to trial, but these police sweeps had the intended effect of cowing the population at large.

22. *GS*, vol. I, p. 125. This is the first 'memoir', which was composed by police using Sorge's statements.

23. Guerin and Chatel, *Camarade Sorge*.

24. *GS*, vol. 1, p. 129.

25. See *Bungei Shunju*, July 1994. After his release, Bickerton went back to England and wrote an article, 'Third Degree in Japan', describing his ordeal in Japan (*Manchester Guardian Weekly*, 27 July 1934).

26. Interview with Ishido Kiyotomo.

8. MOSCOW, SUMMER 1935

1. *GS*, vol. 1, p. 236, p. 361.
2. *GS*, vol. 3, p. 64.
3. Sorge memoir.
4. Poretsky, *Our Own People*.
5. Kuusinen, *Der Gott Stürzt Seine Engel*.
6. Massing, *This Deception*.
7. *Der Spiegel*, 13 June-3 October 1951.
8. Ibid.

9. 'IT'S HARD HERE, REALLY HARD'

1. Interview with Ishii Hanako.
2. *GS*, vol. 1, p. 124.
3. *GS*, vol. 2, p. 274.
4. *GS*, vol. 4, p. 171.
5. *GS*, vol. 3, p. 631.
6. *GS*, vol. 2, p, 8.
7. *GS*, vol. 3, pp. 64-5.
8. Interview with Eta Harich-Schneider.
9. *Der Spiegel*, 13 June-3 October 1951.

10. Kuusinen, *Der Gott Stürzt Seine Engel*.

11. Ibid.

12. Eugene Moosa, Associated Press story, 26 February 1936.

13. *GS*, vol. 2, p. 229.

14. Interview with Ishii Hanako; see also Ishii, *Ningen Zoruge*.

15. There are two widely differing versions of what happened to Katya's pregnancy. According to Russian government officials, she was in poor health and the pregnancy was terminated to save the mother. However, Yamasaki Yoshiko, the widow of Branko Vukelic, recalls that in 1965 a senior official at the Soviet Embassy in Tokyo told her that Katya had given birth to a girl, and that the child, who never saw her father, was sent to an orphanage in 1943, following Katya's death, and brought up under a different name, unaware that she was Sorge's daughter. After Sorge was designated a Hero of the Soviet Union in 1964, a frantic effort was made to track down the long-lost daughter, to no avail. The facts of this episode remain obscure.

16. Kuusinen, *Der Gott Stürzt Seine Engel*.

17. Ibid.

18. Sorge memoir.

19. *GS*, vol. 1, p. 254–5.

20. There is a farcical footnote to this saga. Dr Friederich Hack – the German arms salesmen who, on behalf of Ribbentrop, was using his extensive military contacts in Tokyo to promote a climate conducive to an alliance between Germany and Japan – confided to Sorge that the German Secret Services were aware that Soviet agents were posted outside the homes of Ribbentrop, Canaris and Oshima in Berlin. They had 'even taken photos during the secret negotiations for the Anti-Comintern Pact'. But, Dr Hack boasted, he had foiled the watchers by personally serving as go-between among the three senior officials. Sorge lost no time in relaying this to Moscow. Later he told Japanese interrogators that it was his reports that had led the Russians to watch the trio in the first place, and that after he reported Dr Hack's boast, he too became a target of Soviet surveillance.

21. Krivitsky, *I was Stalin's Agent*.

22. The importance of this traffic is underlined by General George Marshall in a top secret letter written in 1944: 'Our main basis of information regarding Hitler's intentions in Europe is obtained from Baron Oshima's messages from Berlin reporting his interviews with Hitler and other officials to the Japanese Government. These are still in the codes involved in the Pearl Harbor events' (quoted from Lewin, *The American Magic*).

23. Professor Christopher Andrew, interview with author. Professor Andrew said: 'At what point the Russians had broken the Japanese diplomatic code used for dispatches sent from the embassy in Moscow to Tokyo is not clear. But they appear to have had sufficient expertise and technology for this task, though it was not until World War Two that they succeeded in breaking the highest-grade cyphers. The Soviets inherited the most successful tradition of cryptanalysis in the world, and they were putting more resources into it than anybody else'.

24. Interview with Ishii Hanako.

25. Ishii, *Ningen Zoruge*.

26. Interview with Ishii Hanako.

27. Gunther Stein, a German journalist, came to Japan in 1936 as correspondent of the *News Chronicle* and *Financial News* of London. As a Jew, he was unable to work

for the German newspaper *Berliner Tageblatt*, which he had represented in London and Moscow. Stein won recognition as an expert on the Far East with *Made In Japan* (1935) and *Far East in Ferment* (1936). It is entirely possible that during his stay in Moscow Stein was given instructions to contact his compatriot in Tokyo. Indeed, it is conceivable that Stein had already been recruited to work for the Soviet cause before he arrived in Japan.

Sorge told police that he had found Stein 'very helpful to my work'. He said 'I think you could think of him as a reserve force or back-up.' This is how he described their first meeting:

> About 1932, he left Moscow and travelled to China, Hong Kong, Switzerland and London, and when he heard I was in China he tried to meet me, but I had left by then, and so we missed each other. We were both delighted when we met at a press conference at the Foreign Ministry in Tokyo, some time in the spring of 1936. At the beginning we discussed politics but later I hinted that apart from journalism I had some other work. He agreed he would help me with it' (*GS*, vol. 4, p. 135).

Stein allowed Clausen to use his house as a transmitting station, and Sorge trusted him to the extent of asking him to liaise with Ozaki when he (Sorge) was ill. In addition, he brought to the network the political and diplomatic information he gathered from the British and American embassies.

Interestingly, Clausen recalled (*GS*, vol. 4, p. 280) that in 1937 Stein and Sorge discussed a hush-hush Japanese army establishment located near Harbin and researching weapons to spread cholera and plague. Only a tiny handful of army and government people knew of its existence at the time. It was not until the 1970s that the gruesome secret of the germ warfare programme emerged in Japan.

Stein left Japan for London in the early part of 1938 to complete his naturalization as an Englishman. After the war, he was identified as a member of the Sorge ring by General Charles Willoughby. He flatly denied the allegation.

28. *GS*, vol. 3, pp. 3–8.

29. *GS*, vol. 1, p. 124.

30. *GS*, vol. 3, pp. 3–8.

31. Like Ozaki and many of his influential friends Ushiba had attended *Ichiko*, the elite college that trained students for Tokyo University. *Ichiko* is the acronym for *Tokyo Daiichi Koto Gakko*.

32. Kazami was appointed minister of justice in Konoye's second cabinet, formed in July 1940.

33. Two months later, Ozaki rose to even greater prominence with an outstanding book, *Arashi ni Tatsu Shina* (China in the Midst of a Storm). In September 1937, he wrote an article that demonstrated an acute understanding of the strength and direction of Chinese nationalism. He argued that the greatest disaster taking place in China was not that the Nanking government of Chiang Kai-shek was on the verge of collapse: 'It is rather that the Chinese nationalist movement is rapidly turning to the left.'

34. *GS*, vol. 1, p. 152.

35. H. T. Cook and T. F. Cook, *Japan At War: An Oral History*.

36. *GS*, vol. 2, p. 222.

37. Meissner, *The Man with Three Faces*. Meissner's book is a sprinkling of facts in a pudding of fiction. The author asserts that Clausen and Vukelic were among his

wedding guests on 22 September 1937 – one of many amusing distortions in the book. The idea that Vukelic, who had no relations with the German Embassy, would have been invited is utterly preposterous. Neither man is in the wedding portrait. Moreover, we have the word of one of the guests, Wolfgang Galinksy, that neither Clausen nor Vukelic was present at the function.

38. Ibid.

39. Interview with Wolfgang Galinksy.

40. Germans were outnumbered two to one, by both Americans and Britons, up to the end of 1940, when the new partnership between Japan and Germany changed the balance. The dominant voice in the foreign community was Anglo-Saxon. The *Japan Advertiser* was published by an American, and like its rival the *Japan Times* catered mainly for American and British residents. (The *Advertiser* was closed by the government in late 1940 and its title merged with the *Japan Times*; it was seen as too 'pro-American'.) Together with British papers shipped in from Hongkong and Shanghai, these constituted the main news diet of the non-Anglo-Saxons too.

Nationals of these countries mixed easily, and this mitigated the foreigner's sense of isolation. Excluded from all but the periphery of Japanese society, Germans, British and Americans shared what Erwin Wickert describes as the 'solidarity of Whites against Japanese'. This changed with the outbreak of war in Europe in September 1939. Socializing between nationals of the warring countries became much rarer. After the signing of the Axis alliance in September 1940, the divisions were deliberately accentuated by the Japanese authorities. Germans and Italians were put on a pedestal, designated as friends of Japan, in a (vain) attempt to spare them from the hostility directed against all foreigners.

41. Interview with Frieda Weiss.

42. *Der Spiegel*, 13 June–3 October 1951.

43. Interview with Frieda Weiss.

44. Kuusinen, *Der Gott Stürzt Seine Engel*. That evening she had made an appointment at the Goto flower-shop near Roppongi Crossing to meet a German-speaking woman who guided him to Sorge's house. She did not know the identity of this woman, but thought she was 'Sorge's assistant'. She learned from Sorge only that the woman was married to a 'chemist with connections to the Soviet Embassy'. Just before Christmas 1937 she was asked by the Fourth Department to go to the railway station in Moscow with an officer to pick up a couple arriving on the Siberian express – since only she knew what they looked like. When the couple got off the train she recognized the wife as the blonde woman who had previously come to her as Sorge's messenger. They too had obeyed the order to return. Aino Kuusinen wrote many years later: 'They were put in a waiting car, and then they disappeared. Soon it would be my turn to disappear for nine years.' This indicates an additional dimension to the ring that the Japanese police failed to uncover. Aino, arrested as an 'enemy of the people', was subjected to a harsh interrogation by NKVD that would steal fifteen months of her life, the prelude to years in prison camps. She was sentenced to eight years in a punishment camp for 'counter-revolutionary activities'. There was no trial or legal process of any kind. Her ordeal began on the first of January. During the interrogation she was questioned about General Berzin and his successor General Uritsky, as well as about Sorge.

45. Aino's account, converted into direct speech without elaboration. See Kuusinen, *Der Gott Stürzt Seine Engel*.

46. Kuusinen, *Der Gott Stürzt Seine Engel*.

47. Interview with Professor Christopher Andrew.
48. Kuusinen, *Der Gott Stürzt Seine Engel*.
49. Sorge memoir.
50. Ibid.
51. Morin, *East Wind Rising*.
52. Interview with Kase Toshikazu.
53. Russian archives. The letters, which were normally transmitted on microfilm by courier, do not mention the name of the country where Sorge is serving. But Katya must have guessed that the country was Japan; among the typically Japanese gifts he sent her was an *obi*, the sash worn around the kimono.
54. Interview with Eta Harich-Schneider.
55. Ibid.
56. Interview with Ishii Hanako.
57. Ott message to Berlin, 23 February 1942.
58. *Der Spiegel* 13 June–3 October 1951.
59. Harich-Schneider, *Charaktere und Katastrophen*.
60. Russian archives.
61. This cable was intercepted by Japanese monitoring agencies. 'Green Box' was the code-name used by the Russians for the Japanese army.
62. *GS*, vol. 4, p. 282.
63. Scholl was of inestimable value as a source of sensitive information, as Sorge acknowleged. Like the other service attachés at the embassy, he liaised between the *Abwehr* and the espionage sections of the Japanese army and navy General Staffs. See Chapman, *The Price of Admiralty*.
64. Interview with Yoshikawa Mitsusada.
65. Russian archives.
66. Scholl returned to Berlin to be promoted to the rank Lieutenant-Colonel. Wenneker was made a rear-admiral and given the command of the pocket battleship *Deutschland*. He was reassigned to Tokyo in 1940.
67. *GS*, vol. 1, p. 251.
68. *GS*, vol. 1, p. 171.
69. *GS*, vol. 3, p. 175.
70. Sorge did, however, have excellent contacts in the Japanese army who may have been useful as unwitting informants. Conveniently, the Japanese War Ministry and General Staff Headquarters were literally within shouting distance of the German Embassy, and relations between staff officers and the German service attachés were on a firm footing. We know that Eugen Ott and his successor as military attaché, Colonel Matzky, were happy to introduce Sorge to their army contacts, and naval attaché Wenneker did likewise – although Moscow had less interest in navy affairs.

    In this way Sorge got to know staff officers who had trained or served as attachés in Germany and who often walked across the road, from the rear of General Headquarters, and through the embassy's back entrance. After his arrest, Sorge mentioned a handful of names. He admitted to knowing a powerful friend of Germany, Muto Akira, before he was promoted to the rank of general. Akira occupied key positions at General Headquarters, and then at the War Ministry. He also named Colonel Managi Takanobu, Major Saigo Jugo and Major Yamagata Arimitsu, all staff officers involved in liaising with the German Embassy. This liaison often took place in establishments served by geisha. In his memoir Sorge does not elaborate on his relationships with these men. Prosecutors avoided probing this delicate aspect of the case, presumably out of a prudent desire to avoid friction with the military authorities.

71. *GS*, vol. I, p. 441 The judicial records are ambiguous about the timing of Odai's recruitment. One of the charges against him refers to the disclosure of information on the Changkufeng border clash between Japan and the Soviet Union, which occurred in July 1938. Clausen believed that Odai was working for the ring through Miyagi before February 1939.

72. Russian archives.

73. *GS*, vol. 4, p. 76.

74. *GS*, vol. 3, p. 176.

75. *GS*, vol. 1, p. 240.

76. Ibid, p. 240.

77. Ibid, p. 241.

78. *GS*, vol. 4, p. 281.

79. *GS*, vol. 1, p. 241.

80. Feis, *The Road to Pearl Harbor.*

81. *GS*, vol. 1, pp. 269–70.

82. Ibid.

83. Grew, *Ten Years in Japan.*

84. Fleisher, *Our Enemy Japan.*

85. Morin, *East Wind Rising.*

86. Chapman, *The Price of Admiralty.*

87. Interview with Wolfgang Galinsky. Galinsky, then a junior diplomat at the German Consulate-General in Kobe, was making one of his regular business trips to Tokyo. 'In the garden with Frau Stahmer,' he wrote in his diary for Saturday 28 September 1940. Following the embassy reception he went to lunch at the Imperial Hotel, and then to the nearby Takarazuka Theatre with Ursula Ott, the ambassador's daughter, and Franz Krapf, a third secretary in the Economic Section, 'Then to Lohmeyer's. Early to bed,' he concluded his entry for that day.

88. Sorge memoir.

89. Interview with Eta Harich-Schneider; see also Harich-Schneider, *Charaktere und Katastrophen.*

90. *GS*, vol. 3, pp. 8 and 64–5.

91. Ibid.

92. Ibid.

93. Ibid, p. 224.

94. *GS*, vol. 4, pp. 101–2. The police discovered the report when they searched Clausen's house following his arrest.

95. The first venture Clausen launched in Japan, an export–import business, did not go well. The Fourth Department had to come up with more capital, and Clausen established a company to manufacture and sell presses for making industrial blueprints. This got off the ground in the summer of 1937, and by April 1938 he had moved to a central location in Shimbashi, close to the Imperial Hotel. When the business prospered he built a new factory in Miyamura-cho in the Azabu ward of Tokyo (*GS*, vol. 3, p. 159.), and in February 1941 the firm, called M. Clausen Shokai, was converted into a joint stock company. Clausen's share of the capital was 85,000 yen, and three partners each owned 5,000 yen worth of stock.

96. Chapman, *The Price of Admiralty.*

97. Ibid.
98. Russian archives. This message was radioed by Clausen on 29 December 1940.

10. WINTER AND SPRING 1941

1. Nagai, *Danchotei Nichijo*, literally 'Dyspepsia House Days'. One of the most popular Japanese novelists of the twentieth century, Nagai Katu (1879–1959) secretly kept a caustic diary during the war years that was eventually published after Japan's defeat.
2. Tolischus, *Tokyo Record*.
3. Interview with Yamasaki Yoshiko.
4. Based on Vukelic's prison statement, converted into direct speech; see *GS*, vol. 3, p. 621.
5. Ibid.
6. Ibid.
7. Nagai, *Danchotei Nichijo*.
8. *GS*, vol. 1, p. 271, *inter alia*, rendered into direct speech.
9. Ostensibly, Urach had come to Japan on behalf of the German Foreign Ministry to conclude a press agreement with the Japanese. However, Sorge believed he had orders to investigate whether Japan would aid its German ally by attacking Singapore, and whether Japan could be counted on to join in a war against Russia.
10. Kase was a young diplomat in Matsuoka's entourage. More than half a century later, a photograph capturing the moment when the Japan–Soviet neutrality pact was signed can be seen in a prominent position in the living room of Kase's home in Kamakura. Kase looks at the picture, in which he stands behind Matsuoka's chair in Molotov's office in the Kremlin, and chuckles. The Germans, he says, were hoist by their own petard. Hitler and Ribbentrop distrusted their Japanese allies and told them nothing about the impending attack on Russia, with the result that Matsuoka went on to Moscow to seek a rapprochement. 'Germany had volunteered to help Japan improve its relations with the Soviet Union when Germany was on friendly terms with Moscow. But when we arrived at the Kremlin for those negotiations, relations between Berlin and Moscow were already beginning to deteriorate,' says Kase. 'So instead of [using] the friendship between the Soviet Union and Germany [to improve our relations with Moscow] we used the hostility developing between the two at that time.' If, however, Hitler had taken Matsuoka into his confidence about his plans, it is improbable that Japan would have signed the neutrality pact with the Soviet Union. Stalin might then have faced a Japanese invasion in the East, as well as by Germany in the West, and the Second World War might have taken a very different course.
11. On 17 April, when Matsuoka's train was steaming slowly through the Urals, veiled suggestions appeared in the Japanese press that the neutrality pact was a 'new sword' which Japan could use to approach the United States, Great Britain and China. The metaphor was a clumsy one, but this was one of the first opaque allusions in the press to secret moves to settle tensions between Japan and the United States by diplomatic means.
12. *GS*, vol. 1, p. 272.
13. Ibid.
14. *GS*, vol. 2, p. 176.
15. *GS*, vol. 1, p. 272.

16. *GS*, vol. 2, p. 273.
17. Schellenberg, *The Schellenberg Memoirs*.
18. Interview with Frieda Weiss.
19. Interview with Dr Fred de la Trobe.
20. Ritgen also served as editor of the *NS-Partei Korrespondenz*, the official organ of the Nazi party.
21. Schellenberg, *The Schellenberg Memoirs*.
22. Ibid.
23. Ibid.
24. Colonel Meisinger had left his wife behind in Germany. In Tokyo his consort was the former mistress of Heinrich Himmler, the internal security chief. She followed Meisinger to Japan, only to be abandoned soon afterwards; in the summer of 1941 the colonel took up with a young German refugee from the Dutch East Indies, after hiring her as his secretary.
25. Kordt, *Nicht aus den Akten*.

11. MAY 1941

1. Russian archives. The full text of the telegram runs as follows:

I discussed the German–USSR relationship with German Ambassador Ott and the naval attaché. Ott said that Hitler is absolutely determined to crush USSR and get hold of the European part of the Soviet Union and use it as a grain and raw materials base to put the whole of Europe under German control.

Ambassador and attaché both agreed that two critical dates are approaching as regards German–USSR relationship. The first date is on the completion of sowing in USSR. After end of sowing, war against USSR can start at any moment, as Germany merely has to gather the harvest.

The second critical moment concerns the negotiations between Germany and Turkey. War will be inevitable if USSR creates difficulties concerning Turkey's acceptance of German demands.

Possibility of outbreak of war at any moment is very high, because Hitler and his generals are confident that a war with USSR will not hamper conduct of war against Britain in the least.

German generals estimate the Red Army's fighting capacity is so low that they believe the Red Army will be destroyed in the course of a few weeks. They believe the defence system in the German–Soviet border zone is extremely weak.

Decision on start of war against USSR will be taken by Hitler alone either as early as May, or following the war with England.

However, Ott, who is personally against such a war, feels so sceptical at the present time that he already advised Prince Urach to leave for Germany in May.

2. *GS*, vol. 1, p. 248.
3. In Sorge's words, 'It was extremely easy for me to get acquainted with them – most brought letters of introduction from Etzdorf, Dirksen, Matzky, Wenneker, Scholl, Lietzmann, or the *Frankfurter Zeitung* or somewhere else, and some of them had been given special instructions by General Thomas.' *GS*, vol. 1, p. 248.

4. Ibid p. 274.

5. Ibid.

6. Correspondence with Erwin Wickert.

7. Interviews with W. Galinsky and F. de la Trobe.

8. Interview with Eta Harich-Schneider; see also Harich-Schneider, *Charaktere und Katastrophen.*

9. See Kordt, *Nicht aus den Akten,* and Wickert, *Mut und Übermut.*

10. Kordt, *Nicht aus den Akten.*

11. Ibid.

12. Foreign Minister Matsuoka was far from pleased at the initiative taken in his absence. When the liaison conference between government and Imperial Headquarters reached a decision on 18 April, Matsuoka's train was steaming across the Siberian tundra in the direction of home. The conference decided that Japan would not place the Axis pact in jeopardy – but neither would it withdraw the olive branch Ambassador Nomura was tentatively proffering to the Americans in Washington. Japan wanted to have its cake and eat it. The pro-German foreign minister was not consulted.

13. Wickert, *Mut und Übermut.*

14. See *GS,* vol. 2, p. 188.

15. Schellenburg, *The Schellenberg Memoirs.*

16. Ibid.

17. *Der Spiegel.*

18. Ibid.

19. Ibid.

20. Interview with Ishii Hanako; see also Ishii, *Ningen Zoruge.*

21. Direct speech based on *GS,* vol. 1, p. 278.

22. Russian archives.

23. Ibid.

24. *GS,* vol. 1 p. 278.

25. Wickert, *Mut und Übermut.*

26. *GS,* vol. 1 p. 419 and p. 278.

27. As it happened, Meisinger had gone to Shanghai shortly before Sorge arrived. The new police attaché wished to acquaint himself with the resident German diplomats, Nazi functionaries, and the Gestapo operation in Shanghai, which he was to supervise from Tokyo. It is likely that the colonel was too busy expanding his network of informants to keep a close watch on Sorge, preferring to spend his time cooking up grandiose schemes. He was introduced to Trebitsch Lincoln, a legendary figure who had spied for both Britain and Germany in the First World War, and who now, in the guise of a Buddhist abbot, was prepared to offer his services to the Reich once again.

Lincoln's plan was to infiltrate Tibet and arrange for its use as a military base to wage war against British India. Meisinger was impressed by Lincoln's esoteric credentials, and telegraphed the State Security Service (RHSA) to boast of his would-be recruit. Unfortunately the German consul-general found out what was going on, and quickly informed his superiors in Berlin that Lincoln was a political adventurer, with no Buddhist connections of significance. The result was a stinging rebuke for Meisinger from Foreign Minister Ribbentrop, who reminded the police attaché that 'the self-evident assumption for his posting to the Tokyo embassy was that he concern himself exclusively with the police questions within his purview' (quoted by Erwin Wickert in *Mut und Übermut*).

28. Chapman, *The Price of Admiralty*.
29. Ibid.
30. Harich-Schneider, *Charaktere und Katastrophen*.
31. Interview with Eta Harich-Schneider.
32. Ibid.
33. *GS*, vol. 1, p. 274.
34. Russian archives.
35. *GS*, vol. 4, p. 164 re 'corner' and vol. 1, p. 274. When did the meeting between Scholl and Sorge take place in the Imperial Hotel? The police record of the interrogation on 30 December 1941 has this sub-heading: 'Regarding receipt of advance information on the German opening of hostilities against the Soviet Union, from person concerned with the German embassy (20 May 1941)'.

Clearly this date was provided by Sorge. But we know that Sorge had a tendency to forget or to deliberately blur the dates of his activities. For instance, he told prosecutors that his trip to Shanghai took place 'from the end of April to (*itatte*) May.' But we know he was at the embassy on the 17th, that his laissez-passer was issued by the Foreign Ministry that day, and that he drafted a telegram to Moscow dated 19 May.

If Sorge had met Scholl on the 20th, leaving for Shanghai on the next day, it seems unlikely that he would have delayed sending his information from Scholl until 1 June. Besides, Sorge specifically states in the June 1 dispatch that Scholl left Berlin on 6 May. Even with the luckiest combination of trains and flights the journey took fourteen days. There is an additional clue suggesting that Sorge had left for Shanghai by the time Scholl arrived in Tokyo. Eta Harich-Schneider writes in her memoirs that Herr Scholl came to dinner at the residence on 20 May, and that he and the ambassador spoke a good deal about Sorge: 'both gentlemen were unanimous in praising his work and reliability'.

This witness is certain that Sorge was no longer in Tokyo by that day. If Richard had been in the city, there is little doubt that he would have been invited to dinner as well; he and Scholl were old friends, eager to meet again after a long separation. Moreover, Sorge's testimony makes two references to dinner at the Imperial Hotel with Scholl; even if Richard had not been invited to the residence on 20 May, it is unlikely that Scholl would have required two meals that night.

The '20 May' figure appears to be another case of the haphazard way in which police interrogators tried (with the help of back issues of the *Asahi* newspaper) to pinpoint dates of events that had occurred months or years previously.

36. Based on *GS*, vol. 1, p. 274.
37. The message in its entirety runs as follows:

Expected start of German–Soviet war around 15 June is based exclusively on information which Lieutenant-Colonel Scholl brought with him from Berlin, which he left on 6 May for Bangkok. He is taking up post of attaché in Bangkok.

Ott stated that he could not receive information as regards this directly from Berlin, and only has Scholl's information.

In conversation with Scholl I noticed that on the issue of the sortie against the USSR Germans are paying much attention to the fact of a big tactical error which – according to Scholl – the USSR committed.

According to German viewpoint the fact that the USSR defence line is on the whole laid out to face the German line without any big line branching off constitutes the greatest error. This will make it possible to smash the Red Army in the first big battle. Scholl stated that the most powerful thrust error will be delivered by the left flank of the German Army'.

This message prompted a flurry of scribbles by Sorge's superiors. On the telegram there are two underlined notes referring to errors in the text. And the last sentence has a big question mark beside it: the Fourth Department chiefs were clearly puzzled by the words 'left flank'. They could not know that Richard had written something else; that the incomprehensible phrase was the work of a wireless operator who no longer had his heart in his work.

12. JUNE 1941

1. It is not clear why this important dispatch was not sent out earlier. Clausen told interrogators that Sorge gave him so many messages warning of the German invasion that he delayed transmitting some of them, and threw others away. *GS*, vol. 3, p. 197.

2. Interview with Frieda Weiss. Fraulein Weiss was the young woman who visited the Clausens' house to give Anna German lessons.

3. In this cable, Wenneker also reported that senior Japanese naval officers had told him they had abandoned the idea of attacking Singapore, as Germany wanted, because of fears that they would then have to confront not only Britain but the US as well. For the same reason, senior commanding officers felt that Japan should not enter the war, even if German naval vessels came under fire from American warships escorting supply ships across the Atlantic to Britain. Wenneker could not restrain himself from bemoaning the insipidity of Germany's Far Eastern ally: 'When one recalls with what enthusiasm the Japanese went about acceding to the Three Powers' Pact, this more recent trend is a matter of deep disappointment' (Chapman, *The Price of Admiralty*).

4. Harich-Schneider, *Charaktere und Katastrophen*.

5. Sorge commented to interrogators that his complete lack of personal ambition helped assure him the respect and trust of the career-oriented German diplomats.

6. Interview with Eta Harich-Schneider.

7. Harich-Schneider, *Charaktere und Katastrophen*.

8. Ibid.

9. Interview with Eta Harich-Schneider.

10. Ibid.

11. Interview with Kawai Teikichi; also Kawai, *Aru Kakumeika no Kaiso*.

12. Ibid.

13. Ibid.

14. Interview with Eta Harich-Schneider; also Harich-Schneider, *Charaktere und Katastrophen*.

15. By mid-June, the German General Staff under General Franz Halder had assembled, in East Prussia, Poland, Slovakia and Hungary, the largest field force in German history. Though the subjugation of Western Europe was not yet complete, Hitler – consumed by distrust of Stalin – could wait no longer to fulfil his dream of conquering the East and destroying Bolshevism.

On Friday 20 June a force of 150 divisions, three million men and 3,000 tanks was poised along an 1,800-mile front stretching from the Baltic Sea in the north to the Black Sea in the south. In their command posts behind this line, Generals Leeb, Rundstedt and Bock awaited the final order from the High Command in Berlin.

16. Russian archives.

17. Harich-Schneider, *Charaktere und Katastrophen*; interview with Eta Harich-Schneider. She recalled: 'Richard had reached a state where he needed someone in whom he could have absolute trust, to unburden himself. He felt he had no friends, and in that time and place, I felt I had none either. He bared his soul to me, and I mine to him.'

18. Ibid.

19. Interview with Eta Harich-Schneider.

20. Schellenberg, *The Schellenberg Memoirs*; also *GS*, vol. 1, for the comments of the local Nazi party branch; Wickert, *Mut und Übermut*; interview with Eta Harich-Schneider.

21. Harich-Schneider, *Charaktere und Katastrophen*.

22. Interview with Eta Harich-Schneider.

23. Harich-Schneider, *Charaktere und Katastrophen*.

24. Ibid.

25. Kordt, *Nicht aus den Akten*.

26. Interview with Dr Fred de la Trobe.

27. Wickert, *Mut und Übermut*.

28. Ibid.

29. Prince Konoye was taken aback by the news – it put him in mind of the earlier 'act of betrayal' when Germany out of the blue signed a non-aggression treaty with Russia in 1939. Hitler's 'insincerity' in embarking on the invasion of Russia without prior consultation so upset the delicate prince that he pondered (though only briefly) whether to pull Japan out of the Three Powers Pact. There was no doubt in his mind that this alliance did not apply now that Germany had attacked Russia, rather than the other way round. It was also a great relief for Konoye that Japan (perhaps more by good luck than by prescient diplomacy) now had a neutrality pact with Moscow.

While Konoye affected dismay, there was satisfaction in some circles that, as a result of the fight between Hitler and Stalin, the Russian menace to Japan had been blown away by a 'divine wind'. The prince now had to cope with his volatile foreign minister, the loose cannon-ball in his cabinet. Matsuoka was quite prepared to scrap the agreement he had signed in the Kremlin a few weeks earlier, and join forces with the Germans in slaying the Bolshevik bear.

30. Interview with Kase Toshikazu; also Kase, *Journey to the Missouri*.

31. Zhukov, *The Memoirs of Marshal Zhukov*.

32. A 1973 study published in Russia found that Moscow received no fewer than eighty-four separate warnings that a German attack was in the offing. 'A similar study today would probably raise the total to over a hundred' (Andrew and Gordievsky, *KGB, The Inside Story of its Foreign Operations from Lenin to Gorbachev*).

Leonard Trepper, an agent for Red Army Intelligence in Occupied France, provided Moscow with advance warning of the original date of the invasion, 15 May, then with a revised date. He finally told his controller that it would take place on 22 June. On 21 June Harro Schulze-Boysen, who ran an intelligence network in Berlin, provided confirmation that the invasion was set for the next day. See Trepper, *The Great Game*.

33. Russian archives.

34. Andrew and Gordievsky, *KGB, The Inside Story.*

35. Guerin and Chatel, *Camarade Sorge.*

36. Newman (ed.), *How I Got that Story.*

37. Kordt, *Nicht aus den Akten.*

38. Ibid.

39. *Der Spiegel,* 13 June–3 October 1951.

40. Ibid.; interview with Eta Harich-Schneider.

41. Interview with Ohashi Hideo.

42. Conversation is based on official records. See *GS*, vol. 2, pp. 257–8; vol. 2 , p. 187; vol. 1, pp. 204–5; vol. 1, pp. 279–80; and vol. 1, pp. 283–4.

43. *GS*, vol. 1, p. 204.

44. Sorge had tried his hand at exerting political influence in the German Embassy on a number of occasions, notably to try to ward off the encircling alliance between Japan and Germany that the Russians feared so much. In the months prior to the signing of the anti-Comintern pact in November, 1936, he had tried to deflect Germany from a political–military entente with Japan. In discussions with Ambassador Dirksen and Military Attaché Ott he argued that it was not in Germany's national interest to antagonize Russia; Hitler would do better to join hands with Stalin to confront their real enemies, Britain and France.

Sorge would later concede that his arguments had little effect. He was not deterred by the realization that German policy was dictated by Berlin, and that Ott was in effect a glorified messenger-boy whose voice carried little weight in Ribbentrop's Foreign Ministry, and even less in Hitler's *Reichskanzlei.* But he persisted in stressing the negatives of a binding partnership between Germany and Japan. After they had consummated the Three Powers Pact, it quickly became clear that Germany and Japan were dreaming different dreams in the shared bed. From early 1941 Ambassador Ott and his colleagues were constantly irritated by Japan's half-hearted co-operation. Sorge observed the strains in the Axis with satisfaction, and reported on them to Moscow.

It has to be remembered that during these years, right up to the eve of war, Sorge could air pro-Russian sentiments in the embassy without provoking offence or suspicion. There was nothing heretical about his strategic analysis. Hitler himself, after weighing the pros and cons of an alliance with Stalin, eventually settled for a non-aggression pact, while Foreign Minister Ribbentrop beavered away at a scheme to tie Russia into the Axis until well into 1941.

45. *GS*, vol. 1, p. 204.

46. Ibid.

47. Ibid.

48. Interview with Kawai Teikichi; see also Kawai, *Aru Kakumeika no Kaiso.*

49. Miyagi had recruited Hokkaido-born Taguchi Ugenta as an informant, despite his communist past. Taguchi became a party member in 1927, was arrested in 1928, and served a prison term for subversion. Miyagi enlisted him to report on economic matters concerning Hokkaido.

Taguchi was a member of the 'ring within a ring' that Miyagi set up to broaden the scope of his intelligence-gathering. Other recruits included Kuzumi Fusako and Yamano Masazano, both of whom had spent time in prison because of their membership of the Communist Party.

Miyagi also enlisted a translator, Akiyama Koji, whom he had first met in

California in 1931. Akiyama, a communist sympathizer without a regular job, was paid a small fee, never exceeding 100 yen a month, for this work. See *GS*, vol. 3, p. 361 re Hokkaido map. The Seishido bookshop still exists in Roppongi.

50. Tolischus, *Tokyo Record*.

51. *GS*, vol. 2, p. 179. Ozaki could not remember whether Saionji gave him the information in his office at the South Manchurian Railway building or in the Asia Restaurant on the sixth floor.

52. Interview with Eta Harich-Schneider. See also Harich-Schneider, *Charaktere und Katastrophen*.

53. Russian archives.

54. *GS*, vol. 4, p. 83.

55. Ibid.

56. *GS*, vol. 4, p. 165 Sorge said that he did not know the source of the revealing Araki interview, but thought it had been obtained from a secretary of General Ugaki with whom Miyagi had established a good rapport.

57. *GS*, vol. 2, p. 178; see also vol. 3, p. 347 for Miyagi's version.

13. JULY 1941

1. See Butow, *Tojo and the Coming of War*. Government officials spoke of an event of awesome significance – this was only the fourth such conference since the outbreak of the 'China Incident' in July 1937.

2. Tolischus, *Tokyo Record*.

3. Army Chief of Staff Sugiyama Gen reported this to the 2 July conference. See Coox, *Nomonhan: Japan Against Russia, 1939*, vols 1 and 2.

4. Shimotamae et al., *Kokusai Supai Zoruge no Shinjitsu* (The Truth about Sorge the International Spy). According to Saionji's testimony, he found out about the resolutions of the imperial conference from a navy officer, Commander Fujii, who was then working in the military affairs section of the Navy Ministry (*GS*, vol. 3, p. 495). By the time Saionji met Ozaki he had spoken with Commander Fujii, and immediately grasped the direction of the new national policy.

5. During his interrogation, Ozaki stated that he had spoken to Miyagi *before* briefing Sorge in person. Sorge told prosecutors that Ozaki came to report to him 'five or six days' after the conference, see *GS*, vol. 2, p. 288. Sorge's actual words were 'five or six months', In a later interrogation Sorge corrected this mistake.

It is interesting to note that on 5 July Sorge recorded in his diary that he made a 200-yen payment to 'O' (for 'Otto', Ozaki's code-name) for expenses. It is not clear whether Ozaki had already talked to Saionji by this time. See *GS*, vol. 4, p. 226.

6. These dates indicate that Ozaki gave Sorge his own briefing on the situation after that weekend.

7. Kase, *Journey to the Missouri*.

8. *GS*, vol. 1, pp. 275–6.

9. Ibid., p. 288.

10. Ibid., p. 275.

11. Russian archives.

12. Russian archives. It is worth mentioning, as an example of the caution with which Clausen's testimony should be approached, that he could not recall sending a message that contained the words 'imperial conference' (*GS*, vol. 3, p. 205). How-

ever, judging from the Russian translation, Sorge apparently described it as 'conference in presence of emperor' in his English text. Clausen, working in a language not his own, may indeed not have realized that Sorge was referring to an imperial conference.

13. *GS*, vol. 3, p. 205.

14. Ibid. Note that the Centre ordered a change in code-names in June. Sorge became 'Inson', although he continued to use 'Ramsay' into early July. Ozaki became 'Invest'; Clausen 'Insop'; Miyagi 'Intari'; Vukelic 'Inkel'.

15. Ibid.

16. Interview with Robert Guillain. Guillain's account challenges the generally accepted view that Sorge learned about the outcome of the conference several days after it took place. 'Sorge knew about it two or three hours later,' Guillain said. However, if Sorge had the information in his hands on 2 July, he took time to verify it and to ensure that he had interpreted it correctly; from the available evidence, we see that his first report to Moscow was not drafted until 10 July.

17. Interview with Robert Guillain.

18. Harich-Schneider, *Charaktere und Katastrophen*.

19. Wickert, *Mut und Übermut*; interview with Eta Harich Schneider.

20. *Japan Times and Advertiser*, 16 July 1941, letters to editor.

21. Ibid., 20 July 1941. Interestingly, almost identical grumbles by foreign residents about Japan's ambivalent attitude towards the outside world can often be found in the letters column of the modern-day *Japan Times*.

22. *GS*, vol. 1, p. 276.

23. Ibid. Nehmitz's report apparently claimed that the Soviet air force had fifty advanced bombers capable of air strikes against Japan. Ott handed the attaché's report to Matsuoka in early July. Sorge refers to this in his 10 July dispatch, but here the number of advanced bombers is given as 300.

24. Ibid., p. 457.

25. This section is based on Sorge's testimony. see *GS*, vol. 1, p. 419.

26. Ibid.; also based on interview with Eta Harich-Schneider.

27. Harich-Schneider, *Charaktere und Katastrophen*.

28. This was especially the case after the outbreak of war with Russia, which severed the umbilical cord of the Trans-Siberian railway. Ott then became a virtual *generalissimo* with enormous power over the 200 Germans cut adrift from the homeland. When he wished, he could use his influence to secure berths on vessels for those Germans with urgent reasons to leave Japan, assist distressed nationals in a number of ways – or deny requests for passport renewals, and instigate investigations by the Gestapo. On the whole, he appears to have acted with restraint, seeing himself as a father figure to the German community.

29. Harich-Schneider, *Charaktere und Katastrophen*, and interview with Eta Harich-Schneider.

30. Nagai, *Danchotei Nichijo*. As Nagai suggests, Japan was indeed learning from Nazi Germany. Political parties had been abolished in 1940, and replaced by the Imperial Rule Assistance association, a meaningless body since the army and navy refused to support it. An American journalist noted that 'regimentation and government control were already far advanced, and were to be extended manyfold. Nazi experts were sitting in the various ministries, helping to draft decrees under the National Mobilization Act.' Their overriding aim was to ensure that the military got priority in the allocation of manpower and raw materials. See Tolischus, *Tokyo Record*.

31. Sorge memoir.

32. *GS*, vol. 2, p. 238. Ozaki was unable to recall whether the meeting took place in his office, or in the sixth-floor restaurant of the Mantetsu building.

33. It was out of a sense of duty to Ozaki that Miyagi continued to work for the ring. The relationship between these two men is interesting in the Japanese social context: in Japan, most enduring relationships are founded on an initial formal introduction, but Miyagi had presented himself to Ozaki out of the blue. Moreover, they were separated by a wide gap in education and social standing. Ozaki, though only two years the senior, was *erai* – great and famous; the Okinawan was poor, untutored and not well connected. In a status-conscious society, it says much for Ozaki's generous and broad-minded character that he adopted Miyagi as a friend, rather than a subordinate, and treated him with generosity and consideration. Ozaki also took it upon himself to supplement the meagre allowance Miyagi received from Sorge.

34. *GS*, vol. 1, p. 293.

35. Nagai, *Danchotei Nichijo*.

36. *Japan Times and Advertiser*, 17 July 1941.

37. Tolischus, *Tokyo Record*.

38. Kawai, *Aru Kakumeika no Kaiso*, and interview with Kawai Teikichi.

39. Ibid.

40. *GS*, vol. 1, p. 420.

41. The build-up was code-named Kantokuen, an acronym for Kwantung Army Special Manoeuvres. Over the summer of 1941 the Kwantung Army grew in strength from 400,000 to 700,000.

42. Russian archives.

14. AUGUST 1941

1. Hitler and Ribbentrop had divergent ideas about how to harness Japan to German strategy. The former was of the view that the Japanese should be encouraged to expand into Southeast Asia, and tie down British forces in the region. This view would eventually prevail. Ribbentrop, however, thought the Japanese could more usefully be deployed against the Soviet Far East, and as late as August 1941 was still hankering after Japanese intervention against Russia.

2. *GS*, vol. 4, p. 94.

3. In addition, Clausen's diary records no transmissions for the early part of August – although this in itself is not conclusive evidence: we know for instance that he *did* send a radio message on 7 August, although the diary contains no reference to it.

4. *GS*, vol. 3, p. 198.

5. Based on Sorge's and Ozaki's testimony. See *inter alia GS*, vol. 2, p. 182.

6. Sorge was aware, for instance, that Tokyo tried to keep Berlin in the dark about the progress of the Japan–US negotiations.

7. Russian archives.

8. Russian archives. The cable is dated 11 August 1941.

9. See Coox, *Nomonhan: Japan against Russia, 1939*.

10. Harich-Schneider, *Charaktere und Katastrophen*.

11. *GS*, vol. 3, p. 198. Sorge's text was found by police in Clausen's house.

12. Russian archives. If the first half of this telegram exists, it has not been released

by the Russian authorities. Note that in the original texts found at Clausen's house (and in the ring's traffic intercepted by the Japanese authorities, and later decoded by Clausen in prison) most names of officials appear in code. Thus, Ribbentrop appears as 'Ricardo', Ambassador Ott as 'Anna'. In the version submitted to top Soviet officials, the actual names have been substituted, except in the case of members of the Sorge network. The versions are otherwise identical, but it must be remembered that both are translations (one Russian, one Japanese) of messages that Sorge wrote in English.

13. During the interrogation, Clausen said that he sent the first part, and suppressed the second. This is the reverse of what really happened. Clausen's reasoning was curious. He told the examining magistrate that the information in the first part was important, but that the Russians had lots of spies in Manchuria, so they would have known about it already. Therefore, Japan's interests were not harmed by sending this part of the message. Clausen said he did *not* send the second part, which is contained in a telegram released recently by the Russians. He gave the following reason in prison:

> The reason I did not send the latter part of the manuscript is this: it said that the petroleum reserve of the Japanese army had greatly diminished. This was very important to Japan and nobody else knew that sort of thing except us. As my way of thinking was changing at that time, I could not bring myself to transmit such information to Moscow (*GS*, vol. 3, p. 183).

This is a cautionary example of the confusion and unreliability of Clausen's testimony.

14. Ishii, *Ningen Zoruge*; interview with Ishii Hanako.

15. William J. Hood's introduction to Krivitsky, *In Stalin's Secret Service*. In similar vein, Sorge was convinced that he led a spy ring without parallel: 'Even in the Moscow Centre the fact that I penetrated to the heart of the embassy and used it for my intelligence activity was regarded as absolutely amazing, and quite unprecedented', he boasted to interrogators (*GS*, vol. 1 p. 227). Sorge could not of course have known that Soviet agents in the 1930s infiltrated foreign embassies in other capitals, and penetrated the highest levels of government in Germany and Britain. Isolated as he was, it was perhaps an understandable foible to assume that his own exploits were singular and exceptional.

16. Ishii, *Ningen Zoruge*, interview with Ishii Hanako.

17. Interviews with Ishii Hanako, Togo Ise and Frieda Weiss. Frieda Weiss, a young woman who had typed out some of Sorge's newspaper reports, and partnered him for the tango at German Club parties, was one of the very few foreigners residing permanently in Karuizawa in 1941. Sorge may have been unaware of this: he did not contact her during his trips to the resort town that summer.

18. It has been suggested that Sorge and Helma Ott had known each other before their encounter in Japan, and that they had first met in the political turmoil of Munich in 1919. The Ott's daughter, Ursula ('Ulli') holds a different view: 'My mother certainly did not meet Sorge at the time of the Munich uprising in 1919, and I am sure she knew nothing about his political position' (correspondence with author). It is likely that Ott was well aware of his wife's radical views at the time of their marriage in 1921. In Tokyo's German colony many years later, Helma still retained a reputation for being 'slightly pink'.

19. Interview with Eta Harich-Schneider.

20. Ibid.

21. *GS*, vol. 1, p. 294.

22. Ibid. It is not clear from Sorge's testimony when in August he heard about Kodai's letter.

23. Harich-Schneider, *Charaktere und Katastrophen*; interview with Eta Harich-Schneider.

24. Ibid.

25. Based on the text of Wenneker's cable to Berlin, and the text drafted by Sorge. See Chapman, *The Price of Admiralty*; also *GS*, vol. 4, p. 95 and vol. 3, p. 203.

26. Wenneker relayed a summary of his discussions with navy officers in a long message to Berlin on Friday 22 August, which began: 'Japan will not attack Russia. It is estimated that its [Russia's] collapse will occur, at latest, in the winter, and there is no desire to sacrifice on an operation whose success cannot be guaranteed and which would not solve the urgent problem of raw material supply, even if it were successful' (Chapman, *The Price of Admiralty*).

27. Was Clausen telling his interrogators the truth? In view of the proven unreliability of his testimony, we cannot exclude the possibility that the telegram *was* sent, and that a copy survives in Russian archives. The original text was discovered when police search Clausen's house. see *GS*, vol. 3, p. 203.

28. Russian archives.

29. Ibid.

30. *GS*, vol. 2, p. 182–3.

31. *GS*, vol. 4, p. 96.

32. *GS*, vol. 2, p. 239.

33. *GS*, vol. 3, p. 183. Some doubt remains about how much of the text was actually radioed to Moscow; among the telegrams released so far by the Russians there is none that corresponds to Sorge's manuscript. For Sorge's text, see *GS*, vol. 4, p. 96.

34. Ishii, *Ningen Zoruge*.

35. Interview with Ishii Hanako.

36. Ibid.

37. Ibid.

38. Ozaki was on his way to deliver a lecture at the Yubetsu plant of the Japan Paper Recycling Company in northern Japan. This was the company in which Ozaki, using his connnections, secured employment for Kawai. See Kawai, *Aru Kakumeika no Kaiso*.

39. Interview with Kawai Teikichi.

15. SEPTEMBER 1941

1. Sorge informed his controller about Ozaki's journey in the last part of the report transmitted on 26 or 27 August. However, Clausen told interrogators that he had omitted this paragraph from the material he radioed.

2. *GS*, vol. 2, p. 193.

3. Ibid, p. 246.

4. Kase, *Journey to the Missouri*.

5. Nagai, *Danchotei Nichijo*.

6. Ibid.

7. Interview with Eta Harich-Schneider.

8. Harich-Schneider, *Charaktere und Katastrophen*.

9. Ibid.

10. Ibid.

11. Interview with Eta Harich-Schneider.

12. *GS*, vol. 4, p. 99.

13. Russian archives.

14. Russian archives.

15. Both telegrams are dated 14 September – which was also the day of transmission – but this is not necessarily when Sorge drafted the texts. Ozaki had already left on his Manchurian journey ten days before, and it is reasonable to assume that Sorge would have tried to get this important information to Moscow earlier if atmospheric conditions permitted.

16. *GS*, vol. 2, p. 183, and vol. 4, p. 97, converted into direct speech.

17. According to Clausen's diary, nothing was radioed to Moscow between 14 September and 4 October. The only entry is for 27 September, when Clausen noted 'transmission impossible'.

18. Russian state archives. The telegram released by the Defence Ministry contains only a portion of the text found by police and reproduced in *GS*, vol. 4, p. 97. Clausen apparently radioed the text in three parts.

19. Wickert, *Mut und Übermut*.

20. Interview with Eta Harich-Schneider; see also Harich-Schneider, *Charaktere und Katastrophen*.

21. *GS*, vol. 3, p. 249. Ozaki at first thought it was on 20 September that he had seen Saionji's draft and reported its contents to Sorge. See *GS*, vol. 2, p. 374. Later he corrected himself, and said it was probably a week later. See *GS*, vol. 2, p. 386. It is impossible to date the event with accuracy.

22. *GS*, vol. 2, p. 190.

23. Ibid p. 374.

24. *GS*, vol. 4, p. 98.

16. OCTOBER 1941

1. Tolischus, *Tokyo Record*.

2. Konoye memoir.

3. In the words of historian Herbert Feis, 'He [Konoye] was a prisoner, willing or unwilling, of the terms precisely prescribed in conferences over which he presided.' See Feis, *The Road to Pearl Harbor*, for an excellent account of the countdown to the Pacific War.

4. Interview with Eta Harich-Schneider.

5. Ibid.

6. Clausen's practice was to leave certain components in the houses from which he transmitted, so that his radio would fit snugly into the bag. According to Yamasaki Yoshiko, two boxes of equipment were still lying in an upstairs cupboard when police arrived on 18 October.

7. Ishii, *Ningen Zoruge*.

8. Interview with Ishii Hanako. She *believes* this last encounter took place on Sorge's birthday, but her recollection of dates has faded; she is more confident that it was 'around the beginning of October'.

9. Interview with Eta Harich-Schneider.

10. Based on *GS*, vol. 2, pp. 251–2.

11. *GS*, vol. 4, p. 81.

12. Ibid.

13. *GS*, vol. 1, p. 464.

14. Sorge memoir.

15. A day or two later, missionaries in Niigata remarked sadly that the postman hadn't brought their *Deutscher Dienst*; they clearly missed the little newsletter that Sorge pasted together with such disdain. See Harich-Schneider, *Charaktere und Katastrophen*.

16. Clausen first met 'Joe' at Vukelic's house in 1939; he did not discover his real name until police showed him Miyagi's photograph. See *GS*, vol. 4, p. 253.

17. A handwritten analysis of Japan–US relations, dated 5 October, was discovered by police in Clausen's house. This was Miyagi's report, translated and written out in pen, probably by Akiyama Koji (the handwriting is not Sorge's): 'The development of the negotiations has been contrary to Japanese expectations,' the memo says. Roosevelt's answer to the latest Japanese proposals was likely to be negative. The Americans, it seemed, were apparently not willing even to grant the Japanese wish for a face-saving settlement. 'Japan is preparing the southward advance. There is no way of knowing how the situation will develop. However, it would seem that the prediction of war will turn out to be true' (*GS*, vol. 4, p. 92).

We believe Okinawan brought these notes on 7 October, but there is a possibility the delivery took place on 6 October. (Because of discrepancies in the testimony of various members of the ring, it is sometimes difficult to pinpoint when events took place. Sometimes Sorge, Ozaki, Miyagi and Clausen contradicted themselves concerning dates, at the various stages of their interrogation.)

Subsequently, Miyagi talked to Ozaki again, and was obliged to revise his report. According to Miyagi's testimony, he went to Nagasaka-cho on 8 October to deliver the revised version. In any case, all the effort by Ozaki, Miyagi and Akiyama was in vain. The memo was not transmitted by radio, nor was it among the items handed over to Serge from the Soviet Embassy on 10 October. Like so much of the material generated by the ring, it never reached the Fourth Department.

18. During August, the intelligence bureau of the South Manchurian Railway in Tokyo was engaged on an important project: an intricate study of Japan's war-making capabilities, manpower that could be mobilized, naval oil reserves, and other secret data. Furthermore, Ozaki and his colleagues analysed and documented the imperatives that led to Japan's decision to confront the United States and Britain, rather than join the German invasion of the Soviet Union. The report had a deceptively innocuous title: 'An Investigation of the Influence exerted by the New Situation on Japan's Politics and Economics'. Like many other confidential reports produced by the South Manchurian Railway's researchers, this one found its way into Sorge's hands. Ozaki put a copy in his briefcase, and took it home. Miyagi hand-copied portions of it, and had Akiyama Koji translate them into English. After his arrest, Miyagi told police he gave Sorge the first part of the text by 3 September (*GS*, vol. 4, p. 470). The available evidence suggests that he delivered the final part on 7 October.

19. Harich-Schneider, *Charaktere und Katastrophen*.

20. The facts are somewhat different. Grew, ever ready to give the Japanese the benefit of any doubt, told his audience: 'I have never believed that our two countries would come to a break; I do not think so now.' But he also reiterated his govern-

ment's position that international dealing must rest on certain basic principles and that there could be no compromise with these principles. America's insistence that Japan adhere to these tenets – respect for territorial integrity of all nations, non-interference in the internal affairs of other countries, non-disturbance of the status quo in the Pacific – stuck in the gullets of the Japanese, and proved an insuperable obstacle to an acccommodation between the two countries. However, Grew's speech clearly sounded spicier in the retelling, and Sorge got the impression that the ambassador had accused the Japanese government of being utterly untrustworthy. See *GS*, vol. 1, p. 429; Grew, *Ten Years in Japan*; Feis, *The Road to Pearl Harbor.*

21. *GS*, vol. 4, pp. 348–9. The exact day is hard to pinpoint. In his testimony Vukelic recalled the conversation with Sorge as taking place some time in early October. Sorge used the term 'Lenin group' to refer to the old Bolsheviks and their followers, wiped out by Stalin's purge. Among their number was Nikolai Bukharin, chief of the Comintern from 1926 until 1929. As we have seen, during his Comintern period Sorge found special favour with Bukharin; when the latter was expelled from the Politburo in 1929, Sorge lost his protection. The timing of his transfer to Red Army Intelligence coincided with Bukharin's fall from grace. In 1941 he still felt vulnerable as a survivor of the 'Lenin group'.

22. Knightley, *The Second Oldest Profession*: The Kim Philby quote is from his memoirs, *My Silent War* (MacGibbon & Kee, London, 1968), cited by Knightley.

23. Evidence exists that police showed an interest in Ozaki as early as the beginning of 1940. See Kazama, *Aru Hangyaku*; also Miyashita Hiroshi, *Tokko no Kaiso.*

24. *GS*, vol 4, p. 261.

25. Based on *GS,*, vol. 1, pp. 278–9; Harich-Schneider, *Charaktere und Katastrophen*; interview with Eta Harich-Schneider.

26. *GS*, vol. 2, p. 388.

27. Ibid.

28. According to one version, the two were captured by police when they came to visit Miyagi's lodging house in the Roppongi district. However, a former *Tokko* officer stated in his memoirs that Miyagi and his ring of helpers had long been under police surveillance. See Miyashita, *Tokko no Kaiso.*

29. At the eleventh hour, Konoye was handed one last chance to avert a war. As he knew, there was disagreement in the navy on the wisdom of going to war with the US. Now, from the upper echelons of the army, word reached Konoye that if the navy explicitly stated its opposition to war, the army might fall in line. The prince at once sounded out the navy, but was told that there could be no such official renunciation. It came down to a question of face: neither of the rival services would be first to 'chicken out' of the war plan.

On the night of 14 October, Tojo sent a messenger to Konoye's residence. The war minister had heard that the navy was reluctant to go to war while refusing to make its position clear. Tojo was indignant that state policy sanctioned by the emperor (on 6 September) was being called into question. It was an unforgiveable dereliction of duty. Tojo's message urged Konoye to take responsibility: the only honourable course was for the cabinet to resign *en masse*. See Feis, *The Road to Pearl Harbor.*

30. Ozaki's prison letters, collected in Ozaki, *Aijo wa Furu Hoshi no Gotoku.*

31. Ibid.

32. Newman, *How I Got that Story*; also police records.

33. *GS*, vol. 3, p. 229.

34. Ibid.

35. *GS,,* vol. 4, p. 254.

36. Ibid, p. 81.

37. *GS,* vol. 3, p. 229.

38. *GS,* vol. 4, p. 254.

39. *GS,* vol. 3, p. 229.

40. In prison Sorge remarked that the most vulnerable links in his network were the Japanese nationals. He was satisfied up to the end that the Europeans had not compromised the ring; certain that he, Clausen, Vukelic (and, previously, Gunther Stein) had covers sound enough to withstand the closest scrutiny by police. But the wide circles of acquaintances radiating from each Japanese member potentially included people who had attracted the attention of the police. Despite his consciousness of the risk, Sorge conceded that Japanese collaborators were indispensable to the success of the ring. And despite his concerns, he screened few of the peripheral agents recruited by Miyagi.

41. *GS,* vol. 1, p. 479.

42. This account of events on 17 October is drawn from the prison testimony of Sorge, Vukelic and Clausen; Clausen's post-war recollections; and interview with Yamasaki Yoshiko.

43. Kawai, *Aru Kakumeika no Kaiso.*

44. Description of arrest based on interviews with Yoshikawa and Ohashi.

45. *GS,* vol. 4, p. 114.

46. *GS,* vol. 3, p. 230.

47. Ibid.

48. Clausen remarked: 'Recalling what I had heard the previous night, I had a premonition that something more serious than a mere car accident was in the wind' (Guerin and Chatel, *Camarade Sorge*).

49. Interview with Yamasaki Yoshiko.

50. Harich-Schneider, *Charaktere und Katastrophen.* Only in August 1951 – almost ten years later – did Eta discover the exact time and date of Sorge's arrest. She then looked up her diary entry for 18 October 1941: 'Something told me that was the day of the terrible dream. And so it was – I had that frightening dream at the very moment Sorge was arrested. It portended the fate that befell him later. Reading what I had written, I was shaken, and deeply saddened. The guilt I felt that day has never left me.' Interview with Eta Harich-Schneider.

51. 'At the time of my arrest, the discovery of between 800 and 1,000 books at my home proved a considerable source of annoyance to the police. Most of these books were on Japan' (Sorge memoir).

52. Tolischus, *Tokyo Record.*

17. PAYING THE PRICE

1. *GS,* vol. 1, p. 102.

2. Wickert, *Mut und Übermut.*

3. US Army Intelligence (G-2) report on Sorge affair.

4. Harich-Schneider, *Charaktere und Katastrophen.*

5. Ibid.

6. Ibid.

7. Ibid.; also interview with Eta Harich-Schneider.

8. Interview with Yoshikawa Mitsusada.

9. Ibid.

10. Hearings before the Committee on Un-American Activities, Washington, August 1951.

11. Ohashi, *Shinso Zoruge Jiken.*

12. Interview with Yoshikawa Mitsusada.

13. Hearings before the Committee on Un-American Activities, 14.

14. Interview with Ohashi Hideo.

15. Interview with Yoshikawa Mitsusada. He was one of several judicial officials involved with the case who in 1949 provided US Military Intelligence with affidavits claiming that Sorge, Clausen, Ozaki and Vukelic were never tortured or subjected to undue pressure. The Americans wanted to use these affidavits to refute Agnes Smedley's contention that the statements made by members of the ring were extracted by violence and were therefore worthless. In his sworn statement, Yoshikawa said that he 'personally attended the investigations as a witness on frequent occasions to see that torture and other coercive methods were not employed. Of course, I never resorted to torture or other coercive methods in my own investigations of Richard Sorge and Kawai Teikichi, but assumed throughout as gentlemanly an attitude as possible.' However, it is not hard to imagine that Yoshikawa avoided witnessing unpleasant scenes by absenting himself when police used strong-arm methods.

16. Interview with Yoshikawa Mitsusada.

17. Interview with Ishii Hanako.

18. Tolischus, *Tokyo Record.* The author was deported from Japan after a farcical trial. His account offers an insight into Japanese police procedures at the time.

19. Interview with Yoshikawa Mitsusada.

20. A prisoner still undergoing trial (*miketsuin*) had to wear this contraption over the head whenever he left his cell.

21. *Der Spiegel,* 13 June–3 October 1951.

22. Interviews with Yoshikawa Mitsusada and Ohashi Hideo. In Ohashi's recollection, Sorge uttered only two sentences, while Ott said nothing:

> Eventually, Sorge muttered in German: 'I want to say good-bye to you.' A Foreign Ministry official attending translated this into Japanese. 'Please convey my best wishes to your wife and daughter.' Sorge's voice trailed away. There were tears in his eyes. He was unable to find any more words. When the interpreter finished speaking, Ambassador Ott seemed about to say something, but his face went pale with shock, and he just stared at Sorge, speechless, with a pained look. Sorge must have felt distress at having deceived Ambassador Ott, who had put his trust in him. Sorge simply nodded, and left the room in silence (Ohashi, *Shinso Zoruge Jiken*).

Ohashi surmised that the ambassador's questions about the prisoner's treatment and food were directed at Yoshikawa *after* he and Sorge had left the room.

23. Interview with Ohashi Hideo; also Ohashi, *Shinso Zoruge Jiken.*

24. *GS,* vol. 3, p. 109.

25. 'Word-group', *gogun* in Japanese, refers not to words, but to the five-digit clusters into which the text was segmented after being encoded into numerals.

26. *GS,* vol. 3, p. 178.

27. Interview with Ohashi Hideo. See also Matsuhashi and Ohashi, *Zoruge to no Yakosuku.*

28. Interview with Ishii Hanako. Sorge had promised to contact her by telegram, as her mother's house lacked a telephone.

29. Interview with Yoshikawa Mitsusada.

30. 'Sorge never confided to me the truth about the character and function of our organization,' Vukelic wrote in his prison memoir. *GS*, vol. 3, p. 628.

31. *GS*, vol. 1, p. 329.

32. Sorge was charged under the Peace Preservation Law and National Defence Security Law. Both carried a maximum penalty of death. However, had Sorge been charged only under the latter, he might have had a better chance of getting off with a long prison sentence. The National Defence Security Law came into force on May 10, 1941, and could not be applied retroactively. Students of the case argue that it was a travesty of justice to try Sorge under the Peace Preservation Law.

33. Interview with Ohashi Hideo. Ohashi expressed indignation at the way his seniors in the *Tokko* fabricated a memoir, based on Sorge's answers during the interrogation conducted principally by himself (Ohashi). The former policeman revealed that the memoir was composed as if Sorge had written it himself. Ohashi points out that 'If Sorge had prepared the document there had to be an orginal in German or English, but no such thing existed.' The second memoir was written by Sorge himself under Yoshikawa's direction.

34. Sorge memoir.

35. *GS*, vol. 1, p. 329.

36. Ohashi, *Shinso Zoruge Jiken*.

37. There can be little doubt the Russians were quick to learn of the arrests. A Soviet diplomat was a neighbour of Clausen's (which is unlikely to have been a coincidence), and would have alerted the embassy at once.

38. Ohashi, *Shinso Zoruge Jiken*.

39. *GS*, vol. 4, p. 237.

40. Ibid.

41. Interview with Ohashi Hideo.

42. Interview with Yoshikawa Mitsusada.

43. *GS*, vol. 1, p. 302.

44. Interview with Yoshikawa Mitsusada.

45. Russian state archives (KGB).

46. *GS*, vol. 1, p. 106.

47. Ibid, p. 109.

48. Ibid, p. 102.

49. 'We never got any tip-off from Meisinger, the Germans never gave us any information casting doubt on Sorge. What they said afterwards – that's all lies,' Yoshikawa told the author.

50. Mader, *Dr. Sorge-Report*.

51. Kawai, *Aru Kakumeika no Kaiso*. In these memoirs, Kawai said that this glimpse of Sorge through the peep-hole of a cell door was 'the first since we parted in the summer of 1932'. They had met for the last time in China: although Kawai later assisted Sorge's network in Tokyo, their paths did not cross again.

Kawai's suspicion that he had been under close surveillance for almost a year was confirmed when he was arrested, and recognized one of the policemen as the shadowy figure who had tailed him across Tokyo. Later he discovered the identity of this man – Omata Ken, an assistant inspector in the *Tokko*'s First Section.

52. Ozaki, *Kaiso no Ozaki Hotsumi.*

53. At this stage of the judicial process, Sorge sought to revise parts of his earlier testimony. For instance, he now said that Ozaki was *not* a member of the Comintern, that Kawai Teikichi had not worked for the ring in Japan, and that he had joined the Nazi party not in Germany, but only after arriving in Tokyo.

54. *GS*, vol. 1, p. 480.

55. Ibid, p. 580.

56. *GS*, August, 1962.

57. Interview with Yamasaki Yoshiko.

58. Willoughby, *Shanghai Conspiracy.*

59. Three members of Ozaki's Shanghai sub-ring also succumbed in prison: Kawamura Yoshio (15 December 1942), Funakoshi Hisao (27 February 1945) and Mizuno Shigeo (22 March 1945).

60. Ozaki, *Aijo no Furu Hoshi no Gotoku.*

61. *GS*, vol. 1, p. 276.

62. Krushchev wrote in his memoirs that from the available material it was impossible to determine 'whether we used the material from Sorge strategically, or tactically, against Germany'.

63. John Erickson, *The Road to Stalingrad.*

64. Andrew and Gordievsky, *KGB, The Inside Story.*

65. Japanese Self-Defence Agency's war history, quoted in Coox, *Nomonhan: Japan Against Russia.*

66. Ibid.

67. Nishizato, *Kakumei no Shanghai de.* Nishizato was arrested in June 1942 on suspicion of espionage. Nakanishi Kou, another of Ozaki's friends, was also picked up. Nakanishi served for a while in the South Manchurian Railway, while Nishizato worked as a journalist, and both had held civilian posts with the Japanese army in China. They shared Ozaki's passionate belief in the justice of the Chinese revolutionary struggle, and decided that they could be most effective by collaborating with Ozaki's intelligence activities. The two passed Japanese military secrets to the Chinese Communist Party, and were also conduits to the Russians. Ozaki was the point at which the China ring and the Sorge network intersected. But they were distinct organizations, and police investigators handled them as separate cases.

In August 1945 Nishizato and Nakanishi were sentenced to life imprisonment, but were freed in October after American troops landed in Japan and liberated political prisoners. After the war, both became prominent figures in the Japan Communist Party, which may explain why their personal memoirs of their time in China contain few hard facts about their espionage on behalf of the Chinese communists. Nor do their accounts illuminate how their network tied in with that run by Sorge. To this day, relatively little is known about the workings of the China ring, which was Ozaki's own creation.

68. *Der Spiegel,* 13 June–3 October 1951.

69. Ibid. Sorge instructed his lawyer to sell his worldly goods and give Anna Clausen the proceeds, together with his bank balances, providing a total amount of over 10,000 yen. See *Gendai Shiryo Geppo,* August 1962.

70. Trepper, *The Great Game.* Tominaga Kyoji was a senior Japanese officer who had held a number of important posts in the War Ministry, including that of chief of the personnel division. The encounter described in Leopold Trepper's book took

place in a Soviet prison cell after the general was captured at the end of the war by the Russians in Manchuria, and before he was taken to Khabarovsk to testify at the trial of Japanese war criminals.

71. Ibid.

72. Ibid.

73. Kase, *Journey to the Missouri*.

74. Ibid.; interview with Kase Toshikazu. Kase is convinced that the Japanese side, made keenly aware of Moscow's lack of concern for Sorge, would not have wished to embarrass their Russian hosts by alluding to the issue on an occasion such as this. The contrary view is that of a Russian diplomat, identified as Ivanov, quoted in Shimotanae, *Kokusai Supai Zoruge no Shinjitsu*.

75. Ozaki, *Kaiso no Ozaki Hotsumi*.

EPILOGUE

1. Willoughby, *Shanghai Conspiracy*.

2. Ibid.

3. Ibid.

4. The thesis that Sorge was traded to the Soviet Union was first propagated in Meissner's *The Man with Three Faces*. An energetic proponent of the theory was Dr Karl Kindermann (who, although he was Jewish, is believed to have served as an informant of Gestapo Colonel Meisinger). Kindermann acted as interpreter when German officials tried in vain to persuade Japan to extradite Sorge. In 1976, he wrote a series of newspaper articles for the *Japan Times* alleging that Sorge was in fact handed over to the Russians at the Manchuria–Siberian frontier. Kindermann offered only hearsay evidence in support of his claim, but was totally convinced that the information was reliable. Moreover, he found it impossible to accept that the Japanese government ordered Sorge's execution on 7 November, a sacred anniversary for the Soviet Union. Japan was desperately anxious to retain Soviet goodwill, he argued, and selecting 7 November would have been 'an act not only politically unwise and stupid but also tasteless' (*Japan Times*, 24 November 1976). However, Imoto Daikichi, a prosecutor during the wartime period, and a post-war procurator-general, said that it was through 'pure chance' that the execution coincided with the anniversary of the Bolshevik Revolution.

5. Interview with Ishii Hanako.

Bibliography

PRIMARY SOURCES

Obi Toshito (ed.) *Gendaishi Shiryo, Zoruge Jiken* (Materials on Modern History), 4 vols (Misuzu Shobo, Tokyo, vols 1–3, 1962, vol. 4, 1971).
US House of Representatives, 82nd Congress, First Session: Committee on Un-American Activities (US Government Printing Office, Washington, DC, 1951).
German Foreign Office Archives, file on Sorge case.
Russian Ministry of Defence and KGB archives.

BOOKS CONNECTED WITH THE SORGE AFFAIR

In English

Deakin, F. W. and Storry, G. R., *The Case of Richard Sorge* (Chatto and Windus, London, 1966).
Johnson, Chalmers, *An Instance of Treason* (Stanford University Press, Stanford, CA, 1964).
Meissner, Hans-Otto, *The Man With Three Faces* (Rinehart, New York, 1955).
Prange, Gordon, *Target Tokyo*, (McGraw Hill, New York, 1984).
Willoughby, Charles A., *Shanghai Conspiracy* (E. P. Dullin, New York, 1952).

In German

Kordt, Erich, *Nicht aus den Akten* (Deutsche Verlagsanstalt, Stuttgart, 1950).
Mader, Julius, *Dr. Sorge-Report* (Militarverlag der Deutschen Demokratischen Republik, Berlin, 1984).
– Stuchlick, Gerhard and Pehnert, Horst, *Dr. Sorge Funkt aus Tokyo* (Militarverlag, Berlin, 1966).

In Japanese

Ishii, Hanako, *Ningen Zoruge* (The Man Sorge) (Keiso Shobo, Tokyo,1967).
Kawai, Teikichi, *Aru Kakumeika no Kaiso* (Memoirs of a Revolutionary) (Nihon Shuppan Kyokai, Tokyo, 1953).
Kazama, Michitaro, *Aru Hangyaku: Ozaki Hotsumi no Shogai* (A Case of Treason: The Life of Ozaki Hotsumi) (Shinseido, Tokyo, 1950).
Matsuhashi, Tadamitsu and Ohashi, Hideo, *Zoruge to no Yakusoku wo Hatasu* (Keeping a Promise Made to Sorge) (Origin Shuppan Centre, Tokyo 1988).
Miyashita, Hiroshi, *Tokko no Kaiso* (Recollections of a Tokko Agent) (Tabata Shoten, Tokyo, 1978).

Nakanishi, Ko, *Chugoku Kakumei no Arashi no naka de* (Within the Tempest of China's Revolution) (Aoki Shoten, Tokyo, 1975).

Nishizato, Tatsuo, *Kakumei no Shanghai de* (In the Shanghai of the Revolution) (Nitchu Shuppan, Tokyo, 1977).

Ohashi, Hideo, *Shinso Zoruge Jiken* (published by author, 1977).

Ozaki, Hotsuki, *Zoruge Jiken* (The Sorge Affair) (Chuo Koronsha, Tokyo, 1963).

— (ed.) *Kaiso no Ozaki Hotsumi* (Recollections of Ozaki Hotsumi) (Keiso Shobo, Tokyo, 1979).

Ozaki, Hotsumi, *Aijo wa Furu Hoshi no Gotoku* (Love is Like a Falling Star) (Sekai Hyonronsha, Tokyo, 1946).

Shimotomae, Nobuo, with NHK Reporters, *Kokusai Supai Zoruge no Shinjitsu* (The Truth about Sorge the International Spy) (Kadokawa Shoten, Tokyo, 1992).

Watabe, Tomiya, *Itsuwari no Rakuin* (The Stigma of a Falsehood) (Gogatsu Shobo, Tokyo, 1993).

In Russian

Dementyeva, I., Agayanyants, N. and Yakovlev, Y., *Tovaritch Sorge* (Comrade Sorge) (Sovietskaya Rossiya, Moscow, 1965).

In French

Guerin, Alain and Chatel, Nicole, *Camarade Sorge* (Julliard, Paris, 1965).

NEWSPAPER AND MAGAZINE ARTICLES CONNECTED WITH THE SORGE AFFAIR

In English

Kindermann, Karl, series of articles on Sorge case, *Japan Times*, 20, 21, 23, 24 November 1976.

In German

Sorge, Christiane, 'Mein Mann – Richard Sorge', *Weltwoche*, December 1964.

'Herr Sorge Sass Mit zu Tische', series of articles, *Der Spiegel*, 13 June–3 October 1951.

In Japanese

Guillain, Robert, 'Kaiso no Zoruge Jiken' (Recollections of the Sorge Case), *Chuo Koron*, April 1972.

Ikoma, Yoshitoshi, 'Zoruge Kaiso' (Sorge Recollections) *Misuzu*, March 1962.

Ito, Ritsu, 'Nihon no Yuda to Yobarete' (Designated the Japanese Judas), *Bungei Shunju*, February, March, April 1993.

— 'Sanshu Supai Nozaka Sanzo' (Triple Spy Nozaka Sanzo), *Bungei Shunju*, January 1994.

Ohashi, Hideo, 'Watakushi wa Zoruge o Toraeta', (I Arrested Sorge), *Sunday Mainichi*, 2 July 1961.

Yamamoto, Makiko, interviewed in *Sunday Mainichi*, 28 September 1980, 'Watakushi ga Zoruge wo Utta' (I Gave Sorge Away).

GENERAL WORKS

In English

Andrew, Christopher, and Gordievsky, Oleg, *KGB, The Inside Story of its Foreign Operations from Lenin to Gorbachev* (Hodder and Stoughton, London, 1990).

Behr, Edward, *Hirohito. Behind the Myth* (Hamish Hamilton, London, 1989).

Buton, R. J. C., *Tojo and the Coming of War* (Princeton University Press, Princeton, NJ, 1961).

Chamberlin, William Henry, *Japan Over Asia* (Little, Brown, Boston, MA, 1937).

Chapman, John M. W., *The Price of Admiralty* (Ripe, East Sussex, 1984).

Cook, Maruko Taya and Cook, Theodore F., *Japan at War: An Oral History* (New York Press, New York, 1992).

Coox, Alvin D., *Nomonhan: Japan Against Russia, 1939*, vols 1 and 2 (Stanford University Press, Stanford, CA, 1985).

Dirksen, Herbert von, *Moscow, Tokyo, London* (Hutchinson, London, 1951).

Dupuy, T. N., *A Genius For War, The German Army and General Staff, 1807-1945* (Macdonald and Jane's, London, 1977).

Erickson, John, *The Road to Stalingrad* (Panther Books, London, 1983).

Feis, Herbert, *The Road to Pearl Harbor* (Princeton University Press, Princeton, NJ, 1950).

Fleisher, Wilfrid, *Our Enemy Japan* (Doubleday, New York, 1942).

Grew, Joseph, *Ten Years In Japan* (Simon and Schuster, New York, 1944).

Haslam, Jonathon, *The Soviet Union and the Threat from the East, 1933-41* (Macmillan, London, 1992).

Hughes, Richard, *Foreign Devil* (André Deutsch, London, 1972).

Johnson, Paul, *A History of the Modern World* (Weidenfeld and Nicholson, London, 1983).

Kase Toshikazu, *Journey to the Missouri* (Yale University Press, New Haven, CT, 1950).

Knightley, Phillip, *The Second Oldest Profession* (André Deutsch, London, 1983).

Krivitsky, Walter G., *In Stalin's Secret Service* (University Publications of America, 1985).

– *I was Stalin's Agent* (Hamish Hamilton, London, 1939).

Lewin, Ronald, *The American Magic* (Hutchinson, London, 1982).

MacKinnon, Janice R. and Mackinnon, Stephen R., *Agnes Smedley. The Life and Times of an American Radical* (University of California Press, Berkeley, 1988).

Massing, Hede, *This Deception* (Duell, Sloan and Pearce, New York, 1951).

Morin, Relman, *East Wind Rising* (Alfred A. Knopf, New York, 1960).

Newman, Joseph, *Goodbye Japan* (L. B. Fischer, New York, 1942).

– (ed.), *How I Got that Story* (Overseas Press Club of America, New York, 1967).

Oda, James, *Secret Embedded in Magic Cables* (published by author, 1993).

Piggott, Francis, *Broken Thread* (Gale and Polden, Aldershot, 1950).

Pincher, Chapman, *Their Trade is Treachery* (Sidgwick and Jackson, London, 1981).

– Too Secret too Long (Sidgwick and Jackson, London, 1984).

Poretsky, Elizabeth, *Our Own People* (Oxford University Press, 1969).

Sansom, Katharine, *Sir George Sansom and Japan: A Memoir* (Diplomatic Press, Tallahassee, FL, 1972).

Schellenberg, Walter, *The Schellenberg Memoirs* (André Deutsch, London, 1956).
Seth, Ronald, *Secret Servants* (Farrar, Straus and Cuhady, New York, 1957).
Stein, Gunther, *Made in Japan* (Methuen, London, 1935).
– *Far East in Ferment* (Methuen, London, 1936).
Tiltman, H. Hessell, *The Far East Comes Nearer* (J. B. Lippincott, Philadelphia and London, 1937).
Tsuji Masanobu, *Singapore, The Japanese Version* (Ure Smith, Sydney, 1960).
Tolischus, Otto, *Tokyo Record* (Hamish Hamilton, London, 1943).
Trepper, Leopold, *The Great Game* (Michael Joseph, London, 1977).
Wright, Peter, *Spycatcher* (Viking, New York, 1987).
Zacharias, Ellis M., *Secret Missions* (G. P. Putnam's Sons, New York, 1946).

In German

Deutsche Botschafter in Japan, 1860–1973 (Deutsche Gesellschaft für Natur- und Volktumerkunde Ostasians, Tokyo, 1974).
Harich-Schneider, Eta, *Charaktere und Katastrophen* (Ullstein, Berlin, 1978).
Kuusinen, Aino, *Der Gott Sturzt Seine Engel* (Verlag Fritz Molden, Vienna, 1972).
Sieburg, Friedrich, *Die Stahlerne Blume* (Societats-Verlag, Frankfurt, 1939).
Werner, Ruth, *Sonjas Rapport* (Verlag Neues Leben, Berlin, 1977).
Wickert, Erwin, *Mut und Übermut* (Deutsche Verlagsanstalt, Stuttgart, 1991).

In Japanese

Hiyama Yoshiaki, *Stalin Ansatsu Keikaku* (The Plan to Assassinate Stalin) (Tokuma Shoten, Tokyo, 1978).
Nagai Kafu, *Danchotei Nichijo* (Nagai diaries) (Iwanami Shoten, Tokyo, 1987).

Index